THE MAGAZINE FOR ENTREPRENEURS

Venture's

GUIDE TO INTERNATIONAL VENTURE CAPITAL

BY THE EDITORS OF VENTURE, THE MAGAZINE FOR ENTREPRENEURS

SIMON AND SCHUSTER ☐ NEW YORK

Copyright © 1983, 1984, 1985 by Venture Magazine, Inc.
All rights reserved
including the right of reproduction
in whole or in part in any form
Published by Simon and Schuster
A Division of Simon & Schuster, Inc.
Simon & Schuster Building
Rockefeller Center
1230 Avenue of the Americas
New York, New York 10020
SIMON AND SCHUSTER and colophon are registered trademarks of Simon & Schuster, Inc.
Designed by Steve Phillips Design, Inc.
Manufactured in the United States of America
1 2 3 4 5 6 7 8 9 10

Library of Congress Cataloging in Publication Data
The Editors of Venture Magazine
Venture's guide to international venture capital.
                Includes index.
1. Venture capital—Directories. 2. Small business investment companies—
Directories. I. Venture (New York, N.Y.: 1979)
HG64.V46 1985   332.6'6   84-27629
ISBN 0-671-55698-3

The following chapters in this work have been previously published in Venture Magazine:
"Money for the Asking," June, 1983.
"What Investors Hate Most About Business Plans," June, 1984.
"Holding On to Equity," May, 1983.

ACKNOWLEDGMENTS

The Editors of VENTURE, The Magazine for
Entrepreneurs, wish to thank the following people for
the many hours spent researching, editing,
proofreading, inputting, designing, and promoting this
book: Marion Arkin, Andrea Fishman,
Michele H. Fleischer, Mary Frances Hildebrandt,
Nancy Koch, Stephen Krampf, Lee Kravitz,
Christopher M. Lehman, Jeannie Mandelker,
Barbara Presley Noble, Frank Russo, Steve Phillips,
and Webster Williams.

CONTENTS

Articles

Directory

CONTENTS

WHAT VENTURE CAPITALISTS WANT

The fast-pace and big-ticket deals of today's venture capital industry often leave new entrepreneurs intimidated. But, in reality, venture financing is just a modern version of a venerable old game: A venture capitalist invests in young companies in fields where the risks are high but the potential rewards are great; the entrepreneur's goal is to secure as much capital as necessary at the lowest price, without sacrificing much equity ownership in his or her business. The venture capitalist, in turn, seeks the greatest possible return for his or her support—at the very least, a return of 25% to 30% compounded annually. Seven to 10 years after the company's startup, when it's either sold through a public stock offering or is acquired by another company, the investors recoup their money.

Unlike traditional lenders, venture capitalists take an active role in managing the companies they invest in, often serving on the board of directors. Some demand a bigger role in company operations than others do. Explains John Pappajohn, president of Pappajohn Capital Resources in Des Moines, Iowa: "I'm really in the business of putting together good ideas and good people with money, of financing companies at startup and then keeping close tabs on them until they go public." Because entrepreneurs don't always have managerial experience, venture capitalists may help in

> **"WE'RE LEARNING HOW TO FIND EMERGING GROWTH COMPANIES AND MOVE THEM SUCCESSFULLY FROM INFANCY TO MATURITY"**

long-term planning, marketing, and personnel development. Pappajohn, for one, isn't bashful about being an active adviser to the presidents of the companies in his portfolio. "I call them every day and I make them millions," he says.

The venture capitalists are making millions, too, and that's attracting hundreds of new investors. In 1976, private venture partnerships took in $600 million in new capital from investors. In 1984, that figure hit $3.2 billion, and the total venture capital pool reached a record of nearly $16 billion. Between 1977 and 1984 the number of professional venture firms more than doubled to almost 500. The growth is not yet over. "Venture capital is moving into the mainstream of American and world corporate finance," says David Brophy, professor of finance at the University of Michigan. The reason, he and others believe, is that high-risk investment strategies have evolved from a game of hunches to a well-honed art. "The most important thing that's happened in the last six or seven years is that we're learning how to find emerging growth companies and move them successfully from infancy to maturity," Brophy explains.

Tax incentives also have encouraged much of the venture capital boom. Congress lowered the capital gains tax from 49% to 28% in 1979 and then to 20% in 1981, encouraging many hitherto reluctant investors to reach deep into their pockets. Another boost came in 1979, when the Dept. of Labor ruled that pension managers could participate in venture capital without violating the "prudent man" rule, which had effectively discouraged such investment since 1974. That freed a small percentage of the $800 billion in pension assets in the U.S. for venture investment.

A groundswell of entrepreneurs has risen to satisfy the desire of venture capitalists to invest in new companies. An entrepreneurial revolution has been sweeping America in the decade since the baby-boom generation came of age. Finding corporate ranks clogged and often distrusting big institutions, young, ambitious executives have moved out to blaze their own trails, particularly in high-technology industries such as computers, communications, and biotechnology. New business incorporations in 1984 alone topped 675,000, an all-time high.

And with better funding, added experience, and more investment opportunities to choose from, venture firms have broadened their traditional reach. Many firms still favor high-technology industries and startups, but others have begun investing in nontechnological fields and in the later stages of a company's development. Indeed, venture capital firms are almost as varied as the com-

"MORE THAN EVER, THE NAME OF THE [VENTURE CAPITAL] GAME IS MANAGEMENT. IF YOU FIND A COMPANY WITH THE RIGHT HORSES, YOU BACK IT TO THE HILT. OTHERWISE, YOU THINK TWICE"

panies they invest in. The most prevalent type is an independent private venture firm, which can be either an investment partnership or a privately held corporation. Other venture firms include Small Business Investment Companies (SBICs), Minority Enterprise Small Business Investment Companies (MESBICs), merchant banking firms, and investment banking houses. A growing number of major industrial corporations, commercial bank holding companies, and other financial institutions also have subsidiaries or divisions involved in venture investment. Not every investment opportunity is right for every venture firm, and entrepreneurs should approach funds that best match their needs.

INDEPENDENT PRIVATE VENTURE FIRMS

In general, independent private venture firms are the major source of venture capital. These firms, which are typically structured as limited partnerships, supply equity financing to new and expanding businesses. They raise pools of capital from a wide range of investors: corporations, insurance companies, pension funds, university endowments, and wealthy individuals. And while most have at least $10 million in investment capital, the largest manage capital pools of $100 million or more.

Although a growing number of independent venture firms are looking to back consumer-oriented businesses, they generally favor technology-based industries in high-growth fields. (This usually means a total potential market of at least $20 million and preferably $100 million within five years.) They invest in everything from seed and startup situations to leveraged buyouts (for stage definitions, see box). While some will do any type of deal, others may have a clear preference for either early-round or later-round financing.

SMALL BUSINESS INVESTMENT COMPANIES

For entrepreneurs seeking funds for companies with more modest growth potential, SBICs are a plentiful source of capital. SBICs were created by Congress in 1958 as a vehicle for providing equity capital and long-term loans to new and expanding small businesses. While SBICs are privately owned and managed, they are licensed and regulated by the Small Business Administration and are eligible to receive federal loans to augment their private capital.

In general, SBICs will consider a wider range of industries than will limited-partnership venture firms. The larger SBICs have private capital ranging from $1 million to more than $30 million and, like venture partnerships, they invest in everything from startups to leveraged buyouts. Not all SBICs make venture capital investments per se, and some make straight loans exclusively to taxicab owners, grocery stores, distributorships, or other small businesses. Since SBICs borrow much of their money from the SBA and need to repay these loans plus interest to the government, they are reluctant to risk tying up all their money in nonoperating companies or startups. Consequently, most SBICs lend money—at rates slightly higher than they borrow from the SBA—and they often build options to buy stock into their loans.

THE SEVEN STAGES OF VENTURE CAPITAL FINANCING

With more investment opportunities to choose from, venture firms are beginning to specialize in companies in certain stages of development and in specific industries.

When a company is formed it is commonly funded in three stages, which all fall under the term of early-stage financing:

Seed Financing. Investors provide small amounts of capital for entrepreneurs to investigate a business concept and transform it into a tangible business plan.

Startup Financing. Entrepreneurs receive a larger amount of capital to fund product development and initial marketing.

First-Round Financing. This enables a company to develop a prototype and to begin manufacturing and selling its product.

Once a company is generating revenue, it seeks later-round financing, which includes:

Second-Round Financing. Investors offer initial expansion capital for a firm already in business.

Third-Round Financing. In some circumstances, third-round financing involves millions of dollars earmarked to expand a company's existing plant, revamp a marketing strategy, or improve an existing product.

Mezzanine or Bridge Financing. This round keeps a company growing until it can go public. It is meant to last no more than a year.

Leveraged Buyouts. Some venture funds also help finance leveraged buyouts (LBOs) to enable management to acquire control of the firm—or to help an entrepreneur acquire a business. In an LBO deal, the company's assets are used for collateral.

MINORITY ENTERPRISE SMALL BUSINESS INVESTMENT COMPANIES

A source of financing for entrepreneurs belonging to one of eight specified minority groups (Black, Indian, Eskimo, Mexican, Puerto Rican, Cuban, Philippine, or Oriental) is the Minority Enterprise Small Business Investment Company. MESBICs are SBICs that are required to invest in small businesses owned by "individuals from groups underrepresented in the free-enterprise system." They also provide money to entrepreneurs from economically disadvantaged groups, such as Vietnam veterans and the handicapped. While they follow the same general guidelines as SBICs—and use the same criteria to evaluate their portfolio companies—MESBICs often have the additional goal of creating more minority jobs or company ownership. As a result, they target considerably lower rates of return than other venture capitalists do.

OTHER OPTIONS

For those considering taking their companies public within a year, a good source of later-stage financing might be found at a venture capital subsidiary of a bank holding company or at either a merchant banking firm or an investment banking house. A bank holding company can allocate as much as 5% of its capital to its venture capital subsidiary, which typically makes commitments ranging from $1 million to $5 million a deal. While investment bankers and merchant bankers will sometimes invest their own capital in a venture deal, they more typically act as an intermediary between investors and companies, often acting as advisers in leveraged buyouts, mergers, and acquisitions.

At the same time, growing numbers of major corporations—for example, General Electric Co., The Lubrizol Corp., and Xerox Corp.—have launched venture capital divisions to cash in on the extraordinarily high returns they've seen from venture capital pools. These corporations typically look for products, markets, and technologies that are related to their own operations—or for situations that will help them diversify. In addition to direct investments, corporations have become a major funding source for independent venture firms.

There may be plenty of venture capital around and a growing number of venture capitalists, but it's not as easy as it was just a couple of years ago to raise money. As this book goes to press, the word in the venture capital industry is retrenchment. In the past year, the market for initial public offerings (IPOs) has

cooled down dramatically. (Venture capitalists look forward to the day when a portfolio company goes public because it gives them a chance to sell off their shares.) In 1983, a record 888 companies went public and raised an astonishing $12.6 billion in capital. But, according to *Going Public*, an industry newsletter published in Philadelphia that tracks the IPO market, only 548 companies went public in 1984, and they raised a comparatively modest $3.8 billion. As a result, say experts, venture firms have been forced to prop up their existing portfolio companies instead of cashing in and moving on to new companies. Many expect this trend to continue well into 1985.

At the same time, more venture firms than ever are trying to raise money. As of Feb. 1, 1985, 87 firms

THERE'S AN EVOLUTION GOING ON IN THE VENTURE CAPITAL INDUSTRY. THE OLD MODEL—THE INVESTOR WHO COULD DEAL WITH ANY TYPE OF VENTURE—IS NO LONGER POSSIBLE. BECAUSE OF THE INTENSE COMPETITION FOR MONEY AND DEALS, THERE'S MORE SPECIFIC TARGETING

were seeking to raise $2.5 billion, according to Venture Economics, a research firm located in Wellesley Hills, Mass. Yet, as analysts point out, raising new money is harder than it was a year ago—especially for dozens of new, unestablished venture managers who don't have a track record. "Now that the IPO market has cooled off, investors are becoming more cautious and more picky," explains Richard Testa, a partner in the Boston law firm of Testa, Hurwitz & Thibeault, who specializes in venture capital. "For venture capitalists, fundraising is no longer a question of making two or three phone calls, then opening some mail."

Ironically, many see today's malaise as a direct result of yesterday's boom. In 1983, when enthusiasm among investors for high-tech growth companies reached a feverish pitch, the IPO fervor pushed the price/earnings ratios of some high-tech stocks several times higher than the ratios of proven blue chip companies. Not surprisingly, the heated IPO market encouraged scores of new investors and entrepreneurs to enter

the venture business. Analysts say that many of these fledgling risk investors hoped to make a quick killing by running up the prices of deals, especially in later-stage financings. "As the value of the IPO market went up, so did the valuations of deals at earlier stages," says one venture capitalist. "A lot of people new to the field were willing to accept these inflated valuations where, given the same situation, experienced venture capitalists would have declined."

Expectations were so inflated that few analysts were surprised when the bubble burst. And the strain has been particularly apparent in the high-tech arena. According to *Going Public*, the average price/earnings ratio of high-tech companies declined from 27 in the first half of 1983—the last time the IPO market boomed—to 12 in the third quarter of 1984, a drop of over 50% in how the public investor perceives the value of these stocks. Moreover, while 23% of the firms that went public in 1983 were either high-tech manufacturing or computer companies, only 16% fell into those categories in 1984.

While that's bad news for entrepreneurs—especially for entrepreneurs in those high-tech industries—most experienced venture capitalists see the period of retrenchment as a blessing in disguise. Says Peter C. Wendell, general partner in Sierra Ventures/Wood River Capital in Menlo Park, Calif.: "Now that the bloom is off the rose, I detect a greater willingness on the part of entrepreneurs to be flexible in terms of valuation and to look more toward the long-term building up of their companies." And Brophy, the professor of finance at the University of Michigan, notes that the market is already "coming back down to reality. As valuations continue to come down in second- and third-round deals, I think we're going to see a more competitive marketplace, where fairpricing risks are rewarded by fair returns on investments."

Another new trend that is changing the way venture capitalists operate is the rise of venture capital megafunds—the most visible byproduct of the 1983 fundraising bonanza. A few years ago, $30 million was considered a mammoth venture fund. Then in 1983, a half-dozen firms raised individual funds of $100 million or more.

Some venture capitalists warn of two dangers lurking behind the megafunds: the pressure to invest the burgeoning capital quickly, and the lack of both time and personnel to manage investments effectively. "The [venture capital] industry was built to be small so that the venture capitalist could have an active role in managing emerging companies," explains Ramon V. Reyes, an associate of Nazem & Co., a New York venture firm. "The more money you have, the more you can invest. But in some situations, because you're running so hard to invest your money, there might be a tendency to get sloppy."

Partners at the megafunds are well aware of these dangers. "The significant issue now is how venture capitalists managing large amounts of money will come to grips with managing their firms," says Brook H. Byers, general partner of Kleiner, Perkins, Caufield & Byers, San Francisco, which sparked the spate of large-scale funding when it raised $150 million in 1983. His own solution: "We only hire senior partners with significant operating experience. And, no matter what the business cycle is, we keep our investments at a steady flow—five commitments each quarter, in the range of $1 million to $3 million each." Still, the pressure of investing and managing these growing pools of capital—a pressure felt by hundreds of venture firms—has made venture firms as a whole less inclined to back either inexperienced entrepreneurs or poorly run companies. Explains one analyst: "There are a lot of war stories in this industry about venture capitalists who miraculously turned around a company that had been verging on bankruptcy. But talk to the same venture capitalists in private, and, 9 times out of 10, they'll tell you that a company is a big loser for them if it requires too much hand-holding." Venture firms are still willing to take an active role in managing their porfolio companies, but they are becoming much more discriminating in their choices of companies. As Reyes puts it: "More than ever, the name of the game is management. If you find a company with the right horses, you back it to the hilt. Otherwise, you think twice."

On the opposite end of the megafunds are the boutique firms, another recent trend. Since 1982, more than two dozen funds have been started that invest only in the earliest stages of a company. By investing small amounts of capital in exchange for large chunks of equity, this new breed of "seed specialist" sets its sights on returns of as high as 50% on investments. At the same time, notes one analyst, some of the more enterprising firms have begun "poking around laboratories, hoping to find scientists who have the expertise to manage investments effectively."

But specialization isn't limited to any one breed of venture capitalist; it is becoming characteristic of the entire industry. "There's an evolution going on in the structuring of the industry," notes Brophy. "The old model, in which the venture capitalist was a generalist, confident that he could deal with any type of venture, is no longer possible. Because of the intense competition for money and deals, we're seeing much more targeting of specific areas of technology and growth."

Venture firms are also becoming more specialized in the way they staff and raise funds. To stay abreast, "funds are tending to devote more people to specific areas of technology," says Brophy. "And there is an influx of people with operating backgrounds, people who have been successful in molding companies and getting products out the door."

For managers who wish to buy their companies, one new area of specialization is the leveraged buyout (LBO)—broadly speaking, when a company is purchased by a group of investors and financed mainly by borrowing against the

THE TREND IS CLEAR: MORE VENTURE CAPITAL IS BEGETTING MORE ENTREPRENEURIAL ACTIVITY, AND MORE ENTREPRENEURIAL ACTIVITY IS BEGETTING MORE VENTURE CAPITAL

company's assets. In addition to increasing their investments in LBOs, several firms are establishing independent funds to separate LBOs from traditional portfolio investments. The reason: "LBOs represent a significant departure from the traditional orientation of venture capital companies toward [startup] high-tech companies where assets are intangible," says Brophy. In LBOs, the assets are tangible and provide hard collateral for debt. "You might have both LBOs and traditional venture capital funds under the same roof, but the two are quite different things."

While the venture capital industry is undergoing dramatic changes, though, some things remain the same. For instance, the industry is still concentrated in a handful of states. Just four of these states—New York, California, Massachusetts, and Connecticut—accounted for 71% of the new money raised in 1984. Nearly 35% of the total capital raised went to venture firms in Northern California, the home of Silicon Valley. But, according to Venture Economics, which tracks this information, venture capital is also beginning to spread well beyond these traditional centers. For instance, in 1984, there was a significant increase in money raised by venture firms in Colorado, Pennsylvania, Illinois, and New Jersey.

And venture capital is no longer an exclusively American domain; it's rapidly becoming an international phenomenon. The reason, says Reyes, "is an increasing awareness that venture capital plays a very real role in the economic development process." Japan has an embryonic venture capital industry, as does Singapore, the United Kingdom, and continental Europe. "The European arena is particularly aware that it has been leapfrogged by the United States in terms of technology," says Reyes. "And now, in addition to forming alliances with U.S. firms, they are trying to develop a venture environment by cultivating a risk-taking psychology in their own countries, which are traditionally conservative."

One indication of the European venture boom has been the growth of the European Venture Capital Association, founded in Brussels, Belgium, in 1983. The association now is comprised of more than 80 firms in the United Kingdom and Western Europe, and, according to Robert A. Ceurvorst, its secretary general, the membership role is expanding every month. Since many of these firms invest in American companies—or offer important links to overseas markets—they are becoming a rich resource for fledgling American firms, especially in high-tech areas like electronics. The spirit of entrepreneurship is particularly alive in France, where government-fostered changes in the capital markets and tax laws now encourage the use of American-style venture techniques.

And the French are not alone. In the past, foreign investors would typically channel their money through U.S. venture capitalists for investment in American companies. But now, more and more foreigners are generating their own funds for investment both in their own countries and abroad, often with U.S. venture capitalists acting as co-investors and consultants. In Japan there are more than 20 active venture funds, including several either affiliated with or managed by such blue-chip American firms as Hambrecht & Quist.

The trend—both here and abroad—is clear. More venture capital is begetting more entrepreneurial activity, and more entrepreneurial activity is begetting more venture capital. According to analysts, this trend should continue well into the future. As Brophy puts it: "In the race for technological growth and development, investors throughout the world are beginning to see the tremendous value that lies in cultivating the partnership of venture capitalists and entrepreneurs."

—Lee Kravitz

MONEY FOR THE ASKING

Art Caisse was minding his own business during the summer of 1982 when a partner from Sutter Hill Ventures, the prestigious Palo Alto, Calif., venture capital firm, plucked him away from his job as vice-president for research of Tymshare Inc. Sutter Hill, unsolicited, offered him a loan and an office in its own suite to get started on any computer communications ideas he had in mind. Sure enough, six months later Caisse's Cohesive Network Corp., Los Gatos, Calif., received funding of $2 million—from Sutter Hill, along with Bessemer Venture Partners—leaving Caisse controlling 50% of the stock. "It's been like a fairy tale," says the Cohesive Network Corp. board chairman.

A nice story—and a true one. But in the real world, venture capital is rarely handed out on a silver platter—particularly to nontechnology startups. The paradox is that the demand from a throng of first-time entrepreneurs has kept pace with the unprecedented supply of cash.

Indeed, with the competition for startup capital so fierce, business hopefuls may find that their most valuable skills are those needed to pry cash loose from venture capitalists' reserves. Experiences of the most adroit, practiced fundraisers are giving other entrepreneurs the ammunition to stride confidently to the bargaining table and extract yeses from venture capitalists. Following are some rules to help first-timers tap venture capital.

Now is an opportune time to deal, so don't sell yourself short. On average, startups are raising capital at higher valuations than ever before. This means entrepreneurs are giving up less equity in exchange for *more* cash. "Never has there been a better time to start a company," insists David Marquardt, general partner of Technology Venture Investors, Menlo Park, Calif. He figures the 26 investments his fund made in high-tech startups between 1981 and 1983 were valued between $1.5 million and $2.4 million *before* the venture capital investment was counted, leaving their entrepreneurs between 40% and 50% of the equity on average. That compares to a valuation range of $500,000 to $1.5 million in 1980, when management typically ended up with 20% to 30%.

Be realistic, however. Only top high-tech managers are extracting such extravagant prices. Venture capitalists are generally not interested unless investments have the potential to return about 10 times their money within five

VENTURE CAPITAL IS PLENTIFUL, BUT SO ARE ENTREPRENEURS. RIGHT NOW, THE COMPETITION FOR MONEY IS AS HOT AS EVER

years. Without big winners, venture funds would be unable to give their investors the minimum 35% to 60% compounded annual returns they require. Historically, technology-oriented companies have done best.

Hence, The Early Stages Co., San Francisco, places relatively low valuations on the consumer goods and services companies it specializes in. A $1 million Early Stages investment in 1983 could typically buy 60% to 80% of the equity in such companies.

Be prepared to bargain. In 1982, Nubar Hagopian and Kenneth Foster set out to raise $800,000 for Magnetite Inc., a Boston manufacturer of an interior, magnetic storm window used in the retrofit market. Investors led by EAB Venture Corp. demanded 60% of the stock, and insisted that the money be structured as debt—half in notes and half in debentures convertible into stock. Hagopian and Foster countered by offering just 40% of the stock, and insisted on being able to earn back 10% of it in three years if Magnetite came within 75% of its sales projections. EAB held firm at 60%, but offered a 20% earn-back option. Finally, Hagopian and Foster traded an extra seat on the board of directors to get the earn-out equity upfront: The investing group got majority control of the board and 40% of Magnetite. Hagopian and Foster got 30% each by taking the 20% earn-out equity upfront, which they would have kept if they had satisfied the earn-out provision.

But sometimes plans go astray. And Magnetite provides a good example of why it's important to set realistic goals. Per the agreement with the investors, Hagopian and Foster were to meet a goal of $1.9 million pretax profit by November, 1985, or the 60:40 ratio would flip in favor of the investors. The Magnetite executives conceded that they wouldn't meet the specified goal. The investors pumped in an additional $800,000 between 1983 and 1984, and gained control of 60% of the company. Now Hagopian and Foster own a 40% share of Magnetite, but still have seats on the six-person board.

Develop a prototype, strategy, and management team—even if that means getting seed capital elsewhere. Even for an experienced engineering executive who came out of a subsidiary of Xerox Corp. such as Richard Charlton, "It's difficult to get venture capital with just a wild-eyed proposition," as he says. To gain negotiating leverage, Charlton completed a research and development contract with Dysan Corp., a computer disk maker, before soliciting for his own rigid disk company, Charlton Associates, Irvine, Calif. The contract paid him $1 million, which helped him refine some technical processes. "By the time we let venture capitalists even look at us," he says, "we could prove our technology would work." In April, 1982—seven months after incorporating—he raised $2 million for only 25% of the company, and his second round ballooned from $3 million to $5 million for another 20% in January, 1983.

As the number of capital sources has mushroomed, some investors are dropping the requirement that entrepreneurs risk their own cash. But even with $150,000 of their own cash, the three founders of Pensa Inc., a Portland, Ore., maker of athletic shoes, couldn't get so much as an appointment with investors. "It's no wonder," says Scott Taylor, vice-president for finance. The president was a former basketball coach, and the marketing plan called for meeting billion-dollar competitors in a hopeless national advertising campaign.

Henry Hillman Jr., scion of the wealthy Pittsburgh family that owns and operates The Hillman Co., invested $250,000 in September, 1982—but with strings attached. With 20% of Pensa's stock, a seat on the four-man board, and complete control of operations, Hillman reorganized management (including the addition of a new, qualified president), remapped the marketing strategy, and rewrote the business plan. Pensa's renewed search for venture capital turned up two offers, and Taylor says, "Some of the same venture capitalists who were shaking their heads before [were then] nodding."

Don't shotgun your business plan to investors at random. Instead, get referrals from attorneys, accountants, even stockbrokers and bankers who can recommend you to a venture capital firm interested in your industry. Cold calls in all but the hottest of deals are long shots, says Harvey Mallement, managing director of Harvest Ventures, New York. "We've never done a deal from a cold call."

An attorney versed in venture financing can get you a better deal. Investment contracts are tricky enough to warrant venture expertise. Unlikely to find a venture attorney anywhere near Broken Arrow, Okla.—headquarters for George W. Moody Inc.—George

Moody decided to rely on his own experience in writing contracts. But in the midst of negotiations with First Chicago Investment Corp., the voluminous legal clauses overwhelmed him. Feigning "dumb engineer," Moody says he asked his investor's attorney to explain the trappings, although not on a formal retainer basis. The attorney obliged and suggested Moody challenge some detrimental clauses. Moody warns, "It's not a recommended strategy, but if he agrees to help you out, the lawyer is essentially obligated to tell you everything."

Never deal under pressure. As it turned out, Moody feels he didn't get the best possible deal. Because of erratic payments from his customers for the flight-simulation equipment he manufactures, Moody was short of cash in Au-

---

WHEN ASKED HOW MUCH THE COMPANY WAS WORTH, "WE FROZE. IT WAS LIKE STARTING A SKI RACE AT THE BOTTOM OF THE HILL"

---

gust, 1982, when First Chicago provided an interim credit line guarantee from its parent company, a bank. "That obligated us to whatever venture capital deal they offered, as long as it was reasonable," Moody says. Had he not waited until a month before he needed capital, he might have saved 20% of his equity. Instead, he gave up 45% for $500,000 in convertible debentures and $3.5 million in nonconvertible debentures.

If you have a choice of venture capitalists, don't necessarily grab the one that offers the best price. D'Lites of America Inc., a Norcross, Ga., franchisor of low-calorie fast-food restaurants, turned down at least four investment offers for a $2.3 million deal led by William Blair Venture Partners of Chicago. Founder and board chairman Doug Sheley chose the geographically dispersed consortium of five firms organized by Blair because he figures it can provide a network to help screen potential franchisees and provide them with financing contacts in the states where he intends to sell franchises. Sheley lowered his original proposal of $5 a share to $4 a share.

Negotiate with a valuation in mind. There are at least half a dozen ways to determine a company's value, each yielding a different figure. But almost any one is a place to begin bargaining. Venture capitalists often start by estimating the projected earnings of the first

profitable year (the first chance to cash out), multiplied by some price-earnings ratio of similar companies. By applying their desired rate of return to that valuation, they work backward to come up with the amount of equity they must get to achieve that goal. "We had firm answers for all of their questions about technology, markets, and products," Charlton says of his first few interviews with venture firms. "But as soon as they asked how much the company was worth, we froze. It made us vulnerable, like starting a ski race at the bottom of the hill."

If you are extra confident, consider playing venture capitalists off against one another. Just be sure it doesn't backfire. In this market, a strong negotiator with a desirable company can virtually command his own deal, within reason. Still, many investors won't play a bidding game. Trip Hawkins was prepared to walk away from any investor—and he let them know it—and take out a bank loan to tide over his software startup, Electronic Arts, San Mateo, Calif. But he knew he had a hot ticket the day he left a marketing spot at Apple Computer in April, 1982, and began receiving calls from venture capitalists.

Probably due to his Apple connection, Hawkins took space in the office of Don Valentine, an Apple backer and operations man whose participation Hawkins set as a priority. When it was time to negotiate, Hawkins asked for $2 million for "substantially less than 50% of the equity," and Valentine responded with a less favorable deal. Careful to avoid an auction, Hawkins agreed to talk with three more firms, each aware of Valentine's interest. That helped spur their interest, "like blood for the sharks to feed on," he says. To his dismay, all three came back with similar proposals.

Eventually, Hawkins met with Kleiner, Perkins, Caufield & Byers, another premiere San Francisco firm. Kleiner, Perkins agreed to a compromise deal. Hawkins went back to Valentine, willing to sacrifice his participation only after Kleiner, Perkins became a strong backup. But Valentine accepted the new deal, as did Sevin Rosen Partners Limited, Dallas.

Seeing someone like Electronic Arts President Hawkins talk his way into an improved deal has an element of poetic justice to it. Venture capitalists, by virtue of practice, have an edge in negotiating and won't hesitate to use it. Still the best deal, most will tell you, is a "win-win" deal, where everybody's happy. "After all," says a veteran investor, "we have to work with the guys for years afterward." —Jon Levine

HOW TO WRITE A BUSINESS PLAN THAT WORKS

"The business plan is the only chance you've got to see a venture capitalist," says Brent T. Rider, president of Union Venture Corp., the venture capital subsidiary of Union Bank, Los Angeles. "It's absolutely critical."

Chances are writing a business plan will be a tough exercise. Plans must be promotional, substantive, and succinct. Most venture capitalists prefer that proposals total no more than 50 pages, and some draw the line at 25. At the same time, plans must be comprehensive. A too-sketchy plan is often viewed as evidence entrepreneurs haven't done their homework, sure grounds for rejection. All projections should be based on a five-year time period, which may be hard to envision for companies with minuscule or no revenue, or no products in existence. Yet every figure should be defensible in some way.

There is no such thing as a perfect plan. Venture capitalists openly disagree on several aspects, such as whether to include résumés for a proposed board of directors and how detailed market research should be. Prescribed formats are virtually nonexistent, and the struc-ture that succeeds brilliantly with one plan may fall flat with another. A plan for a startup that would intrigue venture sources probably will be turned down flat by a bank. Even the few "givens," like length guidelines, don't always hold. Union Ventures has funded plans as brief as 15 pages and as long as 250. As Rider

A TYPICAL TIME FRAME FOR WRITING A BUSINESS PLAN RUNS FROM ONE TO SIX MONTHS, DEPENDING ON HOW COMPLICATED THE PLAN BECOMES AND HOW MUCH TIME CAN BE DEVOTED TO IT

explains, "When it comes to business plans, about the only rule is that there really aren't any rules."

Yet venture capitalists say they know a good plan when they see one. That usually begins with a clever sense of what the plan needs to convey. "Business plans have to confront the old 'who, when, where, why, and how,'" says Dr. James McN. Stancill, associate professor of finance at the University of South-ern California in Los Angeles. "You have to tell people everything they could possibly want to know." Most importantly, a plan should stress what makes a venture truly unique and worthy of investment *now*.

Begin the plan with a one- to two-page summary of the proposed venture: its purpose, significant product features, market potential, capital requested, and technical and operational milestones. Give financial projections, including when you expect to break even, and investor profit potential. Keep it clear and readable, since venture capitalists inundated by business plans may never glance past the summary. And steer away from hype or slogans: "Madison Avenue doesn't belong in a business plan," Rider points out. You may want to write the summary last, when you're best able to sort out the relevant information. Whatever happens, don't skip this section. "If we have to read an entire plan," says Rider, "we won't."

Next comes the table of contents. List sections and major subsections, but save the details for discussion in the text. From here on, the order is up to you. A typical agenda: summary, table of contents, company description, prod-ucts, market analysis and strategy, technology/research and development, competition, manufacturing and operations, management and ownership, organization and personnel, financial data, and appendices. Or you can lead with your major strength, such as proprietary technology or first-class management, followed by your second-strongest suit, and so on. As long as all of the information is included, "it's a question of how early you lay out your aces," says Ron Stephens, senior consultant of ADL Inc. Ventures Group in San Francisco, a startup-oriented division of management consulting giant Arthur D. Little & Co. Stephens usually favors the high-card-first strategy, which he refers to as the "algorithm" method. Not only are many entrepreneurs more comfortable getting right to the point, he says, but also "venture capitalists want the bottom line, financial and otherwise, as quickly as they can get it."

Whatever format you settle on, it's helpful to lead with a background sketch of the company, if it exists. Describe when it was formed, where, by whom, and with what funds. Where did the idea come from in the first place? Trace any changes in capitalization, management, ownership, operating activity, and structure. Give current general information: What business you're in, what the principal products or services are, and what markets and applications you're seeking. Make clear why someone else can't generate the same product or tap the same market with minimal effort—"distinctive competence," in entrepreneurial jargon. "There has to be some barrier to entry when somebody decides to compete with you," says G. Bradford Jones, a principal of Brentwood Associates, Los Angeles. This, he points out, is inevitable if the concept is as good as you're saying it is.

Next, move on to individual sections. Jones suggests striving for an overall tone that doesn't assume venture capitalists know intimate details of an industry. But don't underestimate venture capitalists' savvy, either.

Give a complete description of products ready for the market and improvements over existing, conventional products. Cite primary applications and any proposed enhancements (and the timetable over which enhancements would occur). Describe product models and prices. If no product yet exists, describe prototypes or cite evidence that proves your product is viable. Depending on the technology involved, you can use this section or set up a separate technology/research and development section to address related issues.

For a section on technology/R&D, discuss your proprietary technology and the feasibility of gaining patent protection, or explain why you need not apply for a patent. Touch on how comprehensive and effective patents or copyrights are likely to be. Is there any other way to protect your technology? Describe R&D activity to be pursued and products likely to be introduced within the next five years.

This is also the place to describe new technologies that may become practical during the next five years and how they will affect product design. Cite any factors that may limit their development or acceptance, and how you believe you can overcome those obstacles. Discuss R&D risks, regulatory requirements or the need to gain approval from a government agency, and propose R&D milestones *and* standards by which to judge

BEGIN THE PLAN WITH A BRIEF SUMMARY. WRITE IT LAST, WHEN YOU'RE BEST ABLE TO SORT OUT THE RELEVANT INFORMATION. VENTURE CAPITALISTS DON'T HAVE TIME TO READ AN ENTIRE PLAN

whether goals have been reached. Don't include copies of patent documents, correspondence with regulators, and the like. Venture capitalists don't necessarily understand or care about minute technical details early on and may view such inserts as unnecessary padding.

Just how much to reveal about proprietary information is another issue. At least as far as the essence of the material is concerned, you don't have much choice. Venture capitalists almost universally refuse to sign nondisclosure agreements, and in the cases where they will, it's only after they have a pretty good idea of what the technology is all about. One reason is that nondisclosure agreements can be so broadly written that venture capitalists argue they can't pursue their business if they sign. Another reason is time. "We couldn't afford to wait for a legal review of each and every document," Jones says. If it's any comfort, reputable venture capitalists maintain they keep business plans confidential. Many will turn down the opportunity to view plans if they already have investments along similar lines, something that can be easily checked out in advance by phone. And if they do bring in outside experts, it should be only with the knowledge and consent of the entrepreneurs involved—and the understanding those experts will agree not to disclose what they learn.

On the other hand, you're probably taking a risk every time you send out a plan. "There's not much way around that," concludes Jeffrey Scheinrock, a partner in Big Eight accounting firm Arthur Young and Co. and director of its entrepreneurial services group in Los Angeles. The consolation is that technology can often be described without being revealed. Rider suggests stating what is proprietary, what the advantages are, and what the technology yields. "You can still tell us enough," he argues. "We're not going to know how to mix the eye of newt and toe of frog anyway." What's more, venture capitalists tend to suspect technology that *can* be fully revealed in the confines of a business plan, says Jones. "If something is that simple, there's a question about whether it can be protected once the product is released." But venture capitalists aren't likely to fund something they don't think they fully understand, so be prepared for full disclosure on request.

Under the section on market analysis and marketing strategy describe the industry your company is in, its size, and how large it will be in 5 and 10 years. Give its chief characteristics and describe major trends. Then focus on the market segment *specifically* addressed by the product: size, historical and projected growth rates, and market data sources.

The actual marketing plan is critical. "This is where technical types tend to fall apart," suggests USC's Stancill. "If you don't know how you're going to sell your product, you're in trouble." Describe your complete marketing strategy (including market-share objectives and desired product and company image), proposed distribution method, promotion, pricing, geographical penetration, and field service. Since no startup can do everything at once, explain how you'll set priorities. On the selling side, describe how you'll identify and contact prospective customers (telephone marketing, in-person visits, direct mail), your level of selling effort (number of sales people, full- or part-time), efficiency (how many sales calls each person can generate), conversion rates (number of calls per demonstration, number of demonstrations per sale), and how long each activity will take per person. Estimate initial order size, and the likelihood and size of repeat orders. Describe the structure of your sales organization, commission plans, and any other sales incentives.

If your product is already available, cite any current test accounts or active accounts with present and expected volume and reorder rates. Give inventory and distribution network costs and projections. Trace your product's introduction and marketing and selling efforts up to the present. Give sales terms, current order backlog, and a comparison with backlogs in earlier periods. Describe any existing customer agreements and marketing or selling agreements. Define your selling cycle (Does it run from production to delivery or from sale to payment?) and detail the length of the steps within it. What is your product-pricing strategy now and for the next five years? Describe customers' buying habits and the likely impact of your product on how customers do business, such as cost savings. Will customers need to retool production lines or alter their organizational structures once they've bought?

Finally, describe how segments and applications will change over the next five years. Focus on showing how a product fits into the market as described. "We see a lot of proposals for office-automation systems," says Jones, "but it's hard to understand how customers would justify buying them. They just don't seem to fulfill a specific need."

Market research performed by outside sources is "very important," Scheinrock says. "Your assumptions aren't necessarily going to be accepted." Most venture capitalists agree that some research is probably helpful. But market research studies can sometimes run $30,000 or more, and Rider warns research isn't particularly meaningful if you're introducing a revolutionary product. When demand is difficult to project, "sometimes you just have to guess," he says. Others prefer entrepreneurs describe markets themselves rather than rely on commissioned studies. Jones says, "It shows they understand."

The next order of business might be a section on the competition. Name the companies you'll be competing with, including the likelihood that other startups may soon enter the field. For each, give sales volume and market share and describe competitive advantages and disadvantages. Many venture capitalists also like to see an equivalent price/performance matrix (a graph that shows how your product compares with the competition), although Jones cautions a matrix should include buying factors if products are similar in price and performance. Describe competitors' distribution, inventory, marketing, and selling procedures. Detail industry competitive practices and any major competitive risks. For instance, will you threaten the strategic objectives of competitors—and thus provide them considerable incentive to destroy you—or will you have a more limited impact? Do you

require liaisons with manufacturers or distributors which may be reluctant to support your product for fear of alienating your competitors, or for warranty or liability reasons?

Honesty is crucial throughout your plan, but that's especially true when it comes to describing competition. "Say as much as you can," advises Rider. Far from injuring your chances of being funded, you'll be doing yourself a favor. "If we're able to find out more than someone seems to know," Rider says, "he's probably not going to raise money from us." Stancill points out you may also be protecting yourself from legal liability, since you could be sued for fraud later on if the deal goes sour.

In the area of manufacturing and operations, cite necessary production

FOR A SECTION ON THE COMPETITION, NAME THE COMPANIES YOUR FIRM WILL BE COMPETING WITH, INCLUDING THE LIKELIHOOD THAT OTHER STARTUPS MAY SOON ENTER THE FIELD. DESCRIBE COMPETITIVE ADVANTAGES AND DISADVANTAGES

equipment and costs, historical and projected, and major equipment lead times. Describe production or assembly facilities and methods, average production time per unit (current and projected), and unit cost by major material and labor components. Give current production-facility capacity and project your needs over the next five years. Cite essential raw materials and their sources, availability, costs, and contract and supplier limitations (including single suppliers and lead times). Describe existing or imminent labor agreements. If portions of manufacturing will be subcontracted, which ones and how? Detail costs for production at different volume levels.

When you get to the section on management and ownership, provide background information on all top management: length of time with the company (on a full- or part-time basis) and current compensation and extent of financial interest. Include a current and projected organizational chart, whether or not all the members of your team are already on board. If any key managers are missing, say so. (Don't bring in someone mediocre just to fill out this section.) Describe how you plan to attract and compensate key people (stock,

incentive bonus, and so on). Make certain to differentiate between managerial responsibilities and ownership, even if the individuals involved are the same. List any directors and their stock holdings, along with a complete roster of other stockholders. Name any individuals or entities holding notes, options, warrants, or other special rights, and describe each agreement. Identify any limitations on management, such as non-competition agreements in force, and provide a legal opinion of their validity or applicability. How much stock is currently issued and authorized? How many shares do you propose?

Provide résumés for all top management. According to Stancill, résumés should show achievements: begin with your most recent job, describe your specific responsibilities and the extent to which you had profit-and-loss accountability. If possible, give profit levels achieved during your tenure. "You're trying to show you can make money," Stancill points out. Jones likes a tabular format with dates, company affiliation, position, and so on, for each individual, including colleges attended, majors, and degrees awarded. If a company is highly technical, include résumés for senior engineers and R&D staff as well.

Naming a board of directors is a thornier question. Rider doesn't like to see résumés for a proposed board, preferring to structure the board to the mutual satisfaction of management and venture backers later on. Jones disagrees. "Being affiliated with qualified people is an advantage," he argues. Stephens suggests taking the middle ground by identifying two or three individuals who have indicated their willingness to serve on a board, but only if the startup will clearly benefit from their expertise. Provide essential background on each, but skip résumés. And don't bother naming prestigious law and accounting firms in an effort to impress venture capitalists with your contacts. Many venture firms have cozy relationships with lawyers and accountants, and prefer to steer startups into familiar hands.

Under organization and personnel, describe the rest of your current and proposed structure: number of people needed in each capacity, compensational methods and levels, and pension and profit-sharing structure.

Give historical financial information up to the most recent month, and if prior-year losses have occurred, detail amounts and reasons. Include pro forma profit-and-loss statements monthly for the first year, quarterly for the next two years, and annually for another two to three years. If the company won't break even for more than two years, include quarterly statements up to breakeven. This section should also include cash-flow statements (monthly for two years, quarterly or annually for the next three years). Provide source-and-use-of-funds documents based on two different equity assumptions, with breakeven points clearly identified in each case. Finally, provide pro forma balance sheets quarterly or annually for five years.

The five-year requirement may seem impossible to meet with any degree of accuracy—and often is. "There's a great deal of blue sky beyond two years," agrees Stephens. One solution is to generate three scenarios for the five-year period: conservative projections based on a weak market, aggressive projections based on robust demand, and something more realistic in between. If there isn't space to detail from all three scenarios, provide highlights from each.

Next, explain any key assumptions and show how numbers were derived, "so somebody can really read the blooming thing," says Stancill. "They may not agree with you, but at least they can follow your reasoning." If you're guessing, say so—and why. For instance, you may not yet have rented office space, but can explain how much rents are running per square foot in the general location you're seeking. Detail categories carefully. You don't need to say how many pencils you're buying, but "general administrative expenses" isn't enough. "Large or unusual numbers should always be explained," Rider advises. Stick to reasonable estimates, and avoid the so-called "1% trap." Giving market size and suggesting a mere 1% share would generate phenomenal revenue is common—and useless—according to venture capitalists. Stancill queries, "How do you know you can get 1%?"

Explain how you expect the capitalization process to go, including initial and subsequent venture capital financings and the extent to which existing investors will be diluted at each stage. Don't forget proposed R&D partnership funds and other possible sources of funds. Make sure assumptions fit the scenario you've developed so far: Figures on unit sales, selling price, and other concerns should correlate directly with the background material presented in the manufacturing and marketing sections. Unless development time is unusually long, don't try to project beyond five years. Show the company's probable market value based on the price/earnings ratios of similar companies. Include statements of accounts receivable and payable. But, cautions Scheinrock, "It's important to only put in what matters."

A note on salaries: Venture capital-ists like them lean, with financial payoffs coming when your team accomplishes what it set out to achieve. But salaries for the management team shouldn't be too low, says Stancill. "It raises questions about whether you're really worth what you say you're worth."

Should you explicitly state what you're willing to accept in terms of capital and equity? That depends. Rider believes giving some indication is "appropriate," particularly since venture capitalists tend to discount whatever entrepreneurs request anyway. But be aware that statement could become a liability. Should the deal be funded for much less than you ask or your equity shaved substantially, Jones counters, you may not want that record languishing in someone's files as evidence you

> **VENTURE CAPITALISTS LIKE SALARIES LEAN, WITH FINANCIAL PAYOFFS COMING WHEN YOUR TEAM MEETS ITS GOAL. BUT DON'T MAKE SALARIES TOO LOW; IT MAY RAISE QUESTIONS ABOUT YOUR REAL VALUE TO THE VENTURE**

didn't really mean what you said. "It just doesn't serve any purpose," Jones says. Being highly unrealistic about pricing could also put off investors who might otherwise seriously consider the deal, but believe a ballooned estimate indicative of future problems.

The appendix is a catchall section for whatever didn't seem to fit earlier: additional notes to financial statements, professional references, detailed market studies, further technical background, articles from trade journals, and other supporting documents. You may also want to include pictures or drawings of products and prototypes. Some entrepreneurs also opt to put résumés here. Don't worry if the appendices seem to swell quickly—it's common for appendices to be as long as a plan's actual text.

Bank financing is another matter. Banks don't lend equity capital, which means loans to raw startups must be guaranteed by the individual principals. Principals must prove net worth or assets sufficient for repayment, information venture capitalists may never request. On the other hand, a bank probably requires much less aggregate information. Your plan's summary and management and financial sections may be enough—and in the case of financial statements, pro formas are far less important than historical data. "We're looking for a secondary source of repayment," explains Cathy Allen, president of Metrobank, Torrance, Calif., which caters to entrepreneurs. "If we come in to a startup at all, it has to be through the back door."

If your venture already has a track record, banks still may not be interested in seeing your entire business plan. But chances are banks will want to see financial pro formas as an indication of your company's ability to repay. What's more, banks will require accounts receivable aging statements (accounts receivable for 30, 60, and 90 days) to find out how likely you are to collect outstanding funds. That tells a bank whether you're able to pay your debts. If you're requesting a loan to purchase specific pieces of equipment, make sure to include written estimates for the items. As with venture capital sources, the plan's organization is up to you. Says Allen, "A good banker is capable of putting the pieces together."

If that sounds like a lot of work, you're right. "Everybody thinks drafting a business plan is a lot easier than it is," says Scheinrock. A typical time frame runs from one to six months, depending on how complicated the plan becomes and how much time entrepreneurs are able to devote. For example, Minoru Tonai, vice-president and general manager of Symbolics Inc., Cambridge, Mass., spent three months as primary architect of the startup's plan in 1980. Symbolics wanted to develop hardware to use a symbolic language created at the Massachusetts Institute of Technology. But because the symbolic-language workstation was a new concept, "we were guessing all the time," says Tonai. The venture was funded for $6 million in 1981. Smiles Tonai, "Everyone thought it would cost a lot less until we put the plan together."

The entrepreneurs who launched GigaBit Logic Inc. of Newbury Park, Calif., managed to draft their plan in just two months in late 1981. But not without their own set of problems: GigaBit manufactures integrated circuits based on gallium arsenide, not industry-standard silicon. "We didn't have to differentiate ourselves," says President and Chairman Fred Blum. "We had to prove the technology was viable." Apparently they succeeded: GigaBit received $1 million in seed capital in 1982, and venture backers later upped the ante to $9 million. "We probably did more extensive planning than most people," says Blum, whose original plan totaled more than 75 pages, "but we felt it was the only way to make our case."

—Michelle Bekey

WHAT INVESTORS HATE MOST ABOUT BUSINESS PLANS

They live on his desktop at work, fatten his briefcase coming home, and sit on his lap during long plane trips. A venture capitalist can never get away from business plans. They pour into his office like the tide, and, like the tide, they are swept right back out: Ninety-nine out of 100 business plans that are received by venture capitalists are never funded.

During any given year, large venture capital firms typically receive 500 to 1,500 business plans in the mail. Surprisingly, most are read. But only about 10% of those plans make it past the first reading, and only 10% of those are ever funded. "Most venture capitalists are so inundated with business plans that they

ONLY 1% OF BUSINESS PLANS GET FUNDED, SO MAKE THEM SHORT, NEAT (BUT NOT TOO NEAT), AND SHOW HOW YOU COULD PUT THE CASH TO GOOD WORK

are looking for something in the plan that will let them say no, and quickly," confesses James Lally, general partner of Kleiner, Perkins, Caufield & Byers' Palo Alto, Calif., office. For the entrepre-

neur, the odds are slim indeed.

There are certainly no hard-and-fast rules regarding business plans. An all-star team with proprietary products and a ready market is likely to get a nod even if the business plan is the back of a damp cocktail napkin. Even so, it's likely the entrepreneur will still be asked to write a formal plan, if only to enforce the discipline required to do so. For the rest of us, the simple understanding that business plans are serious summations of strategy, not sales gimmicks, will go a long way.

Most venture capitalists think of business plans in terms of inches. A report that is no more than 1/4-to-1/2-in. thick, loosely bound in a clear plastic cover, will do nicely. George Crandell, a general partner with Los Angeles venture capital firm Brentwood Associates, remembers the other extreme: Two cardboard boxes arrived at his office containing 12 volumes of looseleaf notebooks. "We knew we weren't going to read them," he says.

Venture capitalists are not impressed with computer-generated scenarios in business plans. Such electronic theatrics tend to accomplish little, while needlessly padding already adequate proposals. "One thing VisiCalc has done for the world is make business plans 50% larger," says Mary Jane Elmore, general partner of Institutional Venture Partners, Menlo Park, Calif. "We want to know if somebody really sat and thought about those numbers, or if they just punched them in."

A business plan must show clearly and concisely the nature of the new company and its market, the amount of money needed, sales and earnings forecasts, and the makeup of the management team. The word venture capitalists most love to describe a good business plan is "crisp." Like a job-seeker's resume, a business plan's purpose in life is to secure an interview for its writer.

Although some potential investors may say they look at a business plan that arrives "over the transom," a proposal sent in the mail without a phone call first might as well be dead on arrival. Referral calls from well-connected friends or associates make a big difference. An introduction from an entrepreneur whose company has already been funded by the venture capital firm gets the best results. Lacking such evidence of good connections, an introductory call from an attorney or accountant who knows the firm will often do the trick.

Often, the best strategy is simply avoiding the obvious turnoffs. "At 3000 Sand Hill Road we get people carrying a sackful of business plans passing them out like calling cards," says Robert Burr, senior vice-president of General Electric Venture Capital Corp., which has a branch office in the Menlo Park office complex that's home to 28 venture capital firms.

The quickest way for an entrepreneur to get a business plan rejected is to send it to a venture capitalist who doesn't fund that kind of business. Kleiner, Perkins' Lally says about one-third of all plans received by his firm, which favors high-tech ventures, are tossed out on those grounds. A little research by the entrepreneur will uncover the kinds of businesses a venture capitalist is willing to consider. Most firms keep lists of preferred or avoided investments.

Venture capitalists vary in the amount of importance they assign to business plans. Donald Lucas, a Menlo Park, Calif., venture capitalist for 28 years, says the plans all tend to look alike after a while. He focuses on referrals and the experience of the management team. Brentwood Associates' George Crandell, on the other hand, says a business plan is like a contract between entrepreneur and investor. "You had better be prepared to live with the numbers you put in there and be judged by them," he says. "The most highly regarded managers are those who lay out what they are going to do and get it done."

Regardless of the import of the document in question, venture capitalists

"A BUSINESS PLAN SHOULDN'T READ LIKE A SALES BROCHURE WITH A LOT OF FLOWERY NONESSENTIALS. IT SHOULD GET TO THE POINT"

agree that it is only the first step. As Gerald S. Casilli, general partner of Genesis Capital, puts it, "The value of a business plan is in the process. The important part is the thinking that goes on to come up with it."

With the odds stacked against the entrepreneur, a venture capitalist's first impressions—of the initial phone call or the executive summary at the front of the business plan—are key to getting a personal audition. "The first 30 seconds," says Bill Lanphear, general partner of The Early Stages Co., San Francisco, "are about as important as those first few seconds of eye contact when people are romancing."

Investors usually expect a business plan to be neatly typed and purged of poor grammar and spelling errors, but too polished a business plan can raise the eyebrows of venture capitalists. "If a guy thinks form is more important than substance, then he's missing the point of a business plan," says Steven Merrill, managing partner of Merrill, Pickard, Anderson & Eyre, San Francisco. Herbert Shaw, limited partner of Shaw Venture Partners, Portland, Ore., agrees. "It shouldn't read like a sales brochure with a lot of flowery nonessentials," he says. "It should get to the point."

Venture capitalists strongly advise against using outside consultants to help develop a business plan. "A professionally prepared business plan is a turnoff if the entrepreneur is not the guiding force

behind it," says Dan Case, vice-president of venture capital at Hambrecht & Quist, San Francisco. "If it's not really [an entrepreneur's] business plan, venture capitalists see through it very quickly," warns David Thompson, partner and national coordinator for venture finance at Deloitte Haskins & Sells, New York. Thompson's unit at the Big Eight accounting firm offers entrepreneurs help in obtaining venture capital backing.

A venture capitalist will trash a plan as quickly as a maître d'hôtel in a chic restaurant will turn away a man in sneakers, so it is important for entrepreneurs to avoid common errors that send up red flags to the seasoned business-plan reader. "If a detailed description of the competition isn't in there, I'm willing to turn it down on the spot," says Roger Borovoy, general partner of Sevin Rosen Bayless Borovoy, Sunnyvale, Calif. The first things he reads in a business plan are the resumes of the management team. A quick turnoff is the plan that leaves blank spaces for alleged employees whose identity, for one reason or another, can't be divulged. "Don't bother with future draft choices," he quips.

Most venture capitalists don't want financial statements with long-term forecasts down to the last nickel. They do expect projections of factors such as sales, earnings, and cash flow on a monthly basis for the first or second year and on a quarterly basis for five years. If the venture's team lacks financial experience, the gap will not escape notice. "A lot of plans use assumptions on receivables of 30 days," notes Lally. "That's a big red flag. It's not the way the real world runs."

And if there is one thing that is sure to leave a venture capitalist with a bitter aftertaste, it's an entrepreneur who seems more eager to spend money than earn it. Ken Tingey of Ventana Growth Fund, San Diego, recalls a plan from one early-stage company whose 30 employees were earning an average salary of $35,000. "In an entrepreneurial environment," he says, "you don't get high salaries. You get stock." Tingey also recalls a plan where five founders had factored in $500-a-month lease payments for cars. Needless to say, the deal wasn't funded—at least not by Ventana.

Sometimes, of course, the aftertaste left by a spendthrift entrepreneur can be strong without being bitter. One Christmas season, a seeker of venture capital sent Steven Merrill a business plan accompanied by a small bottle of Remy Martin cognac and a plastic glass. "Needless to say, I never read it," recalls the venture capitalist. "But I drank the bottle." —Sabin Russell

HOLDING ON TO EQUITY

When Edwin Lee and Matt Biewer founded Pro-Log Corp., they had two requisites: It would be far from the job-hopping atmosphere they deplored in Los Angeles, and it would be free from fast-buck pressures imposed by outside investors.

Lee, Biewer, and a third colleague, Keith Rosburg, located Pro-Log, a maker of microprocessor components, in Monterey, Calif., remote from almost anything except cypresses and sea lions. And they stoutly retained full equity control. Says Lee: "We wanted a fun organization where there was commitment toward building things well." Twelve years later, Pro-Log is a solidly established company with 1984 sales of $20.4 million. Lee and his partners still own 60% of the company, with the rest held by family, friends, and employees.

Lee is not the first to dream of such independence. Many of those who hold on to their equity remain, to be sure, on the small side. But a handful of such independently controlled companies have surpassed the $100 million mark and a very few, most notably $1 billion-in-sales Wang Laboratories, are approaching the status of giants.

Founders of such firms tend to have more business talent than most. And even for entrepreneurs, they hold high self-esteem. Richard McVickers and his wife own Ven-Tel Inc., a Santa Clara, Calif., modem maker. Declares McVickers: "Without venture capitalists you don't have a lot of people to coordinate with. Decisions are better and faster."

In addition many companies that remain essentially in the hands of their founders fall into one of the following categories:
■ Companies that generate substantial sales right at the start as a way to pay-as-you-go.
■ Companies with entrepreneurs who willingly absorb debt rather than look for equity-based capital.
■ Companies with unique products that discourage competition and thus can sustain high margins.
■ Companies with entrepreneurs that survive with less capital; at a more mature stage, investors will put up money for less of the action.

Even founders who are not adverse to outsiders' advice see advantages in maintaining control. Edward Colbert never intended to hold all the stock in Data Instruments Inc., a Lexington, Mass., maker of measuring and automation equipment. But when he bought the company from Tyco Laboratories in 1977, he paid with a note that Tyco subordinated to Colbert's bank debt, eliminating his need for outside investors. Now, eight years later, Colbert believes majority ownership allowed him to avoid "the whims of the public markets."

WHILE CONVENTIONAL WISDOM HOLDS THAT 10% OF A MAJOR COMPANY IS BETTER THAN 100% OF A SMALL ONE, MANY ENTREPRENEURS CLAIM THEY CAN HAVE IT BOTH WAYS

To be sure, many entrepreneurs need capital to gobble up market share early on. Founders who do maintain control must have the right product at the right moment. David Brophy, professor of business administration at the University of Michigan in Ann Arbor, says such companies must "be able to generate enough retained earnings so that sales keep pace with sales opportunities and the ability to finance."

Entrepreneurs may find they have sufficient sales only in retrospect. When Fred Molinari founded Marlboro, Mass.-based Data Translation Inc., the 1974 recession and a law suit challenging Molinari's right to Data Translation's technology discouraged investors. So Molinari began the company, which builds analog measurement instruments that communicate with digital computers, with only $700 in savings and a $5,000 loan from a bank Molinari did not tell about the suit.

Molinari then contracted for advertising space, taking advantage of electronics publications' 60-day credit waivers. Resulting sales, with margins 65% above manufacturing cost, paid for the ads and more. Although Molinari's ads revealed Data Translation's product to competitors, he claims that its properties were so unfamiliar that he held a one-year jump on the competition. A $25,000 order for devices to measure oil flow along the Alaska pipeline gave the company another boost. "It was just one thing after another," recalls Molinari.

Data Translation grew steadily until May, 1981, when the company had sales of $4.8 million, Molinari sold 20% to C.R. Investments, of which Cavendish Investing Ltd. of Canada is a general partner, for $2 million. "Because we waited so long," states Molinari, "we had to give away less." Today, Molinari holds, along with his family, about 44% of a company that had $15 million in sales in 1984, up 40% over 1983. At press time, Data Translation was registering to go public.

Most entrepreneurs attempt a low profile at first. With limited competition, they can keep profit margins high to prepare for growth. In 1955, when Donald Bently, then residing in Berkeley, Calif., developed a transducer to measure vibration in rotating machinery, for example, he based it on little-known eddy-current technology. "I had no competitors," Bently recalls about his early mail-order business. Only after 10 years and at a time when his company, now known as Bently Nevada Corp., Minden, Nev., obtained $1 million in sales did the competition begin to react. But by then, Bently says, "I was the industry leader." Bently Nevada had $50 million in revenues in 1983. Today, there are 54 sales and service offices worldwide. Stock, with the exception of a few shares in employee hands, all belongs to Bently.

Service companies can find hard-to-copy niches, too. By building a network of franchises that specialize in pizza delivery, Thomas Monaghan, chairman of the board and president of Domino's Pizza Inc., Ann Arbor, Mich., for example, found an approach competitors hesitate to copy. "Delivery is a pain in the neck," he says.

Monaghan built a successful regional chain, but flopped in 1969 when he tried to take it national with strong centralized management and controls. When profits plummeted, his bankers removed him. But Monaghan got a second chance 10 months later when a franchisee rebellion forced the bankers to bring him back. By 1973, Domino's had paid off creditors and was expanding again. This time Monaghan succeeded with decentralized regional management plus further standardization of the pizza-making operation. Today, Domino's has 2,000 stores and over $385 million in sales, and Monaghan holds close to 95% of the company. Through his struggles, Monaghan turned down every offer of equity financing. "Success was just a matter of time," he says deadpan.

Sometimes whole industries lend themselves to owner control if the entry costs are low enough and the profits are high enough. Today, the industry most accessible to independents is software. The niches are plentiful, demand high, and access to computers on which to write so easy that several substantial software firms are springing up in which the founders remain in firm control. Fred Gibbons, John Page, and Janelle Bedke started Software Publishing Corp., Mountain View, Calif., by buying their own $2,000 computer. Working nights and weekends, they developed their first product, PFS:FILE. Currently, they provide a family of integrated software for Apple, IBM, and selected MS-DOS computers.

Software Publishing's founders obtained $1.2 million in venture capital in return for only 35% of their equity three years after starting their company. Bedke, now vice-president of marketing, says the three, all Hewlett-Packard alumni, wanted control in order to give the company the "stability" that H-P had when David Packard and William Hewlett were leading their company through its formative years. According to Bedke, Software Publishing's 1984

sales were $23.5 million. The company went public in 1984.

Some entrepreneurs maintain control simply by holding down the need for capital. Although several modem manufacturers had already built strong market positions when Richard McVickers entered the field in 1975, he offered nothing truly distinctive in Ven-Tel's product. Nor did he resort to cutting prices. Instead of building an engineering staff, McVickers farmed out product design to freelance engineers. He also offered distributors 50% margins (compared with the 20% industry standard) in return for payment within 10 short days.

With such tactics, McVickers found the cash flow to fund a company that had annual sales of $10 million in 1982.

While conventional wisdom holds that 10% of a major firm beats 100% of a small one, many founders claim to have it both ways. Says Bently: "I've seen companies short $1 million go public and then have enormous expenses fighting the SEC."

FOUNDERS WHO MAINTAIN MAJORITY CONTROL TEND TO HAVE MORE BUSINESS TALENT THAN MOST AND TO POSSESS HIGH SELF-ESTEEM—EVEN FOR ENTREPRENEURS

Bently believes many difficulties simply go away if you let them. Every five years Bently Nevada came up against "a wall right in front of you." Seventeen years ago, Bently had to supplement his transducers with new monitoring systems to read them. "We needed many more people and parts than we could afford," he says. But time lags incurred in hiring and buying materials stretched out capital. The problem "diffused." Whatever his company's short-term capital needs, Bently covers them with short-term bank loans.

Lee claims that majority control at Pro-Log has allowed him the luxury of idealism. One example of Pro-Log's idealistic point of view, he maintains, is the company's decision to publicize the specifications of its STD bus (the electrical and physical interconnect standard for microprocessors). Pro-Log opened itself up to severe competition, but the action helped establish the bus as an industry standard. Longer-term acceptance of the bus virtually assured Pro-Log of about 10% of the $100 million market, Lee says. But had Pro-Log's

fate been in the hands of outside investors, the company might have been forced "to try to make more money in the short-run," by keeping the design proprietary.

Indeed, it is the long-term that entrepreneurs always come back to. Says Colbert of Data Instruments: "During the time the entrepreneur has control, he can create the culture the company needs to reach long-term objectives." With his corporate culture in place, Colbert says he has no qualms about giving up control. In 1980, Hambrecht & Quist took 20% of the company.

A classic case of hanging on too long is that of Michael and Charity Cheiky, who founded Ohio Scientific in 1975. Their technically advanced, low-cost computers built company sales to $20 million. Recalls Charity Cheiky: "We were determined to do things our own way." But Ohio Scientific needed capital to maintain market share against competitors and the Cheikys finally sold to M/A Comm, which soon divested it. Although $1 million richer from the sale, the Cheikys were without a company.

The Cheikys have moved to Santa Barbara, Calif. Michael is chairman and vice-president of development for Santa Barbara Labs, which manufactures advanced executive workstations that are voice activated and pictorially prompted. Michael provided the seed money, and he managed to get $10 million in venture capital in two rounds of financing. He says that Santa Barbara Labs is now shipping products to Fortune 500 companies.

Charity is also busy with her DEMI venture, which does research on high-energy battery systems. To date there is no venture financing, but a limited partnership for research and development. The Cheikys have modified their position on venture financing. "Our attitude has changed," says Charity Cheiky. "We want a management team in which risk and responsibility are spread."

None other than Edwin Lee of Pro-Log is now considering outside financing. A turning point came four years ago when, "enthusiasm within the company began dropping off." Profits have too, from 10% of sales to below 2%. To counteract the blahs, Pro-Log's founders set more ambitious growth goals, including $88 million in sales by 1989. Lee and his colleagues have begun beefing up R&D and might even consider venture capital as a way to bring in board members to help take the company public.

That would add outside pressure, no doubt, but Lee seems prepared. "Venture capitalists," he says, "have their obligations, too."

—G. Thomas Gibson

DIRECTORY

INTRODUCTION

In compiling this directory, the Editors of Venture, the Magazine for Entrepreneurs, contacted more than 1,200 firms actively involved in financing deals in the United States, Canada, the United Kingdom, Europe, Israel, and Asia. Of the firms contacted, 957 are listed on the following pages.

The directory portion of this book is broken down into two main sections: Domestic Listings and Foreign Listings.

DOMESTIC LISTINGS

Under this heading there are 780 firms divided into six subsections: Venture Firms: $10 Million and Up, Venture Firms: Under $10 Million, Small Business Investment Companies: $3 Million and Up, Small Business Investment Companies: Under $3 Million, Minority Enterprise Small Business Investment Companies: $1.5 Million and Up, and Minority Enterprise Small Business Investment Companies: Under $1.5 Million.

The first group, venture firms, consists of U.S.-based firms that fall under one of the following types: independent private venture firms; merchant and investment banking houses; corporations, bank holding companies, and other financial institutions with venture capital subsidiaries or divisions; community development corporations; and various consulting and advisory firms that specialize in venture financing. The first section within the venture firms category covers those organizations that had a minimum of $10 million in paid-in capital or invested more than $4 million in venture deals in 1983. The second group consists of those firms that did not meet these criteria because they were smaller, newly formed, or did not provide data by which to categorize them. Within each category the firms are listed alphabetically by the states in which they are located.

The next subsection covers the Small Business Investment Companies (SBICs). They are privately capitalized venture firms, which are licensed by the Small Business Administration (SBA) and are eligible to leverage and augment their funds with SBA money. The SBIC category is divided into two groups. To make it into the first section, an SBIC had to have at least $3 million in combined SBA leverage and private capital or made at least $1 million in investments in 1983. The second group consists of those firms that were less active, just starting out, or did not provide any financial data. Again, all firms located within both SBIC sections are arranged alphabetically by state.

The third area under the Domestic Listings category details Minority Enterprise Small Business Investment Companies (MESBICs). MESBICs are chartered by the SBA to make investments in small businesses owned by members of minority groups, Vietnam veterans, and the handicapped. The dividing line for MESBICs was a minimum of $1.5 million in combined SBA leverage and private capital or $750,000 in investments in 1983. The under $1.5 million category consists of those funds that were smaller, newly formed, or did not provide any financial information to indicate their proper grouping. In both sections, the MESBIC listings are arranged alphabetically by state.

FOREIGN LISTINGS

While American venture capitalists dominate the industry, firms in other countries are also investing in emerging growth companies both here and abroad. The second section of this directory consists of 177 firms located in Canada, the United Kingdom, Europe, Israel, and Asia. With the exception of Canada, the firms are broken out alphabetically by their respective countries. In Canada, venture firms are arranged according to province.

WHAT'S IN THE LISTINGS

In each listing you'll find a firm's name, address, phone number, year founded, and affiliation, where applicable. In most cases, the firms have provided their total paid-in capital and 1983 investment history, which includes the dollars invested and the number of deals made. Following the total investment figures, you'll find an average investment figure, which was derived from the 1983 investment totals. In the case of the foreign listings, the total paid-in capital, total investments, and average investment figures are provided in both the country's currency and in the U.S. dollar equivalent. (The U.S. rate was based on the exchange rate for December 31, 1984.) When a firm did not supply information for a specific area within a listing, "N.A." was inserted to denote the data was not available. In the case of funds formed in late 1983 or in 1984, "New Fund" appears in the 1983 investment history section.

The listings in both venture firms sections contain breakouts of the 1983 investment history: Seed/Startup refers to early-stage deals; Later Stage covers second-, third-, and fourth-round financings; Follow-On refers to investments in existing portfolio companies; and Buyouts details investments in leveraged buyouts.

The next area that appears in all listings is Project Preferences. Each firm was asked to characterize its preference in terms of location, industry, and stage of financing. Location: Most venture capitalists like to invest close to home, because it enables them to monitor their investments. Yet many firms seek deals in a variety of places, and others will invest anywhere they find an attractive opportunity.

While some firms cited one or two specific industries as their preference, most firms wanted to be labeled according to one of the the following categories: Diversified (will consider investing in a variety of industries covering the entire spectrum of high-technology and non-high-technology fields), High Technology (invests primarily or exclusively in high-tech industries and is willing to consider a wide range of companies within the high-tech field), and Diversified Non-High Technology (invests primarily in areas outside the realm of high technology—e.g., basic manufacturing, transportation, or grocery stores—and will consider a broad spectrum of industries).

Under the Stages heading, firms were asked to specify their preferences according to seed, startup, first, second, later (defined as third- and fourth-round financing), and buyouts (defined as leveraged buyouts). Finally, the listings contain information on a firm's principals, people who can be contacted, and its branches.

VENTURE FIRMS:
$10 MILLION AND UP

Arizona

CORONADO FUND

800 N. Swan Rd., Suite 130
Tucson, AZ 85711
602/326-6778

Year Founded: 1980
Type: Private V.C. Firm
Total Paid-In Capital: Not Provided

1983 Investment History:

Stage	Dollars Invested	No. of Deals
Seed/Startup	0	0
Later Stage	$4,000,000	6
Follow-On	0	0
Buyouts	0	0
Total Investments	$4,000,000	0
Average Investment	$ 666,667	

Project Preferences
Geographical: Southwest
Industries: High Technology, Computers, Electronics
Stages: First, Second

Principals: W. Ross Humphreys, Part.; James M. Strickland, Part.
Contact: Either

FBS VENTURE CAPITAL CO.

6900 E. Camelback Rd.
Scottsdale, AZ 85251
602/941-2160

Year Founded: 1960
Type: Private V.C. Firm
Affiliation: FBS Venture Capital Corp.; Community Investment Enterprises Inc.
Total Paid-In Capital: $20,000,000

1983 Investment History:

Stage	Dollars Invested	No. of Deals
Seed/Startup	N.A.	N.A.
Later Stage	N.A.	N.A.
Follow-On	N.A.	N.A.
Buyouts	N.A.	N.A.
Total Investments	$2,000,000	6
Average Investment	$ 333,333	

Project Preferences
Geographical: AZ, CO, MN
Industries: Diversified, Medical, Computers, Electronics
Stages: Startup, First, Second

Principals: William B. McKee, Pres.; R. Randy Stolworthy, V.P.; Stephen R. Buchanan, Investment Off.
Contact: Stephen Buchanan

Branches: 7515 Wayzata Blvd., Suite 110, Minneapolis, MN 55426, 612/544-2754. *Contacts:* W. Ray Allen, Exec. V.P.; John Howell Bullion, V.P.
3000 Pearl St., Suite 206, Boulder, CO 80301, 303/442-6885. *Contact:* Brian Johnson, V.P.

GREYHOUND CAPITAL CORP.

1201 Greyhound Tower
Phoenix, AZ 85077
602/248-6032

Year Founded: 1979
Type: Corp. V.C. Subsidiary
Affiliation: Greyhound Corp.
Total Paid-In Capital: Not Provided

1983 Investment History:

Stage	Dollars Invested	No. of Deals
Seed/Startup	$2,500,000	7
Later Stage	$4,500,000	3
Follow-On	$ 700,000	2
Buyouts	0	0
Total Investments	$7,700,000	12
Average Investment	$ 641,667	

Project Preferences
Geographical: Anywhere in U.S.
Industries: High Technology
Stages: Startup, Buyouts

Principals: O.E. Swanky, Pres.; E. Allen Henson, Sr. V.P. & Gen. Mgr.; Del Lawin, Dir. Venture Technology Analysis; David A. Bays, V.P. Venture Investments
Contact: E. Allen Henson, David A. Bays

Branch: 8 New England Executive Park, Burlington, MA 01803, 617/272-8110. *Contact:* John Schroeder, Dir. Venture Investment Development.

SUNVEN PARTNERS LP

2402 E. Arizona Biltmore Circle*
Phoenix, AZ 85016
602/957-7933

Year Founded: 1984
Type: Private V.C. Firm
Affiliation: Hambrecht & Quist; Wescot Capital Corp.
Total Paid-In Capital: $21,000,000

1983 Investment History: New Fund

Project Preferences
Geographical: Anywhere in U.S., Southwest
Industries: High Technology (only in Southwest), Media Communications
Stages: Startup, First, Second, Later, Buyouts

Principals: F. Wesley Clelland, Gen. Part.; Scott Eller, Gen. Part.; Karl Eller, Gen. Part.
Contact: F. Wesley Clelland, Scott Eller

*After August 1, 1985, address will be: 702 E. McDowell, Phoenix, AZ 85006, 602/957-7933

California

ALPHA PARTNERS

2200 Sand Hill Rd., Suite 250
Menlo Park, CA 94025
415/854-7024

Year Founded: 1982
Type: Private V.C. Firm
Total Paid-In Capital: $13,500,000

1983 Investment History:

Stage	Dollars Invested	No. of Deals
Seed/Startup	N.A.	N.A.
Later Stage	N.A.	N.A.
Follow-On	N.A.	N.A.
Buyouts	N.A.	N.A.
Total Investments	$4,300,000	7
Average Investment	$ 614,286	

Project Preferences
Geographical: West Coast
Industries: High Technology, Healthcare
Stages: Seed, Startup, First

Principals: Samuel Urcis, Gen. Part.; Brian J. Grossi, Gen. Part.; Ruth Scott, Gen. Part.; Wallace F. Davis, Gen. Part.
Contact: Any of Above

ARSCOTT, NORTON & ASSOCIATES

369 Pine St., Suite 506
San Francisco, CA 94104
415/956-3386

Year Founded: 1979
Type: Private V.C. Firm
Total Paid-In Capital: $70,000,000

1983 Investment History:

Stage	Dollars Invested	No. of Deals
Seed/Startup	$ 2,400,000	5
Later Stage	$ 2,300,000	3
Follow-On	$ 9,700,000	11
Buyouts	0	0
Total Investments	$14,400,000	19
Average Investment	$ 758,895	

Project Preferences
Geographical: Anywhere in U.S., Silicon Valley
Industries: Diversified, Telecommunications, Information Processing, Semiconductors
Stages: Seed, Startup, First, Second, Later

Principals: David G. Arscott, Gen. Part.; Dean C. Campbell, Gen. Part.; Leal F. Norton, Gen. Part.
Contact: Any of Above

ASSET MANAGEMENT CO.

1417 Edgewood Dr.
Palo Alto, CA 94301
415/321-3131

Year Founded: 1965
Type: Private V.C. Firm
Total Paid-In Capital: $65,000,000

1983 Investment History:

Stage	Dollars Invested	No. of Deals
Seed/Startup	$3,400,000	8
Later Stage	$1,800,000	3
Follow-On	0	0
Buyouts	0	0
Total Investments	$5,200,000	11
Average Investment	$ 472,727	

Project Preferences
Geographical: West Coast
Industries: High Technology
Stages: Seed, Startup, First

Principals: Craig C. Taylor, Gen. Part.; Daniel P. Flamen, Gen. Part.; Franklin P. Johnson Jr., Gen. Part.
Contact: Any of Above

ASSOCIATED VENTURE INVESTORS

3000 Sand Hill Rd., Bldg. 1, Suite 105
Menlo Park, CA 94025
415/854-4470

Year Founded: 1982
Type: Private V.C. Firm
Affiliation: AVI Management Partners
Total Paid-In Capital: $20,000,000

1983 Investment History:

Stage	Dollars Invested	No. of Deals
Seed/Startup	$4,000,000	5
Later Stage	$ 800,000	1
Follow-On	$1,200,000	3
Buyouts	0	0
Total Investments	$6,000,000	9
Average Investment	$ 666,667	

Project Preferences
Geographical: Silicon Valley
Industries: Electronics
Stages: Seed, Startup, First

Principals: Peter Wolken, Gen. Part.
Contact: Peter Wolken

BAY PARTNERS

1927 Landings Dr., Suite B
Mountain View, CA 94043
415/961-5800

Year Founded: 1976
Type: Private V.C. Firm
Total Paid-In Capital: $59,000,000

1983 Investment History:

Stage	Dollars Invested	No. of Deals
Seed/Startup	$ 4,000,000	9
Later Stage	$ 1,800,000	3
Follow-On	$ 6,800,000	12
Buyouts	0	0
Total Investments	$12,500,000	24
Average Investment	$ 520,833	

Project Preferences
Geographical: West Coast
Industries: High Technology
Stages: Seed, Startup, First

Principals: John Bosch, Gen. Part.; John Freidenrich, Gen. Part.; W. Charles Hazel, Gen. Part; Terry Morris, Assoc.
Contact: Any of Above

BECKMAN INSTRUMENTS INC.

2500 Harbor Blvd.
Fullerton, CA 92634
714/871-4848

Year Founded: 1935
Type: Public V.C. Firm
Affiliation: SmithKline Beckman Corp.
Total Paid-In Capital: Not Provided

1983 Investment History:

Stage	Dollars Invested	No. of Deals
Seed/Startup	0	0
Later Stage	0	0
Follow-On	$10,000,000	1
Buyouts	0	0
Total Investments	$10,000,000	1

Project Preferences
Geographical: Anywhere in U.S.
Foreign: Western Europe
Industries: Diagnostic & Scientific Instrumentation, Biotechnology
Stages: Seed, Startup*

Principals: Louis T. Rosso, Pres.; Nathaniel Brenner, Mgr. Corp. Planning.
Contact: Nathaniel Brenner

*With intent to buy out

BERLINER ASSOCIATES

535 Middlefield Rd., Suite 240
Menlo Park, CA 94025
415/324-1231

Year Founded: 1970
Type: Private V.C. Firm
Total Paid-In Capital: $10,000,000

1983 Investment History:

Stage	Dollars Invested	No. of Deals
Seed/Startup	N.A.	N.A.
Later Stage	N.A.	N.A.
Follow-On	N.A.	N.A.
Buyouts	N.A.	N.A.
Total Investments	$1,500,000	3
Average Investment	$ 500,000	

Project Preferences
Geographical: CA
Industries: High Technology, Medical, Genetic Engineering
Stages: Seed, Startup, First, Second

Principals: David L. Berliner, Man. Dir.; Martha L. Berliner, Man. Dir.
Contact: Either

BLALACK—LOOP INC.

696 E. Colorado Blvd., Suite 220
Pasadena, CA 91101
818/449-3411

Year Founded: 1969
Type: Private V.C. Firm
Total Paid-In Capital: Not Provided

1983 Investment History:

Stage	Dollars Invested	No. of Deals
Seed/Startup	$6,500,000	3
Later Stage	0	0
Follow-On	$2,000,000	1
Buyouts	0	0
Total Investments	$8,500,000	4
Average Investment	$2,125,000	

Project Preferences
Geographical: West Coast
Industries: High Technology
Stages: Second

Principals: Charles M. Blalack, Chair.
Contact: Charles M. Blalack

BRENTWOOD ASSOCIATES

11661 San Vicente Blvd., Suite 707
Los Angeles, CA 90049
213/826-6581

Year Founded: 1979
Type: Private V.C. Firm
Affiliation: Brentwood Capital Corp.
Total Paid-In Capital: $138,590,000

1983 Investment History:

Stage	Dollars Invested	No. of Deals
Seed/Startup	$22,600,000	23
Later Stage	0	0
Follow-On	$19,000,000	40
Buyouts	0	0
Total Investments	$41,500,000	63
Average Investment	$ 659,365	

Project Preferences
Geographical: Anywhere in U.S., West Coast
Industries: High Technology
Stages: Seed, Startup, First, Buyouts

Principals: G. Bradford Jones, Prin.; Brian P. McDermott, Assoc.; George M. Crandell Jr., Gen. Part.; B. Kipling Hagopian, Gen. Part.; Timothy M. Pennington III, Gen. Part.; Frederick Warren, Gen. Part.; Roger C. Davisson, Gen. Part.; Michael J. Forticq, Gen. Part.; Leslie R. Shaw, V.P. Finance
Contact: G. Bradford Jones, Brian P. McDermott

BRYAN & EDWARDS

3000 Sand Hill Road, Bldg. 2, Suite 260
Menlo Park, CA 94025
415/854-1555
•
600 Montgomery St.
San Francisco, CA 94111
415/421-9990

Year Founded: 1962
Type: Private V.C. Firm
Total Paid-In Capital: Not Provided

1983 Investment History:

Stage	Dollars Invested	No. of Deals
Seed/Startup	$4,500,000	11
Later Stage	$1,600,000	4
Follow-On	$1,500,000	9
Buyouts	0	0
Total Investments	$7,600,000	24
Average Investment	$ 316,667	

Project Preferences
Geographical: Anywhere in U.S., West Coast
Industries: High Technology, Biotechnology, Healthcare
Stages: Seed, Startup, First, Second, Later

Principals (Menlo Park): William C. Edwards, Part.; Guy Conger, Part.
Contact (Menlo Park): Guy Conger
•
Principals (San Francisco): Allan R. Brudos, Part.; Robert W. Ledoux, Part.
Contact (San Francisco): Robert W. Ledoux

BUSINESS RESOURCE INVESTORS

2001 Gateway Pl., Suite 200 W.
San Jose, CA 95110
408/280-5075

Year Founded: 1983
Type: Private V.C. Firm
Total Paid-In Capital: $25,000,000

1983 Investment History: New Fund

Project Preferences
Geographical: Southwest
Industries: High Technology, Telecommunications, Medical Technology, Robotics, Computer-Related
Stages: Seed, Startup, First

Principals: G.R. (Jerry) Schoonhoven, Gen. Part.; Philip R. Thomas, Gen. Part.
Contact: G.R. Schoonhoven

CAPITAL MANAGEMENT SERVICES INC.

3000 Sand Hill Rd., Bldg. 4, Suite 280
Menlo Park, CA 94025
415/854-3927

Year Founded: 1973
Type: Private V.C. Firm
Affiliation: Sequoia Capital
Total Paid-In Capital: $160,000,000

1983 Investment History:

Stage	Dollars Invested	No. of Deals
Seed/Startup	$ 6,300,000	8
Later Stage	$ 5,400,000	6
Follow-On	$ 4,200,000	10
Buyouts	0	0
Total Investments	$15,900,000	24
Average Investment	$ 662,500	

Project Preferences
Geographical: West Coast
Industries: High Technology
Stages: Seed, Startup, First

Principals: Donald T. Valentine, Part.; Gordon Russell, Part.; Pierre Lamond, Part.; Walter Baumgartner, Part.; Jonathan Hamren, Part.; Robert Spencer, Part.
Contact: Any of Above

CHAPPELL & CO.

1 Lombard St.
San Francisco, CA 94111
415/397-5094

Year Founded: 1980
Type: Investment Banking Firm
Total Paid-In Capital: Not Provided

1983 Investment History:

Stage	Dollars Invested	No. of Deals
Seed/Startup	$15,000,000	8
Later Stage	0	0
Follow-On	0	0
Buyouts	0	0
Total Investments	$15,000,000	8
Average Investment	$ 1,875,000	

Project Preferences
Geographical: CA
Industries: High Technology, Semiconductors, Biotechnology, Software, Telecommunications
Stages: Seed, Startup, First, Buyouts*

Principals: Robert H. Chappell, Pres.; Charles Stephen Chapman, V.P., Leverage; N. Colin Lind, V.P. Venture Capital
Contact: Michael Hsieh, Asst. V.P.

*Buyouts in agribusiness only.

CHURCHILL INTERNATIONAL

444 Market St., 25th Floor
San Francisco, CA 94111
415/398-7677

Year Founded: 1978
Type: Investment Banking and Consulting Firm
Total Paid-In Capital: $70,000,000

1983 Investment History:

Stage	Dollars Invested	No. of Deals
Seed/Startup	$ 2,500,000	4
Later Stage	$ 2,500,000	5
Follow-On	$18,200,000	15
Buyouts	0	0
Total Investments	$23,200,000	24
Average Investment	$ 966,667	

Project Preferences
Geographical: Northeast, West Coast, Southwest, TX
Industries: High Technology, Advanced Materials, Artificial Intelligence, Communications, Computer-Related, Semiconductors, Testing & Measurement Equipment
Stages: Startup, Second, Later, Buyouts

Principals: Louis L. Davis, Chair.
Contact: Roy G. Helsing, V.P.

Branches: 545 Middlefield Rd., Suite 160, Menlo Park, CA 94025, 415/328-4401. *Contact:* Roy G. Helsing, V.P.
9 Riverside Rd., Weston, MA 02193, 617/893-6555. *Contact:* Julie B. Dunbar, Mgr. of Corp. Communications.

CONTINENTAL CAPITAL VENTURES

555 California St., Suite 5070
San Francisco, CA 94104
415/989-2020

Year Founded: 1959
Type: Private V.C. Firm
Total Paid-In Capital: $21,000,000

1983 Investment History:

Stage	Dollars Invested	No. of Deals
Seed/Startup	$5,300,000	9
Later Stage	$1,500,000	3
Follow-On	$1,100,000	3
Buyouts	0	0
Total Investments	$7,900,000	15
Average Investment	$ 526,667	

Project Preferences
Geographical: West Coast
Industries: High Technology, Medical Technology
Stages: Seed, Startup, First

Principals: William A. Boeger, Gen. Part.; Frank G. Chambers, Gen. Part.; Lawrance A. Brown Jr., Gen. Part.; Donald R. Scheuch, Gen. Part.
Contact: Any of Above

Branch: 3000 Sand Hill Rd., Bldg. 1, Suite 135, Menlo Park, CA 94025, 415/854-6633. *Contact:* Same as Above

CROSSPOINT VENTURE PARTNERS

P.O. Box 10101
1015 Corporation Way
Palo Alto, CA 94303
415/964-3545

Year Founded: 1979
Type: Private V.C. Firm
Total Paid-In Capital: $18,000,000

1983 Investment History:

Stage	Dollars Invested	No. of Deals
Seed/Startup	$12,000,000	22
Later Stage	0	0
Follow-On	0	0
Buyouts	0	0
Total Investments	$12,000,000	22
Average Investment	$ 545,455	

Project Preferences
Geographical: Anywhere in U.S.
Industries: High Technology, Communications, Electronic Components, Instrumentation, Medical
Stages: Seed

Principals: John Mumford, Man. Gen. Part.; Jim Willenborg, Gen. Part.; Roger Barry, Gen. Part.; William Cargile, Gen. Part.
Contact: Any of Above

Branches: 4600 Campus Dr., Suite 3, Newport Beach, CA 92660, 714/852-1611. *Contact:* Robert A. Hoff, Gen. Part.
6 New England Executive Park, Suite 400, Burlington, MA 01803, 617/229-8920. *Contact:* Frederick J. Dotzler, Gen. Part.

DOUGERY, JONES & WILDER

3 Embarcadero Center, Suite 1980
San Francisco, CA 94111-4060
415/434-1722

Year Founded: 1981
Type: Private V.C. Firm
Total Paid-In Capital: $75,000,000

1983 Investment History: Stage	Dollars Invested	No. of Deals
Seed/Startup	$ 6,500,000	6
Later Stage	$ 3,500,000	3
Follow-On	$ 1,000,000	1
Buyouts	0	0
Total Investments	$11,000,000	10
Average Investment	$ 1,100,000	

Project Preferences
Geographical: West, Southwest
Industries: Diversified, Medical Energy
Stages: Any

Principals: David A. Jones, Gen. Part.; Henry L.B. Wilder, Gen. Part.
Contact: Either

Branches: 2 Lincoln Centre, 5420 LBJ Freeway, Suite 1100, Dallas, TX 75240, 214/960-0077. *Contact:* A. Lawson Howard, Assoc.
2105 Landings Dr., Mountain View, CA 94043, 415/968-4820. *Contact:* John Dougery, Gen. Part.

THE EARLY STAGES CO.

244 California St., Suite 300
San Francisco, CA 94111
415/986-5700

Year Founded: 1978
Type: Private V.C. Firm
Total Paid-In Capital: $10,500,000

1983 Investment History: Stage	Dollars Invested	No. of Deals
Seed/Startup	$2,300,000	5
Later Stage	$1,300,000	6
Follow-On	$1,400,000	4
Buyouts	0	0
Total Investments	$5,000,000	15
Average Investment	$ 333,333	

Project Preferences
Geographical: West Coast
Industries: High Technology, Consumer Products & Services
Stages: Startup, First, Second

Principals: Michael G. Berolzheimer, Gen. Part.; William P. Lanphear IV, Gen. Part.; Frank W. "Woody" Kuehn, Gen. Part.
Contact: Any of Above

EMC II VENTURES PARTNERS

8950 Villa La Jolla Dr., Suite 2132
La Jolla, CA 92037
619/455-0362

Year Founded: 1980
Type: Private V.C. Firm
Affiliation: McKewon Securities
Total Paid-In Capital: $30,000,000

1983 Investment History: Stage	Dollars Invested	No. of Deals
Seed/Startup	$1,000,000	1
Later Stage	0	0
Follow-On	$3,000,000	3
Buyouts	0	0
Total Investments	$4,000,000	4
Average Investment	$1,000,000	

Project Preferences
Geographical: Southwest
Foreign: West Germany, Austria, Switzerland
Industries: Diversified, Healthcare, Aerospace, Electronics
Stages: Seed, Startup, First

Principals: Ray McKewon, Gen. Part.; Hans Schoepflin, Gen. Part.; Bradley B. Gordon, Gen. Part.; Alan Grant, Gen. Part.
Contact: Any of Above

ENTERPRISE PARTNERS

18003 Skypark Circle, Suite A
Irvine, CA 92714
714/261-9124

Affiliation: Hambrecht & Quist; Mayfield Fund
Year Founded: 1985
Type: Private V.C. Firm
Total Paid-In Capital: $25,000,000

1983 Investment History: New Fund

Project Preferences
Geographical: Southern CA
Industries: Healthcare & Medical Technology, Electronics, Communications, Computer-Related Products
Stages: Startup, First, Second

Principals: Charles Martin, Man. Gen. Part.
Contact: Charles Martin

GIRARD CAPITAL INC.

9191 Towne Centre Dr., Suite 370
San Diego, CA 92122
619/457-5114

Year Founded: 1976
Type: Private V.C. Firm
Total Paid-In Capital: Not Provided

1983 Investment History: Stage	Dollars Invested	No. of Deals
Seed/Startup	$ 4,000,000	4
Later Stage	0	0
Follow-On	0	0
Buyouts	$ 6,000,000	2
Total Investments	$10,000,000	6
Average Investment	$ 1,666,667	

Project Preferences
Geographical: West Coast
Industries: High Technology
Stages: Startup, Buyouts

Principals: R.B. Woolley Jr., Pres.; E. Sam Gudmundson, V.P.; W. Creighton Gallaway, V.P.; Irby McMichael, V.P.; Sanjay Subhedar, V.P.
Contact: E. Sam Gudmundson, W. Creighton Gallaway, Sanjay Subhedar

BRUCE GLASPELL & ASSOCIATES

57 Post St., Suite 513
San Francisco, CA 94104
415/781-1313

Year Founded: 1973
Type: Private V.C. Firm
Total Paid-In Capital: Not Provided

1983 Investment History:

Stage	Dollars Invested	No. of Deals
Seed/Startup	N.A.	N.A.
Later Stage	N.A.	N.A.
Follow-On	N.A.	N.A.
Buyouts	N.A.	N.A.
Total Investments	$9,000,000	13
Average Investment	$ 692,308	

Project Preferences
Geographical: Anywhere in U.S.
Foreign: Western Europe
Industries: Diversified
Stages: Any

Principals: Bruce Glaspell, Gen. Part.
Contact: Bruce Glaspell

GLYNN VENTURES

3000 Sand Hill Rd., Bldg. 2, Suite 210
Menlo Park, CA 94025
415/854-2215

Affiliation: Glynn Capital Management Co.
Year Founded: 1983
Type: Private V.C. Firm
Total Paid-In Capital: $22,000,000

1983 Investment History:

Stage	Dollars Invested	No. of Deals
Seed/Startup	$ 200,000	1
Later Stage	$2,500,000	7
Follow-On	$ 600,000	2
Buyouts	0	0
Total Investments	$3,300,000	10
Average Investment	$ 330,000	

Project Preferences
Geographical: West Coast, Boston
Industries: Software, Digital Communications, Computer-Aided Graphics & Design, Segments of VLSI Industry
Stages: Second

Principals: John W. Glynn Jr., Gen. Part.
Contact: John W. Glynn Jr.

HAMBRECHT & QUIST

235 Montgomery St.
San Francisco, CA 94104
415/576-3300

Affiliation: Hamco Capital Corp.; Rainier Venture Partners; Mohr Ventures; SunVen Partners; Enterprise Partners
Year Founded: 1968
Type: Private V.C. Firm; Investment Banking Firm
Total Paid-In Capital: $450,000,000*

1983 Investment History:

Stage	Dollars Invested	No. of Deals
Seed/Startup	$20,000,000	20
Later Stage	$27,000,000	35
Follow-On	$22,000,000	51
Buyouts	0	0
Total Investments	$69,000,000	106
Average Investment	$ 650,943	

Project Preferences
Geographical: Anywhere in U.S.
Foreign: Canada, U.K.
Industries: High Technology, Computer-Related
Stages: Startup, First, Second

Principals: William R. Hambrecht, Pres.; W. Denman Van Ness, Sr. Investment Part.; D. Kirkwood Bowman, Sr. Investment Part.; Grant M. Inman, Sr. Investment Part.; Bob O. Evans, Sr. Investment Part.; Theodor H. Heinrichs, Sr. Investment Part.; Robert J. Kunze, Man. Dir.; Kenneth L. Guernsey, Admin. Gen. Part.
Contact: Robert J. Kunze

Branches: 1 Hollis St., Suite 102, Wellesley, MA 02181, 617/237-2099. *Contact:* Robert M. Morrill, Sr. Investment Part.
4800 LeJeune Rd., Coral Gables, FL 33146, 305/447-0423. *Contact:* Modesto A. Maidique, Sr. Investment Part.

*Figure is over $450 million.

INSTITUTIONAL VENTURE PARTNERS

3000 Sand Hill Rd., Bldg. 2, Suite 290
Menlo Park, CA 94025
415/854-0132

Year Founded: 1980
Type: Private V.C. Firm
Total Paid-In Capital: $57,000,000

1983 Investment History:

Stage	Dollars Invested	No. of Deals
Seed/Startup	$ 5,200,000	4
Later Stage	$ 5,000,000	6
Follow-On	$ 7,300,000	12
Buyouts	0	0
Total Investments	$17,500,000	22
Average Investment	$ 795,455	

Project Preferences
Geographical: West Coast, Southwest
Industries: High Technology
Stages: Seed, Startup, First, Second

Principals: John K. Poitras, Gen. Part.; Reid W. Dennis, Gen. Part.; Mary Jane Elmore, Gen. Part.
Contact: Any of Above

INTERWEST PARTNERS

2620 Augustine Dr. Suite 201
Santa Clara, CA 95054
408/727-7200

Year Founded: 1979
Type: Private V.C. Firm
Total Paid-In Capital: $88,600,000

1983 Investment History:

Stage	Dollars Invested	No. of Deals
Seed/Startup	$ 3,900,000	8
Later Stage	$ 6,600,000	12
Follow-On	$ 6,400,000	22
Buyouts	$ 1,600,000	2
Total Investments	$18,500,000	44
Average Investment	$ 420,454	

Project Preferences
Geographical: Anywhere in U.S.
Industries: High Technology
Stages: Seed, Startup, First

Principals: W. Scott Hedrick, Gen. Part.; Wallace R. Hawley, Gen.
    Part.; Robert R. Momsen, Gen. Part.; Eugene F. Barth, Gen. Part.;
    Philip T. Gianos, Gen. Part.
Contact: Any of Above

INVESTORS IN INDUSTRY VENTURES

450 Newport Center Dr., Suite 250
Newport Beach, CA 92660
714/720-1421

Affiliation: Investors in Industry Group (England)
Year Founded: 1982
Type: Corp. V.C. Subsidiary
Total Paid-In Capital: $100,000,000

1983 Investment History:

Stage	Dollars Invested	No. of Deals
Seed/Startup	$2,000,000	4
Later Stage	0	0
Follow-On	0	0
Buyouts	0	0
Total Investments	$2,000,000	4
Average Investment	$ 500,000	

Project Preferences
Geographical: West Coast
Foreign: U.K.
Industries: Diversified, Communications, Computer-Related,
    Electronic Components & Instrumentation, Genetic
    Engineering, Healthcare Products & Services
Stages: Seed, Startup, First

Principals: Geoff Taylor, Pres.; Frederick M. Haney; Anna Henry
Contact: Any of Above

KLEINER, PERKINS, CAUFIELD & BYERS

4 Embarcadero Center, Suite 3520
San Francisco, CA 94111
415/421-3110

Year Founded: 1972
Type: Private V.C. Firm
Total Paid-In Capital: $227,000,000

1983 Investment History:

Stage	Dollars Invested	No. of Deals
Seed/Startup	$14,000,000	12
Later Stage	$12,000,000	7
Follow-On	$15,000,000	24
Buyouts	0	0
Total Investments	$41,000,000	43
Average Investment	$ 953,488	

Project Preferences
Geographical: West Coast, CA
Industries: High Technology, Medical Research
Stages: Startup, First

Principals: Thomas J. Perkins, Gen. Part.; Brook H. Byers, Gen. Part.;
    Frank J. Caufield, Gen. Part.; John Doerr, Gen. Part.
Contact: Any of Above

Branch: 2 Embarcadero Place, 2200 Geng Rd., Suite 205, Palo Alto,
    CA 94303, 415/424-1660. *Contact:* James P. Lally, Gen. Part.;
    Floyd Kvamme, Gen. Part.

LATIGO VENTURES

23410 Civic Center Way, Suite E-2
Malibu, CA 90265
213/456-5539

Affiliation: Latigo Capital Partners
Year Founded: 1982
Type: Private V.C. Firm
Total Paid-In Capital: $10,000,000

1983 Investment History:

Stage	Dollars Invested	No. of Deals
Seed/Startup	N.A.	N.A.
Later Stage	N.A.	N.A.
Follow-On	N.A.	N.A.
Buyouts	N.A.	N.A.
Total Investments	$3,400,000	13
Average Investment	$ 261,538	

Project Preferences
Geographical: Anywhere in U.S.
Industries: High Technology, Restaurants, Medical Technology
Stages: First, Second, Later

Principals: Robert Peterson, Gen. Part.; Donald Peterson, Gen. Part.
Contact: Either

MAYFIELD FUND

2200 Sand Hill Rd.
Menlo Park, CA 94025
415/854-5560

Year Founded: 1969
Type: Private V.C. Firm
Total Paid-In Capital: $200,000,000

1983 Investment History:

Stage	Dollars Invested	No. of Deals
Seed/Startup	N.A.	13
Later Stage	N.A.	5
Follow-On	N.A.	14
Buyouts	N.A.	0
Total Investments	$20,000,000	32
Average Investment	$ 625,000	

Project Preferences
Geographical: West Coast
Industries: High Technology, Computers, Communications, Biotechnology
Stages: Any

Principals: Thomas J. Davis Jr., Gen. Part.; F. Gibson Meyers Jr., Gen. Part.; Glenn M. Mueller, Gen. Part.; Norman A. Fogelsong, Gen. Part.; A. Grant Heidrich III, Gen. Part.; Michael J. Leventhal, Gen. Part.
Contact: Norman A. Fogelsong

MELCHOR VENTURE MANAGEMENT INC.

170 State St., Suite 220
Los Altos, CA 94022
415/941-6565

Year Founded: 1959
Type: Private V.C. Firm
Total Paid-In Capital: $20,000,000

1983 Investment History:

Stage	Dollars Invested	No. of Deals
Seed/Startup	$3,500,000	14
Later Stage	0	0
Follow-On	$1,500,000	4
Buyouts	0	0
Total Investments	$5,000,000	18
Average Investment	$ 277,778	

Project Preferences
Geographical: CA
Industries: High Technology, Communications, Computer-Related, Electronic Components, Medical Technology, Energy/Natural Resources
Stages: Seed, Startup

Principals: Jack L. Melchor, Pres.; Gregory S. Young, V.P.; Richard H. Frank, V.P.
Contact: Gregory S. Young, Richard H. Frank

MENLO VENTURES

3000 Sand Hill Rd.
Menlo Park, CA 94025
415/854-8540

Year Founded: 1976
Type: Private V.C. Firm
Total Paid-In Capital: $120,000,000

1983 Investment History:

Stage	Dollars Invested	No. of Deals
Seed/Startup	$ 4,100,000	7
Later Stage	$10,000,000	14
Follow-On	$ 1,200,000	8
Buyouts	$ 4,800,000	4
Total Investments	$20,100,000	33
Average Investment	$ 609,091	

Project Preferences
Geographical: Anywhere in U.S.
Industries: High Technology
Stages: Any

Principals: H. DuBose Montgomery, Gen. Part.; Kenn E. Joy, Gen. Part.; Kirk L. Knight, Gen. Part.; Douglas C. Carlisle, Gen. Part.; Richard P. Magnusen, Gen. Part.
Contact: Any of Above

MERRILL, PICKARD, ANDERSON & EYRE

2 Palo Alto Square, Suite 425
Palo Alto, CA 94306
415/856-8880

Year Founded: 1980
Type: Private V.C. Firm
Affiliation: Bank of America
Total Paid-In Capital: $93,000,000

1983 Investment History:

Stage	Dollars Invested	No. of Deals
Seed/Startup	$ 7,000,000	7
Later Stage	$ 7,000,000	6
Follow-On	$ 5,000,000	5
Buyouts	0	0
Total Investments	$19,000,000	18
Average Investment	$ 1,055,556	

Project Preferences
Geographical: Anywhere in U.S.
Industries: High Technology, Computers, Computer Peripherals, Telecommunications
Stages: Startup, First, Second

Principals: Steven L. Merrill, Man. Part.; James C. Anderson, Gen. Part.; Chris A. Eyre, Gen. Part.; W. Jeff Pickard, Gen. Part.; Stephen E. Coit, Gen. Part.
Contact: W. Jeff Pickard

MONTGOMERY SECURITIES

600 Montgomery St.
San Francisco, CA 94111
415/627-2000

Year Founded: 1983
Type: Investment Banking Firm
Total Paid-In Capital: $46,000,000

1983 Investment History:

Stage	Dollars Invested	No. of Deals
Seed/Startup	0	0
Later Stage	0	0
Follow-On	$23,000,000	37
Buyouts	0	0
Total Investments	$23,000,000	37
Average Investment	$ 621,622	

Project Preferences
Geographical: Anywhere in U.S.
Industries: High Technology
Stages: Later*

Principals: Thomas W. Weisel Sr., Part.; Alan L. Stein, Part. & Dir.
  Corp. Fin.; James Pelkey
Contact: Any of Above

*Specializing in bridge financing.

MORGAN STANLEY VENTURES INC.

101 California St., Suite 2400
San Francisco, CA 94111
415/576-2340

Affiliation: Morgan Stanley Inc.
Year Founded: 1984
Type: Corp. V.C. Subsidiary
Total Paid-In Capital: $50,000,000

1983 Investment History: New Fund

Project Preferences
Geographical: Anywhere in U.S.
Industries: High Technology, Medical & Biotechnology, Computer
  Systems & Software, Telecommunications, Semiconductors,
  Automation
Stages: First, Second, Later

Principals: Fred A. Middleton, Pres.; Nancy Burrus, Sr. Assoc.;
  Robert Kitts, Sr. Analyst
Contact: Any of Above

MURISON, HELLER & PARTNERS

Belmont Shores
1301 Shoreway Rd., Suite 301
Belmont, CA 94002
415/593-2885

Year Founded: 1982
Type: Investment intermediary for British institutional investors
  in U.S.
Total Paid-In Capital: Not Provided

1983 Investment History:

Stage	Dollars Invested	No. of Deals
Seed/Startup	0	0
Later Stage	$12,000,000	5
Follow-On	0	0
Buyouts	0	0
Total Investments	$12,000,000	5
Average Investment	$ 2,400,000	

Project Preferences
Geographical: Anywhere in U.S.
Industries: High Technology
Stages: Later

Principals: Andrew Murison, Part.; David Heller, Part.; Ralph Vaerst,
  Part.; Dieter Mahrenbach, Assoc. Part.; L. Butcher, Assoc. Part.
Contact: David Heller

Branch: Pooting Manor, Crockham Hill, Edenbridge, Kent, TN8 653,
  England, 44/7-328-6624. *Contact:* Andrew Murison

NATIONAL INVESTMENT MANAGEMENT INC.

23133 Hawthorne Blvd.
Torrance, CA 90505
213/373-8944

Year Founded: 1977
Type: Private V.C. Firm
Affiliation: Lombard Sycamore Fund; Sycamore Fund L.P.
Total Paid-In Capital: $25,000,000

1983 Investment History:

Stage	Dollars Invested	No. of Deals
Seed/Startup	N.A.	N.A.
Later Stage	N.A.	N.A.
Follow-On	N.A.	N.A.
Buyouts	N.A.	N.A.
Total Investments	$3,000,000	6
Average Investment	$ 500,000	

Project Preferences
Geographical: Anywhere in U.S.
Industries: Diversified
Stages: Second, Later, Buyouts

Principals: Richard D. Robins, Pres.; Kenneth R. Finn, Part.
Contact: Either

NEW ENTERPRISE ASSOCIATES LP

1025 Russ Bldg.
235 Montgomery St.
San Francisco, CA 94104
415/956-1579

•

1119 St. Paul St.
Baltimore, MD 21202
301/244-0115

Year Founded: 1978
Type: Private V.C. Firm
Total Paid-In Capital: $186,000,000

1983 Investment History:

Stage	Dollars Invested	No. of Deals
Seed/Startup	$ 7,100,000	15
Later Stage	$ 7,500,000	15
Follow-On	$ 6,900,000	34
Buyouts	0	0
Total Investments	$21,500,000	64
Average Investment	$ 335,938	

Project Preferences
Geographical: Anywhere in U.S.
Industries: High Technology, Computer Hardware & Software, Medical, Energy Alternatives, Telecommunications, Semiconductors
Stages: Startup, Second

Principals (San Francisco): C. Richard Kramlich, Man. Gen. Part.; C. Cornelius Bond Jr., Gen. Part.; C. Woodrow Rea Jr., Gen. Part.; R. John Armor, Assoc.; Nancy Dorman, Assoc.
Contact (San Francisco): Nancy Dorman

•

Principals (Baltimore): Frank A. Bonsal Jr., Gen. Part.; Charles Newhall III, Gen. Part.; Arthur Marks, Gen. Part.; Currin W. Harvey, Special Part.
Contact (Baltimore): Any of Above

OSCCO VENTURES

3000 Sand Hill Rd., Bldg. 4, Suite 140
Menlo Park, CA 94025
415/854-2222

Year Founded: 1962
Type: Private V.C. Firm
Total Paid-In Capital: $25,600,000

1983 Investment History:

Stage	Dollars Invested	No. of Deals
Seed/Startup	N.A.	N.A.
Later Stage	N.A.	N.A.
Follow-On	N.A.	N.A.
Buyouts	N.A.	N.A.
Total Investments	$2,000,000	4
Average Investment	$ 500,000	

Project Preferences
Geographical: West Coast, Southwest
Industries: Diversified
Stages: Seed, Startup

Principals: F. Ward Paine, Gen. Part.; Stephen E. Halprin, Gen. Part.; James G. Rudolph, Gen. Part.
Contact: Any of Above

PACIFIC MANAGEMENT LTD.

655 Montgomery St., Suite 1410
San Francisco, CA 94111
415/362-6117

Year Founded: 1983
Type: Private V.C. Firm
Total Paid-In Capital: $17,000,000

1983 Investment History:

Stage	Dollars Invested	No. of Deals
Seed/Startup	0	0
Later Stage	$1,300,000	4
Follow-On	0	0
Buyouts	0	0
Total Investments	$1,300,000	4
Average Investment	$ 325,000	

Project Preferences
Geographical: CA
Industries: High Technology, Computer-Related, Telecommunications, Medical Technology
Stages: Later

Principals: Robert M. Stafford, Gen. Part.; Robert M. Sutton, Gen. Part.; Anthony S. Hooker, Gen. Part.; Jean Hadfield, Assoc.
Contact: Robert M. Stafford, Jean Hadfield

PACIFIC TECHNOLOGY VENTURE FUND

332 Pine St., Suite 610
San Francisco, CA 94104
415/956-3926

Year Founded: 1981
Type: Private V.C. Firm
Total Paid-In Capital: $10,000,000

1983 Investment History:

Stage	Dollars Invested	No. of Deals
Seed/Startup	N.A.	N.A.
Later Stage	N.A.	N.A.
Follow-On	N.A.	N.A.
Buyouts	N.A.	N.A.
Total Investments	$1,200,000	8
Average Investment	$ 150,000	

Project Preferences
Geographical: West Coast
Foreign: Japan
Industries: High Technology, Communications, Computer-Related
Stages: Startup, First, Second

Principals: Patrick J. McGovern, Chair.; Lore Harp, Pres.
Contact: Lore Harp

Branch: Pacific Technology Ventures Co. Ltd., Imperial Tower, Room 5B-3, 1-1-1 Nchisaiwai-Cho, Chiyoda-Ku, 100, Tokyo, Japan, 03/501-8027. *Contact:* Kojiro Watanabe, Pres.

PACIFIC VENTURE PARTNERS

3000 Sand Hill Rd., Bldg. 4, Suite 175
Menlo Park, CA 94025
415/854-2266

Year Founded: 1983
Type: Private V.C. Firm
Total Paid-In Capital: $15,200,000

1983 Investment History: Not Provided

Project Preferences
Geographical: West Coast
Industries: High Technology, Biomedical
Stages: Startup, First, Second

Principals: James C. Balderston, Gen. Part.; Anthony T. Ellis, Gen. Part.; Rigdon Currie, Gen. Part.
Contact: Any of Above

PARAGON PARTNERS

3000 Sand Hill Rd., Bldg. 2, Suite 190
Menlo Park, CA 94025
415/854-8000

Year Founded: 1984
Type: Private V.C. Firm
Total Paid-In Capital: $40,000,000

1983 Investment History: New Fund

Project Preferences
Geographical: Anywhere in U.S.
Industries: High Technology, Computer-Related
Stages: Startup, First, Second

Principals: Jess Marzak, Gen. Part.; Robert F. Kibble, Gen. Part.;
   John S. Lewis, Gen. Part.
Contact: Any of Above

PARIBAS TECHNOLOGY—USA

101 California St., Suite 3150
San Francisco, CA 94111
415/788-2929

Affiliation: Bank Paribas (France)
Year Founded: 1981
Type: Private V.C. Firm
Total Paid-In Capital: $28,000,000*

1983 Investment History: Stage	Dollars Invested*	No. of Deals
Seed/Startup	$1,500,000	4
Later Stage	0	0
Follow-On	$2,500,000	4
Buyouts	0	0
Total Investments	$4,000,000	8
Average Investment	$ 500,000	

Project Preferences
Geographical: Anywhere in U.S.
Industries: High Technology, Computers, Semiconductors, Medical,
   Biotechnology, Telecommunications
Stages: Seed, Startup, First, Second

Principals: Thomas G. McKinley, Prin.; Vincent Worms, Prin.
Contact: Either

*Figures solely for U.S. fund.

PEREGRINE ASSOCIATES

606 Wilshire Blvd., Suite 602
Santa Monica, CA 90401
213/458-1441

Affiliation: Montgomery Ventures
Year Founded: 1981
Type: Private V.C. Firm
Total Paid-In Capital: $44,000,000

1983 Investment History: Stage	Dollars Invested	No. of Deals
Seed/Startup	N.A.	4
Later Stage	N.A.	4
Follow-On	N.A.	2
Buyouts	0	0
Total Investments	$8,000,000	10
Average Investment	$ 800,000	

Project Preferences
Geographical: Anywhere in U.S.
Industries: Diversified, Electronics, Medicine
Stages: Any

Principals: Frank LaHaye, Gen. Part.; Gene I. Miller, Gen. Part.
Contact: Either

WAYNE L. PRIM & ASSOCIATES

3000 Sand Hill Rd., Bldg. 1, Suite 285
Menlo Park, CA 94025
415/854-7860

Year Founded: 1960
Type: Private V.C. Firm
Total Paid-In Capital: $10,000,000

1983 Investment History: Stage	Dollars Invested	No. of Deals
Seed/Startup	0	0
Later Stage	$5,000,000	9
Follow-On	$2,000,000	6
Buyouts	0	0
Total Investments	$7,000,000	15
Average Investment	$ 466,667	

Project Preferences
Geographical: Anywhere in U.S.
Industries: High Technology, Electronics
Stages: Seed, Startup, First, Second, Later

PRINCETON/MONTROSE PARTNERS

2331 Honolulu Ave., Suite G
Montrose, CA 91020
818/957-3623

Year Founded: 1981
Type: Private V.C. Firm
Total Paid-In Capital: $17,175,000

1983 Investment History: Stage	Dollars Invested	No. of Deals
Seed/Startup	N.A.	7
Later Stage	0	0
Follow-On	N A	3
Buyouts	0	0
Total Investments	$4,500,000	10
Average Investment	$ 450,000	

Project Preferences
Geographical: Anywhere in U.S.
Foreign: Western Europe
Industries: Diversified, Food Products & Distribution, Agribusiness
   Technology, Energy/Natural Resources
Stages: Any

Principals: Donald R. Stroben, Man. Gen. Part.; Charles I. Kosmont,
   Gen. Part.; Peter R. Rossmassler, Gen. Part.
Contact: Charles I. Kosmont

Branch: 1000 Herrontown Rd., Princeton, NJ 08540,
   609/921-1590. *Contact:* Ronald R. Hahn, Man. Gen. Part.; Peter R.
   Rossmassler, Gen. Part.

R&D FUNDING CORP.

1290 Ridder Park Dr., Suite 1
San Jose, CA 95131
408/293-0990

Year Founded: 1983
Type: Corp. V.C. Subsidiary
Affiliation: Prudential Bache Securities
Total Paid-In Capital: $68,000,000

1983 Investment History:

Stage	Dollars Invested	No. of Deals
Seed/Startup	$ 3,300,000	1
Later Stage	0	0
Follow-On	$22,000,000	3
Buyouts	0	0
Total Investments	$25,300,000	4
Average Investment	$ 6,325,000	

Project Preferences
Geographical: Anywhere in U.S.
Industries: High Technology
Stages: Second, Later

Principals: Hugh McClung, Pres.
Contact: Hugh McClung

RIORDAN VENTURE MANAGEMENT

523 W. Sixth St.
Los Angeles, CA 90014
213/629-4824

Year Founded: 1983
Type: Private V.C. Firm
Total Paid-In Capital: $150,000,000

1983 Investment History:

Stage	Dollars Invested	No. of Deals
Seed/Startup	$ 8,000,000	8
Later Stage	$ 3,000,000	4
Follow-On	$ 5,000,000	5
Buyouts	0	0
Total Investments	$16,000,000	17
Average Investment	$ 941,176	

Project Preferences
Geographical: West Coast
Industries: High Technology, Computers, Medical, Semiconductors
Stages: Any

Principals: Richard Riordan, Sr. Part.; Chris Lewis, V.P.
Contact: Either

ROBERTSON, COLEMAN, & STEPHENS VENTURE FUND

1 Embarcadero Center, Suite 3100
San Francisco, CA 94111
415/781-9700

Year Founded: 1978
Type: Private V.C. Firm; Investment Banking Firm
Total Paid-In Capital: $57,000,000

1983 Investment History:

Stage	Dollars Invested	No. of Deals
Seed/Startup	$ 5,300,000	11
Later Stage	$19,600,000	32
Follow-On	$ 8,600,000	38
Buyouts	0	0
Total Investments	$33,500,000	81
Average Investment	$ 413,580	

Project Preferences
Geographical: Anywhere in U.S.
Industries: High Technology, Healthcare, Communications
Stages: Any

Principals: Christopher H. Covington, Part. & Dir. Corp. Finance; Sanford R. Robertson, Part.; Paul H. Stephens, Part.; Robert L. Cummings, Part.; Robert Colman, Part.
Contact: Sanford R. Robertson, Paul H. Stephens, Robert L. Cummings

ROTHSCHILD, UNTERBERG, TOWBIN VENTURES

3000 Sand Hill Rd., Bldg. 3, Suite 260
Menlo Park, CA 94025
415/854-2576

Affiliation: L.F. Rothschild, Unterberg, Towbin
Year Founded: 1983
Type: Private Venture Firm
Total Paid-In Capital: $20,000,000*

1983 Investment History: New Fund

Project Preferences
Geographical: Anywhere in U.S.
Foreign: U.K.
Industries: High Technology, Electronics, Telecommunications, Medical Technology, Vertical Applications of Computer Systems
Stages: Startup, First, Second

Principals: J. Michael Gullard, Gen. Part.; Thomas A. Tisch, Gen. Part.
Contact: Either

*Paid-in capital figure as of 12/10/84; in process of closing.

SAN MARINO GROUP

57 Post St., Suite 513
San Francisco, CA 94104
415/781-1313

Year Founded: 1972
Type: Private V.C. Firm
Total Paid-In Capital: Not Provided

1983 Investment History:

Stage	Dollars Invested	No. of Deals
Seed/Startup	$4,000,000	4
Later Stage	$3,000,000	3
Follow-On	0	0
Buyouts	0	0
Total Investments	$7,000,000	7
Average Investment	$1,000,000	

Project Preferences
Geographical: Anywhere in U.S.
Foreign: West Europe
Industries: Diversified, Telecommunications, Computer-Related, Natural Resources, Finance
Stages: Any

Principals: Bruce Glaspell, Gen. Part.
Contact: Bruce Glaspell

SECURITY PACIFIC CAPITAL CORP.

4000 MacArthur Blvd., Suite 950
Newport Beach, CA 92660
714/754-4780

Affiliation: Security Pacific National Bank
Year Founded: 1963
Type: Corp. V.C. Subsidiary
Total Paid-In Capital: Not Provided

1983 Investment History:

Stage	Dollars Invested	No. of Deals
Seed/Startup	$ 8,300,000	5
Later Stage	0	5
Follow-On	$ 940,000	4
Buyouts	$28,600,000	12
Total Investments	$44,240,000	26
Average Investment	$ 1,701,538	

Project Preferences
Geographical: Anywhere in U.S.
Industries: Diversified, Manufacturing, Chain Retailing, Communications, Healthcare Management
Stages: Any

Principals: Timothy Hay, Pres.; Gregory Forest, Exec. V.P.; Brian Jones, Sr. V.P.; John Gear, V.P.; James B. McElwee, V.P.; Alvin Brizzard, V.P.; Everett Cox, Investment Off.; Dimitry Bosky, Investment Off.; James McGoodwin, Investment Off.
Contact: John Gear, Brian Jones, James B. McElwee

Branches: 333 South Hope St., H25-4, Los Angeles, CA 90071, 213/613-5215. *Contact:* John Padgett, V.P.; Tony Stevens, V.P.
P.O. Box 512, Washington, PA 15301, 412/223-0707. *Contact:* Daniel Dye.
50 Milk St., 15th Floor, Boston, MA 02109, 617/542-7601. *Contact:* Michael Cronin, V.P.

SIERRA VENTURES

3000 Sand Hill Rd., Bldg. 1, Suite 280
Menlo Park, CA 94205
415/854-9096

Year Founded: 1982
Type: Private V.C. Firm
Affiliation: Wood River Capital
Total Paid-In Capital: $40,000,000

1983 Investment History:

Stage	Dollars Invested	No. of Deals
Seed/Startup	$1,800,000	5
Later Stage	$ 800,000	3
Follow-On	$4,500,000	15
Buyouts	0	0
Total Investments	$7,100,000	23
Average Investment	$ 308,696	

Project Preferences
Geographical: West Coast, NY, Boston
Industries: High Technology, Information Systems, Computer-Related
Stages: First, Second

Principals: Peter C. Wendell, Gen. Part.; Vincent H. Tobkin, Gen. Part.
Contact: Either

Branch: 615 Madison Ave., New York, NY 10022, 212/758-5954. *Contact:* Gilbert Lamphere, Gen. Part.; Thomas Barron, Gen. Part.

SOFINNOVA INC.

3 Embarcadero Center
San Francisco, CA 94111
415/362-4021

Year Founded: 1977
Type: Private V.C. Firm
Affiliation: Sofinnova SA (France)
Total Paid-In Capital: $41,000,000

1983 Investment History:

Stage	Dollars Invested	No. of Deals
Seed/Startup	$1,800,000	6
Later Stage	$2,000,000	4
Follow-On	$1,200,000	5
Buyouts	0	0
Total Investments	$5,000,000	15
Average Investment	$ 333,333	

Project Preferences
Geographical: Anywhere in U.S.
Industries: High Technology, Electronics, Medical, Biotechnology
Stages: Startup, First, Second

Principals: Jean Bernard Schmidt, Pres.; Jacques Vallee, Gen. Part.
Contact: Jacques Vallee

SOUTHERN CALIFORNIA VENTURES

9920 La Cienega Blvd., Suite 510
Inglewood, CA 90301
213/216-0544

Year Founded: 1983
Type: Private V.C. Firm
Total Paid-In Capital: $15,000,000

1983 Investment History:

Stage	Dollars Invested	No. of Deals
Seed/Startup	N.A.	3
Later Stage	N.A.	3
Follow-On	N.A.	1
Buyouts	0	0
Total Investments	$2,500,000	7
Average Investment	$ 357,143	

Project Preferences
Geographical: Southern CA
Industries: Diversified
Stages: Seed, Startup, First

Principals: B. Allen Lay, Gen. Part.; Jay Raskin, Gen. Part.
Contact: Either

Branch: 2102 Business Center Dr., Irvine, CA 92715, 714/752-9341.
Contact: Robert Johnson, Prin.

SUTRO & CO. INC.

201 California St.
San Francisco, CA 94111
415/445-8576

Year Founded: 1858
Type: Brokerage Firm
Total Paid-In Capital: Not Provided

1983 Investment History:

Stage	Dollars Invested	No. of Deals
Seed/Startup	$ 6,000,000	2
Later Stage	0	0
Follow-On	$ 6,000,000	2
Buyouts	0	0
Total Investments	$12,000,000	4
Average Investment	$ 3,000,000	

Project Preferences
Geographical: West Coast
Industries: Diversified, Medical & Healthcare, Telecommunications, Computer Hardware & Software
Stages: Startup, Later

Principals: Ross L. Cobb, Chair.; Robert L. Woodberry, Pres.; Charles D. Murphy III, Sr. V.P.
Contact: Any of Above

SUTTER HILL VENTURES

2 Palo Alto Square, Suite 700
Palo Alto, CA 94306
415/493-5600

Year Founded: 1962
Type: Corp. V.C. Subsidiary
Affiliation: Genstar Corp.
Total Paid-In Capital: Not Provided

1983 Investment History:

Stage	Dollars Invested	No. of Deals
Seed/Startup	$ 3,500,000	7
Later Stage	$ 3,500,000	4
Follow-On	$ 7,000,000	16
Buyouts	0	0
Total Investments	$14,000,000	27
Average Investment	$ 518,519	

Project Preferences
Geographical: Anywhere in U.S.
Industries: High Technology, Medical, Communications
Stages: Seed, Startup, First

Principals: Paul M. Wythes, Gen. Part.; G. Leonard Baker Jr., Gen. Part.; David L. Anderson, Gen. Part.; William H. Younger Jr., Gen. Part.
Contact: Any of Above

TAYLOR & TURNER

220 Montgomery St., Penthouse 10
San Francisco, CA 94014
415/398-6821

Year Founded: 1982
Type: Private V.C. Firm
Total Paid-In Capital: $18,500,000

1983 Investment History:

Stage	Dollars Invested	No. of Deals
Seed/Startup	$2,700,000	6
Later Stage	0	0
Follow-On	0	0
Buyouts	$ 300,000	1
Total Investments	$3,000,000	7
Average Investment	$ 428,571	

Project Preferences
Geographical: Anywhere in U.S.
Industries: Diversified
Stages: Startup, Second, Buyouts

Principals: Dr. William H. Taylor II, Part.; Marshall C. Turner Jr., Part.
Contact: Either

Branches: Rotan Mosle Technology Partners Ltd., Republicbank Center, 700 Louisiana, Suite 3800, Houston, TX 77002, 713/236-3180. *Contact:* John Jaggers, Assoc.
VenWest, Westinghouse Bldg., Gateway Center, Pittsburgh, PA 15222, 412/642-5858. *Contact:* John Brock

TECHNOLOGY FUNDING INC.

2000 Alameda de las Pulgas
San Mateo, CA 94403
415/345-2200

Year Founded: 1979
Type: Private V.C. Firm
Total Paid-In Capital: $17,000,000

1983 Investment History:

Stage	Dollars Invested	No. of Deals
Seed/Startup	$2,550,000	5
Later Stage	$2,780,000	4
Follow-On	0	0
Buyouts	0	0
Total Investments	$5,330,000	9
Average Investment	$ 588,888	

Project Preferences
Geographical: Anywhere in U.S.
Industries: High Technology, Software, Computers, Telecommunications
Stages: Startup, First, Second, Later

Principals: Charles R. Kokesh, Part.; Frank R. Pope, Part.; John A. Griner III, Part.; David N. Hartford, Part.; Eugene J. Fischer, Part.; Cowfy Wadia, Corp. Finance Assoc.
Contact: Eugene Fischer, Cowfy Wadia

TECHNOLOGY VENTURE INVESTORS

3000 Sand Hill Rd., Bldg. 4, Suite 210
Menlo Park, CA 94025
415/854-7472

Year Founded: 1980
Type: Private V.C. Firm
Total Paid-In Capital: $69,000,000

1983 Investment History:

Stage	Dollars Invested	No. of Deals
Seed/Startup	$ 6,100,000	7
Later Stage	$ 2,100,000	3
Follow-On	$ 6,200,000	19
Buyouts	0	0
Total Investments	$14,400,000	29
Average Investment	$ 496,552	

Project Preferences
Geographical: West Coast
Industries: High Technology
Stages: Any

Principals: Burton J. McMurtry, Gen. Part.; David F. Marquardt, Gen. Part.; James F. Bochnowski, Gen. Part.; Pete Thomas, Assoc.; Robert C. Kagle, Assoc.; James A. Katzman, Assoc.
Contact: Any of Above

U.S. VENTURE PARTNERS

2180 Sand Hill Rd., Suite 300
Menlo Park, CA 94025
415/854-9080

Year Founded: 1981
Type: Private V.C. Firm
Total Paid-In Capital: $150,000,000

1983 Investment History:

Stage	Dollars Invested	No. of Deals
Seed/Startup	$ 8,000,000	11
Later Stage	$12,000,000	31
Follow-On	0	0
Buyouts	0	0
Total Investments	$20,000,000	42
Average Investment	$ 476,190	

Project Preferences
Geographical: West Coast, Northeast
Foreign: Anywhere
Industries: High Technology, Specialty Retailing
Stages: Any

Principals: Robert Sackman, Gen. Part.; Stuart G. Moldaw, Gen. Part.; William K. Bowes Jr., Gen. Part.; Roderick C.M. Hall, Gen. Part.; H. Joseph Horowitz, Gen. Part.; Bruce J. Boehm, Gen. Part.; Jane H. Martin, Gen. Part.
Contact: Any of Above

VANGUARD ASSOCIATES

300 Hamilton Ave., Suite 500
Palo Alto, CA 94301
415/324-8400

Year Founded: 1981
Type: Private V.C. Firm
Total Paid-In Capital: $40,000,000

1983 Investment History:

Stage	Dollars Invested	No. of Deals
Seed/Startup	$3,000,000	6
Later Stage	$3,000,000	4
Follow-On	$2,000,000	4
Buyouts	0	0
Total Investments	$8,000,000	14
Average Investment	$ 571,429	

Project Preferences
Geographical: Anywhere in U.S., West Coast
Industries: High Technology, Biotechnology, Computer Hardware & Software, Telecommunications, Medical Equipment & Instrumentation
Stages: Seed, Startup

Principals: Douglas DeVivo, Gen. Part.; Jack Gill, Gen. Part.; David Rammler, Gen. Part.
Contact: Any of Above

VENTANA GROWTH FUND

19600 Fairchild, Suite 150
Irvine, CA 92715
714/476-2204

Year Founded: 1971
Type: Private V.C. Firm
Total Paid-In Capital: $20,000,000

1983 Investment History:

Stage	Dollars Invested	No. of Deals
Seed/Startup	N.A.	N.A.
Later Stage	N.A.	N.A.
Follow-On	N.A.	N.A.
Buyouts	N.A.	N.A.
Total Investments	$2,250,000	4
Average Investment	$ 562,500	

Project Preferences
Geographical: West Coast
Industries: Healthcare, Electronics, Communications, Energy-
  Conservation Products
Stages: Second, Later

Principals: Thomas O. Gephart, Sr. Gen. Part.; Duwaine Townsen, Sr.
  Gen. Part.; Kenneth B. Tingey, Part.
Contact: Thomas O. Gephart, Duwaine Townsen

WALDEN CAPITAL

303 Sacramento St.
San Francisco, CA 94111
415/391-7225

Year Founded: 1974
Type: Private V.C. Firm
Affiliation: Walden Capital Corp.
Total Paid-In Capital: $30,000,000

1983 Investment History:

Stage	Dollars Invested	No. of Deals
Seed/Startup	$3,800,000	6
Later Stage	$1,100,000	2
Follow-On	$1,300,000	6
Buyouts	0	0
Total Investments	$6,200,000	14
Average Investment	$ 442,857	

Project Preferences
Geographical: West Coast
Industries: High Technology
Stages: Seed, Startup, First

Principals: Arthur S. Berliner, Gen. Part.; George S. Sarlo, Gen. Part.;
  Lip-Bu Tan, Gen. Part.
Contact: Any of Above

Branch: 1001 Logan Bldg., Seattle, WA 98101, 206/623-6550.
  Contact: Ted Wight, Gen. Part.

WEISS, PECK & GREER VENTURE ASSOCIATES LP

555 California St., Suite 4760
San Francisco, CA 94104
415/622-6864

Year Founded: 1984
Type: Private V.C. Firm
Total Paid-In Capital: $94,000,000

1983 Investment History: New Fund

Project Preferences
Geographical: Anywhere in U.S.
Foreign: Anywhere
Industries: High Technology, Computer-Related, Electronics,
  Medical & Healthcare, Energy
Stages: Seed, Startup, First

Principals: Philip Greer, Man. Gen. Part.; John C. Savage, Gen. Part.;
  Robert J. Loarie, Gen. Part.; Eugene M. Weber, Gen. Part.
Contact: Any of Above

Branch: 265 Franklin St., Boston, MA 02109, 617/423-7500. *Contact:*
  Ralph T. Linsalata, Gen. Part.

WEYERHAEUSER VENTURE CO.

21515 Hawthorne Blvd., Suite 310
Torrance, CA 90503
213/543-2661

Affiliation: Weyerhaeuser Co.
Year Founded: 1970
Type: Corp. V.C. Subsidiary
Total Paid-In Capital: Not Provided

1983 Investment History:

Stage	Dollars Invested	No. of Deals
Seed/Startup	$30,500,000	24
Later Stage	0	0
Follow-On	0	0
Buyouts	0	0
Total Investments	$30,500,000	24
Average Investment	$ 1,270,833	

Project Preferences
Geographical: Southwest, Southeast, Northwest, West Coast, Rocky
  Mountains, AK
Industries: Real Estate Development
Stages: Any

Principals: Donald E. Lans, Pres.; Ronald S. Bliss, Sr. V.P.
Contact: Either

Branches: 1510 W. Cape Dr., San Mateo, CA 94404, 415/341-5663.
  Contact: Peter Klein, V.P.
401 Park Pl., Suite 415, Kirkland, WA 98033, 206/822-5588. *Contact:*
  Daniel Fulton, Sr. V.P.

Colorado

THE CENTENNIAL FUND

600 S. Cherry St., Suite 1400
Denver, CO 80222
303/329-9474

Affiliation: Daniels & Associates Inc.
Year Founded: 1981
Type: Private V.C. Firm
Total Paid-In Capital: $28,000,000

1983 Investment History:

Stage	Dollars Invested	No. of Deals
Seed/Startup	$3,350,000	7
Later Stage	$2,140,000	2
Follow-On	$3,370,000	6
Buyouts	0	0
Total Investments	$8,860,000	15
Average Investment	$ 590,667	

Project Preferences
Geographical: Anywhere in U.S.
Industries: Communications
Stages: Seed, Startup, First

Principals: G. Jackson Tankersley Jr., Gen. Part.; Steven C. Halstedt, Gen. Part.; Larry H. Welch, Gen. Part.
Contact: Any of Above

COLUMBINE VENTURE FUND LTD.

5613 Denver Technological Center Parkway, Suite 510
Englewood, CO 80111
303/694-3222

Year Founded: 1983
Type: Private V.C. Firm
Total Paid-In Capital: $35,000,000

1983 Investment History: Not Provided

Project Preferences
Geographical: Mountain States
Industries: High Technology
Stages: Seed, Startup, First

Principals: Mark Kimmel, Gen. Part.; David R. Miller, Gen. Part.; Terry E. Winters, Gen. Part.; Sherman J. Muller, Gen. Part.; Duane D. Pearsall, Gen. Part.
Contact: Any of Above

THE HILL PARTNERSHIP

885 Arapahoe Ave.
Boulder, CO 80302
303/442-5151

Year Founded: 1982
Type: Private V.C. Firm
Total Paid-In Capital: $12,000,000

1983 Investment History:

Stage	Dollars Invested	No. of Deals
Seed/Startup	N.A.	N.A.
Later Stage	N.A.	N.A.
Follow-On	N.A.	N.A.
Buyouts	N.A.	N.A.
Total Investments	$4,000,000	16
Average Investment	$ 250,000	

Project Preferences
Geographical: West Coast, Mountain States
Industries: High Technology, Computer-Related
Stages: Seed, Startup, First

Principals: John G. Hill, Part.; Paul J. Kirby, Part.; Robert H. Keeley, Part.
Contact: Any of Above

EJ PITTOCK & CO. INC.

7951 E. Maplewood, Suite 230
Englewood, CO 80111
303/740-7272

Year Founded: 1974
Type: Investment Banking Firm
Total Paid-In Capital: Not Provided

1983 Investment History:

Stage	Dollars Invested	No. of Deals
Seed/Startup	$ 7,500,000	7
Later Stage	0	0
Follow-On	$ 7,500,000	8
Buyouts	0	0
Total Investments	$15,000,000	15
Average Investment	$ 1,000,000	

Project Preferences
Geographical: CO, Mountain States, New York City
Industries: High Technology, Medical, Computers
Stages: Any

Principals: Robert Fitzner, Pres.
Contact: Robert Fitzner

STEPHENSON MERCHANT BANKING

899 Logan St.
Denver, CO 80203
303/837-1700

Year Founded: 1969
Type: Merchant Banking Firm
Total Paid-In Capital: $30,000,000

1983 Investment History:

Stage	Dollars Invested	No. of Deals
Seed/Startup	$ 1,400,000	3
Later Stage	$ 1,100,000	3
Follow-On	$ 1,200,000	3
Buyouts	$ 7,200,000	7
Total Investments	$10,900,000	16
Average Investment	$ 681,250	

Project Preferences
Geographical: West, Southwest
Industries: Diversified, Publishing, Oil & Gas Service, Communications
Stages: Any

Principals: A. Emmet Stephenson Jr., Sr. Part.; John Browne
Contact: Either

Connecticut

ADVEST INC.*

6 Central Row
Hartford, CT 06103
203/525-1421

Year Founded: 1894
Type: Investment Banking Firm
Total Paid-In Capital: Not Provided

1983 Investment History:

Stage	Dollars Invested	No. of Deals
Seed/Startup	N.A.	N.A.
Later Stage	N.A.	N.A.
Follow-On	N.A.	N.A.
Buyouts	N.A.	N.A.
Total Investments	$5,000,000	4
Average Investment	$1,250,000	

Project Preferences
Geographical: East Coast
Industries: High Technology, Biotechnology
Stages: Seed, Startup, First, Later, Buyouts

Principals: John Everets Jr., Exec. V.P.
Contact: John Everets Jr.

Branch: 99 High Street, Suite 1740, Boston, MA 02110, 617/423-7287. *Principals:* Herbert S. French Jr., Sr. V.P.; Hugh F. Bennett, V.P.; Thomas A. Fitzgerald, V.P.

*Formerly: Burgess & Leith Inc.

FAIRCHESTER ASSOCIATES

2777 Summer St.
Stamford, CT 06905
203/357-0714

Year Founded: 1958
Type: Private V.C. Firm
Total Paid-In Capital: $10,000,000

1983 Investment History:

Stage	Dollars Invested	No. of Deals
Seed/Startup	0	0
Later Stage	$2,000,000	1
Follow-On	$2,000,000	1
Buyouts	0	0
Total Investments	$4,000,000	2
Average Investment	$2,000,000	

Project Preferences
Geographical: East Coast
Industries: Diversified, Healthcare, Publishing, Electronics
Stages: Second

Principals: William R. Knobloch, Pres.; C.W. Knobloch Jr., V.P. & Sec.
Contact: William R. Knobloch

FAIRFIELD VENTURE MANAGEMENT CO. INC.

999 Summer St.
Stamford, CT 06905
203/358-0255

Year Founded: 1981
Type: Private V.C. Firm
Total Paid-In Capital: $30,000,000

1983 Investment History:

Stage	Dollars Invested	No. of Deals
Seed/Startup	$2,700,000	6
Later Stage	$2,000,000	3
Follow-On	$1,700,000	8
Buyouts	0	0
Total Investments	$6,400,000	17
Average Investment	$ 376,471	

Project Preferences
Geographical: Anywhere in U.S.
Industries: High Technology
Stages: Any

Principals: Randall R. Lunn, Chair.; John C. Garbarino, Pres.; Oakes Ames, Gen. Part.; Edmund M. Olivier, Gen. Part.; Pedro A. Castillo, Dir.; Eugene E. Pettinelli, V.P.; Thomas D. Berman, Assoc.
Contact: Oakes Ames

Branch: Fairfield Venture Partners, 4000 MacArthur Blvd., Suite 3000, Newport Beach, CA 92660, 714/955-1408. *Contact:* Edmund M. Olivier, Gen. Part.

GENERAL ELECTRIC VENTURE CAPITAL CORP.

3135 Easton Tpke.
Fairfield, CT 06431
203/373-3333

Affiliation: General Electric Co.
Year Founded: 1969
Type: Corp. V.C. Subsidiary
Total Paid-In Capital: Not Provided

1983 Investment History:

Stage	Dollars Invested	No. of Deals
Seed/Startup	$ 2,000,000	4
Later Stage	$39,000,000	6
Follow-On	$47,000,000	15
Buyouts	0	0
Total Investments	$88,000,000	25
Average Investment	$ 3,520,000	

Project Preferences
Geographical: Anywhere in U.S., CA, MA
Industries: High Technology, Computers, Electronics, Communications, Medical Instrumentation
Stages: Any

Principals: Harry T. Rein, Pres. & CEO; Stephen L. Green, V.P. & Treas.
Contact: Harry T. Rein

Branches: Exchange Pl., 14th Floor, Boston, MA 02109, 617/227-7299. *Contact:* Andrew C. Bangser, V.P.
3000 Sand Hill Rd., Bldg. 1, Suite 230, Menlo Park, CA 94025, 415/854-8092. *Contact:* Robert L. Burr, Sr. V.P.; Eric A. Yang, V.P.
33 Riverside Ave., Westport, CT 06880, 203/373-3525. *Contact:* James J. Fitzpatrick, Sr. V.P.; David C. Fries, Sr. V.P.

OAK INVESTMENT PARTNERS

257 Riverside Ave.
Westport, CT 06880
203/226-8346

Year Founded: 1978
Type: Private V.C. Firm
Total Paid-In Capital: $235,000,000

1983 Investment History:

Stage	Dollars Invested	No. of Deals
Seed/Startup	$16,400,000	20
Later Stage	0	0
Follow-On	$14,700,000	33
Buyouts	0	0
Total Investments	$31,100,000	53
Average Investment	$ 586,792	

Project Preferences
Geographical: Anywhere in U.S., West Coast, Northeast
Foreign: U.K.
Industries: High Technology, Data Communications, Office Automation, Software
Stages: Any

Principals: Stewart H. Greenfield, Chair.; Edward F. Glassmeyer, Pres.; Ginger M. More, Part.; Jeffrey D. West, Part.; Michael D. Kaufman, Part.; Dennis Sisco, Part.; Catherine A. Pierson, Part.
Contact: Any of Above

OXFORD PARTNERS

Soundview Plaza
1266 Main St.
Stamford, CT 06902
203/964-0592

Year Founded: 1981
Type: Private V.C. Firm
Total Paid-In Capital: $56,000,000

1983 Investment History:

Stage	Dollars Invested	No. of Deals
Seed/Startup	$2,400,000	4
Later Stage	$2,200,000	4
Follow-On	$2,700,000	9
Buyouts	$1,000,000	2
Total Investments	$8,300,000	19
Average Investment	$ 436,842	

Project Preferences
Geographical: Anywhere in U.S.
Industries: High Technology
Stages: Any

Principals: Kenneth W. Rind, Gen. Part.; Cornelius "Neil" T. Ryan, Gen. Part.; William R. Lonergan, Gen. Part.; Janice DeLong, Assoc.
Contact: Janice DeLong

Branch: Oxcal Venture Corp., 233 Wilshire Blvd., Suite 730, Santa Monica, CA 90401, 213/458-3135. *Contact:* Steven Birnbaum, Gen. Part.

PRIME CAPITAL MANAGEMENT CO. INC.

1 Landmark Square, Suite 800
Stamford, CT 06901
203/964-0642

Year Founded: 1981
Type: Private V.C. Firm
Total Paid-In Capital: $26,200,000

1983 Investment History:

Stage	Dollars Invested	No. of Deals
Seed/Startup	$3,100,000	6
Later Stage	$1,800,000	3
Follow-On	$2,400,000	9
Buyouts	0	0
Total Investments	$7,300,000	18
Average Investment	$ 405,556	

Project Preferences
Geographical: Anywhere in U.S.
Industries: High Technology, Computers, Telecommunications, Medical Technology, Robotics
Stages: Startup, First, Second, Later

Principals: Theodore H. Elliott Jr., Chair.; Dean E. Fenton, Pres.; H. Thomas Gnuse, V.P.
Contact: Dean E. Fenton

...ANCIAL ...S INC.

...0

...rm
...al: $60,000,000

1983 Investment History:

Stage	Dollars Invested	No. of Deals
Seed/Startup	$1,500,000	3
Later Stage	$2,000,000	5
Follow-On	$ 800,000	4
Buyouts	$3,500,000	2
Total Investments	$7,800,000	14
Average Investment	$ 557,143	

Project Preferences
Geographical: Anywhere in U.S.
Industries: High Technology, Computers, Healthcare, Communications
Stages: Any

Principals: Robert M. Williams, Part.; George E. Thomassy III, Part.; Howard C. Landis, Part.; Robert R. Sparacino, Part.; John V. Titsworth, Part.
Contact: George E. Thomassy III

SAUGATUCK CAPITAL CO.

999 Summer St.
Stamford, CT 06905
203/348-6669

Affiliation: Hawley & Associates
Year Founded: 1982
Type: Private V.C. Firm
Total Paid-In Capital: $25,000,000

1983 Investment History:

Stage	Dollars Invested	No. of Deals
Seed/Startup	N.A.	N.A.
Later Stage	N.A.	N.A.
Follow-On	N.A.	N.A.
Buyouts	N.A.	N.A.
Total Investments	$3,500,000	4
Average Investment	$ 875,000	

Project Preferences
Geographical: Anywhere in U.S.
Industries: Diversified, Communications, Transportation, Industrial Equipment & Products, Financial Services, Oil & Gas Services, Healthcare
Stages: Second, Later, Buyouts

Principals: Frank J. Hawley Jr., Gen. Part.; Alexander H. Dunbar, Gen. Part.; Norman W. Johnson, Gen. Part.
Contact: Any of Above

VISTA VENTURES INC.

36 Grove St.
New Canaan, CT 06840
203/972-3400

Type: Private V.C. Firm
Total Paid-In Capital: $60,000,000

1983 Investment History:

Stage	Dollars Invested	No. of Deals
Seed/Startup	N.A.	8
Later Stage	N.A.	1
Follow-On	N.A.	8
Buyouts	0	0
Total Investments	$9,000,000	17
Average Investment	$ 529,412	

Project Preferences
Geographical: Anywhere in U.S.
Foreign: Japan, U.K.
Industries: Diversified, Communications, Healthcare, Information Systems
Stages: Any

Principals: Gerald B. Bay, Man. Part.; John Tomlin, Part.; Dr. Edwin Snape, Part.; Robert Cummins, Part.
Contact: Any of Above

Branch: 610 Newport Center Dr., Newport Beach, CA 92660, 714/720-1416. *Contact:* Any of Above

District of Columbia

ALLIED CAPITAL CORP.

1625 I St., NW, Suite 603
Washington, D.C. 20006
202/331-1112

Year Founded: 1959
Type: Public V.C. Firm
Total Paid-In Capital: $54,000,000

1983 Investment History:

Stage	Dollars Invested	No. of Deals
Seed/Startup	$ 500,000	3
Later Stage	$ 7,500,000	46
Follow-On	$ 1,000,000	6
Buyouts	$ 3,000,000	18
Total Investments	$12,000,000	73
Average Investment	$ 164,384	

Project Preferences
Geographical: Anywhere in U.S.
Industries: Diversified
Stages: Second, Later, Buyouts

Principals: George C. Williams II, Chair.; David J. Gladstone, Pres.; Brooks Brown, Sr. V.P.; Joan Barra, Asst. V.P.
Contact: Joan Barra

Branch: 1 Financial Plaza, Suite 1614, Ft. Lauderdale, FL 33394, 305/763-8484. *Contact:* George C. Williams III, V.P.

NATIONAL CORP. FOR HOUSING PARTNERSHIPS

1133 15th St., NW
Washington, DC 20005
202/857-5700

Affiliation: NCHP Development Corp.; Housing Capital Corp.
Year Founded: 1968
Type: Private V.C. Firm
Total Paid-In Capital: Not Provided

1983 Investment History:

Stage	Dollars Invested	No. of Deals
Seed/Startup	N.A.	N.A.
Later Stage	N.A.	N.A.
Follow-On	N.A.	N.A.
Buyouts	N.A.	N.A.
Total Investments	$49,000,000	49
Average Investment	$ 1,000,000	

Project Preferences
Geographical: Anywhere in U.S.
Industries: Real Estate, Housing
Stages: Any

Principals: George M. Brady Jr., Chair.; William R. Lanius, Asst. Controller—HCC Operations
Contact: Either

Florida

SOUTH ATLANTIC VENTURE FUND LP

220 E. Madison St., Suite 530
Tampa, FL 33602
813/229-7400

Year Founded: 1981
Type: Private V.C. Firm
Total Paid-In Capital: $17,500,000

1983 Investment History: Not Provided

Project Preferences
Geographical: Southeast
Industries: Diversified, Technology-Based
Stages: First, Second

Principals: Donald W. Burton, Gen. Part.
Contact: Sandra Barber, Admin. Part.

VENTURE MANAGEMENT ASSOCIATES INC.

1 Southeast Financial Center
Miami, FL 33131
305/375-6470

Affiliation: Southeast Banking Corp.
Year Founded: 1968
Type: Private V. C. Firm
Total Paid-In Capital: $25,000,000

1983 Investment History:

Stage	Dollars Invested	No. of Deals
Seed/Startup	$3,300,000	10
Later Stage	0	0
Follow-On	$ 300,000	4
Buyouts	0	0
Total Investments	$3,600,000	14
Average Investment	$ 257,143	

Project Preferences
Geographical: Anywhere in U.S., Southeast
Industries: Diversified
Stages: Seed, Startup, First, Buyouts

Principals: C. L. Hofmann, Pres.; John H. Lamothe, V.P.; James R. Fitzsimons Jr., V.P.; Anne Cario, Treas.
Contact: Any of Above

Georgia

PHILIPPS J. HOOK & ASSOCIATES INC.

5600 Roswell Rd., Suite 300
Atlanta, GA 30342
404/252-1994

Year Founded: 1973
Type: Investment Banking Firm
Total Paid-In Capital: Not Provided

1983 Investment History:

Stage	Dollars Invested	No. of Deals
Seed/Startup	$ 500,000	1
Later Stage	$ 2,000,000	2
Follow-On	0	0
Buyouts	$22,500,000	3
Total Investments	$25,000,000	6
Average Investment	$ 4,166,667	

Project Preferences
Geographical: Anywhere in U.S.
Industries: Diversified
Stages: Any

Principals: Philipps J. Hook, Pres.
Contact: Philipps J. Hook

NORO-MOSELEY PARTNERS

100 Galleria Parkway, Suite 1240
Atlanta, GA 30339
404/955-0020

Year Founded: 1983
Type: Private V.C. Firm
Total Paid-In Capital: $43,500,000

1983 Investment History:

Stage	Dollars Invested	No. of Deals
Seed/Startup	$1,300,000	2
Later Stage	$6,500,000	5
Follow-On	0	0
Buyouts	$1,300,000	2
Total Investments	$9,100,000	9
Average Investment	$1,011,111	

Project Preferences
Geographical: Anywhere in U.S., Southeast
Industries: Diversified, High Technology
Stages: Later

Principals: Charles D. Moseley Jr., Pres; Jack R. Kelly Jr., V.P.
Contact: Either

ROBINSON-HUMPHREY/AMERICAN EXPRESS INC.

3333 Peachtree Rd., NE
Atlanta, GA 30326
404/266-6000

Affiliation: Shearson Lehman/American Express
Year Founded: 1894
Type: Investment Banking Firm
Total Paid-In Capital: Not Provided

1983 Investment History:

Stage	Dollars Invested	No. of Deals
Seed/Startup	0	0
Later Stage	$12,000,000	4
Follow-On	0	0
Buyouts	0	0
Total Investments	$12,000,000	4
Average Investment	$3,000,000	

Project Preferences
Geographical: Anywhere in U.S., Southeast
Foreign: U.K., West Germany
Industries: Diversified
Stages: Later

Principals: Ed Croft, Man. Dir. & Dir. Corp. Finance; Sandy Sands, Asst. V.P. & Sec.
Contact: Sandy Sands

Illinois

ALLSTATE INSURANCE CO.

Allstate Plaza E-2
Northbrook, IL 60062
312/291-5733

Affiliation: Allstate Insurance Co.
Year Founded: 1957
Type: Corp. V. C. Subsidiary
Total Paid-In Capital: Not Provided

1983 Investment History:

Stage	Dollars Invested	No. of Deals
Seed/Startup	$17,700,000	12
Later Stage	$20,400,000	11
Follow-On	$12,400,000	18
Buyouts	$5,000,000	1
Total Investments	$55,500,000	42
Average Investment	$1,321,429	

Project Preferences
Geographical: Anywhere in U.S.
Industries: Diversified
Stages: Any

Principals: Donald Johnson, Investment Mgr.; Leonard Batterson, Investment Mgr.; Robert Lestina, Investment Mgr.
Contact: Any of Above

WILLIAM BLAIR VENTURE PARTNERS

135 S. La Salle St., 29th Floor
Chicago, IL 60603
312/853-8250

Affiliation: William Blair & Co.
Year Founded: 1982
Type: Private V.C. Firm
Total Paid-In Capital: $5,000,000

1983 Investment History:

Stage	Dollars Invested	No. of Deals
Seed/Startup	$1,700,000	5
Later Stage	$3,100,000	7
Follow-On	$400,000	3
Buyouts	0	0
Total Investments	$5,200,000	15
Average Investment	$346,667	

Project Preferences
Geographical: Anywhere in U.S., Midwest
Industries: Diversified
Stages: Any

Principals: Samuel B. Guren, Gen. Part.; Scott F. Meadow, Gen. Part.; James E. Crawford III, Gen. Part.
Contact: Samuel B. Guren

CONTINENTAL ILLINOIS VENTURE CORP.

231 S. La Salle St.
Chicago, IL 60697
312/828-8021

Affiliation: Continental Illinois Corp.
Year Founded: 1978
Type: Corp. V.C. Subsidiary
Total Paid-In Capital: Not Provided

1983 Investment History:

Stage	Dollars Invested	No. of Deals
Seed/Startup	0	0
Later Stage	0	0
Follow-On	0	0
Buyouts	$6,200,000	3
Total Investments	$6,200,000	3
Average Investment	$2,066,667	

Project Preferences
Geographical: Anywhere in U.S.
Industries: Diversified
Stages: Buyouts

Principals: John L. Hines, Pres.; William Putze, Sr. V.P.; Seth L. Pierrepont, V.P.; Judith Bultman Meyer, V.P.; Scott E. Smith, Second V.P.; Samuel C. Freitag, Second V.P.; Burton E. McGillivray, Investment Analyst; Edward K. Chandler, Investment Analyst
Contact: Seth L. Pierrepont; Scott E. Smith

FIRST CHICAGO INVESTMENT ADVISORS

3 First National Plaza, Suite 0140
Chicago, IL 60670
312/732-4154

Affiliation: First National Bank of Chicago
Year Founded: 1972
Type: Corp. V.C. Subsidiary
Total Paid-In Capital: Not Provided

1983 Investment History:

Stage	Dollars Invested	No. of Deals
Seed/Startup	$ 500,000	1
Later Stage	$3,000,000	5
Follow-On	$1,900,000	8
Buyouts	$1,500,000	2
Total Investments	$6,900,000	17
Average Investment	$ 405,882	

Project Preferences
Geographical: Anywhere in U.S., Midwest
Industries: Diversified, Information Processing, Communications, Medical & Healthcare
Stages: Startup, First, Second, Later

Principals: John H. Mahar, V.P., Division Head; T. Bondurant French, V.P.; Marshall Z. Greenwald, V.P.; Patrick A. McGivney, V.P.; Daniel Mitchell, V.P.
Contact: Any of Above

FIRST CHICAGO VENTURE CAPITAL CORP.

1 First National Plaza, Suite 2628
Chicago, IL 60670
312/732-5400

Affiliation: First Chicago Corp.
Year Founded: 1961
Type: Corp. V.C. Subsidiary
Total Paid-In Capital: Not Provided

1983 Investment History:

Stage	Dollars Invested	No. of Deals
Seed/Startup	$ 7,500,000	8
Later Stage	$15,900,000	9
Follow-On	$28,900,000	24
Buyouts	$29,800,000	9
Total Investments	$82,100,000	50
Average Investment	$ 1,640,000	

Project Preferences
Geographical: Anywhere in U.S.
Industries: High Technology, Communications, Healthcare, Computer Software
Stages: Any

Principals: John A. Canning Jr., Pres.; Kent P. Dauten, V.P.; Paul R. Wood, V.P.
Contact: Any of Above

Branch: 133 Federal St., Boston, MA 02110, 617/542-9185. *Contact:* Kevin McCafferty, V.P.

FRONTENAC VENTURE CO.

208 S. La Salle St., Suite 1900
Chicago, IL 60604
312/368-0044

Affiliation: Frontenac Capital Corp.
Year Founded: 1970
Type: Private V.C. Firm
Total Paid-In Capital: $55,000,000

1983 Investment History: Not Provided

Project Preferences
Geographical: Midwest, Southwest
Industries: Medical Products & Services, Computer Products & Services
Stages: Any

Principals: Martin J. Koldyke, Gen. Part.; David A.R. Dullum, Gen. Part.; Rodney L. Goldstein, Gen. Part.
Contact: Any of Above

GOLDER, THOMA & CRESSEY

120 S. La Salle St.
Chicago, IL 60603
312/853-3322

Year Founded: 1980
Type: Private V.C. Firm
Total Paid-In Capital: $130,000,000

1983 Investment History:

Stage	Dollars Invested	No. of Deals
Seed/Startup	$ 3,000,000	4
Later Stage	$13,000,000	11
Follow-On	$ 5,500,000	12
Buyouts	0	0
Total Investments	$21,500,000	27
Average Investment	$ 796,296	

Project Preferences
Geographical: Anywhere in U.S.
Industries: Diversified
Stages: Any

Principals: Stanley C. Golder, Gen. Part.; Carl D. Thoma, Gen. Part.; Bryan C. Cressey, Gen. Part.; Bruce V. Rauner, Gen. Part.; Robert M. Chefitz, Sr. Assoc.
Contact: Any of Above

Branch: 17330 Preston Rd., Suite 203-B, Dallas, TX 75252, 214/248-7848. *Contact:* Dan F. Blanchard, Sr. Assoc.

MESIROW FINANCIAL SERVICES INC.

135 S. La Salle St.
Chicago, IL 60603
312/443-5757

Affiliation: Mesirow Capital Corp.
Year Founded: 1981
Type: Brokerage Firm
Total Paid-In Capital: $15,000,000

1983 Investment History:

Stage	Dollars Invested	No. of Deals
Seed/Startup	N.A.	N.A.
Later Stage	N.A.	N.A.
Follow-On	N.A.	N.A.
Buyouts	N.A.	N.A.
Total Investments	$5,500,000	9
Average Investment	$ 611,111	

Project Preferences
Geographical: Anywhere in U.S.
Industries: Diversified
Stages: First, Second, Later, Buyouts

Principals: James C. Tyree, Exec. V.P.
Contact: James C. Tyree

PRINCE VENTURE PARTNERS

1 First National Plaza, Suite 4950
Chicago, Il 60603
312/726-2232

Year Founded: 1978
Type: Private V.C. Firm
Total Paid-In Capital: $25,000,000

1983 Investment History:

Stage	Dollars Invested	No. of Deals
Seed/Startup	N.A.	N.A.
Later Stage	N.A.	N.A.
Follow-On	N.A.	N.A.
Buyouts	N.A.	N.A.
Total Investments	$1,500,000	5
Average Investment	$ 300,000	

Project Preferences
Geographical: Anywhere in U.S.
Industries: Diversified
Stages: First, Second, Later

Principals: Angus Duffey, Part.
Contact: Angus Duffey

Branch: 767 Third Ave., New York, NY 10017, 212/319-6620. *Contact:* James W. Fordyce, Part.

SEIDMAN JACKSON FISHER & CO.

233 N. Michigan Ave.
Chicago, IL 60601
312/856-1812

Year Founded: 1981
Type: Private V.C. Firm
Total Paid-In Capital: $26,200,000

1983 Investment History:

Stage	Dollars Invested	No. of Deals
Seed/Startup	$1,700,000	1
Later Stage	$2,800,000	4
Follow-On	$ 770,000	4
Buyouts	$ 630,000	1
Total Investments	$5,900,000	10
Average Investment	$ 590,000	

Project Preferences
Geographical: Anywhere in U.S.
Industries: Industrial Products & Services
Stages: Startup, First, Second, Later

Principals: David C. Seidman, Gen. Part.; Douglas L. Jackson, Gen. Part.; Margaret G. Fisher, Gen. Part.
Contact: Any of Above

SUCSY, FISCHER & CO.

135 S. La Salle St., Suite 616
Chicago, IL 60603
312/346-4545

Year Founded: 1972
Type: Investment Banking Firm
Total Paid-In Capital: Not Provided

1983 Investment History:

Stage	Dollars Invested	No. of Deals
Seed/Startup	N.A.	N.A.
Later Stage	N.A.	N.A.
Follow-On	N.A.	N.A.
Buyouts	N.A.	N.A.
Total Investments	$5,000,000	5
Average Investment	$1,000,000	

Project Preferences
Geographical: Midwest
Industries: Diversified
Stages: Startup, First, Second, Later, Buyouts

Principals: Lawrence G. Sucsy, Pres.
Contact: Lawrence G. Sucsy

Indiana

CORPORATION FOR INNOVATION DEVELOPMENT

1 N. Capitol, Suite 520
Indianapolis, IN 46204
317/635-7325

Year Founded: 1982
Type: Private V.C. Firm
Total Paid-In Capital: $10,000,000

1983 Investment History:

Stage	Dollars Invested	No. of Deals
Seed/Startup	N.A.	N.A.
Later Stage	N.A.	N.A.
Follow-On	N.A.	N.A.
Buyouts	N.A.	N.A.
Total Investments	$2,700,000	7
Average Investment	$ 385,714	

Project Preferences
Geographical: IN
Industries: Diversified, Medical Instrumentation, Telecommunications, Agri-Research, Biotechnology
Stages: First, Second, Buyouts

Principals: John W. Fisher, Chair.; Richard D. Wood, V. Chair.; Marion C. Dietrich, Pres. & CEO; John T. Hackett, Treas., CFO & Dir.; Berkley W. Duck III, Sec.
Contact: Marion C. Dietrich

Iowa

RW ALLSOP & ASSOCIATES

2750 First Ave., NE, Suite 210
Cedar Rapids, IA 52402
319/363-8971

Year Founded: 1981
Type: Private V.C. Firm
Total Paid-In Capital: $45,000,000

1983 Investment History:

Stage	Dollars Invested	No. of Deals
Seed/Startup	$3,000,000	5
Later Stage	$1,800,000	4
Follow-On	$1,440,000	7
Buyouts	0	0
Total Investments	$6,240,000	16
Average Investment	$ 390,000	

Project Preferences
Geographical: Anywhere in U.S.
Industries: Communications, Software Applications, Industrial Automation, Medical & Health
Stages: Any

Principals: Robert W. Allsop, Gen. Part.; Paul D. Rhines, Gen. Part.
Contact: Either

Branches: 111 W. Port Plaza, Suite 600, St. Louis, MO 63146, 314/434-1688. *Contact:* Robert L. Kuk, Gen. Part.
35 Corporate Woods, Suite 244, 9101 W. 110 St., Overland Park, KS 66210, 913/642-4719. *Contact:* Larry C. Maddox, Gen. Part.
P.O. Box 1368, 815 E. Mason St., Milwaukee, WI 53201, 414/271-6510. *Contact:* Gregory B. Bultman, Gen. Part.

PAPPAJOHN CAPITAL RESOURCES

2116 Financial Center
Des Moines, IA 50309
515/244-5746

Year Founded: 1969
Type: Private V.C. Firm
Total Paid-In Capital: $16,000,000

1983 Investment History:

Stage	Dollars Invested	No. of Deals
Seed/Startup	$5,500,000	11
Later Stage	0	0
Follow-On	$ 100,000	1
Buyouts	0	0
Total Investments	$5,600,000	12
Average Investment	$ 466,667	

Project Preferences
Geographical: Anywhere in U.S., Southern CA
Industries: Medical & Healthcare
Stages: Seed, Startup, First

Principals: John Pappajohn, Pres.
Contact: John Pappajohn

Maryland

BROVENTURE CAPITAL MANAGEMENT INC.

16 W. Madison St.
Baltimore, MD 21201
301/727-4520

Year Founded: 1984
Type: Private V.C. Firm
Total Paid-In Capital: $20,000,000

1983 Investment History: New Fund

Project Preferences
Geographical: Anywhere in U.S., East Coast
Industries: Diversified
Stages: Any

Principals: William Gust, Gen. Part.; Harvey Branch, Gen. Part.
Contact: Either

ALEX. BROWN & SONS INC. ABS VENTURES

135 E. Baltimore St.
Baltimore, MD 21202
301/727-1700, Ext. 7539

Year Founded: 1982
Type: Private V.C. Firm
Total Paid-In Capital: $107,000,000

1983 Investment History: Stage	Dollars Invested	No. of Deals
Seed/Startup	$ 7,900,000	13
Later Stage	$ 9,300,000	19
Follow-On	$ 800,000	5
Buyouts	$ 1,500,000	1
Total Investments	$19,500,000	38
Average Investment	$ 513,158	

Project Preferences
Geographical: Anywhere in U.S.
Industries: High Technology, Healthcare, Software
Stages: Any

Principals: Donald B. Hebb Jr., Part.; Richard L. Franyo, Part.; John M. Nehra, Part.; Bruns H. Grayson, Part.
Contact: Bruns H. Grayson

Massachusetts

AMERICAN RESEARCH & DEVELOPMENT

45 Milk St.
Boston, MA 02109
617/423-7500

Affiliation: Textron Inc.
Year Founded: 1946
Type: Corp. V.C. Subsidiary
Total Paid-In Capital: Not Provided

1983 Investment History: Stage	Dollars Invested	No. of Deals
Seed/Startup	N.A.	5
Later Stage	N.A.	0
Follow-On	N.A.	6
Buyouts	N.A.	0
Total Investments	$5,000,000	11
Average Investment	$ 454,546	

Project Preferences
Geographical: Anywhere in U.S.
Industries: High Technology
Stages: Any

Principals: Charles J. Coulter, Pres.; R. Courtney Whitin Jr., Sr. V.P.; Francis J. Hughes Jr., V.P.; A. Wade Blackman Jr., V.P.; George W. McKinney III, V.P.; Luc Beaubien, Asst. V.P.; Gary M. Katz, Asst. V.P.
Contact: Any of Above

ANALOG DEVICES ENTERPRISES

P.O. Box 280
2 Technology Way
Norwood, MA 02062
617/329-4700

Affiliation: Analog Devices Inc. (Subsidiary of Standard Oil of Indiana)
Year Founded: 1980
Type: Corp. V.C. Subsidiary
Total Paid-In Capital: Not Provided

1983 Investment History: Stage	Dollars Invested	No. of Deals
Seed/Startup	$5,300,000	5
Later Stage	0	0
Follow-On	$3,000,000	4
Buyouts	0	0
Total Investments	$8,300,000	9
Average Investment	$ 922,222	

Project Preferences
Geographical: Anywhere in U.S.
Foreign: Europe
Industries: High Technology, Communications, Industrial Products & Equipment, Electronic Components & Instrumentation
Stages: Any

Principals: Lawrence T. Sullivan, Gen. Mgr.; Robert A. Boole, Dir. Venture Analysis; John J. Wallace, Controller; Pierre Dogan, Mgr. Venture Analysis
Contact: Robert A. Boole

BANCBOSTON CAPITAL INC.

100 Federal St.
Boston, MA 02110
617/434-4012

Affiliation: Bank of Boston Corp.
Year Founded: 1972
Type: Corp. V.C. Subsidiary
Total Paid-In Capital: $100,000,000*

1983 Investment History:

Stage	Dollars Invested	No. of Deals
Seed/Startup	0	0
Later Stage	0	0
Follow-On	0	0
Buyouts	$6,300,000	3
Total Investments	$6,300,000	3
Average Investment	$2,100,000	

Project Preferences
Geographical: Anywhere in U.S.
Foreign: U.K.
Industries: Diversified Non-High Technology, Cable Television, Entertainment
Stages: Later, Buyouts

Principals: Charles R. Klotz, Pres.; Mary J. Reilly, Asst. V.P.; John C. Whistler, Investment Off.; Robert M. Freedman, Investment Assoc.
Contact: Any of Above

*Approximate figure.

RC BERNER & CO.

65 William St., Suite 310
Wellesley, MA 02181
617/237-9472

Affiliation: BKS Associates
Year Founded: 1966
Type: Private V.C. Firm
Total Paid-In Capital: Not Provided

1983 Investment History:

Stage	Dollars Invested	No. of Deals
Seed/Startup	N.A.	1
Later Stage	N.A.	2
Follow-On	N.A.	0
Buyouts	N.A.	1
Total Investments	$14,000,000	4
Average Investment	$ 3,500,000	

Project Preferences
Geographical: Anywhere in U.S.
Industries: Diversified
Stages: Later, Buyouts

Principals: Robert C. Berner, Pres.
Contact: Robert C. Berner

BURR, EGAN, DELEAGE & CO.

1 Post Office Square, Suite 3800
Boston, MA 02109
617/482-8020

•

3 Embarcadero Center, Suite 2560
San Francisco, CA 94111
415/362-4022

Year Founded: 1979
Type: Private V.C. Firm
Total Paid-In Capital: $190,000,000

1983 Investment History:

Stage	Dollars Invested	No. of Deals
Seed/Startup	N.A.	11
Later Stage	N.A.	4
Follow-On	N.A.	24
Buyouts	N.A.	0
Total Investments	$29,000,000	39
Average Investment	$ 743,590	

Project Preferences
Geographical: Anywhere in U.S.
Foreign: U.K.
Industries: Diversified, Computer Hardware & Software, Communications, Health Services, Biotechnology, Optics & Lasers, Electronics, Oil & Gas
Stages: Any

Principals (Boston): William P. Egan, Gen. Part.; Craig L. Burr, Gen. Part.; Esther B. Sharp, Assoc.
Contact: Esther B. Sharp

•

Principals (San Francisco): Jean Bernard Schmidt, Gen. Part.; Shirley Cerrudo, Gen. Part.; Jean DeLeage, Gen. Part.; Thomas Winter, Gen. Part.; Brian Applegate, Gen. Part.
Contact: Any of Above.

THE CHARLES RIVER PARTNERSHIPS

133 Federal St., Suite 602
Boston, MA 02110
617/482-9370

Year Founded: 1970
Type: Private V.C. Firm
Total Paid-In Capital: $134,000,000

1983 Investment History:

Stage	Dollars Invested	No. of Deals
Seed/Startup	$ 7,200,000	10
Later Stage	$ 8,700,000	20
Follow-On	$ 4,300,000	6
Buyouts	0	0
Total Investments	$20,200,000	36
Average Investment	$ 561,111	

Project Preferences
Geographical: Anywhere in U.S., East Coast, West Coast
Industries: High Technology
Stages: Any

Principals: Richard M. Burnes Jr., Gen. Part.; John T. Neises, Gen. Part.; Donald W. Feddersen, Gen. Part.; Robert F. Higgins, Gen. Part.
Contact: Any of Above

CHATHAM VENTURE CORP.

450 Bedford St.
Lexington, MA 02173
617/863-0970

Year Founded: 1982
Type: Private V.C. Firm
Total Paid-In Capital: $22,400,000

1983 Investment History: Stage	Dollars Invested	No. of Deals
Seed/Startup	$3,000,000	5
Later Stage	$3,600,000	5
Follow-On	$ 900,000	3
Buyouts	0	0
Total Investments	$7,500,000	13
Average Investment	$ 576,923	

Project Preferences
Geographical: Anywhere in U.S.
Industries: High Technology, Electronics, Computer Systems,
   Software & Services
Stages: Seed, Startup, First, Second

Principals: Euan C. Malcolmson, Prin.; Stephen J. Gaal, Prin.
Contact: Either

Branches: 1 Plaza Pl. NE, Suite 1500, St. Petersburg, FL 33701,
   813/823-7234. *Contact:* H. Jay Hill, Prin.
   14676 Stoneridge Dr., Saratoga, CA 95070, 408/867-7478.
      Contact: William D. Jobe, Prin.

CLAFLIN CAPITAL MANAGEMENT INC.

185 Devonshire St.
Boston, MA 02110
617/426-6505

Year Founded: 1978
Type: Private V.C. Firm
Total Paid-In Capital: $21,000,000

1983 Investment History: Not Provided

Project Preferences
Geographical: Northeast
Industries: Diversified
Stages: Seed, Startup, First, Second

Principals: Thomas M. Claflin II, Man. Gen. Part.; Lloyd C. Dahmen,
   Man. Gen. Part.; Joseph Stavenhagen, Man. Gen. Part.
Contact: Any of Above

EASTECH MANAGEMENT CO. INC.

1 Liberty Sq., Ninth Floor
Boston, MA 02109
617/338-0200

Year Founded: 1981
Type: Private V.C. Firm
Total Paid-In Capital: $36,000,000

1983 Investment History: Stage	Dollars Invested	No. of Deals
Seed/Startup	N.A.	N.A.
Later Stage	N.A.	N.A.
Follow-On	N.A.	N.A.
Buyouts	N.A.	N.A.
Total Investments	$3,400,000	9
Average Investment	$ 377,778	

Project Preferences
Geographical: New England
Industries: High Technology
Stages: Seed, Startup, First

Principals: G. Bickley Stevens II, Gen. Part.; Fontaine K. Richardson,
   Gen. Part.; Michael H. Shanahan, Assoc.
Contact: Michael H. Shanahan

EG&G INC.

45 William St.
Wellesley, MA 02181
617/237-5100

Year Founded: 1946
Type: Public Co.
Total Paid-In Capital: Not Provided

1983 Investment History: Stage	Dollars Invested	No. of Deals
Seed/Startup	N.A.	N.A.
Later Stage	N.A.	N.A.
Follow-On	N.A.	N.A.
Buyouts	N.A.	N.A.
Total Investments	$5,000,000	5
Average Investment	$1,000,000	

Project Preferences
Geographical: Anywhere in U.S.
Industries: High Technology
Stages: Seed, Startup, Buyouts

Principals: David J. Beaubien, Sr. V.P. New Business Development;
   L. Daniel Valenti, V.P.
Contact: David J. Beaubien

FARRELL, HEALER & CO. INC.

100 Franklin St., Seventh Floor
Boston, MA 02110
617/451-2577

Type: Private V.C. Firm
Total Paid-In Capital: $19,200,000

1983 Investment History:

Stage	Dollars Invested	No. of Deals
Seed/Startup	N.A.	5
Later Stage	N.A.	2
Follow-On	N.A.	10
Buyouts	N.A.	1
Total Investments	$3,500,000	18
Average Investment	$ 194,444	

Project Preferences
Geographical: East Coast, Northeast
Industries: High Technology, Broadcasting
Stages: Seed, Startup, First

Principals: Richard A. Farrell, Pres.; Harry J. Healer Jr., V.P.
Contact: Either

FIDELITY VENTURE ASSOCIATES INC.

82 Devonshire St.
Boston, MA 02109
617/570-6450

Year Founded: 1969
Type: Private V.C. Firm
Total Paid-In Capital: Not Provided

1983 Investment History:

Stage	Dollars Invested	No. of Deals
Seed/Startup	$2,100,000	5
Later Stage	$ 800,000	1
Follow-On	$2,900,000	10
Buyouts	0	0
Total Investments	$5,800,000	16
Average Investment	$ 352,500	

Project Preferences
Geographical: Western U.S., New England
Industries: Diversified, Data Communications, Medical
Instrumentation, Computer Software
Stages: Any

Principals: Thomas F. Stephenson, Pres.; Peter D. Danforth, Gen.
Part.; William R. Elfers, Gen. Part.; Samuel W. Bodman, Gen. Part.;
Donald R. Young, Assoc.
Contact: William R. Elfers; Donald R. Young

GENESIS GROUP INC.

100 Fifth Ave.
Waltham, MA 02154
617/890-4499

Year Founded: 1970
Type: Private V.C. Firm
Total Paid-In Capital: $40,000,000

1983 Investment History:

Stage	Dollars Invested	No. of Deals
Seed/Startup	N.A.	N.A.
Later Stage	N.A.	N.A.
Follow-On	N.A.	N.A.
Buyouts	N.A.	N.A.
Total Investments	$10,000,000	3
Average Investment	$ 3,333,333	

Project Preferences
Geographical: Anywhere in U.S.
Foreign: Europe
Industries: Diversified
Stages: Any

Principals: Arnold L. Mende, Chair.; Henry Starkman, Pres.; David
Ben Daniel, V.P. International; George Selvais, V.P. Finance
Contact: Any of Above

GREYLOCK MANAGEMENT CORP.

1 Federal Street
Boston, MA 02110
617/423-5525

Year Founded: 1965
Type: Private V.C. Firm
Total Paid-In Capital: $100,000,000

1983 Investment History:

Stage	Dollars Invested	No. of Deals
Seed/Startup	$ 9,400,000	12
Later Stage	$ 1,900,000	4
Follow-On	$ 1,000,000	6
Buyouts	0	0
Total Investments	$12,300,000	22
Average Investment	$ 559,090	

Project Preferences
Geographical: Anywhere in U.S.
Industries: Diversified
Stages: Any

Principals: Daniel S. Gregory, Chair.; Robert P. Henderson, V. Chair.;
Charles. P. Waite, Pres.; Henry F. McCance, V.P. & Treas.; Howard
E. Cox Jr., V.P.; David N. Strohm, V.P.
Contact: Henry F. McCance; Howard E. Cox Jr.; David N. Strohm

JOHN HANCOCK VENTURE CAPITAL MANAGEMENT INC.

John Hancock Place, 57th Floor
P.O. Box 111
Boston, MA 02117
617/421-6350

Affiliation: John Hancock Mutual Life Insurance Co.
Year Founded: 1981
Type: Corp. V.C. Subsidiary
Total Paid-In Capital: $148,000,000

1983 Investment History:

Stage	Dollars Invested	No. of Deals
Seed/Startup	$ 3,350,000	6
Later Stage	$20,850,000	23
Follow-On	$ 300,000	2
Buyouts	$ 1,000,000	1
Total Investments	$25,500,000	32
Average Investment	$ 796,875	

Project Preferences
Geographical: Anywhere in U.S.
Industries: High Technology
Stages: Any

Principals: Edward W. Kane, V.P.; D. Brooks Zug, V.P.; William A. Johnston, Sr. Investment Off.; Robert J. Lepkowski, Investment Off.; Nancy C. Raulston, Asst. Investment Off; Laurie J. Thomsen, Asst. Investment Off.
Contact: Any of Above

HARBOUR FINANCIAL CO.

45 Milk St.
Boston, MA 02109
617/426-8106

Affiliation: Kaufman & Co.
Year Founded: 1980
Type: Merchant Banking Firm
Total Paid-In Capital: Not Provided

1983 Investment History:

Stage	Dollars Invested	No. of Deals
Seed/Startup	$1,000,000	1
Later Stage	0	0
Follow-On	0	0
Buyouts	$3,600,000	1
Total Investments	$4,600,000	2
Average Investment	$2,300,000	

Project Preferences
Geographical: Northeast
Industries: Diversified
Stages: Startup, Buyouts

Principals: John R. Schwanbeck, Pres.
Contact: John R. Schwanbeck

INVESTORS IN INDUSTRY CAPITAL

99 High St., Suite 1200
Boston, MA 02110
617/542-8560

Affiliation: Investors in Industry Group, PLC (England).
Year Founded: 1982
Type: Corp. V.C. Subsidiary
Total Paid-In Capital: $100,000,000

1983 Investment History:

Stage	Dollars Invested	No. of Deals
Seed/Startup	0	0
Later Stage	$5,000,000	7
Follow-On	$ 100,000	1
Buyouts	$3,000,000	3
Total Investments	$8,100,000	11
Average Investment	$ 736,364	

Project Preferences
Geographical: Northeast
Foreign: U.K.
Stages: Later, Buyouts

Principals: David R. Shaw, Pres.; William N. Holm Jr., V.P.; Russ J. Salisbury, V.P.; David Warnock, V.P.
Contact: Any of Above

ARTHUR D. LITTLE ENTERPRISES INC.

25 Acorn Park
Cambridge, MA 02140
617/864-5770

Affiliation: Arthur D. Little Inc.
Year Founded: 1984
Type: Corp. V.C. Subsidiary
Total Paid-In Capital: $15,000,000

1983 Investment History: New Fund

Project Preferences
Geographical: Anywhere in U.S., Northeast
Industries: High Technology
Stages: Startup

Principals: Walter J. Cairns, Pres. & CEO; Paul J. Ballantine, Sr. Investment Analyst
Contact: Walter J. Cairns

MATRIX PARTNERS LP

1 Post Office Square
Boston, MA 02109
617/482-7735

Year Founded: 1982
Type: Private V.C. Firm
Total Paid-In Capital: $44,000,000

1983 Investment History:

Stage	Dollars Invested	No. of Deals
Seed/Startup	$ 3,900,000	6
Later Stage	$ 9,200,000	9
Follow-On	$ 1,700,000	4
Buyouts	0	0
Total Investments	$14,800,000	19
Average Investment	$ 778,947	

Project Preferences
Geographical: East Coast, West Coast
Industries: High Technology, Computer-Related
Stages: Startup, First

Principals: Paul J. Ferri, Gen. Part.; W. Michael Humphreys, Gen. Part.
Contact: W. Michael Humphreys

Branch: 224 W. Browkaw Rd., San Jose, CA 95110, 408/298-0270.
  Principals: Glen McLaughlin, Gen. Part.; Frederick K. Fluegel, Gen. Part.; F. Warren Hellman, Gen. Part.

MCGOWAN/LECKINGER

10 Forbes Rd.
Braintree, MA 02184
617/849-0020

Year Founded: 1984
Type: Private V.C. Firm
Total Paid-In Capital: $12,000,000

1983 Investment History: New Fund

Project Preferences
Geographical: Anywhere in U.S.
Industries: Specialty Retailing, Consumer Products & Services
Stages: Any

Principals: James A. McGowan, Gen. Part.; Robert T. Leckinger, Gen. Part.
Contact: Either

MEMORIAL DRIVE TRUST

25 Acorn Park
Cambridge, MA 02140
617/864-5770

Year Founded: 1951
Type: Private V.C. Firm
Total Paid-In Capital: $75,000,000

1983 Investment History: Not Provided

Project Preferences
Geographical: Anywhere in U.S., Northeast
Industries: Electronics, Artificial Intelligence, Robotics, Telecommunications, Oil & Gas
Stages: Startup, Later

Principals: Jean E. deValpine, Administrator & CEO; Paul D. Shuwall, Investment Off.
Contact: Jean E. deValpine

MORGAN HOLLAND VENTURES CORP.

1 Liberty Square
Boston, MA 02109
617/423-1765

Year Founded: 1981
Type: Private V.C. Firm
Total Paid-In Capital: $58,500,000

1983 Investment History:

Stage	Dollars Invested	No. of Deals
Seed/Startup	$ 6,000,000	8
Later Stage	$ 2,000,000	2
Follow-On	$ 2,000,000	3
Buyouts	0	0
Total Investments	$10,000,000	13
Average Investment	$ 769,231	

Project Preferences
Geographical: Anywhere in U.S.
Industries: Diversified, Computer, Communications
Stages: Any

Principals: James F. Morgan, Chair.; Daniel J. Holland, Pres.; Jay Delahanty, V.P.; Thayer Francis Jr., V.P.; Robert L. Rosbe Jr., V.P.
Contact: Daniel J. Holland

NAUTILUS FUND INC.

24 Federal St.
Boston, MA 02110
617/482-8260

Affiliation: Eaton & Howard, Vance Sanders Inc.
Year Founded: 1979
Type: Private V.C. Firm
Total Paid-In Capital: $22,000,000

1983 Investment History.

Stage	Dollars Invested	No. of Deals
Seed/Startup	N.A.	N.A.
Later Stage	N.A.	N.A.
Follow-On	N.A.	N.A.
Buyouts	N.A.	N.A.
Total Investments	$2,000,000	4
Average Investment	$ 500,000	

Project Preferences
Geographical: Anywhere in U.S.
Industries: High Technology, Computer-Related, Telecommunications, Software
Stages: Second, Later

Principals: Landon T. Clay, Pres. & Dir.; Richard A. Spillane Jr., V.P. & Dir.; M. Dozier Gardner, V.P. & Dir.; James B. Hawkes, V.P.; A. Walker Martin, V.P.
Contact: Richard A. Spillane, Jr.

ORANGE-NASSAU INC.

1 Post Office Square
Boston, MA 02109
617/451-6220

Affiliation: Oranje-Nassau Group BV (The Netherlands)
Year Founded: 1980
Type: Private V.C. Firm
Total Paid-In Capital: $135,000,000

1983 Investment History:

Stage	Dollars Invested	No. of Deals
Seed/Startup	$ 4,000,000	5
Later Stage	$ 8,000,000	10
Follow-On	$ 2,000,000	7
Buyouts	$ 4,000,000	8
Total Investments	$18,000,000	30
Average Investment	$ 600,000	

Project Preferences
Geographical: Anywhere in U.S.
Foreign: U.K., The Netherlands, France, Singapore, Malaysia
Industries: Diversified
Stages: Any

Principals: Joost E. Tjaden, Pres.; Linda S. Linsalata, V.P.
Contact: Either

Branches: 1 Galleria Tower, Suite 635, 13355 Noel Rd., Dallas, TX 75240, 214/385-9685. *Contact:* Richard D. Tadler, V.P.
1 Westerly Place, Suite 540, 1500 Quail St., Newport Beach, CA 92660, 714/752-7811. *Contact:* John W. Blackburn, Assoc. & Mgr.

PAINE WEBBER VENTURE MANAGEMENT CO.

100 Federal St.
Boston, MA 02110
617/423-8000

Affiliation: Paine Webber Inc.
Year Founded: 1970
Type: Private V.C. Firm
Total Paid-In Capital: $50,000,000

1983 Investment History:

Stage	Dollars Invested	No. of Deals
Seed/Startup	N.A.	N.A.
Later Stage	N.A.	N.A.
Follow-On	N.A.	N.A.
Buyouts	N.A.	N.A.
Total Investments	$5,000,000	14
Average Investment	$ 357,143	

Project Preferences
Geographical: Anywhere in U.S.
Industries: Diversified
Stages: Startup, First, Second, Later

Principals: Richard A. Charpie, Man. Gen. Part.; William C. Mills, Gen. Part.; Daniel Alexander, Gen. Part.
Contact: Richard A. Charpie

PALMER PARTNERS

300 Unicorn Park Dr.
Woburn, MA 01801
617/933-5445

Year Founded: 1972
Type: Private Venture Firm
Total Paid-In Capital: $35,000,000

1983 Investment History:

Stage	Dollars Invested	No. of Deals
Seed/Startup	N.A.	N.A.
Later Stage	N.A.	N.A.
Follow-On	N.A.	N.A.
Buyouts	N.A.	N.A.
Total Investments	$3,500,000	11
Average Investment	$ 318,182	

Project Preferences
Geographical: Anywhere in U.S.
Foreign: Anywhere
Industries: Diversified
Stages: Any

Principals: William H. Congleton, Gen. Part.; John A. Shane, Gen. Part.; Stephen J. Ricci, Gen. Part.; Karen S. Camp, Part.; Alison J. Seavey, Part.; Michael T. Fitzgerald, Part.
Contact: Any of Above

Branch: 831 Carew Tower, Cincinnati, OH 45202, 513/621-2331. *Contact:* Orval E. Cook, Regional Mgr.

PLANT RESOURCES VENTURE FUND

175 Federal St.
Boston, MA 02110
617/542-5005

Year Founded: 1981
Type: Private V.C. Firm
Total Paid-In Capital: $12,000,000

1983 Investment History:

Stage	Dollars Invested	No. of Deals
Seed/Startup	N.A.	N.A.
Later Stage	N.A.	N.A.
Follow-On	N.A.	N.A.
Buyouts	N.A.	N.A.
Total Investments	$6,000,000	5
Average Investment	$1,200,000	

Project Preferences
Geographical: Anywhere in U.S.
Foreign: Canada, U.K.
Industries: Agricultural Technology, Waste Treatment
Stages: Any

Principals: John R. Hesse, Man. Gen. Part.; Richard C. McGinity, Gen. Part.; Richard O. von Werssowetz, Gen. Part.
Contact: Richard C. McGinity, Richard O. von Werssowetz

SCHOONER CAPITAL CORP.

77 Franklin St.
Boston, MA 02110
617/357-9031

Year Founded: 1958
Type: Private V.C. Firm
Total Paid-In Capital: $25,000,000

1983 Investment History:

Stage	Dollars Invested	No. of Deals
Seed/Startup	$1,000,000	1
Later Stage	$3,000,000	1
Follow-On	$4,000,000	1
Buyouts	0	0
Total Investments	$8,000,000	3
Average Investment	$2,666,667	

Project Preferences
Geographical: Anywhere in U.S.
Industries: Renewable Energy, Communications, Cable TV, Biotechnology
Stages: Second

Principals: Vincent J. Ryan, Pres.; Cynthia C. Heller, Treas.; Bernice E. Braden, V.P.
Contact: Bernice E. Braden

SUMMIT VENTURES

1 Boston Place
Boston, MA 02108
617/742-5500

Year Founded: 1983
Type: Private V.C. Firm
Total Paid-In Capital: $75,000,000

1983 Investment History:

Stage	Dollars Invested	No. of Deals
Seed/Startup	$ 2,000,000	2
Later Stage	$ 3,000,000	2
Follow-On	$20,000,000	4
Buyouts	$ 6,500,000	1
Total Investments	$31,500,000	9
Average Investment	$ 3,500,000	

Project Preferences
Geographical: Anywhere in U.S.
Foreign: Canada
Industries: Technology, Healthcare & Medical
Stages: Any

Principals: E. Roe Stamps IV, Man. Part.; Stephen G. Woodsum, Man. Part.
Contact: Either

TA ASSOCIATES

45 Milk Street
Boston, MA 02109
617/338-0800

Affiliation: Advent Capital Companies
Year Founded: 1963
Type: Private V.C. Firm
Total Paid-In Capital: $410,000,000

1983 Investment History:

Stage	Dollars Invested	No. of Deals
Seed/Startup	$24,620,000	15
Later Stage	$41,550,000	10
Follow-On	$ 9,300,000	10
Buyouts	$ 9,540,000	4
Total Investments	$85,010,000	39
Average Investment	$ 2,179,744	

Project Preferences
Geographical: Anywhere in U.S.
Industries: Computer Technology, Medical Technology, Process Control & Instrumentation
Stages: Any

Principals: Peter A. Brooke, Man. Part.; C. Kevin Landry, Man. Part.; David D. Croll, Man. Part.; Richard H. Churchill Jr., Part.; Jacqueline C. Morby, Part.; P. Andrews McLane, Part.; Donald J. Kramer, Part.; Michael A. Ruane, Part.; Robert D. Daly, Part.; John L. Bunce, Assoc.; Brian J. Conway, Assoc.; Linda C. Wisnewski, Assoc.
Contact: John L. Bunce, Brian J. Conway, Linda C. Wisnewski

Branch: 525 University Ave., Palo Alto, CA 94301, 415/328-1210.
  Contact: Jeffrey T. Chambers, Gen. Part.; Michael C. Child, Assoc.

TURNER REVIS ASSOCIATES

14 Union Wharf
Boston, MA 02109
617/227-9734

Affiliation: First Chicago Venture Capital
Year Founded: 1983
Type: Private V.C. Firm
Total Paid-In Capital: $12,000,000

1983 Investment History:

Stage	Dollars Invested	No. of Deals
Seed/Startup	N.A.	N.A.
Later Stage	N.A.	N.A.
Follow-On	N.A.	N.A.
Buyouts	N.A.	N.A.
Total Investments	$9,000,000	9
Average Investment	$1,000,000	

Project Preferences
Geographical: MA
Industries: Diversified, Computer-Related, Industrial Products, Commercial and Industrial Electronics (Including Hardware & Software Products)
Stages: Seed, Startup, First, Second, Later

Principals: John G. Turner, Gen. Part.; Kenneth J. Revis, Gen. Part.
Contact: Either

UNC VENTURES INC.

195 State St., Suite 700
Boston, MA 02109
617/723-8300

Year Founded: 1971
Type: Private V.C. Firm
Total Paid-In Capital: $30,000,000

1983 Investment History: Not Provided

Project Preferences
Geographical: Anywhere in U.S.
Industries: Diversified, Telecommunications, Aviation,
   Microcomputer Peripherals & Software, Healthcare
Stages: Startup, Later

Principals: Edward Dugger III, Pres.; James W. Norton Jr., V.P.
Contact: Either

VENTURE FOUNDERS CORP.

100 Fifth Ave.
Waltham, MA 02154
617/890-1000

Affiliation: Venture Founders Ltd. (U.K.)
Year Founded: 1971
Type: Private V.C. Firm
Total Paid-In Capital: $47,000,000

1983 Investment History:

Stage	Dollars Invested	No. of Deals
Seed/Startup	$5,900,000	9
Later Stage	0	0
Follow-On	$1,900,000	8
Buyouts	0	0
Total Investments	$7,800,000	17
Average Investment	$ 458,824	

Project Preferences
Geographical: Northeast, Southwest
Foreign: England, Belgium
Industries: High Technology, Healthcare Research & Development
Stages: Seed, Startup, First

Principals: Alexander L.M. Dingee Jr., Pres.; Leonard E. Smollen,
   Exec. V.P.; Ross Yeiter, Treas.
Contact: Any of Above

Michigan

DOAN ASSOCIATES

P.O. Box 1431
Midland, MI 48640
517/631-2471

Affiliation: VCM II Services Co.
Year Founded: 1972
Type: Private V.C. Firm
Total Paid-In Capital: $9,500,000

1983 Investment History *:

Stage	Dollars Invested	No. of Deals
Seed/Startup	$1,700,000	9
Later Stage	$ 300,000	1
Follow-On	$1,800,000	9
Buyouts	$ 300,000	1
Total Investments	$4,100,000	20
Average Investment	$ 205,000	

Project Preferences
Geographical: Anywhere in U.S.
Industries: Life Sciences, Computers & Peripherals, Software,
   Semiconductors, Communications & Information Systems,
   Industrial Automation
Stages: Seed, Startup, First

Principals: Ian R.N. Bund, Man. Gen. Part.
Contact: Ian R.N. Bund

Branches: 10 Fairmount Ave., Chatham, NJ 07928, 201/635-3520.
   Contact: Philip E. McCarthy, Man. Gen. Part.
350 Second St., Suite 7, Los Altos, CA 94022, 415/941-2392.
   Contact: James R. Weersing, Man. Gen. Part.

*Financial history for Doan Associates is combined with financial
   history of its wholly owned SBIC, Doan Resources Corp., page
   136.

MBW VENTURE PARTNERS LP

P.O. Box 1431
Midland, MI 48640
517/631-2471

Affiliation: MBW Management Co.
Year Founded: 1984
Type: Private V.C. Firm
Total Paid-In Capital: $47,000,000*

1983 Investment History: New Fund

Project Preferences
Geographical: Anywhere in U.S.
Industries: Life Sciences, Computers & Peripherals, Software,
   Semiconductors, Communications & Information Systems,
   Industrial Automation
Stages: Seed, Startup, Buyouts

Principals: Ian R.N. Bund., Man. Gen. Part.
Contact: Ian R.N. Bund

Branches: 10 Fairmount Ave., Chatham, NJ 07928, 201/635-3520.
   Contact: Philip E. McCarthy, Man. Gen. Part.
350 Second St., Suite 7, Los Altos, CA 94022, 415/941-2392.
   Contact: James R. Weersing, Man. Gen. Part.

*Preliminary closing.

MICHIGAN INVESTMENT FUND LP

P.O. Box 1431
Midland, MI 48640
517/631-2471

Affiliation: VCM II Services Co.
Year Founded: 1983
Type: Private V.C. Firm
Total Paid-In Capital: $32,300,000

1983 Investment History:

Stage	Dollars Invested	No. of Deals
Seed/Startup	$1,400,000	5
Later Stage	$ 500,000	1
Follow-On	0	0
Buyouts	$1,200,000	1
Total Investments	$3,100,000	7
Average Investment	$ 442,857	

Project Preferences
Geographical: Anywhere in U.S.
Industries: Life Sciences, Computers & Peripherals, Software, Semiconductors, Communications & Information Systems, Industrial Automation
Stages: Seed, Startup

Principals: Ian R.N. Bund, Man. Gen. Part.
Contact: Ian R.N. Bund

Branches: 10 Fairmont Ave., Chatham, NJ 07928, 201/635-3520.
  Contact: Philip E. McCarthy, Man. Gen. Part.
350 Second St., Suite 7, Los Altos, CA 94022, 415/941-2392.
  Contact: James R. Weersing, Man. Gen. Part.

TAURUS FINANCIAL GROUP INC.

601 S. Norton Road, Suite A-8
Corunna, MI 48817
517/743-5729

Year Founded: 1966
Type: Investment Banking Firm
Total Paid-In Capital: Not Provided

1983 Investment History:

Stage	Dollars Invested	No. of Deals
Seed/Startup	$2,000,000	2
Later Stage	$6,000,000	6
Follow-On	0	0
Buyouts	0	0
Total Investments	$8,000,000	8
Average Investment	$1,000,000	

Project Preferences
Geographical: Anywhere in U.S.
Industries: Diversified
Stages: Startup, Second, Later, Buyouts

Principals: Robert Machala, CEO; Robin Mitchell, V.P.; Cory B. Weston, Sec.-Treas.
Contact: Robert Machala

Minnesota

INVESTMENT ADVISERS INC.

P.O. Box 1160
1100 Dain Tower
Minneapolis, MN 55440
612/371-7780

Year Founded: 1983
Type: Private V.C. Firm
Total Paid-In Capital: $50,200,000

1983 Investment History*:

Stage	Dollars Invested	No. of Deals
Seed/Startup	N.A.	N.A.
Later Stage	N.A.	N.A.
Follow-On	N.A.	N.A.
Buyouts	N.A.	N.A.
Total Investments	$500,000	2
Average Investment	$250,000	

Project Preferences
Geographical: Anywhere in U.S.
Industries: High Technology, Computer-Related, Medical Instrumentation, Telecommunications, Artificial Intelligence
Stages: First, Second

Principals: Richard C. Pflager, Sr. V.P.; Mitchell Dann, V.P.
Contact: Sue Craig, Admin. Asst., 612/371-7935

NORWEST VENTURE CAPITAL MANAGEMENT INC.

1730 Midwest Plaza Bldg.
801 Nicollet Mall
Minneapolis, MN 55402
612/372-8770

Affiliation: Norwest Corp.
Year Founded: 1961
Type: Corp. V.C. Subsidiary
Total Paid-In Capital: $215,000,000

1983 Investment History:

Stage	Dollars Invested	No. of Deals
Seed/Startup	$10,900,000	13
Later Stage	$ 3,500,000	4
Follow-On	$11,200,000	28
Buyouts	$ 6,300,000	4
Total Investments	$31,900,000	49
Average Investment	$ 651,020	

Project Preferences
Geographical: Anywhere in U.S.
Industries: High Technology, Computer-Related
Stages: Seed, Startup, First

Principals: Robert F. Zicarelli, Chair. & CEO; Daniel J. Haggerty, Pres. & Chief Operating Officer; John P. Whaley, Treas.; Timothy Stepanek, V.P.; Douglas Johnson, V.P.; Leonard Brandt, V.P.; John Lindahl, V.P.
Contact: Daniel J. Haggerty

Branches: 1300 SW Fifth Ave., Suite 3018, Portland, OR 97201, 503/223-6622. *Contact:* Anthony Miadich, V.P.; Dale Vogel, V.P.
1801 California St., Suite 585, Denver, CO 80202, 303/297-0537.
Contact: Larry Wannacott, V.P.; Mark Dubovoy, V.P.

PATHFINDER VENTURE CAPITAL FUND

7300 Metro Blvd., Suite 585
Minneapolis, MN 55435
612/835-1121

Year Founded: 1980
Type: Private V.C. Firm
Total Paid-In Capital: $72,000,000

1983 Investment History:

Stage	Dollars Invested	No. of Deals
Seed/Startup	$1,000,000	4
Later Stage	$3,000,000	6
Follow-On	$2,000,000	8
Buyouts	0	0
Total Investments	$6,000,000	18
Average Investment	$ 333,333	

Project Preferences
Geographical: Anywhere in U.S.
Industries: High Technology, Computers, Data Communications, Medical Technology
Stages: Startup, First, Second, Later

Principals: Gary A. Stoltz, Part.; Andrew J. Greenshields, Part.; Marvin Booken, Part.; Norman Dann, Part.; Jack Ahrens II, Part.
Contact: Any of Above

PIPER JAFFRAY VENTURES INC.

222 S. Ninth St.
Minneapolis, MN 55402
612/342-6000

Year Founded: 1982
Type: Private V.C. Firm
Total Paid-In Capital: $10,000,000

1983 Investment History:

Stage	Dollars Invested	No. of Deals
Seed/Startup	N.A.	N.A.
Later Stage	N.A.	N.A.
Follow-On	N.A.	N.A.
Buyouts	N.A.	N.A.
Total Investments	$3,000,000	9
Average Investment	$ 333,333	

Project Preferences
Geographical: Anywhere in U.S.
Industries: Diversified
Stages: Any

Principals: R. Hunt Greene, Part.
Contact: R. Hunt Greene

New Jersey

ACCEL PARTNERS

1 Palmer Square
Princeton, NJ 08542
609/683-4500

Year Founded: 1983
Type: Private V.C. Firm
Total Paid-In Capital: $75,000,000

1983 Investment History:

Stage	Dollars Invested	No. of Deals
Seed/Startup	N.A.	N.A.
Later Stage	N.A.	N.A.
Follow-On	N.A.	N.A.
Buyouts	N.A.	N.A.
Total Investments	$1,500,000	5
Average Investment	$ 300,000	

Project Preferences
Geographical: Anywhere in U.S.
Industries: Diversified, Healthcare, Industrial Automation, Semiconductors, Software
Stages: Any

Principals: Arthur C. Patterson, Man. Part.; James R. Swartz, Man. Part.
Contact: Either

Branch: 1 Embarcadero Center, 31st Floor, San Francisco, CA 94111, 415/989-5656. *Contact:* Arthur C. Patterson, Man. Part.; James R. Swartz, Man. Part.

BRADFORD ASSOCIATES

22 Chambers St.
Princeton, NJ 08540
609/921-3880

Year Founded: 1974
Type: Private V.C. Firm
Total Paid-In Capital: Not Provided

1983 Investment History:

Stage	Dollars Invested	No. of Deals
Seed/Startup	0	0
Later Stage	0	0
Follow-On	$ 2,000,000	2
Buyouts	$18,000,000	3
Total Investments	$20,000,000	5
Average Investment	$ 4,000,000	

Project Preferences
Geographical: East Coast, Middle Atlantic, Midwest, Southeast
Industries: Diversified Non-High Technology
Stages: Later, Buyouts

Principals: Bradford Mills, Part.; Winston J. Churchill, Part.
Contact: Either

Branch: Bradford Ventures Ltd., 1212 Ave. of Americas, Suite 1802, New York, NY 10036, 212/221-4620. *Principals:* Barbara L. Mills, Pres. *Contact:* George A. Devala, V.P.; Robert J. Simon, V.P.

DSV PARTNERS III

221 Nassau St.
Princeton, NJ 08542
609/924-6420

Year Founded: 1981
Type: Private V.C. Firm
Total Paid-In Capital: $34,000,000

1983 Investment History:

Stage	Dollars Invested	No. of Deals
Seed/Startup	$4,900,000	9
Later Stage	$ 750,000	2
Follow-On	$1,400,000	9
Buyouts	0	0
Total Investments	$7,050,000	20
Average Investment	$ 352,500	

Project Preferences
Geographical: Anywhere in U.S.
Industries: High Technology
Stages: Seed, Startup, First, Second

Principals: Morton Collins, Gen. Part.; James R. Bergman, Gen. Part.; Robert S. Hillas, Gen. Part.; John K. Clarke, Assoc.
Contact: Any of Above

INNOVEN GROUP

Park 80, Plaza W. One
Saddle Brook, NJ 07662
201/845-4900

Affiliation: Emerson Electric Co.; Monsanto Co.
Year Founded: 1972
Type: Private V.C. Firm
Total Paid-In Capital: $60,000,000

1983 Investment History:

Stage	Dollars Invested	No. of Deals
Seed/Startup	$1,000,000	3
Later Stage	0	0
Follow-On	$5,000,000	20
Buyouts	0	0
Total Investments	$6,000,000	23
Average Investment	$ 260,870	

Project Preferences
Geographical: East Coast
Industries: High Technology
Stages: Startup, First, Second

Principals: Gerald A. Lodge, CEO; Raun J. Rasmussen, Exec. V.P.; John H. Martinson, V.P.; Bart Holaday, V.P.
Contact: Any of Above

JOHNSTON ASSOCIATES INC.

Research Park
300 Wall St., Bldg. O
Princeton, NJ 08540
609/924-3131

Year Founded: 1967
Type: Private V.C. Firm
Total Paid-In Capital: $10,000,000

1983 Investment History:

Stage	Dollars Invested	No. of Deals
Seed/Startup	N.A.	N.A.
Later Stage	N.A.	N.A.
Follow-On	N.A.	N.A.
Buyouts	N.A.	N.A.
Total Investments	$500,000	3
Average Investment	$166,667	

Project Preferences
Geographical: Northeast
Industries: Medical Instrumentation, Biotechnology
Stages: First

Principals: Robert F. Johnston, Pres.; James Mrazek, Man. Dir.
Contact: Either

VENTURTECH II

600 S. Livingston Ave., Suite 207
Livingston, NJ 07039
201/994-9802

Year Founded: 1984
Type: Private V.C. Firm
Total Paid-In Capital: $25,000,000

1983 Investment History: New Fund

Project Preferences
Geographical: Anywhere in U.S.
Industries: Microelectronics
Stages: Startup, First

Principals: E. Max Charlet, Gen. Part.; F.D. Meyercord, Gen. Part.; David C. Costine, Gen. Part.
Contact: E. Max Charlet, David C. Costine

New Mexico

MEADOWS RESOURCES INC.

1650 University, NE, Suite 500
Albuquerque, NM 87102
505/243-7600

Affiliation: Public Service Co. of New Mexico
Year Founded: 1981
Type: Corp. V.C. Subsidiary
Total Paid-In Capital: $128,000,000

1983 Investment History:

Stage	Dollars Invested	No. of Deals
Seed/Startup	$2,500,000	2
Later Stage	0	0
Follow-On	0	0
Buyouts	0	0
Total Investments	$2,500,000	2
Average Investment	$1,250,000	

Project Preferences
Geographical: Southwest NM
Foreign: Anywhere
Industries: Diversified, Computer, Medical, Telecommunications
Stages: Seed, First, Second

Principals: Susanne Keniley, Exec. Aide to the Pres.; John Sarah, Sr. Strategic Planner
Contact: Susanne Keniley

SANTA FE PRIVATE EQUITY FUND

524 Camino del Monte Sol
Santa Fe, NM 87501
505/983-1769

Year Founded: 1983
Type: Private V.C. Firm
Total Paid-In Capital: $20,000,000

1983 Investment History:

Stage	Dollars Invested	No. of Deals
Seed/Startup	$4,500,000	6
Later Stage	0	0
Follow-On	0	0
Buyouts	0	0
Total Investments	$4,500,000	6
Average Investment	$ 750,000	

Project Preferences
Geographical: Anywhere in U.S., Southwest
Industries: High Technology, Computer-Related, Health & Medical
Stages: Startup, First

Principals: A. David Silver, Man. Gen. Part.; Kay Tsunemori, Assoc.; Jesse L. Acker, Special Part.
Contact: A. David Silver, Kay Tsunemori

New York

ADLER & CO.

375 Park Ave.
New York, NY 10152
212/759-2800

Year Founded: 1965
Type: Private V.C. Firm
Total Paid-In Capital: $100,000,000

1983 Investment History:

Stage	Dollars Invested	No. of Deals
Seed/Startup	$ 9,500,000	16
Later Stage	$ 2,100,000	3
Follow-On	$28,500,000	33
Buyouts	0	0
Total Investments	$40,100,000	52
Average Investment	$ 771,154	

Project Preferences
Geographical: Anywhere in U.S., West Coast, Northeast
Industries: Diversified, Healthcare, Communications, Semiconductors, Data Processing, Automatic Equipment & Instrumentation
Stages: Any

Principals: Frederick R. Adler, Gen. Part.; Joy London, Gen. Part.; Robert Daly, Gen. Part.
Contact: Any of Above

Branch: 1245 Oakmead Parkway, Suite 103, Palo Alto, CA 94086, 408/720-8700. *Contact:* James J. Harrison, Gen. Part.; James E. Long, Assoc.

ADVANCED TECHNOLOGY VENTURES

50 Broad St.
New York, NY 10004
212/344-0622

Year Founded: 1980
Type: Private V.C. Firm
Total Paid-In Capital: $65,000,000

1983 Investment History:

Stage	Dollars Invested	No. of Deals
Seed/Startup	$ 6,000,000	7
Later Stage	$ 2,000,000	2
Follow-On	$ 2,900,000	8
Buyouts	0	0
Total Investments	$10,900,000	17
Average Investment	$ 641,176	

Project Preferences
Geographical: Anywhere in U.S.
Industries: High Technology
Stages: Seed, Startup, First

Principals: Albert E. Paladino, Man. Part.; Ralph J. Nunziato, Gen. Part.; Ivan E. Sutherland, Part.; Robert G. Loewy, Part.
Contact: Robert C. Ammerman, Assoc.

Branch: 1000 El Camino Real, Suite 210, Menlo Park, CA 94025, 415/321-8601. *Contact:* Jos C. Henkens, Assoc.

AEA INVESTORS INC.

640 Fifth Ave.
New York, NY 10019
212/757-0333

Year Founded: 1979
Type: Public V.C. Firm
Total Paid-In Capital: $275,000,000

1983 Investment History:

Stage	Dollars Invested	No. of Deals
Seed/Startup	0	0
Later Stage	0	0
Follow-On	0	0
Buyouts	$84,000,000	1
Total Investments	$84,000,000	1

Project Preferences
Geographical: Anywhere in U.S.
Foreign: Western Europe, Southeast Asia
Industries: Diversified
Stages: Buyouts

Principals: Paul N. Leitner, V.P.; Michel Zalewski, V.P.; C. Stephen Clegg, V.P.; Ned Sherwood, V.P.
Contact: C. Stephen Clegg

BESSEMER VENTURE PARTNERS

630 Fifth Ave.
New York, NY 10111
212/708-9300

Year Founded: 1981
Type: Private V.C. Firm
Total Paid-In Capital: Not Provided

1983 Investment History:

Stage	Dollars Invested	No. of Deals
Seed/Startup	$ 2,500,000	4
Later Stage	$ 7,000,000	8
Follow-On	$ 3,900,000	4
Buyouts	0	0
Total Investments	$13,400,000	16
Average Investment	$ 837,500	

Project Preferences
Geographical: Anywhere in U.S.
Foreign: Canada
Industries: Diversified
Stages: Any

Principals: Robert H. Buescher, Part.; William T. Burgin, Part.
Contact: Robert H. Buescher

Branches: 3000 Sand Hill Rd., Menlo Park, CA 94025, 415/854-2200.
  Principals: Robert B. Field, Part.; Neill H. Brownstein, Part.
  Contact: Robert B. Field
83 Walnut St., Wellesley Hills, MA 02181, 617/237-6050. *Contact:* G.
  Felda Hardymon, Part.

BIOTECH CAPITAL CORP.

600 Madison Ave., 21st Floor
New York, NY 10022
212/758-7722

Year Founded: 1979
Type: Private V.C. Firm
Total Paid-In Capital: $14,100,000

1983 Investment History:

Stage	Dollars Invested	No. of Deals
Seed/Startup	$ 500,000	1
Later Stage	$ 300,000	2
Follow-On	$3,000,000	6
Buyouts	0	0
Total Investments	$3,800,000	9
Average Investment	$ 422,222	

Project Preferences
Geographical: Anywhere in U.S.
Industries: Telecommunications, Information Processing,
  Biotechnology
Stages: Seed, Second

Principals: Dr. Earl W. Brian, Chair.; John E. Koonce, V.P. & CFO
Contact: Richard C. Vivian, Sec.-Treas.

BRIDGE CAPITAL INVESTORS

50 Broadway, 29th Floor
New York, NY 10004
212/514-6700

Year Founded: 1982
Type: Private V.C. Firm
Total Paid-In Capital: $51,000,000

1983 Investment History:

Stage	Dollars Invested	No. of Deals
Seed/Startup	0	0
Later Stage	$6,000,000	5
Follow-On	0	0
Buyouts	0	0
Total Investments	$6,000,000	5
Average Investment	$1,200,000	

Project Preferences
Geographical: Anywhere in U.S.
Industries: Diversified, Healthcare, Broadcasting, Data
  Communications
Stages: Later

Principals: Donald P. Remey, Part.; Hoyt J. Goodrich, Part.; William I.
  Spencer, Part.
Contact: Any of Above

BUTLER CAPITAL CORP.

767 Fifth Ave., Sixth Floor
New York, NY 10153
212/980-0606

Year Founded: 1983
Type: Private V.C. Firm
Total Paid-In Capital: $300,000,000

1983 Investment History:

Stage	Dollars Invested	No. of Deals
Seed/Startup	0	0
Later Stage	0	0
Follow-On	0	0
Buyouts	$30,000,000	3
Total Investments	$30,000,000	3
Average Investment	$10,000,000	

Project Preferences
Geographical: Anywhere in U.S.
Industries: Diversified Non-High Technology
Stages: Buyouts

Principals: Gilbert Butler, Man. Part.; Peter Lamb, Part.; Charles
  Sukenik, Part.
Contact: Any of Above

CITICORP VENTURE CAPITAL LTD.

Citicorp Center
153 E. 53 St., 28th Floor
New York, NY 10043
212/559-1127

Affiliation: Citicorp
Year Founded: 1968
Type: Corp. V.C. Subsidiary
Total Paid-In Capital: Not Provided

1983 Investment History:

Stage	Dollars Invested	No. of Deals
Seed/Startup	$23,600,000	28
Later Stage	$18,000,000	13
Follow-On	$16,500,000	31
Buyouts	$21,500,000	10
Total Investments	$79,600,000	82
Average Investment	$ 970,732	

Project Preferences
Geographical: Anywhere in U.S.
Foreign: Anywhere
Industries: Diversified, Healthcare, Information Processing, Energy, Transportation, Communications, Manufacturing
Stages: Any

Principals: James W. Stevens, Chair.; Peter G. Gerry, Pres.; George M. Middlemas, V.P.; Guy de Chazal, V.P.; Stanley Nitzburg, V.P.
Contact: Peter G. Gerry

Branches: 1 Sansome St., Suite 2410, San Francisco, CA 94109, 415/627-6472. *Contact:* J. Matthew Mackowski, V.P.
2200 Geng Rd., Suite 203, Palo Alto, CA 94303, 415/424-8000. *Contact:* David A. Wegmann, V.P.; Allan Rosenberg, V.P.; Larry J. Wells, V.P.
Diamond Shamrock Tower, 717 N. Harwood St., Suite 2920, Lock Box 87, Dallas, TX 75221, 214/880-9670. *Contact:* Thomas F. McWilliams, V.P.; Newall Starks, V.P.

CONCORD PARTNERS

c/o Dillon, Read & Co. Inc.
535 Madison Ave.
New York, NY 10022
212/906-7000

Affiliation: Dillon, Read & Co. Inc.
Year Founded: 1981
Type: Private V.C. Firm
Total Paid-In Capital: $98,500,000

1983 Investment History:

Stage	Dollars Invested	No. of Deals
Seed/Startup	$ 7,600,000	10
Later Stage	$13,600,000	7
Follow-On	$ 4,200,000	8
Buyouts	$ 5,000,000	3
Total Investments	$30,400,000	28
Average Investment	$ 1,085,714	

Project Preferences
Geographical: Anywhere in U.S.
Industries: High Technology, Computer-Related, Communications, Energy, Medical
Stages: Any

Principals: Charles L. Lea Jr., Man. Dir. of Dillon, Read & Co.; Edgar A. Miller, Sr. V.P.; Kevin J. Maher, V.P.; John B. Clinton, V.P.; Peter A. Leidel, Assoc.
Contact: Any of Above

Branch: 600 Montgomery, 38th Floor, San Francisco, CA 94111, 415/362-2400. *Contact:* E. Payson Smith, Part.

CRALIN & CO. INC.

757 Third Ave., Sixth Floor
New York, NY 10017
212/935-1050

Year Founded: 1973
Type: Investment Banking & Brokerage Firm
Total Paid-In Capital: Not Provided

1983 Investment History:

Stage	Dollars Invested	No. of Deals
Seed/Startup	$4,300,000	2
Later Stage	0	0
Follow-On	$2,200,000	1
Buyouts	$2,000,000	1
Total Investments	$8,500,000	4
Average Investment	$2,125,000	

Project Preferences
Geographical: Anywhere in U.S., Southeast, Southwest
Industries: High Technology, Telecommunications, Medical, Alternative Energy, Entertainment, Computer Hardware & Software
Stages: Startup, First, Second, Buyouts

Principals: Jeffrey L. Feldman, Chair.; Richard A. Josephberg, Pres.; Ivan A. Grosz, V. Chair.; Paul Foont, Exec. V.P.; Anthony Hoffman, Dir. Corp. Finance
Contact: Anthony Hoffman

CW GROUP INC.

1041 Third Ave., Second Floor
New York, NY 10021
212/308-5266

Year Founded: 1983
Type: Private V.C. Firm
Total Paid-In Capital: $40,000,000

1983 Investment History:

Stage	Dollars Invested	No. of Deals
Seed/Startup	N.A.	N.A.
Later Stage	N.A.	N.A.
Follow-On	N.A.	N.A.
Buyouts	N.A.	N.A.
Total Investments	$9,000,000	9
Average Investment	$1,000,000	

Project Preferences
Geographical: Anywhere in U.S.
Foreign: Canada, Sweden
Industries: Healthcare, Biological Sciences
Stages: Any

Principals: Walter Channing Jr., Gen. Part.; Barry Weinberg, Gen. Part.; Charles Hartman, Gen. Part.
Contact: Any of Above

DREXEL BURNHAM LAMBERT INC.

55 Broad St.
New York, NY 10004
212/480-6011

Year Founded: 1979
Type: Investment Banking Firm
Total Paid-In Capital: $40,000,0000

1983 Investment History:

Stage	Dollars Invested	No. of Deals
Seed/Startup	0	0
Later Stage	$3,900,000	10
Follow-On	0	0
Buyouts	$2,300,000	4
Total Investments	$6,200,000	14
Average Investment	$ 442,857	

Project Preferences
Geographical: Anywhere in U.S.
Industries: Diversified, Computer-Related, Medical
Stages: Second, Later, Buyouts

Principals: Anthony M. Lamport, Man. Dir.; Frank Kline, V.P. Corp. Finance; Richard Dumler, First V.P.
Contact: Any of Above

F. EBERSTADT & CO. INC.

61 Broadway
New York, NY 10006
212/480-0792

Year Founded: 1934
Type: Investment Banking Firm
Total Paid-In Capital: $40,000,000

1983 Investment History:

Stage	Dollars Invested	No. of Deals
Seed/Startup	N.A.	N.A.
Later Stage	N.A.	N.A.
Follow-On	N.A.	N.A.
Buyouts	N.A.	N.A.
Total Investments	$20,000,000	N.A.

Project Preferences
Geographical: Anywhere in U.S.
Industries: High Technology, Electronics, Healthcare, Biotechnology, Chemicals
Stages: Any

Principals: William H. Janeway, V.P. & Dir.; John D. Hogan, V.P. & Dir.; Jack W. Lasersohn, V.P.; C.F. Stone III, V.P.; Andrew H. Chapman, V.P.; Michael E. Norton, V.P.
Contact: Any of Above

ELRON TECHNOLOGIES INC.

1211 Ave. of the Americas
New York, NY 10036
212/819-1644

Afilliation: Elron Electronic Industries Ltd. (Israel)
Year Founded: 1982
Type: Corp. V.C. Subsidiary
Total Paid-In Capital: $20,000,000

1983 Investment History:

Stage	Dollars Invested	No. of Deals
Seed/Startup	N.A.	N.A.
Later Stage	N.A.	N.A.
Follow-On	N.A.	N.A.
Buyouts	N.A.	N.A.
Total Investments	N.A.	N.A.
Average Investment	$1,500,000	

Project Preferences
Geographical: Anywhere in U.S.
Foreign: Israel
Industries: High Technology
Stages: Seed, Startup

Principals: Gideon Tolkowsky, V.P.
Contact: Dr. Yuval Binur

EUCLID PARTNERS II LP

50 Rockefeller Plaza
New York, NY 10020
212/489-1770

Year Founded: 1983
Type: Private V.C. Firm
Total Paid-In Capital: $25,000,000

1983 Investment History:

Stage	Dollars Invested	No. of Deals
Seed/Startup	N.A.	N.A.
Later Stage	N.A.	N.A.
Follow-On	N.A.	N.A.
Buyouts	N.A.	N.A.
Total Investments	$3,000,000	5
Average Investment	$ 600,000	

Project Preferences
Geographical: Anywhere in U.S.
Industries: High Technology
Stages: Seed, Startup, First, Second, Later

Principals: Milton J. Pappas, Gen. Part.; A. Bliss McCrum Jr., Gen. Part.; Jeffrey T. Hamilton, Gen. Part.; Vivian Lee, Assoc.
Contact: Milton J. Pappas, A. Bliss McCrum Jr.

FAHNESTOCK & CO.

110 Wall St.
New York, NY 10005
212/668-8000

Year Founded: 1881
Type: Investment Banking Firm
Total Paid-In Capital: $18,000,000

1983 Investment History:

Stage	Dollars Invested	No. of Deals
Seed/Startup	0	0
Later Stage	$2,000,000	1
Follow-On	0	0
Buyouts	0	0
Total Investments	$2,000,000	1

Project Preferences
Geographical: Anywhere in U.S.
Foreign: Europe
Industries: Diversified, Manufacturing, Medical
Stages: Startup, Later, Buyouts

Principals: David C. Young II, Gen. Part.; Thomas Grant, Gen. Part.;
Contact: Either

Branch: 5 rue Gaillon, 2EME, Paris, France, 33/1-266-0120.
  Contact: Claude Cellier, Gen. Part.

FIDENAS CORP.

405 Park Ave., Suite 1005
New York, NY 10022
212/308-2240

Affiliation: Fidenas International Bank Ltd. (Nassau, The Bahamas)
Year Founded: 1971
Type: Corp. V.C. Subsidiary
Total Paid-In Capital: Not Provided

1983 Investment History:

Stage	Dollars Invested	No. of Deals
Seed/Startup	$1,000,000	5
Later Stage	$2,500,000	3
Follow-On	$2,500,000	3
Buyouts	0	0
Total Investments	$6,000,000	11
Average Investment	$ 545,455	

Project Preferences
Geographical: Anywhere in U.S.
Industries: Diversified, Genetic Engineering, High Technology,
  Manufacturing, Telephone-Related
Stages: Second

Principals: Joseph Tricomi, Pres.
Contact: Joseph Tricomi

THE FIRST BOSTON CORP.

Park Ave. Plaza, 40th Floor
New York, NY 10055
212/909-2200

Affiliation: The First Boston Corp.
Year Founded: 1932
Type: Corp. V.C. Subsidiary
Total Paid-In Capital: $30,000,000

1983 Investment History:

Stage	Dollars Invested	No. of Deals
Seed/Startup	$1,700,000	8
Later Stage	$5,300,000	14
Follow-On	$1,000,000	6
Buyouts	$ 600,000	2
Total Investments	$8,600,000	30
Average Investment	$ 286,667	

Project Preferences
Geographical: Anywhere in U.S.
Industries: High Technology, Electronics, Medical
Stages: Startup, First, Second

Principals: Denis Newman, Man. Dir.; Brian D. Young, Assoc. V.P.;
  Harold W. Bogle, Assoc.; W. Barry McCarthy, Assoc.; John Kenny,
  Assoc.
Contact: Brian D. Young (Buyouts), Denis Newman, John Kenny

FIRST CENTURY PARTNERSHIP

c/o Smith Barney, Harris Upham & Co. Inc.
1345 Ave. of the Americas
New York, NY 10105
212/399-6382

Affiliation: Smith Barney, Harris Upham & Co. Inc.
Year Founded: 1972
Type: Private V.C. Firm
Total Paid-In Capital: $121,000,000

1983 Investment History:

Stage	Dollars Invested	No. of Deals
Seed/Startup	$2,700,000	4
Later Stage	$1,500,000	2
Follow-On	$1,800,000	5
Buyouts	0	0
Total Investments	$6,000,000	11
Average Investment	$ 545,455	

Project Preferences
Geographical: Anywhere in U.S.
Industries: High Technology
Stages: Seed, Startup, First

Principals: Michael J. Myers, Gen. Part.; David S. Lobel, Gen. Part.;
  Roberto Buaron, Gen. Part.
Contact: Any of Above

Branch: 350 California St., San Francisco, CA 94104, 415/955-1672.
  Contact: C. Byron Adams, Gen. Part.; Walter C. Johnsen, Gen Part.;
  C. Sage Givens, Assoc.; Steven P. Bird, Assoc.

ROBERT FLEMING INC.

630 Fifth Ave.
New York, NY 10111
212/265-6700

Affiliation: Robert Fleming & Co. Ltd. (England)*
Year Founded: 1968
Type: Corp. V.C. Subsidiary
Total Paid-In Capital: Not Provided

1983 Investment History:

Stage	Dollars Invested	No. of Deals
Seed/Startup	0	0
Later Stage	$5,000,000	10
Follow-On	0	0
Buyouts	0	0
Total Investments	$5,000,000	10
Average Investment	$ 500,000	

Project Preferences
Geographical: Anywhere in U.S.
Industries: Diversified
Stages: Later

Principals: Fred Knoll, Research Analyst; Jonathan Simon, Research Analyst
Contact: Either

*Investment-management broker.

FOSTER MANAGEMENT CO.

437 Madison Ave.
New York, NY 10022
212/753-4810

Year Founded: 1972
Type: Private V.C. Firm
Total Paid-In Capital: $52,000,000

1983 Investment History:

Stage	Dollars Invested	No. of Deals
Seed/Startup	N.A.	N.A.
Later Stage	N.A.	N.A.
Follow-On	N.A.	N.A.
Buyouts	N.A.	N.A
Total Investments	$4,200,000	7
Average Investment	$ 600,000	

Project Preferences
Geographical: Anywhere in U.S.
Industries: Diversified, Broadcasting, Healthcare, Transportation, Energy, Home Furniture
Stages: Any

Principals: John H. Foster, Pres.; Michael J. Connelly, Exec. V.P.; Timothy E. Foster, V.P.
Contact: Any of Above

FOUNDERS VENTURES INC.

477 Madison Ave.
New York, NY 10022
212/319-5900

Affiliation: Kenai Corp.
Year Founded: 1969
Type: Investment Banking Firm
Total Paid-In Capital: $45,000,000

1983 Investment History:

Stage	Dollars Invested	No. of Deals
Seed/Startup	$3,500,000	1
Later Stage	0	0
Follow-On	0	0
Buyouts	$5,500,000	1
Total Investments	$9,000,000	2
Average Investment	$4,500,000	

Project Preferences
Geographical: Anywhere in U.S.
Industries: Manufacturing, Consumer Products & Services, Distribution
Stages: Later, Buyouts

Principals: Warren H. Haber, Chair.; John L. Teeger, Pres.; Donn Hartley, V.P. Corp. Development
Contact: Any of Above

GENERAL INSTRUMENT CORP.

767 Fifth Ave.
New York, NY 10153
212/207-6200

Affiliation: General Instrument Corp.
Year Founded: 1974
Type: Corp. Division
Total Paid-In Capital: Not Provided

1983 Investment History:

Stage	Dollars Invested	No. of Deals
Seed/Startup	0	0
Later Stage	$5,000,000	2
Follow-On	0	0
Buyouts	0	0
Total Investments	$5,000,000	2
Average Investment	$2,500,000	

Project Preferences
Geographical: Anywhere in U.S.
Industries: Electronics, Telecommunications, Artificial Intelligence
Stages: Later, Buyouts

Principals: Frank G. Hickey, Chair. & CEO; Paul N. Meyer, V.P. Finance & CFO; Edward R. Kearney, V.P. Investor Relations
Contact: Edward R. Kearney

GEO CAPITAL VENTURES

655 Madison Ave.
New York, NY 10021
212/935-0111

Affiliation: Geo Capital Corp.
Year Founded: 1984
Type: Private V.C. Firm
Total Paid-In Capital: $12,000,000

1983 Investment History: New Fund

Project Preferences
Geographical: Anywhere in U.S.
Industries: High Technology, Data Communications, Software, Medical
Stages: Startup, First

Principals: Irwin Lieber, Gen. Part.; Stephen Clearman, Gen. Part.
Contact: Either

GIBBONS, GREEN, VAN AMERONGEN

600 Madison Ave.
New York, NY 10022
212/832-2400

Year Founded: 1969
Type: Private V.C. Firm
Total Paid-In Capital: Not Provided

1983 Investment History:

Stage	Dollars Invested	No. of Deals
Seed/Startup	N.A.	N.A.
Later Stage	N.A.	N.A.
Follow-On	N.A.	N.A.
Buyouts	N.A.	N.A.
Total Investments	$370,000,000	2
Average Investment	$185,000,000	

Project Preferences
Geographical: Anywhere in U.S.
Industries: Diversified
Stages: Buyouts

Principals: Edward W. Gibbons, Gen. Part.; Lewis W. van Amerongen, Gen. Part.; Todd Goodwin, Gen. Part.
Contact: Any of Above

Branch: 333 S. Grand Ave., Los Angeles, CA 90071, 213/625-0005. *Contact:* Leonard Green, Gen. Part.

THE GREENHOUSE INVESTMENT FUND

4 Cedar Swamp Rd.
Glen Cove, NY 11542
516/759-1982

Affiliation: The Greenhouse Management Corp.
Year Founded: 1981
Type: Private V.C. Firm
Total Paid-In Capital: $19,000,000

1983 Investment History:

Stage	Dollars Invested	No. of Deals
Seed/Startup	$2,000,000	5
Later Stage	$ 300,000	1
Follow-On	$1,600,000	3
Buyouts	0	0
Total Investments	$3,900,000	9
Average Investment	$ 433,333	

Project Preferences
Geographical: Northeast
Industries: Computers, Electronics, Biotechnology
Stages: Seed, Startup, First

Principals: Evelyn Berezin, Pres.; Solomon Manber, Gen. Part.
Contact: Evelyn Berezin

GUINNESS MAHON INC.

535 Madison Ave.
New York, NY 10022
212/355-5400

Affiliation: Guinness Peat Group
Year Founded: 1982
Type: Investment Banking Firm
Total Paid-In Capital: Not Provided

1983 Investment History:

Stage	Dollars Invested	No. of Deals
Seed/Startup	N.A.	N.A
Later Stage	N.A.	N.A.
Follow-On	N.A.	N.A.
Buyouts	N.A.	N.A.
Total Investments	$7,500,000	2
Average Investment	$3,750,000	

Project Preferences
Geographical: Anywhere in U.S.
Foreign: U.K.
Industries: Diversified, Cable Television, Communications, Computers, High Technology, Financial Services
Stages: Later

Principals: Sharyar Aziz, Pres.; Bradford A. Warner Jr., Exec. V.P.; P. Stephen Weil, V.P.
Contact: Any of Above

HAMBRO INTERNATIONAL VENTURE FUND

17 E. 71st St.
New York, NY 10021
212/288-7778

Affiliation: Hambros Bank (England)
Year Founded: 1982
Type: Private V.C. Firm
Total Paid-In Capital: $50,500,000

1983 Investment History:

Stage	Dollars Invested	No. of Deals
Seed/Startup	$ 392,000	3
Later Stage	$ 6,183,000	11
Follow-On	$ 2,932,000	6
Buyouts	$ 3,820,000	3
Total Investments	$13,327,000	23
Average Investment	$ 579,435	

Project Preferences
Geographical: Anywhere in U.S.
Foreign: Anywhere
Industries: Diversified
Stages: Seed, Startup, First

Principals: Edwin A. Goodman, Gen Part.; Anders K. Brag, Gen. Part.; Arthur C. Spinner, Gen. Part.; Frances N. Janis, Assoc.
Contact: Any of Above

Branch: 1 Boston, Pl., Suite 923, Boston, MA 08108, 617/722-7055. *Contact:* Robert S. Sherman, Gen. Part.; Richard A. D'Amore, Gen. Part.

HARRISON CAPITAL INC.

2000 Westchester Ave.
White Plains, NY 10650
914/253-7845

Affiliation: Texaco Corp.
Year Founded: 1980
Type: Corp. V.C. Firm
Total Paid-In Capital: $9,500,000

1983 Investment History:

Stage	Dollars Invested	No. of Deals
Seed/Startup	$2,400,000	5
Later Stage	$3,800,000	4
Follow-On	$3,300,000	10
Buyouts	0	0
Total Investments	$9,500,000	19
Average Investment	$ 500,000	

Project Preferences
Geographical: Anywhere in U.S.
Industries: High Technology
Stages: Seed, Startup, First, Second

Principals: William T. Corl, Pres.; Margaret S. Johns, Assoc., Edward J. Steigauf, Investment Mgr.
Contact: Any of Above

HARVEST VENTURES INC.

767 Third Ave.
New York, NY 10017
212/838-7776

Year Founded: 1976
Type: Private V.C. Firm
Total Paid-In Capital: $54,000,000

1983 Investment History:

Stage	Dollars Invested	No. of Deals
Seed/Startup	$ 1,100,000	4
Later Stage	$ 6,700,000	9
Follow-On	$ 2,800,000	10
Buyouts	0	0
Total Investments	$10,600,000	23
Average Investment	$ 460,870	

Project Preferences
Geographical: East Coast, West Coast
Industries: High Technology
Stages: Seed, Startup, First

Principals: Harvey Wertheim, Man. Dir.; Harvey Mallement, Man. Dir.
Contact: Either

Branch: 3000 Sand Hill Rd., Bldg. 1, Suite 205, Menlo Park, CA 94025, 415/854-8400. *Contact:* Cloyd Marvin, Man. Dir.

EF HUTTON LBO INC.

1 Battery Park Plaza
New York, NY 10004
212/742-5001

Affiliation: E.F. Hutton Group Inc.
Year Founded: 1983
Type: Corp. V.C. Subsidiary
Total Paid-In Capital: Not Provided

1983 Investment History:

Stage	Dollars Invested	No. of Deals
Seed/Startup	N.A.	N.A.
Later Stage	N.A.	N.A.
Follow-On	N.A.	N.A.
Buyouts	N.A.	N.A.
Total Investments	N.A.	N.A.
Average Investment	$7,000,000	

Project Preferences
Geographical: Anywhere in U.S
Industries: Diversified
Stages: Buyouts

Principals: Robert P. Jensen, Chair. & CEO; William T. Warburton, V.P., Treas. & CFO; Robert Edgreen, Sr. V.P.; Stephen E. Adamson, Asst. V.P.
Contact: Robert Edgreen, Robert P. Jensen

Branch: 8 E. Figueroa St., Santa Barbara, CA 93101, 805/965-3091. *Contact:* Robert P. Jensen, Chair. & CEO.

HUTTON VENTURE INVESTMENT PARTNERS INC.

1 Battery Park Plaza, Suite 1801
New York, NY 10004
212/742-3722

Affiliation: E.F. Hutton Group Inc.
Year Founded: 1981
Type: Corp. V.C. Subsidiary
Total Paid-In Capital: Not Provided

1983 Investment History:

Stage	Dollars Invested	No. of Deals
Seed/Startup	$1,900,000	7
Later Stage	$1,900,000	5
Follow-On	$1,400,000	4
Buyouts	0	0
Total Investments	$5,200,000	16
Average Investment	$ 325,000	

Project Preferences
Geographical: Anywhere in U.S.
Industries: High Technology
Stages: Seed, Startup, First, Second, Later

Principals: James E. McGrath, Pres.; Timothy E. Noll, Investment Mgr.; James F. Wilson, Investment Mgr.
Contact: Any of Above

INCO VENTURE CAPITAL MANAGEMENT

1 New York Plaza
New York, NY 10004
212/742-4000

Affiliation: INCO Ltd.
Year Founded: 1975
Type: Corp. V.C. Subsidiary
Total Paid-In Capital: $50,000,000

1983 Investment History:

Stage	Dollars Invested	No. of Deals
Seed/Startup	$ 3,000,000	9
Later Stage	$ 4,000,000	11
Follow-On	$ 5,000,000	19
Buyouts	$ 2,000,000	1
Total Investments	$14,000,000	40
Average Investment	$ 350,000	

Project Preferences
Geographical: Anywhere in U.S.
Foreign: Switzerland
Industries: High Technology, Biotechnology, Medical Technology, Computer-Related, Telecommunications
Stages: Any

Principals: Stuart F. Feiner, Pres.; A. Douglas Peabody, Sr. V.P.
Contact: Either

Branch: P.O. Box 44, First Canadian Place, Toronto, Ontario, Canada M5X 1CR, 416/361-7511.

INVESTECH LP

515 Madison Ave
New York, NY 10022
212/308-5811

Year Founded: 1981
Type: Private V.C. Firm
Total Paid-In Capital: $27,000,000

1983 Investment History: Not Provided

Project Preferences
Geographical: Anywhere in U.S.
Industries: High Technology, Biotechnology, Communications, Information Processing, Software, Industrial Automation, Robotics
Stages: Any

Principals: Sheldon F. Claar, Gen. Part.; Sy L. Goldblatt, Gen. Part.; Carl S. Hutman, Gen. Part.; Tancred V. Schiavoni, Gen. Part.
Contact: Carl S. Hutman, Tancred V. Schiavoni

THE JORDAN CO.

315 Park Ave. S.
New York, NY 10010
212/460-1900

Affiliation: Leucadia National Corp.
Year Founded: 1982
Type: Investment Banking Firm
Total Paid-In Capital: Not Provided

1983 Investment History:

Stage	Dollars Invested	No. of Deals
Seed/Startup	0	0
Later Stage	0	0
Follow-On	0	0
Buyouts	$50,000,000	5
Total Investments	$50,000,000	5
Average Investment	$10,000,000	

Project Preferences
Geographical: Anywhere in U.S.
Foreign: Western Europe, Japan, Hong Kong
Industries: Diversified
Stages: Buyouts

Principals: John W. Jordan II, Man. Part.; David W. Zalaznick, Part.
Contact: Either

KWIAT MANAGEMENT ASSOCIATES

576 Fifth Ave.
New York, NY 10036
212/391-2461

Year Founded: 1981
Type: Private V.C. Firm
Total Paid-In Capital: Not Provided

1983 Investment History:

Stage	Dollars Invested	No. of Deals
Seed/Startup	N.A.	N.A.
Later Stage	N.A.	N.A.
Follow-On	N.A.	N.A.
Buyouts	N.A.	N.A.
Total Investments	$4,000,000	7
Average Investment	$ 571,429	

Project Preferences
Geographical: Anywhere in U.S.
Industries: Diversified, High Technology
Stages: Startup, First, Second

Principals: David S. Kwiat, Dir.; Sheldon F. Kwiat, Dir.; Lowell M. Kwiat, Dir.; Jeffrey M. Greene, Pres.
Contact: Jeffrey M. Greene

LAWRENCE, WPG PARTNERS LP

1 New York Plaza, 30th Floor
New York, NY 10004
212/908-9500

●

555 California St., Suite 4760,
San Francisco, CA 94104
415/622-6864

Year Founded: 1981
Type: Private V.C. Firm
Total Paid-In Capital: $67,100,000

1983 Investment History:

Stage	Dollars Invested	No. of Deals
Seed/Startup	$ 5,600,000	6
Later Stage	$ 1,850,000	2
Follow-On	$12,500,000	19
Buyouts	$ 3,300,000	3
Total Investments	$23,250,000	30
Average Investment	$ 775,000	

Project Preferences
Geographical: Anywhere in U.S.
Foreign: Anywhere
Industries: High Technology, Computer-Related, Electronics, Medical & Healthcare, Energy
Stages: Seed, Startup, First

Principals (New York): Larry J. Lawrence, Man. Gen. Part.; Richard W. Smith, Gen. Part.
Contact: Either

●

Principals (San Francisco): Philip Greer, Man. Gen. Part.; Robert J. Loarie, Gen. Part.; John C. Savage, Gen. Part.; Eugene M. Weber, Assoc.
Contact: Any of Above

MANUFACTURERS HANOVER VENTURE CAPITAL CORP.

140 E. 45th St.
New York, NY 10017
212/808-0109

Affiliation: Manufacturers Hanover Corp.
Year Founded: 1981
Type: Corp. V.C. Subsidiary
Total Paid-In Capital: Not Provided

1983 Investment History:

Stage	Dollars Invested	No. of Deals
Seed/Startup	0	0
Later Stage	$ 3,000,000	5
Follow-On	0	0
Buyouts	$ 8,000,000	8
Total Investments	$11,000,000	13
Average Investment	$ 846,154	

Project Preferences
Geographical: Anywhere in U.S.
Industries: High Technology, Medical, Healthcare, Communications
Stages: First, Second, Later, Buyouts

Principals: Thomas J. Sandleitner, Pres.; Edward L. Koch III, V.P.; Kevin B. Falvey, V.P.
Contact: Thomas J. Sandleitner

MERRILL LYNCH VENTURE CAPITAL INC.

1 Liberty Plaza
165 Broadway
New York, NY 10080
212/766-6215

Affiliation: Merrill Lynch & Co.
Year Founded: 1981
Type: Corp. V.C. Subsidiary
Total Paid-In Capital: $60,000,000

1983 Investment History:

Stage	Dollars Invested	No. of Deals
Seed/Startup	$ 2,000,000	2
Later Stage	$ 4,800,000	4
Follow-On	$ 3,400,000	4
Buyouts	0	0
Total Investments	$10,200,000	10
Average Investment	$ 1,020,000	

Project Preferences
Geographical: Anywhere in U.S.
Industries: High Technology
Stages: Startup, First, Second

Principals: George Kokkinakis, Chair.; Stephen J. Warner, Pres.; R. Stephen McCormick, V.P.; George L. Sing, V.P.
Contact: George Kokkinakis

NAZEM & CO.

600 Madison Ave.
New York, NY 10022
212/644-6433

Year Founded: 1976
Type: Private V.C. Firm
Total Paid-In Capital: $34,500,000

1983 Investment History:

Stage	Dollars Invested	No. of Deals
Seed/Startup	$2,380,000	3
Later Stage	$3,120,000	4
Follow-On	$ 600,000	4
Buyouts	0	0
Total Investments	$6,100,000	11
Average Investment	$ 554,545	

Project Preferences
Geographical: Anywhere in U.S.
Industries: High Technology, Medical, Electronics
Stages: Any

Principals: Fred F. Nazem, Man. Gen. Part.; Peter G. Imperiale, Gen. Part.; Philip E. Barak, CFO; Edward H. Humner Jr., Assoc.; Ramon V. Reyes, Assoc.
Contact: Fred. F. Nazem

NEW VENTURE PARTNERS

119 E. 55th St.
New York, NY 10022
212/371-8210

Affiliation: New Enterprise Associates; Southwest Enterprise
    Associates
Year Founded: 1981
Type: Private V.C. Firm
Total Paid-In Capital: $20,000,000

1983 Investment History: Not Provided

Project Preferences
Geographical: Anywhere in U.S.
Foreign: U.K.
Industries: High Technology, Communications, Computers,
    Software, Medical Products & Diagnostic Equipment, Retail
Stages: Startup, First

Principals: Howard D. Wolfe Jr., Gen. Part.
Contact: Howard D. Wolfe Jr.

NEW YORK SECURITIES CO. INC.

575 Madison Ave.
New York, NY 10022
212/605-0421; 203/655-7488

Year Founded: 1962
Type: Private V.C. Firm; Investment Banking Firm
Total Paid-In Capital: $30,000,000

1983 Investment History: No Investments Made in 1983

Project Preferences
Geographical: Anywhere in U.S.
Foreign: Western Europe, U.K., Japan, Hong Kong, Singapore
Industries: Diversified, Medical-Related, Alternative Energy, Forestry
    Products
Stages: Startup, First, Second, Buyouts

Principals: F. Kenneth Melis, Pres.
Contact: F. Kenneth Melis

NOVATECH RESOURCE CORP.

103 E. 37th St.
New York, NY 10016
212/725-2555

Year Founded: 1980
Type: Private V.C. Firm
Total Paid-In Capital: $70,000,000

1983 Investment History:

Stage	Dollars Invested	No. of Deals
Seed/Startup	$ 5,000,000	6
Later Stage	$ 3,000,000	3
Follow-On	$ 4,100,000	6
Buyouts	$ 2,000,000	1
Total Investments	$14,100,000	16
Average Investment	$ 881,250	

Project Preferences
Geographical: Anywhere in U.S.
Industries: High Technology, Biotechnology, Energy,
    Communications, Computers, Agribusiness
Stages: Startup, First

Principals: Reynald G. Bonmati, Pres.; Charles H. Weight, V.P.; Gerry
    Iannone, Treas.
Contact: Reynald G. Bonmati

ALAN PATRICOF ASSOCIATES INC.

545 Madison Ave.
New York, NY 10022
212/753-6300
Year Founded: 1970
Type: Private V.C. Firm
Total Paid-In Capital: $227,000,000

1983 Investment History:

Stage	Dollars Invested	No. of Deals
Seed/Startup	$ 7,750,000	9
Later Stage	$ 1,850,000	3
Follow-On	$ 5,250,000	20
Buyouts	0	0
Total Investments	$14,850,000	32
Average Investment	$ 464,063	

Project Preferences
Geographical: Anywhere in U.S.
Foreign: France, U.K.
Industries: High Technology
Stages: Any

Principals: Alan J. Patricof, Chair.; Robert G. Faris, Pres.; Lewis
    Solomon, Exec. V.P.; John C. Baker, V.P.; Bill Bottoms, V.P.; James
    Newton, Assoc.
Contact: Lewis Solomon

PENNWOOD CAPITAL CORP.

645 Madison Ave.
New York, NY 10022
212/753-1600

Year Founded: 1979
Type: Investment Banking Firm
Total Paid-In Capital: Not Provided

1983 Investment History:

Stage	Dollars Invested	No. of Deals
Seed/Startup	N.A.	N.A.
Later Stage	N.A.	N.A.
Follow-On	N.A.	N.A.
Buyouts	$32,000,000	3
Total Investments	N.A.	N.A.

Project Preferences
Geographical: East of the Rockies
Industries: Manufacturing, Distribution, Retail
Stages: Buyouts

Principals: Marc C. Ostrow, Pres. & Chair.; James J. Fuld, Jr., Part.
Contact: Marc C. Ostrow

THE PHOENIX PARTNERS

323 E. 53rd St.
New York, NY 10022
212/980-9440

Year Founded: 1982
Type: Private V.C. Firm
Total Paid-In Capital: $16,000,000

1983 Investment History: Not Provided

Project Preferences
Geographical: Anywhere in U.S.
Industries: High Technology, Medical
Stages: Startup, First, Second

Principals: John W. Keefe Jr., Man. Gen. Part.
Contact: John W. Keefe

Branch: 2125 Old Union Square, 600 University St., Seattle, WA
    98101, 206/624-8968. *Contact:* Stuart C. Johnston, Man. Gen.
    Part.

PIONEER VENTURES

113 E. 55th St.
New York, NY 10022
212/980-9090

Year Founded: 1972
Type: Private V.C. Firm
Total Paid-In Capital: $25,000,000

1983 Investment History:

Stage	Dollars Invested	No. of Deals
Seed/Startup	N.A.	N.A.
Later Stage	N.A.	N.A.
Follow-On	N.A.	N.A.
Buyouts	N.A.	N.A.
Total Investments	$3,820,000	29
Average Investment	$ 131,724	

Project Preferences
Geographical: Anywhere in U.S.
Industries: Diversified, Healthcare & Services, Agriculture, Oil & Gas, Food
Stages: Second, Later

Principals: R. Scott Asen, Part.; James G. Niven, Part.; Neil A. McConnell, Part.
Contact: R. Scott Asen; James G. Niven

THE PITTSFORD GROUP

8 Lodge Pole Rd.
Pittsford, NY 14534
716/223-3523

Year Founded: 1975
Type: Private V.C. Firm
Total Paid-In Capital: Not Provided

1983 Investment History:

Stage	Dollars Invested	No. of Deals
Seed/Startup	$ 500,000	1
Later Stage	$4,500,000	3
Follow-On	$3,300,000	3
Buyouts	0	0
Total Investments	$8,300,000	7
Average Investment	$1,185,714	

Project Preferences
Geographical: NY
Foreign: Eastern Canada
Industries: Optics, Lasers, Telecommunications, Office Automation, Information Sciences, Biotechnology
Stages: Startup, First, Second, Later

Principals: Logan M. Cheek, Man. Principal; C.C. Hipkins Jr., Principal
Contact: Logan M. Cheek

QUINCY PARTNERS

P.O. Box 154
Glen Head, NY 11545
516/355-7830

Year Founded: 1971
Type: Private V.C. Firm
Total Paid-In Capital: Not Provided

1983 Investment History:

Stage	Dollars Invested	No. of Deals
Seed/Startup	0	0
Later Stage	0	0
Follow-On	0	0
Buyouts	$29,000,000	2
Total Investments	$29,000,000	2
Average Investment	$14,500,000	

Project Preferences
Geographical: Anywhere in U.S.
Industries: Diversified, Non-High Technology
Stages: Buyouts

Principals: Donald J. Sutherland, Part.
Contact: Donald J. Sutherland

REPRISE CAPITAL CORP.

591 Stewart Ave.
Garden City, NY 11530
516/222-2555

Year Founded: 1984
Type: Private V.C. Firm
Total Paid-In Capital: $50,000,000

1983 Investment History: New Fund

Project Preferences
Geographical: Anywhere in U.S.
Industries: Food Distribution, Consumer-Product Manufacturing
Stages: Later

Principals: Irwin B. Nelson, Pres.
Contact: Irwin B. Nelson

Branches: 8550 Bryn Mawr Ave., Suite 515, Chicago, IL 60631, 312/693-5990. *Contact:* Irwin B. Nelson, Pres.
10000 Santa Monica Blvd., Suite 300, Los Angeles, CA 90067, 213/556-1944. *Contact:* Norman Tulchin, V.P.

REVERE AE CAPITAL FUND

745 Fifth Ave.
New York, NY 10151
212/888-6800

Year Founded: 1971
Type: Investment Banking Firm
Total Paid-In Capital: $36,000,000

1983 Investment History: Not Provided

Project Preferences
Geographical: Anywhere in U.S.
Industries: High Technology
Stages: Later, Buyouts

Principals: Clint Reynolds, Pres.; Joseph C. White, Financial Analyst
Contact: Clint Reynolds

ROTHSCHILD INC.

1 Rockefeller Plaza
New York, NY 10020
212/757-6000

Year Founded: 1967
Type: Private V.C. Firm
Total Paid-In Capital: $302,200,000

1983 Investment History:

Stage	Dollars Invested	No. of Deals
Seed/Startup	$ 8,900,000	14
Later Stage	$ 6,900,000	8
Follow-On	$15,800,000	18
Buyouts	0	0
Total Investments	$31,600,000	40
Average Investment	$ 790,000	

Project Preferences
Geographical: Anywhere in U.S.
Industries: High Technology, Telecommunications, Biotechnology, Healthcare, Applications Software, Components & Peripherals, Office & Factory Productivity
Stages: Startup, First, Second

Principals: Jess L. Belser, Pres.; James C. Blair, Man. Dir.; Douglas S. Luke Jr., Sr. V.P.; Ivan L. Wolff, Sr. V.P.; Thomas L. Phillips Jr., Asst. V.P.; Robert A. Bettigole, Asst. V.P.; Kathryn A. Minckler, Assoc. V.P.
Contact: Jess L. Belser, Pres.

SCHRODER VENTURE MANAGERS

1 State St. Plaza
New York, NY 10004
212/269-6500

Affiliation: Schroder PLC (U.K.)
Year Founded: 1983
Type: Corp. V.C. Sub.
Total Paid-In Capital: $37,500,000

1983 Investment History: New Fund

Project Preferences
Geographical: Anywhere in U.S.
Industries: Diversified
Stages: Startup

Principals: Jeffrey J. Collinson, Man. Dir.; Judith E. Schneider, Dir.
Contact: Either

Branch: 755 Page Mill Rd., Bldg. A, Suite 280, Palo Alto, CA 94304, 415/424-1144. *Contact:* David Walters, Man. Dir.; Michael A. Hentschel, Dir.

SPROUT CAPITAL GROUP

140 Broadway
New York, NY 10005
212/902-2000

Affiliation: Donaldson, Lufkin & Jenrette
Year Founded: 1971
Type: Brokerage House
Total Paid-In Capital: $451,400,000

1983 Investment History:

Stage	Dollars Invested	No. of Deals
Seed/Startup	$ 6,500,000	7
Later Stage	$ 4,200,000	3
Follow-On	$ 3,700,000	7
Buyouts	0	0
Total Investments	$14,400,000	17
Average Investment	$ 847,059	

Project Preferences
Geographical: Anywhere in U.S.
Industries: Diversified
Stages: Any

Principals: Richard E. Kroon, Pres.; Peter T. Grauer, Sr. V.P.; Larry E. Reeder, Sr. V.P.; David L. Mordy, Sr. V.P.; Lloyd D. Ruth, V.P.
Contact: Richard E. Kroon

Branch: 5300 Stevens Creek Blvd., Suite 320, San Jose, CA 95729, 408/554-1515. *Contact:* Gary W. Kalbach, Part.; Nyal D. McMullin, Part.

TESSLER & CLOHERTY INC.

420 Madison Ave.
New York, NY 10017
212/752-8010

Year Founded: 1979
Type: Private V.C. Firm
Total Paid-In Capital: $25,000,000*

1983 Investment History:

Stage	Dollars Invested	No. of Deals
Seed/Startup	N.A.	N.A.
Later Stage	N.A.	N.A.
Follow-On	N.A.	N.A.
Buyouts	N.A.	N.A.
Total Investments	$3,000,000	6
Average Investment	$ 500,000	

Project Preferences
Geographical: Anywhere in U.S.
Industries: Diversified, Telecommunications, Office & Factory Automation, Broadcasting, Communications
Stages: Any

Principals: Daniel Tessler, Chair.; Patricia Cloherty, Pres.
Contact: Either

*Figure is over $25 million.

THOMAR PUBLICATIONS INC.*

383 S. Broadway
Hicksville, NY 11801
516/681-2111

Year Founded: 1974
Type: Investment Banking Firm
Total Paid-In Capital: Not Provided

1983 Investment History:

Stage	Dollars Invested	No. of Deals
Seed/Startup	N.A.	N.A.
Later Stage	N.A.	N.A.
Follow-On	N.A.	N.A.
Buyouts	N.A.	N.A.
Total Investments	$6,000,000	7
Average Investment	$ 857,143	

Project Preferences
Geographical: East Coast
Industries: Diversified, Non-High Technology, Manufacturing, Distribution, Educational Publishing
Stages: Second

Principals: Thomas J. Martin, Pres.; Aileen Martellucci, Exec. V.P.
Contact: Either

*Publishes *The Business Owner.*

TUCKER, ANTHONY & RL DAY INC.

120 Broadway
New York, NY 10271
212/618-7400

Affiliation: John Hancock Mutual Life Insurance Co.
Year Founded: 1892
Type: Corp. V.C. Subsidiary
Total Paid-In Capital: Not Provided

1983 Investment History:

Stage	Dollars Invested	No. of Deals
Seed/Startup	N.A.	N.A.
Later Stage	N.A.	N.A.
Follow-On	N.A.	N.A.
Buyouts	N.A.	N.A.
Total Investments	$20,000,000	3
Average Investment	$ 6,666,667	

Project Preferences
Geographical: Northeast
Industries: Diversified
Stages: Later

Principals: Lee Archer, Man. Dir. & Dir. Corp. Finance
Contact: Lee Archer

Branch: 1 Beacon St., Boston, MA 02108, 617/725-2000.

VENROCK ASSOCIATES

30 Rockefeller Plaza
New York, NY 10112
212/247-3700

Year Founded: 1969
Type: Private V.C. Firm
Total Paid-In Capital: Not Provided

1983 Investment History:

Stage	Dollars Invested	No. of Deals
Seed/Startup	N.A.	9
Later Stage	N.A.	6
Follow-On	0	0
Buyouts	0	0
Total Investments	$12,500,000	15
Average Investment	$ 833,333	

Project Preferences
Geographical: Anywhere in U.S.
Foreign: U.K., Japan
Industries: High Technology
Stages: Any

Principals: Peter O. Crisp, Gen. Part.; Anthony B. Evnin, Gen. Part.; David R. Hathaway, Gen. Part.; Ted H. McCourtney Jr., Gen. Part.; Anthony Sun, Gen. Part.; Henry S. Smith, Gen. Part.
Contact: Any of Above

VENTURE LENDING ASSOCIATES

767 Fifth Ave.
New York, NY 10153
212/980-0606

Year Founded: 1983
Type: Private V.C. Firm
Total Paid-In Capital: $300,000,000

1983 Investment History:

Stage	Dollars Invested	No. of Deals
Seed/Startup	0	0
Later Stage	0	0
Follow-On	0	0
Buyouts	$30,000,000	3
Total Investments	$30,000,000	3
Average Investment	$10,000,000	

Project Preferences
Geographical: Anywhere in U.S.
Industries: Diversified Non-High Technology
Stages: Buyouts

Principals: Peter Lamb, Part.; Charles Sukenik, Part.; Gilbert Butler, Part.
Contact: Any of Above

WARBURG, PINCUS VENTURES INC.

466 Lexington Ave.
New York, NY 10017
212/878-0600

Affiliation: E.M. Warburg, Pincus & Co. Inc.
Year Founded: 1966
Type: Private V.C. Firm
Total Paid-In Capital: $350,000,000

1983 Investment History:

Stage	Dollars Invested	No. of Deals
Seed/Startup	$10,650,000	10
Later Stage	$11,400,000	5
Follow-On	$12,710,000	35
Buyouts	$23,700,000	2
Total Investments	$58,460,000	52
Average Investment	$ 1,124,231	

Project Preferences
Geographical: Anywhere in Continental U.S.
Industries: Diversified
Stages: Any

Principals: Lionel I. Pincus, Chair.; John L. Vogelstein, V. Chair.; Christopher W. Brody, Man. Dir.; Stephen W. Fillo, Man. Dir.; Andrew Gaspar, Man. Dir.; Sidney Lapidus, Man. Dir.; Rodman W. Moorhead III, Man. Dir.; Charles Steinberg, Man. Dir.; Ernest H. Pomerantz, Man. Dir.; Nissan Boury, Man. Dir.; W. Edward Massey, Man. Dir.
Contact: Christopher W. Brody; Sidney Lapidus

WELSH, CARSON, ANDERSON & STOWE

45 Wall St., 16th Floor
New York, NY 10005
212/422-3232

Year Founded: 1979
Type: Private V.C. Firm
Total Paid-In Capital: $81,000,000

1983 Investment History:

Stage	Dollars Invested	No. of Deals
Seed/Startup	$15,300,000	15
Later Stage	$ 2,700,000	2
Follow-On	$14,500,000	12
Buyouts	$ 7,600,000	3
Total Investments	$40,100,000	32
Average Investment	$ 1,253,125	

Project Preferences
Geographical: Anywhere in U.S.
Industries: High Technology, Information Processing, Healthcare
Stages: Startup, First, Second, Buyouts

Principals: Patrick J. Welsh, Gen. Part.; Russell L. Carson, Gen. Part.; Bruce K. Anderson, Gen. Part.; Richard H. Stowe, Gen. Part.; Charles G. Moore, Gen. Part.; Andrew M. Paul, Gen. Part.
Contact: Any of Above

Branch: 855 Valley Rd., Clifton, NJ 07013, 201/470-8900. *Contact:* Bruce K. Anderson, Gen. Part.

JH WHITNEY & CO.

630 Fifth Ave.
New York, NY 10111
212/757-0500

Year Founded: 1946
Type: Private V.C. Firm
Total Paid-In Capital: Not Provided

1983 Investment History:

Stage	Dollars Invested	No. of Deals
Seed/Startup	$13,000,000	12
Later Stage	$ 1,000,000	1
Follow-On	$ 5,600,000	16
Buyouts	$ 4,800,000	3
Total Investments	$24,400,000	32
Average Investment	$ 762,500	

Project Preferences
Geographical: Anywhere in U.S.
Industries: Diversified, Computer-Related, Manufacturing, Medical, Energy & Natural Resources
Stages: Startup, First, Buyouts

Principals: Benno C. Schmidt, Man. Part.; Don E. Ackerman, Part.; Russell E. Planitzer, Part.; Robert E. Pursley, Part.; Edward V. Ryan, Part.; Peter Young, Part.
Contact: Any of Above

Branches: 3000 Sand Hill Rd., Menlo Park, CA 94025, 415/854-0500. *Contacts:* Harry Marshall, Part.; David T. Morganthaler II, Part.; John W. Larson, Part.
1083 San Jacinto Bldg., Houston, TX 77002, 713/224-6757. *Contact:* Levi W. Goodrich, Part.

HERBERT YOUNG SECURITIES INC.

98 Cuttermill Rd.
Great Neck, NY 11021
516/487-8300

Year Founded: 1959
Type: Investment Banking Firm
Total Paid-In Capital: Not Provided

1983 Investment History:

Stage	Dollars Invested	No. of Deals
Seed/Startup	N.A.	N.A.
Later Stage	N.A.	N.A.
Follow-On	N.A.	N.A.
Buyouts	N.A.	N.A.
Total Investments	$10,000,000	8
Average Investment	$ 1,250,000	

Project Preferences
Geographical: Anywhere in U.S.
Foreign: Anywhere
Industries: Diversified
Stages: Any

Principals: Herbert D. Levine, Pres.
Contact: Herbert D. Levine

North Carolina

SOUTHGATE VENTURE PARTNERS/
SOUTHGATE VENTURE PARTNERS II

227 N. Tryon St.
Charlotte, NC 28202
704/372-1410

Year Founded: 1984
Type: Private V.C. Firm
Total Paid-In Capital: $20,000,000

1983 Investment History: New Fund

Project Preferences
Geographical: Anywhere in U.S.
Industries: Diversified
Stages: Any

Principals: Alexander B. Wilkins Jr., Gen. Part.
Contact: Alexander B. Wilkins Jr.

Branches: 400 Perimeter Center Terrace, Atlanta, GA 30346,
   404/395-0750. *Contact:* M. Corbett Hankey
231 Carondolet, New Orleans, LA 70130, 504/525-2112. *Contact:*
   William D. Humphries, Gen. Part.

Ohio

BASIC SEARCH

Park Place
Hudson, OH 44236
216/656-2442; 216/650-4321

Year Founded: 1974
Type: Private V.C. Firm
Total Paid-In Capital: $10,000,000

1983 Investment History:

Stage	Dollars Invested	No. of Deals
Seed/Startup	N.A.	N.A.
Later Stage	N.A.	N.A.
Follow-On	N.A.	N.A.
Buyouts	N.A.	N.A.
Total Investments	$1,500,000	10
Average Investment	$ 150,000	

Project Preferences
Geographical: Midwest
Industries: Diversified
Stages: Any

Principals: Burton D. Morgan, Pres.
Contact: Burton D. Morgan

CARDINAL DEVELOPMENT
CAPITAL FUND

155 E. Broad St.
Columbus, OH 43215
614/464-5550

Year Founded: 1982
Type: Private V.C. Firm
Total Paid-In Capital: $30,000,000

1983 Investment History:

Stage	Dollars Invested	No. of Deals
Seed/Startup	$1,200,000	2
Later Stage	$5,700,000	8
Follow-On	$ 300,000	1
Buyouts	0	0
Total Investments	$7,200,000	11
Average Investment	$ 654,546	

Project Preferences
Geographical: Anywhere in U.S., OH
Industries: Diversified
Stages: Any

Principals: J. Thomas Walker, Part.; Richard Bannon, Part.; John
   Holscher.
Contact: Any of Above

FIRST CITY TECHNOLOGY VENTURES

1801 E. 12th St., Suite 201
Cleveland, OH 44114
216/687-1096

Affiliation: First City Financial Corp., Ltd.
Year Founded: 1983
Type: Private V.C. Firm
Total Paid-In Capital: Not Provided

1983 Investment History:

Stage	Dollars Invested	No. of Deals
Seed/Startup	$3,150,000	3
Later Stage	$1,330,000	3
Follow-On	$ 545,000	4
Buyouts	0	0
Total Investments	$5,025,000	10
Average Investment	$ 502,500	

Project Preferences
Geographical: East Coast, West Coast
Industries: Communications
Stages: Seed, Startup, First

Principals: Morton A. Cohen, Pres. & Chair.; Michael L. Boeckman,
   V.P.; Roger Eaglen, V.P.
Contact: Roger Eaglen

Branch: 33 Yonge St., Toronto, Ontario M5E 1GH, Canada,
   416/864-1688. *Contact:* Morton A. Cohen, Pres. & Chair.

LUBRIZOL ENTERPRISES INC.

29400 Lakeland Blvd.
Wickliffe, OH 44092
216/943-4200

Affiliation: The Lubrizol Corp.
Year Founded: 1979
Type: Corp. V.C. Subsidiary
Total Paid-In Capital: $70,000,000

1983 Investment History:

Stage	Dollars Invested	No. of Deals
Seed/Startup	$2,000,000	2
Later Stage	0	0
Follow-On	0	0
Buyouts	$5,000,000	1
Total Investments	$7,000,000	3
Average Investment	$2,333,333	

Project Preferences
Geographical: Anywhere in U.S.
Foreign: France
Industries: Diversified, Plant Science, Biotechnology, Microbiology, Manufacturing, Genetic Engineering, Energy Storage & Recovery
Stages: Any

Principals: Donald L. Murfin, Pres.; Bruce H. Grasser, V.P.; David R. Anderson, V.P.; James R. Glynn, V.P. Finance.
Contact: Donald L. Murfin

MORGENTHALER MANAGEMENT CORP.

700 National City Bank Bldg.
Cleveland, OH 44114
216/621-3070

Year Founded: 1971
Type: Private V.C. Firm
Total Paid-In Capital: $21,000,000

1983 Investment History:

Stage	Dollars Invested	No. of Deals
Seed/Startup	$ 600,000	2
Later Stage	$2,400,000	5
Follow-On	$1,900,000	9
Buyouts	0	0
Total Investments	$4,920,000	16
Average Investment	$ 306,250	

Project Preferences
Geographical: Anywhere in U.S.
Industries: High Technology
Stages: Startup, First, Second

Principals: David T. Morgenthaler, Pres.; Robert D. Pavey, Exec. V.P.; Robert C. Bellas Jr., V.P.; Paul S. Brentlinger, V.P.
Contact: Any of Above

NATIONAL CITY VENTURE CORP.

P.O. Box 5756
Cleveland, OH 44101
216/575-2491

Affiliation: National City Corp.
Year Founded: 1979
Type: Corp. V.C. Subsidiary
Total Paid-In Capital: Not Provided

1983 Investment History:

Stage	Dollars Invested	No. of Deals
Seed/Startup	$1,000,000	2
Later Stage	$1,200,000	3
Follow-On	$3,000,000	5
Buyouts	0	0
Total Investments	$5,200,000	10
Average Investment	$ 520,000	

Project Preferences
Geographical: Anywhere in U.S.
Industries: Diversified
Stages: Second, Later

Principals: Michael Sherwin, Pres.; Martha A. Barry, V.P.; John B. Naylor, V.P.
Contact: Martha A. Barry, John B. Naylor

SCIENTIFIC ADVANCES INC.

601 W. Fifth Ave.
Columbus, OH 43201
614/294-5541

Affiliation: Battelle Memorial Institute
Year Founded: 1962
Type: Corp. V.C. Subsidiary
Total Paid-In Capital: $16,000,000

1983 Investment History:

Stage	Dollars Invested	No. of Deals
Seed/Startup	$1,400,000	3
Later Stage	$ 500,000	1
Follow-On	$1,100,000	5
Buyouts	0	0
Total Investments	$3,000,000	9
Average Investment	$ 333,333	

Project Preferences
Geographical: Anywhere in U.S.
Industries: High Technology
Stages: Seed, Startup, First, Second, Later

Principals: Charles G. James, Pres.; Thomas W. Harvey, V.P.; Daniel J. Shea, V.P.; Paul F. Purcell, V.P.
Contact: Thomas W. Harvey, Daniel J. Shea, Paul F. Purcell

Oregon

ROSENFELD & CO.

625 SW Washington St.
Portland, OR 97205
503/228-7686

Year Founded: 1977
Type: Private Investment Banking Firm
Total Paid-In Capital: Not Provided

1983 Investment History:

Stage	Dollars Invested	No. of Deals
Seed/Startup	$ 1,000,000	1
Later Stage	0	0
Follow-On	$ 4,000,000	1
Buyouts	$15,000,000	3
Total Investments	$20,000,000	5
Average Investment	$ 4,000,000	

Project Preferences
Geographical: Northwest
Industries: Diversified, Medical Technology, Manufacturing
Stages: Later, Buyouts

Principals: William W. Rosenfeld Jr., Man. Part.
Contact: William W. Rosenfeld Jr.

SHAW VENTURE PARTNERS

851 SW Sixth Ave., Suite 800
Portland, OR 97204
503/228-4884

Year Founded: 1983
Type: Private V.C. Firm
Total Paid-In Capital: $35,000,000

1983 Investment History:

Stage	Dollars Invested	No. of Deals
Seed/Startup	N.A.	N.A.
Later Stage	N.A.	N.A.
Follow-On	N.A.	N.A.
Buyouts	N.A.	N.A.
Total Investments	$4,000,000	6
Average Investment	$ 666,667	

Project Preferences
Geographical: Anywhere in U.S., Northwest
Industries: Diversified
Stages: Any

Principals: Ralph Shaw, Gen. Part.; Herbert Shaw, Ltd. Part.; Alan Dishlip, Ltd. Part.; David Starr, Assoc.
Contact: Any of Above

Pennsylvania

GROTECH PARTNERS LP

2 Glenhardie Corporate Center, Suite 102
Wayne, PA 19087
215/964-1888

Year Founded: 1984
Type: Private V.C. Firm
Total Paid-In Capital: $10,000,000

1983 Investment History: New Fund

Project Preferences
Geographical: East Coast, Middle Atlantic
Industries: Information Processing, Defense Electronics, Telecommunications, Healthcare, Consumer Goods, Service & Distribution, Applications Software
Stages: Startup, Second, Later, Buyouts

Principals: Edward F. Sager Jr., Man. Part.
Contact: Edward F. Sager Jr.

Branch: c/o Baker, Watts & Co.*, 100 Light St., Baltimore, MD 21202, 301/685-2600. *Contact:* E. Rogers Novak Jr., Part.; Frank A. Adams, Part.

*Investment banking firm.

HILLMAN VENTURES INC.

2000 Grant Bldg.
Pittsburgh, PA 15219
412/281-2620

Affiliation: The Hillman Co.
Year Founded: 1983
Type: Corp. V.C. Subsidiary
Total Paid-In Capital: Not Provided

1983 Investment History:

Stage	Dollars Invested	No. of Deals
Seed/Startup	$16,700,000	14
Later Stage	$24,700,000	19
Follow-On	$46,300,000	27
Buyouts	$11,300,000	6
Total Investments	$99,000,000	66
Average Investment	$ 1,500,000	

Project Preferences
Geographical: Anywhere in U.S.
Industries: Diversified
Stages: Any

Principals: Stephen J. Banks, Pres.; Kent L. Engelmeier, V.P.; Jay D. Glass, V.P.; Marc Yagjian, Mgr.; Kenneth H. Levin, Mgr.
Contact: Any of Above

Branch: 40 Orville Dr., Suite 104, Bohemia, NY 11716, 516/563-1790. *Contact:* Catharine L. Burkett, Mgr.

INNOVEST GROUP INC.

1700 Market St., Suite 1228
Philadelphia, PA 19103
215/564-3960

Year Founded: 1968
Type: Private V.C. Firm
Total Paid-In Capital: Not Provided

1983 Investment History:

Stage	Dollars Invested	No. of Deals
Seed/Startup	$ 4,000,000	2
Later Stage	$ 6,000,000	1
Follow-On	0	0
Buyouts	0	0
Total Investments	$10,000,000	3
Average Investment	$ 3,333,333	

Project Preferences
Geographical: Anywhere in U.S., Southeast, East Coast
Industries: Communications, Computer-Related, Office Automation, Electronic Equipment, Robotics, Medical Services, Educational Publishing, Real Estate
Stages: Startup, First, Second

Principals: Richard E. Woosnam, Pres.; Nila K. Sendzik, V.P.
Contact: Either

KEELEY MANAGEMENT CO.

2 Radnor Corporate Ctr.
Radnor, PA 19087
215/293-0210

Year Founded: 1979
Type: Private V.C. Firm
Total Paid-In Capital: Not Provided

1983 Investment History:

Stage	Dollars Invested	No. of Deals
Seed/Startup	0	0
Later Stage	$ 700,000	1
Follow-On	0	0
Buyouts	$12,300,000	1
Total Investments	$13,000,000	2
Average Investment	$ 6,500,000	

Project Preferences
Geographical: Middle Atlantic
Industries: Diversified Non-High Technology, Publishing
Stages: Buyouts

Principals: Robert E. Brown Jr., Esq., V.P.
Contact: Robert E. Brown Jr.

KOPVENCO INC.

1501 Koppers Bldg.
Pittsburgh, PA 15219
412/227-2000

Affiliation: Koppers Co. Inc.
Year Founded: 1980
Type: Corp. V.C. Subsidiary
Total Paid-In Capital: Not Provided

1983 Investment History:

Stage	Dollars Invested	No. of Deals
Seed/Startup	$7,000,000	5
Later Stage	0	0
Follow-On	0	0
Buyouts	0	0
Total Investments	$7,000,000	5
Average Investment	$1,400,000	

Project Preferences
Geographical: Anywhere in U.S.
Industries: Genetic Engineering, Advanced Ceramics
Stages: Seed, Startup

Principals: B. Otto Wheeley, Pres.; J.A. Hams, Dir.; R.E. Spatz, Dir.; R.R. Wingard, V.P. & Dir.; J. Roger Beidler, V.P., Treas. & Dir.; A.W. Lawrence, V.P. & Dir.; H.J. Zeh Jr., V.P. & Dir.; C.P Dorsey, Dir.; B.G. Bartley, Dir.
Contact: C.P. Dorsey

NEPA VENTURE FUND LTD.

201 Ferry St.
Easton, PA 18402
215/235-8022

Year Founded: 1984
Type: Private V.C. Firm
Total Paid-In Capital: $10,000,000

1983 Investment History: New Fund

Project Preferences
Geographical: Middle Atlantic
Industries: High Technology
Stages: Seed, Startup, First, Second

Principals: Frederick J. Beste III, Pres & CEO; Meyer M. Alperin, Chair.; L. Jack Bradt, Sec. & Treas.; Michael G. Bolton, Asst. Sec. & Asst. Treas.; David C. Hall, V.P.
Contact: Frederick J. Beste III

PHILADELPHIA CAPITAL ADVISORS

Philadelphia National Bank Bldg.
Broad & Chestnut Sts.
Philadelphia, PA 19107
215/629-2727

Affiliation: Philadelphia National Bank
Year Founded: 1974
Type: Investment Banking Firm Acting as Intermediary in Venture Deals
Total Paid-In Capital: Not Provided

1983 Investment History:

Stage	Dollars Invested	No. of Deals
Seed/Startup	$ 1,000,000	1
Later Stage	0	0
Follow-On	0	0
Buyouts	$14,000,000	4
Total Investments	$15,000,000	5
Average Investment	$ 3,000,000	

Project Preferences
Geographical: Middle Atlantic
Industries: Diversified, Specialty Chemicals
Stages: Any

Principals: William A. Frack Jr., Pres
Contact: William A. Frack

SAFEGUARD SCIENTIFICS INC.

630 Park Ave.
King of Prussia, PA 19406
215/265-4000

Affiliation: Safeguard Business Systems
Year Founded: 1953
Type: Public V.C. Firm
Total Paid-In Capital: $21,600,000

1983 Investment History:

Stage	Dollars Invested	No. of Deals
Seed/Startup	$1,000,000	1
Later Stage	0	0
Follow-On	0	0
Buyouts	$3,000,000	1
Total Investments	$4,000,000	2
Average Investment	$2,000,000	

Project Preferences
Geographical: Anywhere in U.S.
Industries: High Technology, Software, Data Processing, Telecommunications
Stages: Second, Buyouts

Principals: Warren V. Musser, Chair.; Adolf A. Paier, Pres.
Contact: Either

NARRAGANSETT CAPITAL

40 Westminster St.
Providence, RI 02903
401/751-1000

Year Founded: 1959
Type: Public Co.
Total Paid-In Capital: $120,200,000

1983 Investment History:

Stage	Dollars Invested	No. of Deals
Seed/Startup	$ 900,000	2
Later Stage	$ 1,000,000	4
Follow-On	0	0
Buyouts	$13,500,000	9
Total Investments	$15,400,000	15
Average Investment	$ 1,026,667	

Project Preferences
Geographical: Anywhere in U.S.
Industries: Diversified
Stages: Seed, Startup, First, Buyouts

Principals: Arthur D. Little, Chair.; Robert D. Manchester, Pres.; Roger A. Vanderberg, V.P.; Paul A. Giusti, V.P.; William P. Lane, V.P.; Gregory P. Barber, V.P.
Contact: Any of Above

MASSEY BURCH INVESTMENT GROUP

1 Park Plaza
Nashville, TN 37203
615/329-9448

Year Founded: 1982
Type: Private V.C. Firm
Total Paid-In Capital: Not Provided

1983 Investment History:

Stage	Dollars Invested	No. of Deals
Seed/Startup	$ 8,400,000	6
Later Stage	$ 2,000,000	1
Follow-On	$ 800,000	4
Buyouts	$ 1,200,000	1
Total Investments	$12,400,000	12
Average Investment	$ 1,333,333	

Project Preferences
Geographical: South
Industries: High Technology, Healthcare
Stages: Any

Principals: Jack Massey, Chair.; Lucius E. Burch III, Pres.; Donald M. Johnston, V.P.
Contact: Any of Above

Texas

CAPITAL SOUTHWEST CORP.

12900 Preston Rd., Suite 700
Dallas, TX 75230
214/233-8242

Year Founded: 1981
Type: Public V.C. Firm
Total Paid-In Capital: $19,700,000

1983 Investment History:

Stage	Dollars Invested	No. of Deals
Seed/Startup	$1,200,000	3
Later Stage	$3,500,000	4
Follow-On	$ 400,000	2
Buyouts	0	0
Total Investments	$5,100,000	9
Average Investment	$ 566,667	

Project Preferences
Geographical: Anywhere in U.S.
Industries: High Technology, Energy
Stages: Later, Buyouts

Principals: William R. Thomas, Chair.; J. Bruce Duty, V.P. & Sec.-
  Treas.; Pat Hamner, Investment Assoc.
Contact: Any of Above

BERRY CASH SOUTHWEST PARTNERSHIP

1 Galleria Tower
13355 Noel Rd., Suite 1375
Dallas, TX 75240-6615
214/392-7279

Year Founded: 1983
Type: Private V.C. Firm
Total Paid-In Capital: $25,000,000

1983 Investment History: New Fund

Project Preferences
Geographical: Southwest
Industries: High Technology
Stages: Startup

Principals: Berry Cash, Gen. Part.
Contact: Berry Cash

CRITERION VENTURE PARTNERS

333 Clay St., Suite 4300
Houston, TX 77002
713/751-2408

Affiliation: Criterion Group
Year Founded: 1983
Type: Private V.C. Firm
Total Paid-In Capital: $20,000,000

1983 Investment History: New Fund

Project Preferences
Geographical: Southeast, Southwest
Industries: Diversified, Medical, Telecommunications, Industrial
  Products & Equipment
Stages: Any

Principals: David O. Wicks, Jr., Sr. Part.; Harvard H. Hill Jr., Part.;
  Gregory A. Rider, Part.; Scott M. Albert, Assoc.; Crichton W.
  Brown, Assoc.
Contact: Any of Above

FIRST DALLAS FINANCIAL CO.

3302 Southland Center
Dallas, TX 75201
214/922-0070

Affiliation: May Financial Corp.
Year Founded: 1980
Type: Investment Banking Firm
Total Paid-In Capital: Not Provided

1983 Investment History:

Stage	Dollars Invested	No. of Deals
Seed/Startup	0	0
Later Stage	$ 6,000,000	2
Follow-On	0	0
Buyouts	$ 6,000,000	2
Total Investments	$12,000,000	4
Average Investment	$ 3,000,000	

Project Preferences
Geographical: Southwest
Industries: Diversified
Stages: Later, Buyouts

Principals: John T. McGuire, Pres.
Contact: John T. McGuire

THE FIRST DALLAS GROUP LTD.

300 Campbell Centre
8350 N. Central Expressway
Dallas, TX 75206
214/987-6481

Year Founded: 1981
Type: Private V.C. Firm
Total Paid-In Capital: $25,000,000

1983 Investment History:

Stage	Dollars Invested	No. of Deals
Seed/Startup	N.A.	N.A.
Later Stage	N.A.	N.A.
Follow-On	N.A.	N.A.
Buyouts	N.A.	N.A.
Total Investments	$15,000,000	9
Average Investment	$ 1,666,667	

Project Preferences
Geographical: Anywhere in U.S.
Industries: Diversified
Stages: Seed, Startup, First, Second, Later

Principals: Alvin E. Holland Jr., Pres.
Contact: Alvin E. Holland Jr.

NBR II

P.O. Box 796
Addison, TX 75001
214/233-6631

Year Founded: 1969
Type: Private V.C. Firm
Total Paid-In Capital: Not Provided

1983 Investment History:

Stage	Dollars Invested	No. of Deals
Seed/Startup	N.A.	7
Later Stage	0	0
Follow-On	0	0
Buyouts	N.A.	1
Total Investments	$4,000,000	8
Average Investment	$ 500,000	

Project Preferences
Geographical: Anywhere in U.S.
Industries: High Technology, Electronics, Healthcare & Medical
Stages: Startup, Buyouts

Principals: Richard Hanschen, Pres.
Contact: Richard Hanschen

NEW BUSINESS RESOURCES

4137 Billy Mitchell
Addison, TX 75001
214/233-6631

Year Founded: 1969
Type: Private V.C. Firm
Total Paid-In Capital: Not Provided

1983 Investment History:

Stage	Dollars Invested	No. of Deals
Seed/Startup	N.A.	3
Later Stage	0	0
Follow-On	N.A.	1
Buyouts	N.A.	2
Total Investments	$16,000,000	6
Average Investment	$ 2,666,667	

Project Preferences
Geographical: Southwest
Industries: Diversified, Proprietary Technology
Stages: Startup, Buyouts

Principals: Richard Hanschen, Pres.
Contact: Richard Hanschen

RUST VENTURES LP

114 W. Seventh St., Suite 1300
Austin, TX 78701
512/479-0055

Year Founded: 1979
Type: Private V.C. Firm
Total Paid-In Capital: $35,000,000

1983 Investment History:

Stage	Dollars Invested	No. of Deals
Seed/Startup	$1,100,000	2
Later Stage	$1,800,000	3
Follow-On	$ 800,000	2
Buyouts	0	0
Total Investments	$3,700,000	7
Average Investment	$ 528,571	

Project Preferences
Geographical: Anywhere in U.S.
Industries: High Technology, Healthcare, Medical Technology, Communications, Telecommunications
Stages: Seed, Startup, First, Buyouts

Principals: Jeffrey C. Garvey, Pres.; Joseph C. Aragona, V.P.; Kenneth P. DeAngelis, Man. Dir.; John J. Locy, V.P.; William P. Wood, Part.
Contact: Any of Above.

SEVIN ROSEN MANAGEMENT CO.

5050 Quorum Dr., Suite 635
Dallas, TX 75240
214/960-1744

Year Founded: 1981
Type: Private V.C. Firm
Total Paid-In Capital: $85,000,000

1983 Investment History:

Stage	Dollars Invested	No. of Deals
Seed/Startup	$ 7,500,000	8
Later Stage	$ 7,500,000	4
Follow-On	0	0
Buyouts	0	0
Total Investments	$15,000,000	12
Average Investment	$ 1,250,000	

Project Preferences
Geographical: Anywhere in U.S.
Industries: Electronics-Related
Stages: Startup, First, Second

Principals: L.J. Sevin, Pres.; Jon W. Bayless, V.P.
Contact: Either

Branches: 200 Park Ave., Suite 4503, New York, NY 10016, 212/687-5115. *Contact:* Benjamin M. Rosen, Chair.
1245 Oakmead Parkway, Suite 101, Sunnyvale, CA 94086, 408/720-8590. *Contact:* Roger Borovoy, V.P.

SOUTH WEST ENTERPRISE ASSOCIATES

2 Lincoln Center, Suite 1266
5420 LBJ Freeway
Dallas, TX 75240
214/991-1620

Affiliation: New Enterprise Associates
Year Founded: 1983
Type: Private V.C. Firm
Total Paid-In Capital: $25,000,000

1983 Investment History: Stage	Dollars Invested	No. of Deals
Seed/Startup	$5,000,000	7
Later Stage	0	0
Follow-On	0	0
Buyouts	0	0
Total Investments	$5,000,000	7
Average Investment	$ 714,286	

Project Preferences
Geographical: Southwest, TX
Industries: Communications, Computers, Defense Electronics, Medical Electronics
Stages: Seed, Startup

Principals: Vin Prothro, Man. Gen. Part.
Contact: Vin Prothro

THE SOUTHWEST VENTURE PARTNERSHIPS

300 Convent St., Suite 1400
San Antonio, TX 78205
512/227-1010

Year Founded: 1975
Type: Private V.C. Firm
Total Paid-In Capital: $60,200,000

1983 Investment History: Stage	Dollars Invested	No. of Deals
Seed/Startup	$1,900,000	5
Later Stage	$5,600,000	15
Follow-On	0	0
Buyouts	0	0
Total Investments	$7,500,000	20
Average Investment	$ 375,000	

Project Preferences
Geographical: Southeast, Southwest
Industries: High Technology, Electronics, Biotechnology
Stages: Second

Principals: Michael Bell, Gen. Part.; Charles D. Grojean, Gen. Part.
Contact: Either

Branch: 5080 Spectrum Dr., Suite 1610 E., Dallas, TX 75248, 214/960-0404. *Contact:* J. Edward McAteer, Gen. Part.

SUNWESTERN INVESTMENT FUND

1 Oaks Plaza, Suite 160
6750 LBJ Freeway
Dallas, TX 75240
214/239-5650

Year Founded: 1982
Type: Private V.C. Firm
Total Paid-In Capital: $11,500,000

1983 Investment History: Stage	Dollars Invested	No. of Deals
Seed/Startup	N.A.	N.A.
Later Stage	N.A.	N.A.
Follow-On	N.A.	N.A.
Buyouts	N.A.	N.A.
Total Investments	$3,500,000	10
Average Investment	$ 350,000	

Project Preferences
Geographical: Southwest
Industries: Communications, Software, Advanced Materials, Medical Services, Energy Technology & Services
Stages: Any

Principals: James F. Leary, Pres. & Dir.; Tom H. Delimitros, Sr. V.P. & Dir.; Floyd W. Collins, V.P.
Contact: James F. Leary

TEXCOM VENTURE CAPITAL INC.

P.O. Box 2558
Houston, TX 77252
713/236-5332

Affiliation: Texas Commerce Bancshares
Year Founded: 1982
Type: Corp. V.C. Subsidiary
Total Paid-In Capital: $10,000,000

1983 Investment History: Not Provided

Project Preferences
Geographical: Anywhere in U.S., Southwest
Industries: Diversified, Natural Resources, Healthcare
Stages: Any

Principals: Fred R. Lummis, V.P. & Mgr.; Fred C. Hamilton, Investment Officer
Contact: Either

TRIAD VENTURES LTD.

Attn: Hobby Abshier
P.O. Box 1987
301 W. Sixth St.
Austin, TX 78767
512/472-7171

Affiliation: FSA Investment Inc.; Bentsen Investment Co.; Capital Investments Inc.
Year Founded: 1984
Type: Private V.C. Firm
Total Paid-In Capital: $13,000,000

1983 Investment History: New Fund

Project Preferences
Geographical: TX
Industries: Regional General Industry
Stages: Startup, First, Second

Principals: Hobby Abshier, Gen. Part.; Lloyd M. Bentsen III, Gen. Part.; Nick Stanfield, Gen. Part.
Contact: Hobby Abshier

Virginia

ATLANTIC VENTURE PARTNERS

P.O. Box 1493
Richmond, VA 23212
804/644-5496

Year Founded: 1982
Type: Private V.C. Firm
Total Paid-In Capital: $15,000,000

1983 Investment History:

Stage	Dollars Invested	No. of Deals
Seed/Startup	$1,400,000	3
Later Stage	$1,000,000	2
Follow-On	0	0
Buyouts	$2,500,000	3
Total Investments	$4,900,000	8
Average Investment	$ 612,500	

Project Preferences
Geographical: Southeast
Industries: Diversified
Stages: Any

Principals: Robert H. Pratt, Gen. Part.
Contact: Robert H. Pratt

Branch: 801 N. Fairfax St., Alexandria, VA 22314, 703/548-6026.
   Contact: Wallace L. Bennett, Gen. Part.

Washington

CABLE, HOWSE & COZADD

999 Third Ave., Suite 4300
Seattle, WA 98104
206/583-2700

Year Founded: 1977
Type: Private V.C. Firm
Total Paid-In Capital: $130,700,000

1983 Investment History:

Stage	Dollars Invested	No. of Deals
Seed/Startup	N.A.	N.A.
Later Stage	N.A.	N.A.
Follow-On	N.A.	N.A.
Buyouts	N.A.	N.A.
Total Investments	$29,400,000	40
Average Investment	$ 735,000	

Project Preferences
Geographical: West Coast
Industries: High Technology
Stages: Seed, Startup, First, Second, Later

Principals: Michael A. Ellison, Part.; Elwood D. Howse Jr., Part.;
   Thomas J. Cable, Part.; Bennett A. Cozadd, Part.; Wayne C.
   Wager, Part.
Contact: Michael A. Ellison; Wayne C. Wager

Branch: 101 SW Main, Suite 1800, Portland, OR 97204,
   503/248-9646. *Contact:* L. Barton Alexander, Part.

RAINIER VENTURE PARTNERS

9725 SE 36th St., Suite 300
Mercer Island, WA 98040
206/232-6720

Affiliation: Hambrecht & Quist
Year Founded: 1983
Type: Private V.C. Firm
Total Paid-In Capital. $25,700,000

1983 Investment History: New Fund

Project Preferences
Geographical: Anywhere in U.S., West Coast
Industries: Diversified
Stages: Seed, First, Later

Principals: John Moser, Part.; George Clute, Part.
Contact: Either

Branch: 1 Lincoln Center, Suite 440, 10300 SW Greensburg Rd.,
   Portland, OR 97223, 503/245-5900. *Contact:* Richard H. Drew,
   Part.

VENTURE FIRMS $10 MIL AND UP

Wisconsin

LUBAR & CO. INC.

777 E. Wisconsin Ave., Suite 3060
Milwaukee, WI 53202
414/291-9000

Year Founded: 1977
Type: Private V.C. Firm
Total Paid-In Capital: Not Provided

1983 Investment History:

Stage	Dollars Invested	No. of Deals
Seed/Startup	0	0
Later Stage	0	0
Follow-On	0	0
Buyouts	$13,000,000	1
Total Investments	$13,000,000	1

Project Preferences
Geographical: Anywhere in U.S.
Industries: Food Processing, Energy-Related, Manufacturing
Stages: Later, Buyouts

Principals: Sheldon B. Lubar, Pres.; James C. Rowe, V.P.; William T. Donovan, V.P.; David J. Lubar, V.P.
Contact: James C. Rowe, William T. Donovan, David J. Lubar

WIND POINT PARTNERS LP

1525 Howe St.
Racine, WI 53403
414/631-4030

Year Founded: 1983
Type: Private V.C. Firm
Total Paid-In Capital: $36,000,000

1983 Investment History:

Stage	Dollars Invested	No. of Deals
Seed/Startup	$2,500,000	3
Later Stage	$2,800,000	2
Follow-On	0	0
Buyouts	$1,700,000	1
Total Investments	$7,000,000	6
Average Investment	$1,166,667	

Project Preferences
Geographical: Anywhere in U.S., Midwest
Industries: Diversified, Healthcare, Telecommunications, Electronics, Medical Instrumentation
Stages: Any

Principals: James E. Daverman, Gen Part.; Arthur Del Vesco, Gen. Part.; S. Curtis Johnson, Gen. Part.
Contact: Any of Above

DOMESTIC LISTINGS

VENTURE FIRMS: UNDER $10 MILLION

Alabama

PORTER, WHITE & YARDLEY CAPITAL INC.

P.O. Box 11633
15 N. 21st St., Steiner Bldg.
Birmingham, AL 35203
205/252-3681

Year Founded: 1970
Type: Investment Banking Firm
Total Paid-In Capital: Not Provided

1983 Investment History:

Stage	Dollars Invested	No. of Deals
Seed/Startup	N.A.	N.A.
Later Stage	N.A.	N.A.
Follow-On	N.A.	N.A.
Buyouts	N.A.	N.A.
Total Investments	N.A.	N.A.
Average Investment	$100,000	

Project Preferences
Geographical: Southeast
Industries: Diversified
Stages: Startup

Principals: Thomas K. Yardley, Chair.; James H. White III, Pres.; George W. Porter, Exec. V.P.; John A. Screws, V.P.; James Milton Johnson, V.P.; Marvin B. Claige, V.P.
Contact: Thomas K. Yardley

PRIVATE CAPITAL CORP.

1625 First Alabama Bank Bldg.
Birmingham, AL 35203
205/251-0152

Year Founded: 1973
Type: Private V.C. Firm
Total Paid-In Capital: Not Provided

1983 Investment History:

Stage	Dollars Invested	No. of Deals
Seed/Startup	N.A.	N.A.
Later Stage	N.A.	N.A.
Follow-On	N.A.	N.A.
Buyouts	N.A.	N.A.
Total Investments	$800,000	2
Average Investment	$400,000	

Project Preferences
Geographical: Southeast
Industries: Diversified, Communications, Healthcare Technology
Stages: Later

Principals: William W. Featheringill, Pres.; William P. Acker III, V.P.
Contact: William W. Featheringill

Arizona

O'BRIEN INDUSTRIES

4350 E. Camelback, Suite 120-B
Phoenix, AZ 85018
602/840-6070

Year Founded: 1948
Type: Private V.C. Firm
Total Paid-In Capital: $1,000,000

1983 Investment History:

Stage	Dollars Invested	No. of Deals
Seed/Startup	$1,000,000	4
Later Stage	0	0
Follow-On	0	0
Buyouts	0	0
Total Investments	$1,000,000	4
Average Investment	$ 250,000	

Project Preferences
Geographical: AZ, NM, Southern CA
Foreign: Mexico, Japan, Peru
Industries: Economic Crops for Arid Land
Stages: Startup

Principals: William Howard O'Brien, Pres.
Contact: William Howard O'Brien

California

BANKAMERICA CAPITAL CORP.

555 California St., 42nd Floor
San Francisco, CA 94104
415/622-2245

Affiliation: Bank of America
Year Founded: 1959
Type: Corp. V.C. Subsidiary
Total Paid-In Capital: Not Provided

1983 Investment History:

Stage	Dollars Invested	No. of Deals
Seed/Startup	N.A.	N.A.
Later Stage	N.A.	N.A.
Follow-On	N.A.	N.A.
Buyouts	N.A.	N.A.
Total Investments	$1,617,000	3
Average Investment	$ 539,000	

Project Preferences
Geographical: Anywhere in U.S., West Coast
Industries: Diversified
Stages: Second, Later

Principals: Robert W. Gibson, Pres.; Philip J. Gioia, V.P.; Patrick J. Topolski, V.P.; Roger C. Drufva Jr., V.P.
Contact: Any of Above

CAPITAL FORMATION CONSULTANTS INC.

P.O. Box 798
Diablo, CA 94528
415/820-8030

Year Founded: 1978
Type: Private V.C. Firm
Total Paid-In Capital: Not Provided

1983 Investment History:

Stage	Dollars Invested	No. of Deals
Seed/Startup	$3,000,000	3
Later Stage	0	0
Follow-On	0	0
Buyouts	0	0
Total Investments	$3,000,000	3
Average Investment	$1,000,000	

Project Preferences
Geographical: Anywhere in U.S.
Foreign: Anywhere
Industries: Diversified, Electronics, Real Estate
Stages: Any

Principals: John H. Rohan, Pres.
Contact: John H. Rohan

Branch: 1720 Ala Moana Blvd., Suite 1506-B, Honolulu, HI 96815, 808/949-0544. *Contact:* John H. Rohan

CATALYST TECHNOLOGIES LTD.

1287 Lawrence Station Rd.
Sunnyvale, CA 94089
408/745-1110

Year Founded: 1983
Type: Corp. V.C. Subsidiary
Total Paid-In Capital: $8,300,000

1983 Investment History:

Stage	Dollars Invested	No. of Deals
Seed/Startup	N.A.	N.A.
Later Stage	N.A.	N.A.
Follow-On	N.A.	N.A.
Buyouts	N.A.	N.A.
Total Investments	$3,000,000	7
Average Investment	$ 428,570	

Project Preferences
Geographical: CA
Industries: High Technology
Stages: Seed

Principals: Lawrence Calof, Gen. Part.; John Anderson, Gen. Part.; Nolan K. Bushnell, Gen. Part.
Contact: Any of Above

CDB INC.

4600 Campus Dr.
Newport Beach, CA 92660
714/852-9000

Year Founded: 1973
Type: Investment Banking Firm
Total Paid-In Capital: Not Provided

1983 Investment History:

Stage	Dollars Invested	No. of Deals
Seed/Startup	N.A.	N.A.
Later Stage	N.A.	N.A.
Follow-On	N.A.	N.A.
Buyouts	N.A.	N.A.
Total Investments	$400,000	4
Average Investment	$100,000	

Project Preferences
Geographical: CA
Industries: High Technology, Computers, Electronics, Medical Products
Stages: Seed, Startup, First

Principals: Walter W. Cruttenden III, Pres.; David A. Carlson, V.P.; Donald F. Brosnan, V.P.
Contact: Any of Above

CHARTER VENTURES

525 University Ave., Suite 1500
Palo Alto, CA 94301
415/325-6953

Affiliation: Chavencap Ltd.
Year Founded: 1982
Type: Private V.C. Firm
Total Paid-In Capital: Not Provided

1983 Investment History:

Stage	Dollars Invested	No. of Deals
Seed/Startup	N.A.	N.A.
Later Stage	N.A.	N.A.
Follow-On	N.A.	N.A.
Buyouts	N.A.	N.A.
Total Investments	$1,500,000	5
Average Investment	$ 300,000	

Project Preferences
Geographical: Anywhere in U.S.
Industries: High Technology
Stages: Seed, Startup, First, Second

Principals: A. Barr Dolan, Gen. Part.
Contact: A. Barr Dolan

KIRKWOOD G. COLVIN & ASSOCIATES INC.

4817 Lennox Ave.
Sherman Oaks, CA 91423
818/986-1210

Year Founded: 1969
Type: Private V.C. Firm
Total Paid-In Capital: Not Provided

1983 Investment History: Not Provided

Project Preferences
Geographical: Anywhere in U.S.
Foreign: Canada, Western Europe, South America
Industries: High Technology, Medical, Defense
Stages: Seed, Startup, First, Second

Principals: Kirkwood G. Colvin, Gen. Part.; Joan Colvin, Gen. Part.; Charles Boudakian, Assoc.
Contact: Any of Above

DAVIS SKAGGS CAPITAL

160 Sansome St.
San Francisco, CA 94104
415/393-0274

Affiliation: Shearson Lehman/American Express
Year Founded: 1981
Type: Corp. V.C. Subsidiary
Total Paid-In Capital: Not Provided

1983 Investment History: Stage	Dollars Invested	No. of Deals
Seed/Startup	N.A.	N.A.
Later Stage	N.A.	N.A.
Follow-On	N.A.	N.A.
Buyouts	N.A.	N.A.
Total Investments	$500,000	3
Average Investment	$166,667	

Project Preferences
Geographical: West Coast
Industries: Diversified
Stages: First, Second, Later

Principals: Charles P. Stetson Jr., Pres.
Contact: Charles P. Stetson Jr.

DIEHL, SPEYER & BROWN

1201 Dove St., Suite 570
Newport Beach, CA 92660
714/955-2000

Year Founded: 1978
Type: Investment Banking Firm
Total Paid-In Capital: Not Provided

1983 Investment History: Stage	Dollars Invested	No. of Deals
Seed/Startup	N.A.	N.A.
Later Stage	N.A.	N.A.
Follow-On	N.A.	N.A.
Buyouts	N.A.	N.A.
Total Investments	$3,000,000	5
Average Investment	$ 600,000	

Project Preferences
Geographical: West of Rockies
Industries: High Technology, Medical, Biotechnology, Computers, Artificial Intelligence
Stages: First

Principals: Russell R. Diehl, Man. Part.; Ronald J. Speyer, Man. Part.; Thomas G. Brown, Man. Part.; Michael Henton, Broker; Richard Stasand, Broker
Contact: Any of Above

FIRST CALIFORNIA BUSINESS & INDUSTRIAL DEVELOPMENT CORP.

3931 MacArthur Blvd., Suite 212
Newport Beach, CA 92660
714/851-0855

Affiliation: United Bank SSB
Year Founded: 1976
Type: Corp. V.C. Subsidiary
Total Paid-In Capital: $2,500,000

1983 Investment History: Not Provided

Project Preferences
Geographical: CA
Industries: Diversified, Manufacturing, Real Estate Development
Stages: Startup, Second

Principals: Leslie R. Brewer, Pres.; Harold S. Charney, Sec.
Contact: Leslie R. Brewer

Branch: 130 Montgomery St., Sixth Floor, San Francisco, CA 94104, 415/392-5410. *Contact:* Richard Heath, Chair.

GENESIS CAPITAL LP

20823 Stevens Creek Blvd., Bldg. C2, Suite A
Cupertino, CA 95014
408/446-9690

Year Founded: 1981
Type: Private V.C. Firm
Total Paid-In Capital: Not Provided

1983 Investment History: Not Provided

Project Preferences
Geographical: West Coast
Industries: High Technology, Communications, Computer Hardware & Software, Data Processing, Medical Equipment & Instrumentation, Office Automation
Stages: Any

Principals: Gerald S. Casilli, Gen Part.
Contact: Gerald S. Casilli

Branch: 777 106th Ave NE, Bellevue, WA 98009, 206/454-7211. *Contact:* David E. Kratter, Gen. Part.

GLOVER CAPITAL CORP.

1000 E. Dominguez St.
Carson, CA 90746
213/532-6187

Year Founded: 1983
Type: Private V.C. Firm
Total Paid-In Capital: $1,100,000

1983 Investment History: Not Provided

Project Preferences
Geographical: Anywhere in U.S., West Coast
Industries: Diversified
Stages: Any

Principals: M.D. Glover, Pres.
Contact: M.D. Glover

GRACE VENTURES CORP.

630 Hansen Way
Palo Alto, CA 94304
415/424-1171

Affiliation: W.R. Grace & Co.
Year Founded: 1983
Type: Corp. V.C. Subsidiary
Total Paid-In Capital: Not Provided

1983 Investment History: Stage	Dollars Invested	No. of Deals
Seed/Startup	N.A.	N.A.
Later Stage	N.A.	N.A.
Follow-On	N.A.	N.A.
Buyouts	N.A.	N.A.
Total Investments	$1,900,000	3
Average Investment	$ 633,333	

Project Preferences
Geographical: Anywhere in U.S.
Foreign: Hong Kong, Singapore, Malaysia
Industries: Diversified
Stages: Any

Principals: Dr. Christian F. Horn, Pres.; Dr. Charles A. Bauer, V.P.; Susan A. Woods, Asst. V.P.; William B. Wittmeyer, Asst. V.P.
Contact: Dr. Christian F. Horn

HAPP VENTURES

444 Castro St., Suite 400
Mountain View, CA 94041
415/961-1115

Year Founded: 1982
Type: Private V.C. Firm
Total Paid-In Capital: Not Provided

1983 Investment History:

Stage	Dollars Invested	No. of Deals
Seed/Startup	N.A.	N.A.
Later Stage	N.A.	N.A.
Follow-On	N.A.	N.A.
Buyouts	N.A.	N.A.
Total Investments	$1,500,000	3
Average Investment	$ 500,000	

Project Preferences
Geographical: Anywhere in U.S.
Foreign: Northern Europe, Japan
Industries: High Technology, Computer-Related, Medical
   Technology
Stages: Seed, Startup, First

Principals: William D. Happ, Pres.
Contact: William D. Happ

HOEBICH VENTURE MANAGEMENT INC.

850 Hamilton Ave.
Palo Alto, CA 94301
415/326-5590

Year Founded: 1971
Type: Private V.C. Firm
Total Paid-In Capital: Not Provided

1983 Investment History:

Stage	Dollars Invested	No. of Deals
Seed/Startup	N.A.	N.A.
Later Stage	N.A.	N.A.
Follow-On	N.A.	N.A.
Buyouts	N.A.	N.A.
Total Investments	$200,000	3
Average Investment	$ 66,667	

Project Preferences
Geographical: CA
Industries: High Technology, Computer Hardware & Software,
   Communications
Stages: Seed, Startup

Principals: Christian C.E. Hoebich, Pres.
Contact: Christian C.E. Hoebich

INTERNATIONAL BUSINESS SPONSORS INC.

765 Bridgeway
Sausalito, CA 94965
415/331-2262

Year Founded: 1979
Type: Private V.C. Firm
Total Paid-In Capital: Not Provided

1983 Investment History:

Stage	Dollars Invested	No. of Deals
Seed/Startup	N.A.	N.A.
Later Stage	N.A.	N.A.
Follow-On	N.A.	N.A.
Buyouts	N.A.	N.A.
Total Investments	$1,200,000	4
Average Investment	$ 300,000	

Project Preferences
Geographical: Anywhere in U.S., West Coast
Foreign: Anywhere
Industries: Consumer Products & Services
Stages: Second, Later

Principals: Mel L. Bacharach, Pres.
Contact: Mel L. Bacharach

IRVINE TECHNOLOGY FUNDS

4600 Campus Dr., Suite 201
Newport Beach, CA 92660
714/852-9000

Year Founded: 1981
Type: Private V.C. Firm
Total Paid-In Capital: $2,000,000

1983 Investment History:

Stage	Dollars Invested	No. of Deals
Seed/Startup	N.A.	N.A.
Later Stage	N.A.	N.A.
Follow-On	N.A.	N.A.
Buyouts	N.A.	N.A.
Total Investments	$1,400,000	9
Average Investment	$ 155,556	

Project Preferences
Geographical: Southern CA
Industries: Computer-Related, Biomedical and Medical Industries,
   Proprietary Products
Stages: Seed, Startup

Principals: Walter W. Cruttenden III, Gen. Part.; Donald F. Brosnan,
   Gen. Part.; H.D. Thoreau, Gen. Part.
Contact: Any of Above

ROBERT B. LEISY

P.O. Box 4405
14408 E. Whittier Blvd., Suite B-5
Whittier, CA 90607
213/698-4862

Year Founded: 1972
Type: Consulting Firm
Total Paid-In Capital: Not Provided

1983 Investment History: Not Provided

Project Preferences
Geographical: West Coast
Industries: Diversified, Industrial Products & Services
Stages: Startup, First

Principals: Robert B. Leisy, Pres.
Contact: Robert B. Leisy

VENTURE FIRMS UNDER $10 MIL

MANNING & CO.

29438 Quailwood Dr.
Rancho Palos Verdes, CA 90274
213/377-4335

Year Founded: 1971
Type: Private V.C. Firm
Total Paid-In Capital: Not Provided

1983 Investment History:

Stage	Dollars Invested	No. of Deals
Seed/Startup	N.A.	N.A.
Later Stage	N.A.	N.A.
Follow-On	N.A.	N.A.
Buyouts	N.A.	N.A.
Total Investments	$350,000	2
Average Investment	$175,000	

Project Preferences
Geographical: Southwest, CA
Industries: Diversified, Real Estate, Leisure & Recreational Products
Stages: First, Second, Buyouts

Principals: Dr. Christopher A. Manning, Pres.
Contact: Dr. Christopher A. Manning

LEONARD MAUTNER ASSOCIATES

1434 Sixth St.
Santa Monica, CA 90401
213/393-9788

Year Founded: 1968
Type: Private V.C. Firm; Consulting Firm
Total Paid-In Capital: Not Provided

1983 Investment History:

Stage	Dollars Invested	No. of Deals
Seed/Startup	N.A.	N.A.
Later Stage	N.A.	N.A.
Follow-On	N.A.	N.A.
Buyouts	N.A.	N.A.
Total Investments	N.A.	N.A.
Average Investment	$100,000	

Project Preferences
Geographical: West Coast
Industries: Diversified, Communications, Computers, Electronics
Stages: Startup, First

Principals: Leonard Mautner, Pres.
Contact: Leonard Mautner

MOHR VENTURES

3000 Sand Hill Rd., Bldg. 4, Suite 240
Menlo Park, CA 94025
415/854-7236

Year Founded: 1983
Type: Private V.C. Firm
Total Paid-In Capital: Not Provided

1983 Investment History: New Fund

Project Preferences
Geographical: Western U.S.
Industries: Communications, Computer-Related, Energy &
   Natural Resources, Genetic Engineering, Industrial Products
   & Equipment, Medical
Stages: Seed, Startup, First

Principals: Lawrence G. Mohr, Gen. Part.; Peter Roshko, Assoc.
Contact: Either

MORGAN, OLMSTEAD, KENNEDY & GARDNER INC.

606 S. Olive St.
Los Angeles, CA 90014
213/625-1611

Year Founded: 1936
Type: Investment Banking Firm
Total Paid-In Capital: $7,200,000

1983 Investment History:

Stage	Dollars Invested	No. of Deals
Seed/Startup	N.A.	N.A.
Later Stage	N.A.	N.A.
Follow-On	N.A.	N.A.
Buyouts	N.A.	N.A.
Total Investments	$1,500,000	2
Average Investment	$ 750,000	

Project Preferences
Geographical: West Coast
Foreign: Europe
Industries: Diversified Non-High Technology
Stages: First, Second

Principals: G. Tilton Gardner, Chair.; Bryan Herrman, Pres.
Contact: Richard Drysdale, Consultant

NATURAL RESOURCES FUND

1500 W. Shaw, Suite 404
Fresno, CA 93711
209/226-5513

Year Founded: 1977
Type: Private V.C. Firm
Total Paid-In Capital: $2,500,000

1983 Investment History:

Stage	Dollars Invested	No. of Deals
Seed/Startup	0	0
Later Stage	$3,000,000	2
Follow-On	0	0
Buyouts	0	0
Total Investments	$3,000,000	2
Average Investment	$1,500,000	

Project Preferences
Geographical: West Coast, Southwest, Northwest
Industries: Oil & Gas, Precious Metals
Stages: Startup, First

Principals: John R. Shelburne, Pres.
Contact: John R. Shelburne

PALO ALTO VENTURES INC.

3000 Sand Hill Rd., Bldg. 1, Suite 140
Menlo Park, CA 94025
415/854-8770

Affiliation: Cooper Laboratories Inc.
Year Founded: 1983
Type: Corp. V.C. Subsidiary
Total Paid-In Capital: Not Provided

1983 Investment History:

Stage	Dollars Invested	No. of Deals
Seed/Startup	N.A.	N.A.
Later Stage	N.A.	N.A.
Follow-On	N.A.	N.A.
Buyouts	N.A.	N.A.
Total Investments	$1,500,000	3
Average Investment	$ 500,000	

Project Preferences
Geographical: Anywhere in U.S.
Foreign: Japan, Europe
Industries: Healthcare & Medical
Stages: Second, Later

Principals: Daniel Larson, Man. Dir.
Contact: Daniel Larson

PROTOTYPE FUNDING CORP.

790 Lucerne Drive
Sunnyvale, CA 94086
408/733-3595

Year Founded: 1980
Type: Private V.C. Firm
Total Paid-In Capital: Not Provided

1983 Investment History:

Stage	Dollars Invested	No. of Deals
Seed/Startup	N.A.	N.A.
Later Stage	N.A.	N.A.
Follow-On	N.A.	N.A.
Buyouts	N.A.	N.A.
Total Investments	$1,000,000	2
Average Investment	$ 500,000	

Project Preferences
Geographical: Silicon Valley
Industries: Diversified Non-High Technology
Stages: Any

Principals: Nicholas L. Feakins, Pres.; Jeffie W. Feakins, V.P.
Contact: Either

ARTHUR ROCK & CO.

235 Montgomery St.
San Francisco, CA 94104
415/981-3921

Year Founded: 1961
Type: Private V.C. Firm
Total Paid-In Capital: Not Provided

1983 Investment History: Not Provided

Project Preferences
Geographical: CA
Industries: High Technology
Stages: First

Principals: Arthur Rock, Prin.; Marie Getchel, Admin. Asst.
Contact: Either

SAN JOSE CAPITAL

100 Park Center Plaza, Suite 427
San Jose, CA 95113
408/293-7708

Year Founded: 1977
Type: Private V.C. Firm
Total Paid-In Capital: $4,500,000

1983 Investment History: Not Provided

Project Preferences
Geographical: West Coast
Industries: High Technology, Computers, Telecommunications, Electronics, Medical
Stages: Startup, First

Principals: Daniel Hochman, Gen. Part.; Robert T. Murphy, Gen. Part.
Contact: Either

SECURITY FINANCIAL MANAGEMENT CORP.

100 Bush St., Suite 1905
San Francisco, CA 94104
415/981-8060

Year Founded: 1942
Type: Private V.C. Firm
Total Paid-In Capital: Not Provided

1983 Investment History:

Stage	Dollars Invested	No. of Deals
Seed/Startup	N.A.	N.A.
Later Stage	N.A.	N.A.
Follow-On	N.A.	N.A.
Buyouts	N.A.	N.A.
Total Investments	$500,000	4
Average Investment	$125,000	

Project Preferences
Geographical: West Coast
Industries: Diversified
Stages: Later

Principals: Byron G. Rouda, Pres.
Contact: Byron G. Rouda

SEIDLER AMDEC SECURITIES INC.

515 S. Figueroa St.
Los Angeles, CA 90071-3396
213/624-4232

Year Founded: 1969
Type: Investment Banking Firm
Total Paid-In Capital: Not Provided

1983 Investment History:

Stage	Dollars Invested	No. of Deals
Seed/Startup	N.A.	N.A.
Later Stage	N.A.	N.A.
Follow-On	N.A.	N.A.
Buyouts	N.A.	N.A.
Total Investments	$2,000,000	4
Average Investment	$ 500,000	

Project Preferences
Geographical: West Coast, Southwest
Industries: Diversified
Stages: Second, Later, Buyouts

Principals: Bruce P. Emmeluth, Sr. V.P.; James E. Moore, V.P.; Robert W. Campbell, Asst. V.P.; Joseph Giansante
Contact: Any of Above

SIGMA PARTNERS

224 W. Brokaw Rd., Suite 395
San Jose, CA 95110
408/298-8588

Year Founded: 1984
Type: Private V.C. Firm
Total Paid-In Capital: Not Provided

1983 Investment History: New Fund

Project Preferences
Geographical: Anywhere in U.S., West Coast, Mountain States
Industries: High Technology
Stages: Any

Principals: J. Burgess Jamieson, Gen. Part.
Contact: J. Burgess Jamieson

SILICON VALLEY MANAGEMENT

15474 Via Vaquero
Monte Sereno, CA 95030
408/395-2200

Year Founded: 1982
Type: Consulting Firm
Total Paid-In Capital: Not Provided

1983 Investment History: Stage	Dollars Invested	No. of Deals
Seed/Startup	N.A.	N.A.
Later Stage	N.A.	N.A.
Follow-On	N.A.	N.A.
Buyouts	N.A.	N.A.
Total Investments	$250,000	3
Average Investment	$ 83,333	

Project Preferences
Geographical: West Coast
Industries: High Technology, Computer-Related, Semiconductors, Medical
Stages: Startup

Principals: Dr. Charles H. Sutcliffe, Prin.
Contact: Dr. Charles H. Sutcliffe

STANFORD UNIVERSITY INVESTMENT MANAGEMENT

209 Hamilton Ave.
Palo Alto, CA 94301
415/326-5782

Year Founded: 1970
Type: Institutional Endowment Fund
Total Paid-In Capital: Not Provided

1983 Investment History: Stage	Dollars Invested	No. of Deals
Seed/Startup	N.A.	N.A.
Later Stage	N.A.	N.A.
Follow-On	N.A.	N.A.
Buyouts	N.A.	N.A.
Total Investments	$1,800,000	2
Average Investment	$ 900,000	

Project Preferences
Geographical: Anywhere in U.S.
Foreign: U.K., Germany, Japan, Hong Kong, Australia, Malaysia, Singapore
Industries: Diversified
Stages: Seed, Startup, First

Principals: Rodney H. Adams, University Treasury Dir.
Contact: Rodney H. Adams

TRIANGLE VENTURES

1245 Oakmeade Parkway, Suite 105
Sunnyvale, CA 94086
408/730-9948

Year Founded: 1982
Type: Private V.C. Firm
Total Paid-In Capital: $500,000

1983 Investment History: Stage	Dollars Invested	No. of Deals
Seed/Startup	N.A.	N.A.
Later Stage	N.A.	N.A.
Follow-On	N.A.	N.A.
Buyouts	N.A.	N.A.
Total Investments	$500,000	8
Average Investment	$ 62,500	

Project Preferences
Geographical: West Coast
Industries: Microelectronics, Computer Software
Stages: Seed, Startup

Principals: Thomas A. Skornia, Gen. Part.; Kirsten Olsen, Gen. Part.
Contact: Either

WALLNER & CO.

P.O. Box 8329
La Jolla, CA 92038
619/454-3805

Year Founded: 1975
Type: Private V.C. Firm
Total Paid-In Capital: Not Provided

1983 Investment History: Stage	Dollars Invested	No. of Deals
Seed/Startup	N.A.	N.A.
Later Stage	N.A.	N.A.
Follow-On	N.A.	N.A.
Buyouts	N.A.	N.A.
Total Investments	N.A.	2

Project Preferences
Geographical: Anywhere in U.S.
Foreign: Anywhere
Industries: Diversified Non-High Technology, Manufacturing, Distribution & Wholesale
Stages: Buyouts

Principals: Dr. Nicholas Wallner, Part.
Contact: Nicholas Wallner

WHITNEY VENTURES INC.

444 Castro St., Suite 400
Mountain View, CA 94041
415/960-3525

Year Founded: 1982
Type: Private V.C. Firm
Total Paid-In Capital: $2,000,000

1983 Investment History:

Stage	Dollars Invested	No. of Deals
Seed/Startup	N.A.	N.A.
Later Stage	N.A.	N.A.
Follow-On	N.A.	N.A.
Buyouts	N.A.	N.A.
Total Investments	$1,000,000	10
Average Investment	$ 100,000	

Project Preferences
Geographical: CA
Industries: Computers, Communications, Instrumentation, Semiconductors
Stages: Startup

Principals: Thomas M. Whitney, Pres.
Contact: Thomas M. Whitney

WOODSIDE FUND

850 Woodside Dr.
Woodside, CA 94062
415/368-5545

Year Founded: 1983
Type: Private V.C. Firm
Total Paid-In Capital: Not Provided

1983 Investment History:

Stage	Dollars Invested	No. of Deals
Seed/Startup	N.A.	N.A.
Later Stage	N.A.	N.A.
Follow-On	N.A.	N.A.
Buyouts	N.A.	N.A.
Total Investments	N.A.	9

Project Preferences
Geographical: CA
Industries: Diversified
Stages: Seed, Startup, First, Second

Principals: Vincent M. Occhipinti, Gen. Part.; Charles E. Greb, Gen. Part.; V. Frank Medicino, Gen. Part.; Robert E. Larson, Gen. Part.; William M. Hassebrock, Part.; Thomas R. Blakeslee, Part.
Contact: Vincent M. Occhipinti, V. Frank Medicino

Colorado

CAMBRIDGE VENTURE PARTNERS

Cambridge Bldg., Suite 200
88 Steele St.,
Denver, CO 80206
303/393-1111

Year Founded: 1981
Type: Private V.C. Firm
Total Paid-In Capital: Not Provided

1983 Investment History:

Stage	Dollars Invested	No. of Deals
Seed/Startup	N.A.	N.A.
Later Stage	N.A.	N.A.
Follow-On	N.A.	N.A.
Buyouts	N.A.	N.A.
Total Investments	$3,000,000	6
Average Investment	$ 500,000	

Project Preferences
Geographical: CA, CO
Foreign: U.K.
Industries: High Technology, Medical, Computers
Stages: Seed, Startup, First

Principals: Bruce B. Paul, Man. Part.; Duncan M. Davidson, Part.; Ozzie Malek, Part.; Jack Snyder, Part.
Contact: Bruce B. Paul, Duncan M. Davidson (computers)

INVESTMENT SECURITIES OF COLORADO INC.

4605 Denice Dr.
Englewood, CO 80111
303/796-9192

Year Founded: 1970
Type: Private V.C. Firm
Total Paid-In Capital: Not Provided

1983 Investment History:

Stage	Dollars Invested	No. of Deals
Seed/Startup	N.A.	N.A.
Later Stage	N.A.	N.A.
Follow-On	N.A.	N.A.
Buyouts	N.A.	N.A.
Total Investments	$150,000	2
Average Investment	$ 75,000	

Project Preferences
Geographical: CO
Industries: Diversified, Construction, Medical Instrumentation
Stages: Startup

Principals: Vern D. Kornelsen, Pres.
Contact: Vern D. Kornelsen

VENTURE FIRMS UNDER $10 MIL

Connecticut

ASSET CAPITAL & MANAGEMENT CORP.

608 Ferry Blvd.
Stratford, CT 06497
203/375-0299

Year Founded: 1979
Type: Private V.C. Firm
Total Paid-In Capital: Not Provided

1983 Investment History:

Stage	Dollars Invested	No. of Deals
Seed/Startup	N.A.	N.A.
Later Stage	N.A.	N.A.
Follow-On	N.A.	N.A.
Buyouts	N.A.	N.A.
Total Investments	$3,800,000	20
Average Investment	$ 190,000	

Project Preferences
Geographical: Anywhere in U.S., Northeast
Industries: Manufacturing
Stages: Later

Principals: Ralph Smith, Pres.; Edward L. Marcus, Dir.
Contact: Either

BEACON PARTNERS

71 Strawberry Hill Ave., Suite 614
Stamford, CT 06902
203/348-8858

Year Founded: 1976
Type: Consulting Firm
Total Paid-In Capital: Not Provided

1983 Investment History: Not Provided

Project Preferences
Geographical: Northeast
Industries: Diversified Non-High Technology
Stages: Later, Buyouts

Principals: Leonard Vignola, Part.
Contact: Leonard Vignola

CAMBRIDGE RESEARCH & DEVELOPMENT GROUP

21 Bridge Square
Westport, CT 06880
203/226-7400

Year Founded: 1965
Type: Private V.C. Firm*
Total Paid-In Capital: Not Provided

1983 Investment History: Not Provided

Project Preferences
Geographical: Anywhere in U.S.
Industries: Diversified
Stages: Seed, Startup, First, Second

Principals: Lawrence M. Sherman, Gen. Part.; Kenneth N. Sherman, Gen. Part.; Deborah Gardner O'Connor, Product-Evaluation Mgr.; Gregory F. Zaic, Dir. New Products & Ventures
Contact: Deborah Gardner O'Connor, Gregory F. Zaic

*Specializes in tax-advantaged private placements.

GEMINI ASSOCIATES

16 Pitkin St.
East Hartford, CT 06108
203/528-9674

Year Founded: 1971
Type: Investment Banking Firm
Total Paid-In Capital: Not Provided

1983 Investment History:

Stage	Dollars Invested	No. of Deals
Seed/Startup	N.A.	N.A.
Later Stage	N.A.	N.A.
Follow-On	N.A.	N.A.
Buyouts	N.A.	N.A.
Total Investments	$2,500,000	5
Average Investment	$ 500,000	

Project Preferences
Geographical: Northeast
Industries: Consumer Products & Services, Industrial Products & Equipment
Stages: Startup, First, Second

Principals: G. Stanton Geary, Pres.
Contact: G. Stanton Geary

JAMES B. KOBAK & CO.

774 Hollow Tree Ridge Rd.
Darien, CT 06820
203/655-8764

Year Founded: 1971
Type: Private V.C. Firm
Total Paid-In Capital: Not Provided

1983 Investment History: Not Provided

Project Preferences
Geographical: Anywhere in U.S.
Industries: Communications, Publishing, Mail Order
Stages: Any

Principals: James B. Kobak, Pres.; Hope M. Kobak, V.P.
Contact: Either

MEMHARD INVESTMENT BANKERS

22 Fifth St., Suite 204
Stamford, CT 06905
203/348-6802

Year Founded: 1973
Type: Investment Banking Firm
Total Paid-In Capital: Not Provided

1983 Investment History: Not Provided

Project Preferences
Geographical: Anywhere in U.S.
Foreign: Far East, Europe
Industries: Diversified
Stages: Any

Principals: Richard C. Memhard, Pres.; David G. Bernard, Exec. V.P.; Laura Memhard, Treas.
Contact: Any of Above

THE PACE CONSULTING GROUP

20 Hurlbut St.
West Hartford, CT 06110
203/525-9921

Year Founded: 1970
Type: Consulting Firm*
Total Paid-In Capital: Not Provided

1983 Investment History: Not Provided

Project Preferences
Geographical: Northeast
Industries: Diversified, Manufacturing
Stages: Later

Principals: Gary Brooks, Prin.; Langdon G. Johnson, Prin.
Contact: Gary Brooks

*Specializes in crisis management and turnarounds.

DONALD C. SEIBERT

P.O. Box 704
Old Greenwich, CT 06870
203/637-1704

Year Founded: 1968
Type: Private V.C. Firm
Total Paid-In Capital: Not Provided

| *1983 Investment History:* | | |
Stage	Dollars Invested	No. of Deals
Seed/Startup	N.A.	N.A.
Later Stage	N.A.	N.A.
Follow-On	N.A.	N.A.
Buyouts	N.A.	N.A.
Total Investments	$200,000	2
Average Investment	$100,000	

Project Preferences
Geographical: Anywhere in U.S.
Foreign: Anywhere
Industries: Diversified, Energy & Natural Resources, Robotics
Stages: Any

Principals: Donald C. Seibert, Owner
Contact: Donald C. Seibert

WHITEHEAD ASSOCIATES

15 Valley Dr.
Greenwich, CT 06830
203/629-4633

Year Founded: 1980
Type: Private V.C. Firm
Total Paid-In Capital: Not Provided

| *1983 Investment History:* | | |
Stage	Dollars Invested	No. of Deals
Seed/Startup	N.A.	N.A.
Later Stage	N.A.	N.A.
Follow-On	N.A.	N.A.
Buyouts	N.A.	N.A.
Total Investments	$3,100,000	6
Average Investment	$ 516,667	

Project Preferences
Geographical: Anywhere in U.S.
Industries: Diversified
Stages: Startup, First, Second

Principals: Edwin C. Whitehead, Chair.; Joseph A. Orlando, Pres.;
William E. Engbers, V.P.; Andrew Ziolkowski, Investment Mgr.
Contact: Joseph A. Orlando, William E. Engbers

XEROX VENTURE CAPITAL

800 Long Ridge Rd.
Stamford, CT 06904
203/329-8711

Affiliation: Xerox Corp.
Year Founded: 1976
Type: Corp. V.C. Subsidiary
Total Paid-In Capital: Not Provided

1983 Investment History: Not Provided

Project Preferences
Geographical: Anywhere in U.S.
Industries: Communications, Data Communications,
Software, Office Automation, Computer Graphics
Stages: Startup, First

Principals: L.R. Robinson, Prin.; W.Z. Ludwick, Assoc. Prin.
Contact: Either

Branch: 2029 Century Park E., Suite 740, Los Angeles, CA 90067,
213/278-7940. *Contact:* A. Talbot, Prin.

District of Columbia

BLAKE INVESTMENT GROUP

1101 30th St., NW, Suite 101
Washington, DC 20007
202/833-9031

Year Founded: 1980
Type: Investment Banking & Consulting Firm
Total Paid-In Capital: Not Provided

1983 Investment History: Not Provided

Project Preferences
Geographical: Anywhere in U.S.
Industries: Diversified, Semiconductors, Publishing, Oil & Gas,
Alternative Energy, Industrial Materials, Real Estate
Stages: Any

Principals: Carl W. Blake, Sr. Part.; David D. Brunell, Sr. Part.; Russell
F. Smith, Sr. Part.
Contact: Carl W. Blake

Branch: 43 Charles St., London WlX 7PB, England, 44/1-491-3030.
Contact: Sanford G. Henry, Sr. Part.

MALCOLM BUND & ASSOCIATES INC.

2000 L St., NW
Washington, DC 20036
202/293-2910

Year Founded: 1977
Type: Investment Banking & Consulting Firm
Total Paid-In Capital: Not Provided

1983 Investment History: Not Provided

Project Preferences
Geographical: East Coast
Industries: Diversified
Stages: Second, Later

Principals: Malcolm Bund, Pres.; E. Richard Busse, V.P.
Contact: Either

CORPORATE FINANCE OF WASHINGTON INC.

1326 R St., NW, Suite 2
Washington, DC 20009
202/328-9053

Year Founded: 1976
Type: Investment Banking Firm Acting as Intermediary in Venture Deals
Total Paid-In Capital: Not Provided

1983 Investment History:

Stage	Dollars Invested	No. of Deals
Seed/Startup	N.A.	N.A.
Later Stage	N.A.	N.A.
Follow-On	N.A.	N.A.
Buyouts	N.A.	N.A.
Total Investments	$1,500,000	3
Average Investment	$ 500,000	

Project Preferences
Geographical: East Coast
Industries: Diversified, Communications, Electronics
Stages: First

Principals: Peter W. Gavian, Pres.
Contact: Peter W. Gavian

EWING CAPITAL INC.

1016 16th St., NW, Suite 650
Washington, DC 20036
202/463-8787

Year Founded: 1981
Type: Investment Banking Firm
Total Paid-In Capital: Not Provided

1983 Investment History: Not Provided

Project Preferences
Geographical: Anywhere in U.S.
Industries: Diversified, Communications, Broadcasting, Engineering
Stages: Any

Principals: Samuel D. Ewing Jr., Pres.
Contact: Samuel D. Ewing Jr.

SYNDICATED COMMUNICATIONS INC.

1625 I St., NW
Washington, DC 20006
202/293-9428

Year Founded: 1977
Type: Private V.C. Firm
Total Paid-In Capital: $3,500,000

1983 Investment History:

Stage	Dollars Invested	No. of Deals
Seed/Startup	N.A.	N.A.
Later Stage	N.A.	N.A.
Follow-On	N.A.	N.A.
Buyouts	N.A.	N.A.
Total Investments	$350,000	2
Average Investment	$175,000	

Project Preferences
Geographical: Anywhere in U.S.
Industries: Telecommunications
Stages: Startup

Principals: Herbert P. Wilkins, Pres.; Terry L. Jones, V.P.
Contact: Either

WACHTEL & CO. INC.

1101 14th St., NW
Washington, DC 20005
202/898-1144

Year Founded: 1961
Type: Private V.C. Firm
Total Paid-In Capital: $1,500,000

1983 Investment History:

Stage	Dollars Invested	No. of Deals
Seed/Startup	N.A.	N.A.
Later Stage	N.A.	N.A.
Follow-On	N.A.	N.A.
Buyouts	N.A.	N.A.
Total Investments	$475,000	5
Average Investment	$ 95,000	

Project Preferences
Geographical: East Coast, Midwest
Industries: Data Processing, Service Industries, Electronics, Communications, Computer-Related
Stages: First, Second, Later

Principals: Sidney B. Wachtel, Chair.; John D. Sanders, V.P.; Wendie L. Wachtel, V.P.; Bunnie K. Wachtel, V.P.
Contact: Any of Above

Florida

ACORN VENTURE CAPITAL CORP.

P.O. Box 1328
2401 E. Atlantic Blvd.
Pompano Beach, FL 33061
305/941-2764

Year Founded: 1984
Type: Public V.C. Firm
Total Paid-In Capital: $2,000,000

1983 Investment History: New Fund

Project Preferences
Geographical: Anywhere in U.S.
Industries: Diversified, High Technology, Biomedical, Communications, Computer Hardware & Software
Stages: Second, Later

Principals: Nick Christos, Dir. & Treas.; Peter Christos, Consultant
Contact: Either

ATLANTIC AMERICAN CAPITAL LTD.

Lincoln Center, Suite 851
5401 W. Kennedy Blvd.
Tampa, FL 33609
813/877-8844

Affiliation: Atlantic American Holdings Inc.
Year Founded: 1979
Type: Corp. V.C. Subsidiary
Total Paid-In Capital: Not Provided

1983 Investment History: Not Provided

Project Preferences
Geographical: Anywhere in U.S.
Foreign: Canada
Industries: Communications, Broadcasting, Cable Television
Stages: Second, Later, Buyouts

Principals: J. Patrick Michaels Jr., Pres.; H. Gene Gawthrop, V.P.
Contact: J. Patrick Michaels Jr.

BUSINESS RESEARCH CO.

205 Worth Ave., Suite 307
Palm Beach, FL 33480
305/832-2155

Year Founded: 1961
Type: Private V.C. Firm
Total Paid-In Capital: Not Provided

1983 Investment History:

Stage	Dollars Invested	No. of Deals
Seed/Startup	N.A.	0
Later Stage	N.A.	2
Follow-On	N.A.	0
Buyouts	N.A.	0
Total Investments	N.A.	2

Project Preferences
Geographical: East Coast, Midwest
Industries: Basic Manufacturing
Stages: Later

Principals: George B. Kilborne, Pres.
Contact: George B. Kilborne

Branch: Baystreet Corp., 400 E. 54th St., Apartment 22C, New York, NY 10022, 212/838-0464. *Contact:* George B. Kilborne, Pres.

ELECTRO-SCIENCE MANAGEMENT CORP.

600 Courtland St., Suite 490
Orlando, FL 32804
305/645-1188

Year Founded: 1969
Type: Private V.C. Firm
Total Paid-In Capital: $9,000,000

1983 Investment History:

Stage	Dollars Invested	No. of Deals
Seed/Startup	N.A.	N.A.
Later Stage	N.A.	N.A.
Follow-On	N.A.	N.A.
Buyouts	N.A.	N.A.
Total Investments	$2,500,000	4
Average Investment	$ 625,000	

Project Preferences
Geographical: Anywhere in U.S., Southeast
Industries: High Technology, Computers, Communications, Medical
Stages: Seed, Startup, First

Principals: G. Arthur Herbert, V.P.; John W. Boone, V.P.; Paul F. Curry, V.P.
Contact: G. Arthur Herbert

FIRST AMERICAN INVESTMENT CORP.

2701 S. Bayshore Dr.
Coconut Grove, FL 33133
305/854-6840

Affiliation: HMG Property Investors Inc.
Year Founded: 1981
Type: Corp. V.C. Subsidiary
Total Paid-In Capital: $4,000,000

1983 Investment History:

Stage	Dollars Invested	No. of Deals
Seed/Startup	N.A.	N.A.
Later Stage	N.A.	N.A.
Follow-On	N.A.	N.A.
Buyouts	N.A.	N.A.
Total Investments	$1,500,000	3
Average Investment	$ 500,000	

Project Preferences
Geographical: Southeast
Industries: Real Estate, High Technology
Stages: Startup, Second

Principals: Maurice Wiener, Chair. & Treas.; Joseph N. Hardin Jr., Dir. & Pres.
Contact: Either

INTERSTATE CAPITAL CORP.

701 E. Camino Real
Boca Raton, FL 33432
305/395-8466

Year Founded: 1959
Type: Private V.C. Firm
Total Paid-In Capital: $300,000

1983 Investment History:

Stage	Dollars Invested	No. of Deals
Seed/Startup	N.A.	N.A.
Later Stage	N.A.	N.A.
Follow-On	N.A.	N.A.
Buyouts	N.A.	N.A.
Total Investments	$250,000	3
Average Investment	$ 83,333	

Project Preferences
Geographical: Anywhere in U.S., East Coast
Industries: Electronics, Leisure Activities & Services
Stages: Startup, First, Second

Principals: William C. McConnell Jr., Pres.
Contact: William C. McConnell Jr.

KATHO CAPITAL CORP.

2000 W. Commercial Blvd., Suite 108
Ft. Lauderdale, FL 33309
305/776-5700

Type: Private V.C. Firm
Total Paid-In Capital: Not Provided

1983 Investment History: Not Provided

Project Preferences
Geographical: Anywhere in U.S.
Industries: Diversified
Stages: Any, Startups

Principals: Lionel Reifler, Pres.; Timothy J. Petersen, V.P. Operations
Contact: Either

Georgia

ANATAR INVESTMENTS INC.

Gas Light Tower, Suite 2218
235 Peachtree St.
Atlanta, GA 30303
404/588-0770

Year Founded: 1979
Type: Private V.C. Firm
Total Paid-In Capital: Not Provided

1983 Investment History:

Stage	Dollars Invested	No. of Deals
Seed/Startup	$100,000	1
Later Stage	0	0
Follow-On	$200,000	2
Buyouts	0	0
Total Investments	$300,000	3
Average Investment	$100,000	

Project Preferences
Geographical: Southeast
Industries: Diversified Non-High Technology
Stages: Any

Principals: Douglas A. P. Hamilton, Pres.
Contact: Douglas A. P. Hamilton

CRESCENT MANAGEMENT CO.

5775 Peachtree-Dunwoody Rd., Suite 330C
Atlanta, GA 30342
404/252-8660

Year Founded: 1982
Type: Private V.C. Firm
Total Paid-In Capital: $3,200,000

1983 Investment History:

Stage	Dollars Invested	No. of Deals
Seed/Startup	N.A.	N.A.
Later Stage	N.A.	N.A.
Follow-On	N.A.	N.A.
Buyouts	N.A.	N.A.
Total Investments	$2,000,000	6
Average Investment	$ 333,333	

Project Preferences
Geographical: Southeast
Industries: Diversified
Stages: Later

Principals: Walter M. Wellman, Chair.; John Thomas, Pres.; James R. Johnson, V.P. High-Tech Investments; David W. Howe, V.P. Corp. Finance
Contact: Any of Above

GRUBB & CO.

1500 Tower Pl.
3340 Peachtree Rd.
Atlanta, GA 30026
404/237-6222

Year Founded: 1982
Type: Investment Banking Firm
Total Paid-In Capital: Not Provided

1983 Investment History: Not Provided

Project Preferences
Geographical: Southeast
Industries: Diversified
Stages: Seed, Startup, First

Principals: Stephen B. Grubb, Man. Dir.; David E. Thomas Jr., Dir.
Contact: Either

LENDMAN CAPITAL ASSOCIATES

5 Piedmont Center, Suite 320
Atlanta, GA 30305
404/233-9003

Year Founded: 1982
Type: Private V.C. Firm
Total Paid-In Capital: Not Provided

1983 Investment History:

Stage	Dollars Invested	No. of Deals
Seed/Startup	N.A.	N.A.
Later Stage	N.A.	N.A.
Follow-On	N.A.	N.A.
Buyouts	N.A.	N.A.
Total Investments	N.A.	N.A.
Average Investment	$500,000	

Project Preferences
Geographical: Anywhere in U.S.
Industries: Diversified
Stages: Any

Principals: William M. Lendman, Gen. Part.; Robert H. Friedman, Gen. Part.; Loren J. Rivard, Gen. Part.
Contact: William M. Lendman

Idaho

FIRST IDAHO VENTURE CAPITAL CORP.

P.O. Box 1739
Boise, ID 83701
208/345-3460

Affiliation: First Idaho Corp.
Year Founded: 1976
Type: Corp. V.C. Subsidiary
Total Paid-In Capital: Not Provided

1983 Investment History:

Stage	Dollars Invested	No. of Deals
Seed/Startup	N.A.	N.A.
Later Stage	N.A.	N.A.
Follow-On	N.A.	N.A.
Buyouts	N.A.	N.A.
Total Investments	$800,000	11
Average Investment	$ 72,727	

Project Preferences
Geographical: Northwest
Industries: Communications, Consumer, Distribution
Stages: Second

Principals: Ron J. Twileger, Pres.; Dennis Clark, V.P.
Contact: Dennis Clark

Illinois

THE CAPITAL STRATEGY GROUP INC.

20 N. Wacker Dr.
Chicago, IL 60606
312/444-1170

Year Founded: 1982
Type: Investment Banking Firm
Total Paid-In Capital: Not Provided

1983 Investment History: Not Provided

Project Preferences
Geographical: Midwest
Industries: High-Technology & Low-Technology, Manufacturing & Service Industries for Industrial & Consumer Markets
Stages: Any

Principals: E. von Bauer, Pres.
Contact: E. von Bauer

CR INVESTMENTS

3 First National Plaza, Suite 2725
Chicago, IL 60602
312/346-6038

Affiliation: Cavendish Investing Ltd. (Canada)
Year Founded: 1980
Type: Private V.C. Firm
Total Paid-In Capital: Not Provided

1983 Investment History:

Stage	Dollars Invested	No. of Deals
Seed/Startup	N.A.	N.A.
Later Stage	N.A.	N.A.
Follow-On	N.A.	N.A.
Buyouts	N.A.	N.A.
Total Investments	$500,000	1

Project Preferences
Geographical: Anywhere in U.S.
Industries: High Technology, Electronics, Computer Hardware & Software
Stages: First, Second, Later

Principals: Edward J. Roberts, Pres.
Contact: Edward J. Roberts

IEG VENTURE MANAGEMENT INC.

401 N. Michigan Ave., Suite 2020
Chicago, IL 60611
312/644-0890

Year Founded: 1983
Type: Private V.C. Firm
Total Paid-In Capital: $3,000,000*

1983 Investment History:

Stage	Dollars Invested	No. of Deals
Seed/Startup	N.A.	N.A.
Later Stage	N.A.	N.A.
Follow-On	N.A.	N.A.
Buyouts	N.A.	N.A.
Total Investments	N.A.	N.A.
Average Investment	**	

Project Preferences
Geographical: Midwest
Industries: High Technology
Stages: Startup

Principals: Francis I. Blair, Pres.; Edwin R. Spina, V.P.; Marian M. Zamlynski, V.P. & Operations Mgr.
Contact: Any of Above

*Figure is over $3,000,000; would not disclose actual figure.
**Average falls between $200,000 and $500,000.

LANG CAPITAL CORP.

1301 W. 22nd St., Suite 601
Oak Brook, IL 60521
312/920-8000

Year Founded: 1981
Type: Private V.C. Firm
Total Paid-In Capital: $5,000,000

1983 Investment History:

Stage	Dollars Invested	No. of Deals
Seed/Startup	N.A.	N.A.
Later Stage	N.A.	N.A.
Follow-On	N.A.	N.A.
Buyouts	N.A.	N.A.
Total Investments	$2,300,000	2
Average Investment	$1,150,000	

Project Preferences
Geographical: Anywhere in U.S.
Industries: High Technology, Computers, Telecommunications, Information Processing, Medical Products
Stages: Seed, Startup, First

Principals: Peter D. Lang, Pres.; Jean R. Cada, Sec.
Contact: Peter D. Lang

THE LUKEN CO.

135 S. LaSalle St., Suite 711
Chicago, IL 60603
312/263-4015

Year Founded: 1982
Type: Investment Banking & Advisory Firm
Total Paid-In Capital: Not Provided

1983 Investment History:

Stage	Dollars Invested	No. of Deals
Seed/Startup	N.A.	N.A.
Later Stage	N.A.	N.A.
Follow-On	N.A.	N.A.
Buyouts	N.A.	N.A.
Total Investments	$700,000	4
Average Investment	$175,000	

Project Preferences
Geographical: Midwest
Industries: High Technology, Computers, Distribution
Stages: First, Second

Principals: Donald J. Luken, Pres.
Contact: Donald J. Luken

NORTH AMERICAN CAPITAL GROUP

7250 N. Cicero, Suite 201
Lincolnwood, IL 60646
312/982-1010

Year Founded: 1980
Type: Private V.C. Firm
Total Paid-In Capital: Not Provided

1983 Investment History:

Stage	Dollars Invested	No. of Deals
Seed/Startup	N.A.	N.A.
Later Stage	N.A.	N.A.
Follow-On	N.A.	N.A.
Buyouts	N.A.	N.A.
Total Investments	$3,000,000	3
Average Investment	$1,000,000	

Project Preferences
Geographical: Midwest
Industries: Diversified, Basic Manufacturing, Distribution, Real Estate, Medical Technology, Franchising
Stages: First, Second

Principals: Jeffrey E. Grossman, CEO; Gregory I. Kravitt, Pres.
Contact: Either

VANGUARD CAPITAL CORP.

101 Lions Dr.
Barrington, IL 60010
312/381-2330

Year Founded: 1961
Type: Private V.C. Firm
Total Paid-In Capital: $1,000,000

1983 Investment History:

Stage	Dollars Invested	No. of Deals
Seed/Startup	N.A.	N.A.
Later Stage	N.A.	N.A.
Follow-On	N.A.	N.A.
Buyouts	N.A.	N.A.
Total Investments	N.A.	N.A.
Average Investment	$100,000	

Project Preferences
Geographical: IL
Industries: Diversified
Stages: Seed

Principals: Kenneth M. Arenberg, Pres.
Contact: Kenneth M. Arenberg

Indiana

RHVM

20 N. Meridian St.
Indianapolis, IN 46204
317/635-4551

Year Founded: 1984
Type: Investment Banking Firm
Affiliation: Raffensperger Hughes & Co. Inc.
Total Paid-In Capital: Not Provided

1983 Investment History: New Fund

Project Preferences
Geographical: Midwest
Industries: Diversified
Stages: Any

Principals: Charles L. Rees, Pres.; Russell Breeden III, V.P.; Sam B. Sutphin II, Investment Off.; R. Edward Allen, Investment Off.
Contact: Any of Above

Kentucky

KENTUCKY HIGHLANDS INVESTMENT CORP.

911 North Main St.
London, KY 40741
606/864-5175

Year Founded: 1968
Type: Community Development Corp.
Total Paid-In Capital: $8,000,000

1983 Investment History:

Stage	Dollars Invested	No. of Deals
Seed/Startup	N.A.	N.A.
Later Stage	N.A.	N.A.
Follow-On	N.A.	N.A.
Buyouts	N.A.	N.A.
Total Investments	$750,000	4
Average Investment	$187,500	

Project Preferences
Geographical: KY
Industries: Manufacturing
Stages: Seed, Startup, First

Principals: Steven C. Meng, V. Chair. & CEO; Ray Moncrief, Pres.
Contact: Either

Louisiana

SOUTHERN COOPERATIVE DEVELOPMENT FUND

1006 Surrey St.
Lafayette, LA 70501
318/232-3769

Year Founded: 1969
Type: Private V.C. Firm
Total Paid-In Capital: Not Provided

1983 Investment History: Not Provided

Project Preferences
Geographical: Southeast
Industries: Diversified
Stages: Startup, Second

Principals: Rev. Albert J. McKnight, Pres.; Martial Mirabeau, Sr. V.P.; Marvin Beaulieu, Exec. V.P.
Contact: Vicki Bolden, Gen. Mgr.

TEKMAR VENTURE CAPITAL GROUP

5723 Superior Dr.
Baton Rouge, LA 70816
504/293-1560

Year Founded: 1983
Type: Private V.C. Firm
Total Paid-In Capital: $3,000,000

1983 Investment History: New Fund

Project Preferences
Geographical: Southeast
Industries: High Technology
Stages: Any

Principals: Ron Chaisson, Part.; Mac Wampold, Part.
Contact: Either

Maryland

FIRST FINANCIAL MANAGEMENT SERVICES INC.

7316 Wisconsin Ave., Suite 215
Bethesda, MD 20814
301/951-9670

Year Founded: 1981
Type: Private V.C. Firm
Total Paid-In Capital: Not Provided

1983 Investment History: Not Provided

Project Preferences
Geographical: East Coast
Industries: Diversified
Stages: Startup

Principals: Kendall W. Wilson, Pres.
Contact: Kendall W. Wilson

MERIDIAN VENTURES

21 West Rd.
Baltimore, MD 21204
301/296-1000

Affiliation: Meridian Inc.
Year Founded: 1982
Type: Corp. V.C. Subsidiary
Total Paid-In Capital: Not Provided

1983 Investment History: Stage	Dollars Invested	No. of Deals
Seed/Startup	N.A.	N.A.
Later Stage	N.A.	N.A.
Follow-On	N.A.	N.A.
Buyouts	N.A.	N.A.
Total Investments	$3,000,000	3
Average Investment	$1,000,000	

Project Preferences
Geographical: Anywhere in U.S., Middle Atlantic
Industries: Healthcare, Outdoor Power Equipment, Automotive Subcontractor Companies
Stages: Startup, Second, Later

Principals: Earl L. Linehan, Gen. Part.
Contact: Earl L. Linehan

Massachusetts

ACQUIVEST GROUP INC.

1 Newton Executive Park, Suite 204
Newton, MA 02162
617/527-5757

Year Founded: 1960
Type: Private V.C. Firm
Total Paid-In Capital: Not Provided

1983 Investment History: Not Provided

Project Preferences
Geographical: Anywhere in U.S.
Industries: Diversified, Health-Related, Biotechnology, Publishing
Stages: Later, Buyouts

Principals: S. John Loscocco, Pres.
Contact: S. John Loscocco

AMERVEST CORP.

10 Commercial Wharf W.
Boston, MA 02110
617/723-5230

Year Founded: 1979
Type: Private V.C. Firm
Total Paid-In Capital: Not Provided

1983 Investment History: Not Provided

Project Preferences
Geographical: MA
Industries: Diversified
Stages: First, Second, Later, Buyouts

Principals: Burton Stern, Pres.; Jason S. Rosenberg, Treas.
Contact: Either

THE BOSTON VENTURE FUND INC.

33 Bedford St., Suite 7
Lexington, MA 02173
617/862-0269

Affiliation: Thomas Schinkel & Associates
Year Founded: 1982
Type: Private V.C. Firm
Total Paid-In Capital: $1,000,000

1983 Investment History: Stage	Dollars Invested	No. of Deals
Seed/Startup	N.A.	N.A.
Later Stage	N.A.	N.A.
Follow-On	N.A.	N.A.
Buyouts	N.A.	N.A.
Total Investments	N.A.	3

Project Preferences
Geographical: Northeast
Industries: High Technology, Healthcare, Medical Instruments & Equipment
Stages: Seed, Startup, First

Principals: Thomas Schinkel, Pres.
Contact: Thomas Schinkel

EAST BOSTON COMMUNITY DEVELOPMENT CORP.

72 Marginal St.
East Boston, MA 02128
617/569-5590

Year Founded: 1971
Type: Community Development Corp.
Total Paid-In Capital: Not Provided

1983 Investment History: Stage	Dollars Invested	No. of Deals
Seed/Startup	N.A.	N.A.
Later Stage	N.A.	N.A.
Follow-On	N.A.	N.A.
Buyouts	N.A.	N.A.
Total Investments	$600,000	14
Average Investment	$ 42,857	

Project Preferences
Geographical: Boston
Industries: Manufacturing, Electronics
Stages: Second

Principals: Albert F. Caldarelli, Exec. Dir.; Salvatore J. Colombo, Business Dir.
Contact: Either

FANEUIL HALL ASSOCIATES

1 Boston Place
Boston, MA 02108
617/723-1955

Affiliation: Venture Founders Corp.
Year Founded: 1973
Type: Private V.C. Firm
Total Paid-In Capital: Not Provided

1983 Investment History:		
Stage	Dollars Invested	No. of Deals
Seed/Startup	$ 300,000	1
Later Stage	0	0
Follow-On	$1,000,000	7
Buyouts	0	0
Total Investments	$1,300,000	8
Average Investment	$ 162,500	

Project Preferences
Geographical: East Coast, New England
Industries: Healthcare, Biotechnology, Alternative Energy, Software
Stages: First, Second

Principals: David T. Riddiford, Gen. Part.
Contact: David T. Riddiford

FOSTER DYKEMA CABOT & CO. INC.

50 Milk St.
Boston, MA 02109
617/423-3900

Year Founded: 1964
Type: Investment Banking & Management Firm
Total Paid-In Capital: Not Provided

1983 Investment History:		
Stage	Dollars Invested	No. of Deals
Seed/Startup	N.A.	N.A.
Later Stage	N.A.	N.A.
Follow-On	N.A.	N.A.
Buyouts	N.A.	N.A.
Total Investments	$1,000,000	3
Average Investment	$ 333,333	

Project Preferences
Geographical: Northeast
Foreign: Anywhere
Industries: Diversified
Stages: Second, Later, Buyouts

Principals: Robert E. Gibbons, Pres.; Brinck Lowery, V.P.; Jere H. Dykema, Esq.
Contact: Brinck Lowery

FOWLER, ANTHONY & CO.

20 Walnut St.
Wellesley, MA 02181
617/237-4201

Year Founded: 1976
Type: Private V.C. Firm
Total Paid-In Capital: Not Provided

1983 Investment History: Not Provided

Project Preferences
Geographical: Northeast
Industries: Diversified
Stages: Seed

Principals: John A. Quagliaroli, Pres.
Contact: John A. Quagliaroli

MASSACHUSETTS TECHNOLOGY DEVELOPMENT CORP.

84 State St.
Boston, MA 02109
617/723-4920

Year Founded: 1979
Type: Independent Public Agency
Total Paid-In Capital: $7,000,000

1983 Investment History:		
Stage	Dollars Invested	No. of Deals
Seed/Startup	N.A.	N.A.
Later Stage	N.A.	N.A.
Follow-On	N.A.	N.A.
Buyouts	N.A.	N.A.
Total Investments	$2,500,000	12
Average Investment	$ 208,333	

Project Preferences
Geographical: MA
Industries: High Technology
Stages: Startup, First

Principals: John F. Hodgman, Pres.; Robert J. Crowley, V.P.
Contact: Either

REGENT FINANCIAL CORP.

10 Commercial Wharf W.
Boston, MA 02110
617/723-4820

Year Founded: 1966
Type: Private V.C. Firm
Total Paid-In Capital: Not Provided

1983 Investment History: Not Provided

Project Preferences
Geographical: New England
Industries: Diversified
Stages: Later, Buyouts

Principals: Jason S. Rosenberg, Pres.
Contact: Jason S. Rosenberg

WCCI CAPITAL CORP.

340 Main St., Suite 836
Worcester, MA 01608
617/791-3259

Affiliation: Worcester Cooperation Council Inc.
Year Founded: 1969
Type: Private V.C. Firm
Total Paid-In Capital: $200,000

1983 Investment History: No Investments Made in 1983

Project Preferences
Geographical: MA
Industries: Diversified
Stages: First, Second

Principals: Gerald Garrity, Economic Dev. Dir.
Contact: Gerald Garrity

VENTURE FIRMS UNDER $10 MIL

THE WELLESLEY VENTURE GROUP

65 William St.
Wellesley, MA 02181
617/235-9160

Year Founded: 1979
Type: Private V.C. Firm
Total Paid-In Capital: $3,200,000

1983 Investment History:

Stage	Dollars Invested	No. of Deals
Seed/Startup	N.A.	N.A.
Later Stage	N.A.	N.A.
Follow-On	N.A.	N.A.
Buyouts	N.A.	N.A.
Total Investments	$1,300,000	3
Average Investment	$ 433,333	

Project Preferences
Geographical: Northeast, Middle Atlantic
Industries: High Technology, Telecommunications, Computers, Hardware & Software, Peripherals, Electro-Optics, Photovoltaics, Robotics
Stages: Seed, Startup, First, Second

Principals: Donal B. Barrett, Gen. Part.
Contact: Donal B. Barrett

ZERO STAGE CAPITAL EQUITY FUND

156 Sixth St.
Cambridge, MA 02142
617/876-5355

Year Founded: 1982
Type: Private V.C. Firm
Total Paid-In Capital: $5,000,000

1983 Investment History:

Stage	Dollars Invested	No. of Deals
Seed/Startup	N.A.	N.A.
Later Stage	N.A.	N.A.
Follow-On	N.A.	N.A.
Buyouts	N.A.	N.A.
Total Investments	$500,000	3
Average Investment	$166,667	

Project Preferences
Geographical: Northeast
Industries: High Technology
Stages: Seed

Principals: Paul Kelley, Man. Gen. Part.; Edward B. Roberts, Gen. Part.; Gordon B. Baty, Gen. Part.
Contact: Paul Kelley

Michigan

ALAN-DEAN & CO. INC.

20276 Mack Ave.
Grosse Pointe Woods, MI 48236
313/886-6116

Year Founded: 1982
Type: Private V.C. Firm
Total Paid-In Capital: $100,000

1983 Investment History:

Stage	Dollars Invested	No. of Deals
Seed/Startup	N.A.	N.A.
Later Stage	N.A.	N.A.
Follow-On	N.A.	N.A.
Buyouts	N.A.	N.A.
Total Investments	$1,500,000	4
Average Investment	$ 375,000	

Project Preferences
Geographical: Anywhere in U.S.
Industries: Diversified
Stages: Second, Later

Principals: Marc J. Alan, Pres.; George J. Giuliani
Contact: Marc J. Alan

COMERICA CAPITAL CORP./COMERICA VENTURES CORP.

30150 Telegraph Rd., Suite 245
Birmingham, MI 48010
313/258-5800

Affiliation: Comerica Inc.
Year Founded: 1981
Type: Corp. V.C. Subsidiary
Total Paid In Capital: Not Provided

1983 Investment History:

Stage	Dollars Invested	No. of Deals
Seed/Startup	N.A.	N.A.
Later Stage	N.A.	N.A.
Follow-On	N.A.	N.A.
Buyouts	N.A.	N.A.
Total Investments	$700,000	3
Average Investment	$233,333	

Project Preferences
Geographical: Midwest
Industries: Diversified, Office & Industrial Automation, Communications, Medical
Stages: Any

Principals: John D. Berkaw, Pres.; Debra A. Ball, Asst. V.P.
Contact: Either

VENTURE FIRMS UNDER $10 MIL

HOUSTON & ASSOCIATES INC.

1626 Woodward Ave., Suite 220
Bloomfield Hills, MI 48013
313/332-1625

Affiliation: Houston Funding Inc.
Year Founded: 1971
Type: Private V.C. & Consulting Firm
Total Paid-In Capital: Not Provided

1983 Investment History: Not Provided

Project Preferences
Geographical: Midwest
Industries: Diversified
Stages: Any

Principals: E. James Houston Jr., Pres.
Contact: E. James Houston Jr.

Branch: 9 Hickory Hollow, Birmingham, MI 48010, 313/645-1860.
  Contact: E. James Houston Jr.

LINDENDALE VENTURE DEVELOPMENT INC.

2245 S. State St.
P.O. Box 1368
Ann Arbor, MI 48106
313/761-3440

Affiliation: Bottum Inc.
Year Founded: 1982
Type: Private V.C. Firm
Total Paid-In Capital: Not Provided

1983 Investment History: Not Provided

Project Preferences
Geographical: Midwest
Industries: Diversified
Stages: Startup

Principals: Roger H. Kappler, Pres.
Contact: Roger H. Kappler

Minnesota

DAIN BOSWORTH INC.

100 Dain Tower
Minneapolis, MN 55402
612/371-2711

Affiliation: Inter-Regional Financial Group
Year Founded: 1909
Type: Investment Banking Firm
Total Paid-In Capital: Not Provided

1983 Investment History: Not Provided

Project Preferences
Geographical: Northwest
Industries: High Technology, Data Processing, Medical
Stages: Second, Later, Buyouts

Principals: Douglas R. Coleman Jr., Exec. V.P. Corp. Finance; Peter A. Randall, First V.P., Corp. Finance
Contact: Either

Branches: 1225 17th St., Suite 1800, Denver, CO 80202, 303/294-7301. *Contact:* Harry T. Lewis, Sr. V.P.
999 Third Ave., Suite 1500, Seattle, WA 98104, 206/621-3112.
  Contact: James M. Stearns, V.P.

MICROTECHNOLOGY INVESTMENTS

3400 Comserv Dr.
Eagan, MN 55122
612/681-7581

Affiliation: Control Data Corp.
Year Founded: 1982
Type: Private V.C. Firm
Total Paid-In Capital: Not Provided

1983 Investment History:		
Stage	Dollars Invested	No. of Deals
Seed/Startup	N.A.	N.A.
Later Stage	N.A.	N.A.
Follow-On	N.A.	N.A.
Buyouts	N.A.	N.A.
Total Investments	$1,000,000	2
Average Investment	$ 500,000	

Project Preferences
Geographical: Anywhere in U.S., West Coast, MN
Industries: Personal Computer Software
Stages: Startup, First

Principals: M.M. Stuckey, CEO
Contact: M.M. Stuckey

Branch: 46 Red Birch Court, Danville, CA 94526, 415/838-9319.
  Contact: M.M. Stuckey

MINNESOTA SEED CAPITAL INC.

1660 S. Highway 100
Parkdale Plaza, Suite 146
Minneapolis, MN 55416
612/545-5684

Year Founded: 1980
Type: Private V.C. Firm
Total Paid-In Capital: Not Provided

1983 Investment History: Not Provided

Project Preferences
Geographical: MN
Industries: High Technology
Stages: Startup

Principals: Richard C. Gottier, Pres.; Thomas M. Neitge, V.P.
Contact: Either

PR PETERSON MANAGEMENT CO.

7301 Washington Ave. S.
Edina, MN 55435
612/941-8171

Affiliation: Electro Sensors
Year Founded: 1961
Type: Private V.C. Firm
Total Paid-In Capital: $5,000,000

1983 Investment History:		
Stage	Dollars Invested	No. of Deals
Seed/Startup	N.A.	N.A.
Later Stage	N.A.	N.A.
Follow-On	N.A.	N.A.
Buyouts	N.A.	N.A.
Total Investments	$2,000,000	20
Average Investment	$ 100,000	

Project Preferences
Geographical: MN
Industries: Electronics, Medical
Stages: Startup

Principals: P.R. Peterson, Pres.
Contact: P.R. Peterson

Missouri

DONELAN, PHELPS & CO.

7800 Bonhomme
St. Louis, MO 63105
314/863-0600

Year Founded: 1968
Type: Private V.C. Firm
Total Paid-In Capital: Not Provided

1983 Investment History: Not Provided

Project Preferences
Geographical: Midwest
Industries: Diversified
Stages: Buyouts

Principals: Thomas E. Phelps, Chair.; Mark Lincoln, V.P.
Contact: Either

FINANCO INC

323B E. McCarty
P.O. Box 252
Jefferson City, MO 65102
314/634-6186

Year Founded: 1978
Type: Consulting Firm Arranging Private Placements
Total Paid-In Capital: Not Provided

1983 Investment History: Not Provided

Project Preferences
Geographical: Midwest
Industries: Diversified
Stages: Any

Principals: Jerry Stegall, Pres.
Contact: Jerry Stegall

New Jersey

BROAD ARROW INVESTMENT CORP.

P.O. Box 2231-R
Morristown, NJ 07960
201/766-2835

Year Founded: 1970
Type: Private V.C. Firm
Total Paid-In Capital: $180,000

1983 Investment History:

Stage	Dollars Invested	No. of Deals
Seed/Startup	N.A.	N.A.
Later Stage	N.A.	N.A.
Follow-On	N.A.	N.A.
Buyouts	N.A.	N.A.
Total Investments	$96,000	3
Average Investment	$32,000	

Project Preferences
Geographical: East Coast
Industries: Diversified, Computers & Information Processing, Urban Rehabilitation
Stages: Any

Principals: Charles N. Belim, Pres.
Contact: Charles N. Belim

INVESTMENT PARTNERS OF AMERICA

732 W. 8th St.
Plainfield, NJ 07060
201/561-3622

Affiliation: Product Partners
Year Founded: 1969
Type: Private V.C. Firm
Total Paid-In Capital: $5,000,000

1983 Investment History:

Stage	Dollars Invested	No. of Deals
Seed/Startup	N.A.	N.A.
Later Stage	N.A.	N.A.
Follow-On	N.A.	N.A.
Buyouts	N.A.	N.A.
Total Investments	$1,700,000	3
Average Investment	$ 566,667	

Project Preferences
Geographical: Northeast
Industries: Publishing, Consumer Products & Services, Water & Mineral Exploration, Defense Electronics, Beverage Products
Stages: Second, Later

Principals: Frank J. Abella Jr., Man. Part.; Donald S. Bab, Gen. Part.
Contact: Frank J. Abella Jr.

JOHNSON & JOHNSON DEVELOPMENT CORP.

1 Johnson & Johnson Plaza
New Brunswick, NJ 08933
201/524-6407

Affiliation: Johnson & Johnson
Year Founded: 1973
Type: Corp. V.C. Subsidiary
Total Paid-In Capital: Not Provided

1983 Investment History: Not Provided

Project Preferences
Geographical: Anywhere in U.S.
Industries: Healthcare-Related Technology
Stages: Seed, Startup, First, Second

Principals: Charles M. Anderson, Pres.; Harold R. Werner Jr., Linda A. Cahill, Dir. of New Business Dev.
Contact: Any of Above

MAIN CAPITAL INVESTMENT CORP.

426 Essex St., Suite J
Hackensack, NJ 07601
201/489-2080

Year Founded: 1964
Type: Private V.C. Firm
Total Paid-In Capital: Not Provided

1983 Investment History: Not Provided

Project Preferences
Geographical: Anywhere in U.S.
Industries: Diversified, TV & Film Production, Real Estate
Stages: Any

Principals: Sam Klotz, Pres. & Part.
Contact: Sam Klotz

VENRAY CAPITAL CORP.

981 Route 22
P.O. Box 6817
Bridgewater, NJ 08807
201/725-1020

Year Founded: 1982
Type: Private V.C. Firm
Total Paid-In Capital: $5,000,000

1983 Investment History: Stage	Dollars Invested	No. of Deals
Seed/Startup	N.A.	N.A.
Later Stage	N.A.	N.A.
Follow-On	N.A.	N.A.
Buyouts	N.A.	N.A.
Total Investments	$1,500,000	6
Average Investment	$ 250,000	

Project Preferences
Geographical: Anywhere in U.S.
Industries: Diversified
Stages: Later

Principals: Raymond J. Skiptunis, Pres.
Contact: Raymond J. Skiptunis

New York

ALEPH NULL CORP.

1 Old Country Rd., Box 25
Carle Place, NY 11514
516/742-9527

Year Founded: 1979
Type: Private V.C. Firm
Total Paid-In Capital: $2,500,000

1983 Investment History: Stage	Dollars Invested	No. of Deals
Seed/Startup	N.A.	N.A.
Later Stage	N.A.	N.A.
Follow-On	N.A.	N.A.
Buyouts	N.A.	N.A.
Total Investments	$175,000	4
Average Investment	$ 43,750	

Project Preferences
Geographical: NY, NJ, CT
Industries: High Technology, Electronics, Semiconductors, Computers
Stages: Seed, Startup, First

Principals: Herman Fialkov, Pres.; Richard E. Kopelman, V.P.; Jay M. Fialkov, V.P.
Contact: Any of Above

AMERICAN CORPORATE SERVICES

515 Madison Ave.
New York, NY 10022
212/688-9691

Year Founded: 1958
Type: Private V.C. Firm
Total Paid-In Capital: $5,000,000

1983 Investment History: Stage	Dollars Invested	No. of Deals
Seed/Startup	N.A.	N.A.
Later Stage	N.A.	N.A.
Follow-On	N.A.	N.A.
Buyouts	N.A.	N.A.
Total Investments	$1,500,000	5
Average Investment	$ 300,000	

Project Preferences
Geographical: Anywhere in U.S.
Foreign: U.K.
Industries: High Technology
Stages: Any

Principals: Sanford R. Simon, Pres.; Keith G. Langworthy, V.P.; Michael R. Simon, V.P.
Contact: Sanford R. Simon, Michael R. Simon

ASHWOOD RESOURCES INTERNATIONAL INC.

230 W. 230th St.
Riverdale, NY 10463
212/289-5900

Year Founded: 1976
Type: Private V.C. Firm
Total Paid-In Capital: $9,000,000

1983 Investment History: Not Provided

Project Preferences
Geographical: Anywhere in U.S.
Foreign: Canada
Industries: Oil & Gas, Computer Technology, Medical Technology, Entertainment, Communications
Stages: Startup, Later

Principals: William Ashwood, Pres.; Bud Kavanaugh, V.P.; Peter Segall, Technology Engineer
Contact: William Ashwood

BERNHARD ASSOCIATES

1211 Ave. of the Americas, Suite 2905
New York, NY 10036
212/921-7755

Year Founded: 1983
Type: Private V.C. Firm
Total Paid-In Capital: $3,500,000

1983 Investment History: Stage	Dollars Invested	No. of Deals
Seed/Startup	N.A.	N.A.
Later Stage	N.A.	N.A.
Follow-On	N.A.	N.A.
Buyouts	N.A.	N.A.
Total Investments	N.A.	N.A.
Average Investment	$150,000	

Project Preferences
Geographical: Anywhere in U.S.
Industries: Diversified
Stages: Any

Principals: Robert A. Bernhard, Man. Part.; David N. Nutt, Part.; Fergus Reid III, Part.; Jonathan P. Altman, Part.; Donald Greene, Part.
Contact: David N. Nutt

ARTHUR BIER & CO. INC.

110 E. 59th St., 31st Floor
New York, NY 10022
212/355-7733

Year Founded: 1961
Type: Private V.C. Firm
Total Paid-In Capital: Not Provided

1983 Investment History: Not Provided

Project Preferences
Geographical: Anywhere in U.S.
Industries: Diversified
Stages: Later

Principals: Robert L. Bier, Pres.; Joan S. Bier, Sec.; James H. Mathias, Dir.
Contact: Robert L. Bier

BRAINTREE MANAGEMENT LTD.

59 S. Greeley, Penthouse 7
Chappaqua, NY 10514
914/238-5221

Year Founded: 1976
Type: Private V.C. Firm
Total Paid-In Capital: Not Provided

1983 Investment History:

Stage	Dollars Invested	No. of Deals
Seed/Startup	N.A.	N.A.
Later Stage	N.A.	N.A.
Follow-On	N.A.	N.A.
Buyouts	N.A.	N.A.
Total Investments	$100,000	1

Project Preferences
Geographical: Northeast
Industries: Diversified, Medical Electronics, Plumbing, Reinsurance
Stages: Later

Principals: G.C. Newlin, Pres.
Contact: G.C. Newlin

BUFFALO CAPITAL CORP.

Mt. Morris Rd.
Geneseo, NY 14454
716/243-4310

Affiliation: J.H. Hickman & Co.; The Hickman Corp.
Year Founded: 1983
Type: Merchant Banking Firm
Total Paid-In Capital: $1,500,000

1983 Investment History:

Stage	Dollars Invested	No. of Deals
Seed/Startup	N.A.	N.A.
Later Stage	N.A.	N.A.
Follow-On	N.A.	N.A.
Buyouts	N.A.	N.A.
Total Investments	$2,200,000	6
Average Investment	$ 366,667	

Project Preferences
Geographical: Northeast, S. FL
Foreign: U.K., France, Germany, Latin America
Industries: Diversified
Stages: Seed, Startup, Later, Buyouts

Principals: J.H. Hickman, Chair.
Contact: J.H. Hickman

CHARTERHOUSE GROUP INTERNATIONAL INC.

535 Madison Ave.
New York, NY 10022
212/421-3125

Affiliation: Charterhouse J. Rothschild PLC (England)
Year Founded: 1973
Type: Corp. V.C. Subsidiary
Total Paid-In Capital: Not Provided

1983 Investment History: Not Provided

Project Preferences
Geographical: Anywhere in U.S.
Industries: Diversified
Stages: Later, Buyouts

Principals: Merril M. Halpern, Chair.; Jerome Katz, Pres., CEO; Patricia Riley Merrick, Sr. V.P.
Contact: Patricia Riley Merrick

COLEMAN VENTURES INC.

5909 Northern Blvd.
East Norwich, NY 11732
516/626-3642

Year Founded: 1965
Type: Private V.C. Firm
Total Paid-In Capital: $5,000,000

1983 Investment History:

Stage	Dollars Invested	No. of Deals
Seed/Startup	N.A.	N.A.
Later Stage	N.A.	N.A.
Follow-On	N.A.	N.A.
Buyouts	N.A.	N.A.
Total Investments	$2,500,000	3
Average Investment	$ 833,333	

Project Preferences
Geographical: Anywhere in U.S.
Industries: High Technology, Electronics
Stages: Seed, Startup, First, Buyouts

Principals: Gregory S. Coleman, Pres.; Roger V. Coleman, V.P.
Contact: Gregory S. Coleman

WJP CURLEY

630 Fifth Ave., Suite 2920
New York, NY 10111
212/582-1232

Year Founded: 1978
Type: Private V.C. Firm
Total Paid-In Capital: Not Provided

1983 Investment History:

Stage	Dollars Invested	No. of Deals
Seed/Startup	N.A.	N.A.
Later Stage	N.A.	N.A.
Follow-On	N.A.	N.A.
Buyouts	N.A.	N.A.
Total Investments	$1,800,000	3
Average Investment	$ 600,000	

Project Preferences
Geographical: Anywhere in U.S.
Foreign: Europe, U.K., Ireland
Industries: Energy & Natural Resources, Process Control, Entertainment
Stages: Startup, First

Principals: Walter J.P. Curley
Contact: Walter J.P. Curley

ELF TECHNOLOGIES INC.

103 E. 37th St.
New York, NY 10016
212/625-2555

Affiliation: Inovelf S.A.
Year Founded: 1981
Type: Corp. V.C. Subsidiary
Total Paid-In Capital: Not Provided

1983 Investment History: Not Provided

Project Preferences
Geographical: Anywhere in U.S.
Industries: Energy, Oil-Related, Chemicals, Pharmaceuticals,
    Biotechnology, Food & Agriculture
Stages: Any

Principals: Francois Nicoly, V.P.
Contact: Francois Nicoly

Branch: 7 rue Nélaton, F 75015 Paris, France, 33/1-571-7458.
    Contact: Michel Ronc, Pres. & CEO

FUNDEX CAPITAL CORP.

525 Northern Blvd.
Great Neck, NY 11021
516/466-8550

Affiliation: U.S. Capital Corp.
Year Founded: 1978
Type: Private V.C. Firm
Total Paid-In Capital: $1,000,000

1983 Investment History: Not Provided

Project Preferences
Geographical: Northeast
Industries: Diversified
Stages: First

Principals: Howard F. Summer, Pres.; Martin Albert, V.P.
Contact: Howard F. Summer

G/L CAPITAL CORP.

1414 Ave. of the Americas
New York, NY 10019
212/759-4544

Year Founded: 1981
Type: Corp. V.C. Subsidiary
Total Paid-In Capital: Not Provided

1983 Investment History: Not Provided

Project Preferences
Geographical: Middle Atlantic, Northeast
Industries: Diversified
Stages: Later

Principals: Victor F. Germack, Pres.
Contact: Victor F. Germack

HARRISON ENTERPRISES INC.

5 Norma Lane
Dix Hills, NY 11746
516/673-8914

Year Founded: 1982
Type: Private V.C. Firm
Total Paid-In Capital: Not Provided

1983 Investment History: Not Provided

Project Preferences
Geographical: Anywhere in U.S.
Industries: High Technology, Computer, Medical,
    Telecommunications, Software
Stages: Any

Principals: Shelley A. Harrison, Pres.; Susanne Harrison, V.P.
Contact: Either

HELFER BROUGHTON INC.

4 World Trade Center, Suite 7178
New York, NY 10048
212/938-1350

Affiliation: Helfer Commodities Corp.
Year Founded: 1969
Type: Corp. V.C. Subsidiary
Total Paid-In Capital: $3,000,000

1983 Investment History: Stage	Dollars Invested	No. of Deals
Seed/Startup	N.A.	N.A.
Later Stage	N.A.	N.A.
Follow-On	N.A.	N.A.
Buyouts	N.A.	N.A.
Total Investments	$2,000,000	7
Average Investment	$ 285,714	

Project Preferences
Geographical: Anywhere in U.S.
Industries: High Technology, Medical, Food Distribution
Stages: First, Second

Principals: Joseph Leftoff, Prin.; Richard Helfer, Prin.
Contact: Joseph Leftoff

INTERCOASTAL CAPITAL CORP.

380 Madison Ave.
New York, NY 10017
212/986-0482

Year Founded: 1949
Type: Private V.C. Firm
Total Paid-In Capital: Not Provided

1983 Investment History: Not Provided

Project Preferences
Geographical: East Coast
Industries: Diversified
Stages: Second, Later

Principals: Herbert Krasnow, Pres.
Contact: Herbert Krasnow

ITC CAPITAL CORP.

1290 Ave. of the Americas
New York, NY 10104
212/408-4800

Affiliation: Irving Bank Corp.
Year Founded: 1976
Type: Corp. V.C. Subsidiary
Total Paid-In Capital: Not Provided

1983 Investment History: Not Provided

Project Preferences
Geographical: Anywhere in U.S.
Industries: Diversified
Stages: Buyouts

Principals: J. Andrew McWethy, Exec. V.P. & Gen. Mgr.; Barry A. Solomon, V.P.; Kathleen M. Snyder, Asst. Sec.
Contact: Kathleen M. Snyder

KG CAPITAL CORP.

3100 Monroe Ave.
Rochester, NY 14618
716/586-6015

Year Founded: 1981
Type: Private V.C. Firm
Total Paid-In Capital: $2,000,000

1983 Investment History:

Stage	Dollars Invested	No. of Deals
Seed/Startup	N.A.	N.A.
Later Stage	N.A.	N.A.
Follow-On	N.A.	N.A.
Buyouts	N.A.	N.A.
Total Investments	$2,000,000	12
Average Investment	$ 166,667	

Project Preferences
Geographical: NY
Industries: High Technology, Computer-Related, Semiconductors
Stages: Seed, Startup, First

Principals: Bernard Kozel, Pres.; Dr. Frederick A. Schwertz, V.P
Contact: Either

LAWRENCE VENTURE ASSOCIATES

1 New York Plaza, 30th Floor
New York, NY 10004
212/908-9500

Year Founded: 1984
Type: Private V.C. Firm
Total Paid-In Capital: New Fund

1983 Investment History: New Fund

Project Preferences
Geographical: Eastern U.S.
Industries: High Technology, Medical Services & Technologies, Computer-Related, Electronics
Stages: Seed, Startup, First

Principals: Larry J. Lawrence, Man. Gen. Part.; Richard W. Smith, Gen. Part.
Contact: Either

LEPERCQ, DE NEUFLIZE & CO.

345 Park Ave.
New York, NY 10154
212/702-0205

Year Founded: 1948
Type: Investment Banking Firm
Total Paid-In Capital: Not Provided

1983 Investment History: No Investments Made in 1983

Project Preferences
Geographical: Anywhere in U.S.
Foreign: Europe
Industries: High Technology
Stages: Any

Principals: Marcel Fournier, V.P.
Contact: Marcel Fournier

MIDLAND CAPITAL CORP.

950 Third Ave.
New York, NY 10022
212/753-7790

Year Founded: 1961
Type: Business Development Co.
Total Paid-In Capital: $24,000,000*

1983 Investment History:

Stage	Dollars Invested	No. of Deals
Seed/Startup	0	0
Later Stage	0	0
Follow-On	$360,000	1
Buyouts	0	0
Total Investments	$360,000	1

Project Preferences
Geographical: Anywhere in U.S.
Industries: Precision Manufacturing, Precious Metals, Energy
Stages: Buyouts

Principals: Robert B. Machinist, Man. Dir.; Michael R. Stanfield, Man. Dir.; Edwin B. Hathaway, Asst. V.P., Investment Dept.
Contact: Any of Above

*Approximate figure.

NORTHWOOD VENTURES

420 Madison Ave., 13th Floor
New York, NY 10017
212/935-4679

Year Founded: 1983
Type: Private V.C. Firm
Total Paid-In Capital: Not Provided

1983 Investment History:

Stage	Dollars Invested	No. of Deals
Seed/Startup	N.A.	N.A.
Later Stage	N.A.	N.A.
Follow-On	N.A.	N.A.
Buyouts	N.A.	N.A.
Total Investments	$2,000,000	10
Average Investment	$ 200,000	

Project Preferences
Geographical: Anywhere in U.S.
Industries: Diversified, High Technology
Stages: Any

Principals: Peter G. Schiff, Gen. Part.
Contact: Peter G. Schiff

QUESTEC ENTERPRISES INC.

328 Main St.
Huntington, NY 11743
516/351-1222

Affiliation: Kollmorgen Corp.
Year Founded: 1983
Type: Corp. V.C. Subsidiary
Total Paid-In Capital: $8,000,000

1983 Investment History:

Stage	Dollars Invested	No. of Deals
Seed/Startup	N.A.	N.A.
Later Stage	N.A.	N.A.
Follow-On	N.A.	N.A.
Buyouts	N.A.	N.A.
Total Investments	$300,000	1

Project Preferences
Geographical: Anywhere in U.S.
Foreign: U.K.
Industries: High Technology
Stages: Seed, Startup, First

Principals: William P. Sharpe, Pres.; Charles Lassen, V.P.
Contact: Either

RAIN MILL GROUP INC.

90 Broad St.
New York, NY 10004
212/483-9162

Year Founded: 1976
Type: Private Service Co.
Total Paid-In Capital: Not Provided

1983 Investment History: Not Provided

Project Preferences
Geographical: Anywhere in U.S.
Foreign: Anywhere
Industries: High Technology
Stages: Seed, Startup

Principals: Richard A. Cawley, Pres.; Robin George, V.P.; Jack Rubin, V.P.
Contact: Diane Lupi, Resource Coordinator

RAND CAPITAL CORP.

1300 Rand Bldg.
Buffalo, NY 14203
716/853-0802

Year Founded: 1969
Type: Publicly Traded Investment Firm
Total Paid-In Capital: $5,000,000

1983 Investment History:

Stage	Dollars Invested	No. of Deals
Seed/Startup	N.A.	N.A.
Later Stage	N.A.	N.A.
Follow-On	N.A.	N.A.
Buyouts	N.A.	N.A.
Total Investments	$1,500,000	5
Average Investment	$ 300,000	

Project Preferences
Geographical: Northeast
Industries: Diversified, Communications, Cable Applications
Stages: Any

Principals: George F. Rand III, Chair.; Peter Gilbert, V. Chair.; Donald A. Ross, Pres.; Keith B. Wiley, V.P., Thomas G. Hunt, V.P.
Contact: George F. Rand III, Donald A. Ross, Keith B. Wiley

REGULUS INTERNATIONAL CAPITAL CO. INC.

10 Rockefeller Plaza
New York, NY 10020
212/582-7715

Year Founded: 1975
Type: Private V.C. Firm
Total Paid-In Capital: Not Provided

1983 Investment History:

Stage	Dollars Invested	No. of Deals
Seed/Startup	0	0
Later Stage	$1,000,000	1
Follow-On	0	0
Buyouts	$2,000,000	1
Total Investments	$3,000,000	2
Average Investment	$1,500,000	

Project Preferences
Geographical: Anywhere in U.S.
Foreign: Anywhere
Industries: Printing & Converting Paper, Packaging, Publishing, Building Materials, Chemicals & Coatings
Stages: Any

Principals: Lee H. Miller, Pres.
Contact: Lee H. Miller

SALOMON BROTHERS INC.

1 New York Plaza
New York, NY 10004
212/747-7080

Year Founded: 1906
Type: Investment Banking Firm
Total Paid-In Capital: Not Provided

1983 Investment History: Not Provided

Project Preferences
Geographical: Anywhere in U.S.
Industries: Communications, Electronics, Computers, Information Processing
Stages: Later, Buyouts

Principals: Denis A. Bovin, Man. Dir.
Contact: Denis A. Bovin

MARTIN SIMPSON & CO. INC.

150 Broadway, Suite 1606
New York, NY 10038
212/406-5200

Year Founded: 1973
Type: Public Co.
Total Paid-In Capital: Not Provided

1983 Investment History: Not Provided

Project Preferences
Geographical: Anywhere in U.S.
Foreign: Western Europe, Australia, Hong Kong
Industries: High Technology
Stages: Startup

Principals: Martin Simpson, Pres.; Robert S. Anderson, V.P.
Contact: Either

ALLAN E. SKORA ASSOCIATES

49 W. 12th St., Executive Suite
New York, NY 10011
212/691-9895

Affiliation: Entertainment Funding Group
Year Founded: 1976
Type: Private V.C. Firm
Total Paid-In Capital: Not Provided

1983 Investment History:

Stage	Dollars Invested	No. of Deals
Seed/Startup	$ 850,000	3
Later Stage	$1,700,000	4
Follow-On	$ 500,000	1
Buyouts	$ 250,000	1
Total Investments	$3,300,000	9
Average Investment	$ 366,667	

Project Preferences
Geographical: Anywhere in U.S.
Foreign: Europe, South America, Far & Middle East
Industries: Medical, Computer-Related, Manufacturing, Alternative Energy, Film & Video
Stages: Any

Principals: Allan E. Skora, Pres.
Contact: Alan E. Skora

CHARLES DE THAN GROUP

51 E. 67th St.
New York, NY 10021
212/988-5108

Year Founded: 1970
Type: Private Brokerage & Acquisitions Firm
Total Paid-In Capital: Not Provided

1983 Investment History: Not Provided

Project Preferences
Geographical: Anywhere in U.S.
Foreign: Canada, Australia
Industries: Diversified
Stages: Buyouts

Principals: Charles de Than, Gen. Part
Contact: Charles de Than

TINICUM INC.

885 Second Ave.
New York, NY 10017
212/832-3883

Year Founded: 1974
Type: Private Firm
Total Paid-In Capital: Not Provided

1983 Investment History:

Stage	Dollars Invested	No. of Deals
Seed/Startup	N.A.	N.A.
Later Stage	N.A.	N.A.
Follow-On	N.A.	N.A.
Buyouts	N.A.	N.A.
Total Investments	N.A.	6
Average Investment	$1,000,000	

Project Preferences
Geographical: Northeast, PR
Foreign: Canada, U.K.
Industries: Diversified
Stages: Later, Buyouts

Principals: Eric Ruttenberg, Exec. V.P.
Contact: Eric Ruttenberg

VENCON MANAGEMENT INC.

301 West 53rd St.
New York, NY 10019
212/581-8787

Year Founded: 1972
Type: Private V.C. Firm
Total Paid-In Capital: Not Provided

1983 Investment History: Not Provided

Project Preferences
Geographical: Anywhere in U.S.
Industries: High Technology, Chemicals, Biotechnology
Stages: Startup, Buyouts

Principals: I. Barash, Pres.
Contact: I. Barash

VENTURE CAPITAL FUND OF AMERICA INC.

509 Madison Ave.
New York, NY 10022
212/838-5577

Year Founded: 1983
Type: Private V.C. Firm
Total Paid-In Capital: New Fund

1983 Investment History: New Fund

Project Preferences
Geographical: Anywhere in U.S.
Industries: Diversified, Communications, Medical, Computer-Related, Energy & Natural Resources, Electronic & Industrial Equipment
Stages: Startup, First, Second

Principals: Dayton T. Carr, Part.; Thomas P. Murphy, Part.; M. John Sterba Jr., Part.
Contact: Any of Above

WINTHROP VENTURES

74 Trinity Place, Suite 1100
New York, NY 10006
212/422-0100

Affiliation: Winthrop, Brown & Co. Inc.
Year Founded: 1972
Type: Corp. V.C. Subsidiary; Private Investment Banking Firm
Total Paid-In Capital: Not Provided

1983 Investment History: Not Provided

Project Preferences
Geographical: Anywhere in U.S.
Foreign: Anywhere
Industries: Diversified
Stages: Any

Principals: Cyrus Brown, Pres.; Thomas Wood, V.P.
Contact: Either

North Carolina

RUDDICK INVESTMENT CO.

2290 First Union Plaza
Charlotte, NC 28282
704/333-7144

Affiliation: Ruddick Corp.
Year Founded: 1938
Type: Corp. V.C. Subsidiary
Total Paid-In Capital: $3,000,000

1983 Investment History:

Stage	Dollars Invested	No. of Deals
Seed/Startup	$ 400,000	1
Later Stage	$ 400,000	1
Follow-On	$1,300,000	5
Buyouts	$ 500,000	1
Total Investments	$2,600,000	8
Average Investment	$ 325,000	

Project Preferences
Geographical: Anywhere in U.S.
Foreign: Malaysia, Hong Kong
Industries: Diversified
Stages: Second, Later

Principals: Herman B. McManaway, Pres.; William R. Starnes, V.P.
Contact: Either

Ohio

SHV INVESTMENT FUND

300 Pike St.
Cincinnati, OH 45202
513/621-4014

Affiliation: SHV (The Netherlands)
Year Founded: 1970
Type: Corp. V.C. Subsidiary
Total Paid-In Capital: Not Provided

1983 Investment History:

Stage	Dollars Invested	No. of Deals
Seed/Startup	N.A.	N.A.
Later Stage	N.A.	N.A.
Follow-On	N.A.	N.A.
Buyouts	N.A.	N.A.
Total Investments	$3,000,000	4
Average Investment	$ 750,000	

Project Preferences
Geographical: Anywhere in U.S.
Foreign: The Netherlands
Industries: Oil & Gas, Retail & Wholesale Distribution, Scrap Metal, Food
Stages: Second, Later, Buyouts

Principals: J.D. Zankarnebeek, Pres.
Contact: J.D. Zankarnebeek

SI SOKOL & ASSOCIATES

50 W. Broad St.
Columbus, OH 43215
614/228-2800

Year Founded: 1964
Type: Mergers & Acquisitions Broker
Total Paid-In Capital: Not Provided

1983 Investment History:

Stage	Dollars Invested	No. of Deals
Seed/Startup	0	0
Later Stage	0	0
Follow-On	0	0
Buyouts	$3,000,000	3
Total Investments	$3,000,000	3
Average Investment	$1,000,000	

Project Preferences
Geographical: Anywhere in U.S., OH, PA, IN, KY, WV
Industries: Manufacturing
Stages: Buyouts

Principals: Si Sokol, Pres.; Mohammed Kurmally, V.P.
Contact: Either

Oregon

ORIANS INVESTMENT CO.

529 SW Third Ave., Suite 600
Portland, OR 97204
503/224-7885

Year Founded: 1979
Type: Investment Banking Firm
Total Paid-In Capital: Not Provided

1983 Investment History:

Stage	Dollars Invested	No. of Deals
Seed/Startup	N.A.	N.A.
Later Stage	N.A.	N.A.
Follow-On	N.A.	N.A.
Buyouts	N.A.	N.A.
Total Investments	$3,000,000	5
Average Investment	$ 600,000	

Project Preferences
Geographical: Northwest
Industries: High Technology, Software, Home Fitness, Genetic Engineering
Stages: Seed, First

Principals: Robert J. Orians, Pres.; Gregory A. Kimsey, V.P.
Contact: Either

Pennsylvania

ANCHOR LEASING CORP.

7 Wood St.
Pittsburgh, PA 15222
412/765-0690

Year Founded: 1962
Type: Private V.C. Firm
Total Paid-In Capital: Not Provided

1983 Investment History:

Stage	Dollars Invested	No. of Deals
Seed/Startup	N.A.	N.A.
Later Stage	N.A.	N.A.
Follow-On	N.A.	N.A.
Buyouts	N.A.	N.A.
Total Investments	$500,000	3
Average Investment	$166,667	

Project Preferences
Geographical: PA
Industries: Diversified
Stages: Any

Principals: James H. Rich, Chair.; Charles G. Williams Jr., Pres.
Contact: Either

CAPITAL CORP. OF AMERICA

225 S. 15th St., Suite 920
Philadelphia, PA 19102
215/732-1666; 215/732-3415

Year Founded: 1962
Type: Public Corp.
Total Paid-In Capital: $1,300,000

1983 Investment History:

Stage	Dollars Invested	No. of Deals
Seed/Startup	N.A.	N.A.
Later Stage	N.A.	N.A.
Follow-On	N.A.	N.A.
Buyouts	N.A.	N.A.
Total Investments	$550,000	3
Average Investment	$183,333	

Project Preferences
Geographical: Anywhere in U.S.
Industries: Diversified
Stages: Second, Later, Buyouts

Principals: Martin M. Newman, Pres.
Contact: Martin M. Newman

FOSTIN CAPITAL CORP.

681 Andersen Dr.
Pittsburgh, PA 15220
412/928-8900

Affiliation: Foster Industries Inc.
Year Founded: 1982
Type: Merchant Banking Firm
Total Paid-In Capital: Not Provided

1983 Investment History:

Stage	Dollars Invested	No. of Deals
Seed/Startup	N.A.	N.A.
Later Stage	N.A.	N.A.
Follow-On	N.A.	N.A.
Buyouts	N.A.	N.A.
Total Investments	$3,000,000	10
Average Investment	$ 300,000	

Project Preferences
Geographical: Anywhere in U.S.
Industries: High Technology, Computer-Related, Communications, Medical, Electronics
Stages: Later, Buyouts

Principals: William F. Woods, Pres.; Thomas M. Levine, Exec. V.P.
Contact: Either

HOWARD & CO.

1528 Walnut St., Suite 2020
Philadelphia, PA 19102
215/735-2815

Year Founded: 1972
Type: Investment Banking Firm
Total Paid-In Capital: Not Provided

1983 Investment History: Not Provided

Project Preferences
Geographical: Anywhere in U.S.
Foreign: Western Europe
Industries: Diversified
Stages: Any

Principals: Graeme K. Howard Jr., Part.; Joel S. Lawson III, Part.; T. Patrick Hurley Jr., Part.; Michael A. Cuneo, Venture Assoc.
Contact: Michael A. Cuneo,

PENNSYLVANIA GROWTH INVESTMENT CORP.

1000 RIDC Plaza, Suite 311
Pittsburgh, PA 15238
412/963-9339

Affiliation: Pennsylvania Financial Development Corp.
Year Founded: 1961
Type: Private V.C. Firm
Total Paid-In Capital: Not Provided

1983 Investment History: Not Provided

Project Preferences
Geographical: Midwest, East Coast, Southeast
Industries: Diversified
Stages: Second, Later

Principals: William L. Mosenson, Pres.; Mary G. Dell Exec. V.P.
Contact: Either

VENTURE FIRMS UNDER $10 MIL

PHILADELPHIA CITYWIDE DEVELOPMENT CORP.

Land Title Bldg., Suite 2032
100 S. Broad St.
Philadelphia, PA 19110
215/561-6600

Year Founded: 1977
Type: Economic Development Corp.
Total Paid-In Capital: $3,000,000

1983 Investment History:

Stage	Dollars Invested	No. of Deals
Seed/Startup	$ 423,700	15
Later Stage	$ 595,028	19
Follow-On	0	0
Buyouts	0	0
Total Investments	$1,018,728	34
Average Investment	$ 29,963	

Project Preferences
Geographical: Philadelphia
Industries: Diversified
Stages: Startup, First

Principals: Dean Rosencrantz, Exec. V.P.
Contact: Dean Rosencrantz

PNC VENTURE CAPITAL GROUP

Fifth Ave. & Wood St.
Pittsburgh, PA 15222
412/355-2245

Affiliation: PNC Financial Corp.
Year Founded: 1982
Type: Corp. V.C. Subsidiary
Total Paid-In Capital: $7,500,000

1983 Investment History:

Stage	Dollars Invested	No. of Deals
Seed/Startup	N.A.	N.A.
Later Stage	N.A.	N.A.
Follow-On	N.A.	N.A.
Buyouts	N.A.	N.A.
Total Investments	$1,600,000	4
Average Investment	$ 400,000	

Project Preferences
Geographical: Anywhere in U.S., PA, Middle Atlantic
Industries: Diversified
Stages: Second, Later, Buyouts

Principals: David M. Hillman, Exec. V.P.; Jeffrey H. Schutz, V.P.
Contact: Either

ROBINSON VENTURE PARTNERS

6507 Wilkins Ave.
Pittsburgh, PA 15217
412/661-1200

Year Founded: 1982
Type: Private V.C. Firm
Total Paid-In Capital: $2,000,000

1983 Investment History:

Stage	Dollars Invested	No. of Deals
Seed/Startup	N.A.	N.A.
Later Stage	N.A.	N.A.
Follow-On	N.A.	N.A.
Buyouts	N.A.	N.A.
Total Investments	$525,000	4
Average Investment	$131,250	

Project Preferences
Geographical: Anywhere in U.S., PA, OH, WV
Industries: Computer-Related, Electronic Components, Medical, Communications, Industrial Equipment, Robotics
Stages: Startup, First, Second

Principals: Donald Robinson, Gen. Part.; Steve Robinson, Gen. Part.
Contact: Steve Robinson

SOUTHEASTERN PENNSYLVANIA DEVELOPMENT FUND

3 Penn Center Plaza, Suite 604
Philadelphia, PA 19102
215/568-4677

Year Founded: 1964
Type: State Business Development Corp.
Total Paid-In Capital: Not Provided

1983 Investment History:

Stage	Dollars Invested	No. of Deals
Seed/Startup	N.A.	N.A.
Later Stage	N.A.	N.A.
Follow-On	N.A.	N.A.
Buyouts	N.A.	N.A.
Total Investments	$1,500,000	8
Average Investment	$ 187,500	

Project Preferences
Geographical: PA
Industries: Manufacturing
Stages: First, Second, Later, Buyouts

Principals: Paul A. Mitchell, Pres.
Contact: Paul A. Mitchell

WRK WORKS INC.

2 Davis Ave.
Frazer, PA 19355
215/296-4150

Year Founded: 1978
Type: Private V.C. Firm
Total Paid-In Capital: Not Provided

1983 Investment History:

Stage	Dollars Invested	No. of Deals
Seed/Startup	N.A.	N.A.
Later Stage	N.A.	N.A.
Follow-On	N.A.	N.A.
Buyouts	N.A.	N.A.
Total Investments	$2,000,000	2
Average Investment	$1,000,000	

Project Preferences
Geographical: Anywhere in U.S.
Industries: Diversified, Medical Instruments
Stages: Startup, First

Principals: W.R. Knepshield, Pres.
Contact: W.R. Knepshield

Rhode Island

FLEET GROWTH RESOURCES INC.

111 Westminster St.
Providence, RI 02903
401/278-5597

Affiliation: Fleet Financial Group
Year Founded: 1982
Type: Corp. V.C. Subsidiary
Total Paid-In Capital: Not Provided

1983 Investment History:

Stage	Dollars Invested	No. of Deals
Seed/Startup	0	0
Later Stage	0	0
Follow-On	0	0
Buyouts	$1,200,000	1
Total Investments	$1,200,000	1

Project Preferences
Geographical: Northeast, Middle Atlantic, South, Southeast, Midwest, Southwest
Industries: High Technology, Communications, Software
Stages: Startup, First, Second, Later, Buyouts

Principals: Robert M. Van Degna, Pres.
Contact: Robert M. Van Degna

Branch: 60 State St., Boston, MA 02109, 617/367-6700.
  Contact: Carlton B. Klein, V.P.

MAXWELL CAPITAL CORP.

P.O. Box 813
Providence, RI 02901
401/739-3850

Year Founded: 1979
Type: Private V.C. Firm
Total Paid-In Capital: Not Provided

1983 Investment History:

Stage	Dollars Invested	No. of Deals
Seed/Startup	N.A.	N.A.
Later Stage	N.A.	N.A.
Follow-On	N.A.	N.A.
Buyouts	N.A.	N.A.
Total Investments	$400,000	1

Project Preferences
Geographical: Anywhere in U.S.
Industries: Computer-Related
Stages: Later

Principals: Dana H. Gaebe, Pres.; Robert E. Radican, V.P.
Contact: Robert E. Radican

Tennessee

CAPITAL SERVICES & RESOURCES INC.

5159 Wheelis Dr., Suite 104
Memphis, TN 38117
901/761-2156

Year Founded: 1975
Type: Private V.C. Firm
Total Paid-In Capital: $500,000

1983 Investment History: Not Provided

Project Preferences
Geographical: East Coast, Southeast, Midwest
Industries: Manufacturing, Distribution
Stages: Second, Later

Principals: Charles Y. Bancroft, Treas.
Contact: Charles Y. Bancroft

DAVIS ASSOCIATES CONSULTANTS

P.O. Box 415
Alcoa, TN 37701
615/982-5641

Year Founded: 1969
Type: Private V.C. Firm
Total Paid-In Capital: $2,000,000

1983 Investment History:

Stage	Dollars Invested	No. of Deals
Seed/Startup	N.A.	N.A.
Later Stage	N.A.	N.A.
Follow-On	N.A.	N.A.
Buyouts	N.A.	N.A.
Total Investments	$400,000	30
Average Investment	$ 13,333	

Project Preferences
Geographical: Anywhere in U.S., Southeast
Industries: Diversified
Stages: Seed, Startup, First

Principals: Roger W. Davis, Co-Owner; Matthew S. Davis, Co-Owner
Contact: Either

TENNESSEE EQUITY CAPITAL FUND

1102 Stonewall Jackson
Nashville, TN 37220
615/373-4502

Year Founded: 1978
Type: Private V.C. Firm
Total Paid-In Capital: $2,000,000

1983 Investment History: Not Provided

Project Preferences
Geographical: Anywhere in U.S.
Foreign: Caribbean
Industries: Diversified
Stages: Startup, First, Second, Later, Buyouts

Principals: Walter S. Cohen, CEO
Contact: Walter S. Cohen

Texas

BUSINESS DEVELOPMENT PARTNERS

10805 Pecan Park Rd.
Austin, TX 78750
512/258-1977

Year Founded: 1980
Type: Private V.C. Firm
Total Paid-In Capital: Not Provided

1983 Investment History: Stage	Dollars Invested	No. of Deals
Seed/Startup	N.A.	N.A.
Later Stage	N.A.	N.A.
Follow-On	N.A.	N.A.
Buyouts	N.A.	N.A.
Total Investments	$3,000,000	4
Average Investment	$ 750,000	

Project Preferences
Geographical: Southwest, TX
Industries: High Technology, Computers, Communications, Biotechnology
Stages: Seed, Startup, First

Principals: Robert L. Brueck, Gen. Part.; A.G.W. Biddle, Asst.
Contact: Either

Branch: 6133 Highgate Lane, Dallas, TX 75214. *Contact:* Michael E. Faherty, Gen. Part.

CURTIN & CO.

2050 Houston Natural Gas Bldg.
Houston, TX 77002
713/658-9806

Year Founded: 1974
Type: Investment Banking Firm Acting as Intermediary in Venture Deals
Total Paid-In Capital: Not Provided

1983 Investment History: Not Provided

Project Preferences
Geographical: TX, OK, LA
Industries: Diversified
Stages: Startup, First, Second

Principals: John. D. Curtin Jr., Pres.; Stewart Cureton Jr., V.P.; Charles Armbrust III, V.P.
Contact: Any of Above

DS VENTURES INC.

P.O. Box 152300
Irving, TX 75015-2300
214/659-7205

Affiliation: Diamond Shamrock Corp.
Year Founded: 1981
Type: Corp. V.C. Subsidiary
Total Paid-In Capital: Not Provided

1983 Investment History: Stage	Dollars Invested	No. of Deals
Seed/Startup	0	0
Later Stage	0	0
Follow-On	$3,500,000	6
Buyouts	0	0
Total Investments	$3,500,000	6
Average Investment	$ 583,333	

Project Preferences
Geographical: Anywhere in U.S.
Foreign: U.K., Japan
Industries: High Technology, Chemical-Related
Stages: Seed, Startup, First, Second

Principals: Martin G. White, Pres.; Frank Briden, V.P.; Charles J. Hora, V.P.
Contact: Any of Above

FSA GROUP

301 W. Sixth St.
Austin, TX 78701
512/472-7171

Year Founded: 1979
Type: Investment Banking Firm
Total Paid-In Capital: $5,000,000

1983 Investment History: Not Provided

Project Preferences
Geographical: Southwest, TX
Industries: Diversified
Stages: First, Second

Principals: H.A. Abshier Jr., Chair.; Bradley A. Fowler, Pres.; G. Felder Thornhill, Exec. V.P.; William Ward Greenwood, Sr. V.P.
Contact: Any of Above

GREAT AMERICAN CAPITAL INVESTORS INC.

1006 Holiday
Wichita Falls, TX 76301
817/322-5554

Year Founded: 1978
Type: Private V.C. Firm
Total Paid-In Capital: $300,000

1983 Investment History: No Investments Made in 1983

Project Preferences
Geographical: TX
Industries: Diversified
Stages: Second

Principals: William A. Wylie, Chair.; Doyle Davis, Sr. V.P.
Contact: Either

HICKS & HAAS

750 N. St. Paul, Suite 500
Dallas, TX 75201
214/969-0250

Year Founded: 1984
Type: Merchant Banking Partnership*
Total Paid-In Capital: Not Provided

1983 Investment History: New Fund

Project Preferences
Geographical: Southwest
Industries: Diversified
Stages: Later, Buyouts

Principals: Robert B. Haas, Man. Gen. Part.; Thomas O. Hicks, Man. Gen. Part.
Contact: Either

*Acts as investment partner for managing general partners and limited partnerships.

IDANTA PARTNERS

201 Main St., Suite 3200
Ft. Worth, TX 76102
817/338-2020
Year Founded: 1971
Type: Private V.C. Firm
Total Paid-In Capital: $8,000,000

1983 Investment History:

Stage	Dollars Invested	No. of Deals
Seed/Startup	$1,000,000	1
Later Stage	0	0
Follow-On	$1,000,000	1
Buyouts	0	0
Total Investments	$2,000,000	2
Average Investment	$1,000,000	

Project Preferences
Geographical: Anywhere in U.S.
Industries: Diversified
Stages: Seed, Startup, First, Second

Principals: David J. Dunn, Man. Part.; Dev Purkayastha, Gen. Part.; Steven B. Dunn, Assoc.
Contact: Any of Above

ITEC CAPITAL CORP.

5151 San Felipe, Suite 1420
Houston, TX 77056
713/960-8400

Year Founded: 1956
Type: Public Co.
Total Paid-In Capital: Not Provided

1983 Investment History:

Stage	Dollars Invested	No. of Deals
Seed/Startup	$2,000,000	6
Later Stage	$2,000,000	5
Follow-On	0	0
Buyouts	0	0
Total Investments	$4,000,000	11
Average Investment	$ 363,636	

Project Preferences
Geographical: Anywhere in U.S.
Foreign: Europe, Hong Kong
Industries: Diversified, Medical Technology, Electronics, Basic Manufacturing
Stages: Seed, Later

Principals: Franklin C. Fisher Jr.
Contact: Franklin C. Fisher Jr.

MSI CAPITAL CORP.

650 People's Bank Bldg.
6510 Abrams Rd.
Dallas, TX 75231
214/341-1553
Year Founded: 1976
Type: Private V.C. Firm
Total Paid-In Capital: $500,000

1983 Investment History:

Stage	Dollars Invested	No. of Deals
Seed/Startup	N.A.	N.A.
Later Stage	N.A.	N.A.
Follow-On	N.A.	N.A.
Buyouts	N.A.	N.A.
Total Investments	$250,000	3
Average Investment	$ 83,333	

Project Preferences
Geographical: TX
Industries: Communications, Computer-Related, Energy & Natural Resources, Transportation
Stages: Startup, First

Principals: Nick Stanfield, Pres.; Richard Wirzbick, Investment Analyst
Contact: Either

PORCARI, FEARNOW & ASSOCIATES INC.

1900 W. Loop S., Suite 901
Houston, TX 77207
713/840-7500

Year Founded: 1978
Type: Brokerage Firm
Total Paid-In Capital: Not Provided

1983 Investment History:

Stage	Dollars Invested	No. of Deals
Seed/Startup	N.A.	N.A.
Later Stage	N.A.	N.A.
Follow-On	N.A.	N.A.
Buyouts	N.A.	N.A.
Total Investments	$2,500,000	3
Average Investment	$ 833,333	

Project Preferences
Geographical: Southeast, Southwest
Foreign: Europe, Central America, Hong Kong, Japan
Industries: Diversified
Stages: Startup, First

Principals: Michael T. Fearnow, Chair.; Arthur J. Porcari, Pres.; Alex Budzinski, V.P.
Contact: Any of Above

SCHNITZIUS & CO. LTD.

3410 Republic Bank Center
700 Louisiana St.
Houston, TX 77002
713/222-2170
Year Founded: 1984
Type: Investment Banking Firm
Total Paid-In Capital: New Fund

1983 Investment History: New Fund

Project Preferences
Geographical: Southwest, TX
Industries: Diversified
Stages: Any

Principals: Thomas H. Schnitzius, Gen. Part.
Contact: Thomas H. Schnitzius

VENTURE FIRMS UNDER $10 MIL

TELPAR INC.

P.O. Box 796
Addison, TX 75001
214/233-6631

Year Founded: 1969
Type: Private V.C. Firm
Total Paid-In Capital: Not Provided

1983 Investment History:

Stage	Dollars Invested	No. of Deals
Seed/Startup	$3,500,000	4
Later Stage	0	0
Follow-On	0	0
Buyouts	0	0
Total Investments	$3,500,000	4
Average Investment	$ 875,000	

Project Preferences
Geographical: Anywhere in U.S.
Industries: High Technology, Electronics, Healthcare & Medical
Stages: Startups, Buyouts

Principals: Richard Hanschen, Chair.; Bill Konrad, Pres.
Contact: Either

TEXAS CAPITAL VENTURE INVESTMENTS CORP.

333 Clay St., Suite 2100
Houston, TX 77002
713/658-9961

Affiliation: TeleCom Corp.
Year Founded: 1958
Type: Corp. V.C. Subsidiary
Total Paid-In Capital: Not Provided

1983 Investment History:

Stage	Dollars Invested	No. of Deals
Seed/Startup	N.A.	N.A.
Later Stage	N.A.	N.A.
Follow-On	N.A.	N.A.
Buyouts	N.A.	N.A.
Total Investments	$936,000	5
Average Investment	$187,200	

Project Preferences
Geographical: Southwest
Industries: Diversified
Stages: Second, Later, Buyouts

Principals: W. Grogan Lord, Pres. & Chair.; Larry W. Schumann, Exec. V.P.; Larry Marek, V.P.; David G. Franklin, V.P.; Tom Beecroft, Investment Mgr.
Contact: Larry W. Schumann, David G. Franklin

WEST CENTRAL CAPITAL CORP.

440 Northlake Center, Suite 206
Dallas, TX 75238
214/348-3969

Year Founded: 1964
Type: Private V.C. Firm
Total Paid-In Capital: $350,000

1983 Investment History:

Stage	Dollars Invested	No. of Deals
Seed/Startup	N.A.	N.A.
Later Stage	N.A.	N.A.
Follow-On	N.A.	N.A.
Buyouts	N.A.	N.A.
Total Investments	N.A.	1
Average Investment	$50,000	

Project Preferences
Geographical: TX
Industries: Diversified Non-High Technology, Small Manufacturing
Stages: Second, Later

Principals: Howard W. Jacob, Pres.; Barbara C. Evans, V.P.
Contact: Either

Vermont

NORTHERN COMMUNITY INVESTMENT CORP.

20 Main St.
St. Johnsbury, VT 05819
802/748-5101

Year Founded: 1975
Type: Community Development Corp.
Total Paid-In Capital: Not Provided

1983 Investment History: Not Provided

Project Preferences
Geographical: VT, NH
Industries: Basic Manufacturing
Stages: Second

Principals: Stephen C. McConnell, Pres.
Contact: Stephen C. McConnell

Virginia

HILLCREST GROUP

9 S. 12th St.
Richmond, VA 23219
804/643-7358

Year Founded: 1984
Type: Management Group
Affiliation: UV Capital & James River Capital Associates
Total Paid-In Capital: Not Provided

1983 Investment History: New Fund

Principals: A. Hugh Ewing, III, Gen. Part.; James B. Farinholt Jr., Gen. Part.; John B. Funkhouser, Gen. Part.
Contact: Any of Above

Branch: 1666 K St., NW, Washington, DC 20006, 202/872-6054.
Contact: J. Roderick Heller III, Gen. Part.

RESEARCH INDUSTRIES INC.

123 N. Pitt St.
Alexandria, VA 22314
703/548-3667

Year Founded: 1968
Type: Private V.C. Firm
Total Paid-In Capital: $2,000,000

1983 Investment History:

Stage	Dollars Invested	No. of Deals
Seed/Startup	N.A.	N.A.
Later Stage	N.A.	N.A.
Follow-On	N.A.	N.A.
Buyouts	N.A.	N.A.
Total Investments	$600,000	

Project Preferences
Geographical: Anywhere in U.S.
Industries: High Technology
Stages: Later, Buyouts

Principals: John H. Grover, V.P.
Contact: John H. Grover

Washington

VENTURE SUM

N. 618 Sullivan, Suite 25
Veradale, WA 99037
509/926-3720

Year Founded: 1981
Type: Private V.C. Firm
Total Paid-In Capital: Not Provided

1983 Investment History:

Stage	Dollars Invested	No. of Deals
Seed/Startup	N.A.	N.A.
Later Stage	N.A.	N.A.
Follow-On	N.A.	N.A.
Buyouts	N.A.	N.A.
Total Investments	$1,000,000	5
Average Investment	$ 200,000	

Project Preferences
Geographical: Northwest, CO, CA
Industries: Diversified, Technology-Based
Stages: First, Second, Later

Principals: A.T. Zirkle, Pres.
Contact: A.T. Zirkle

Wisconsin

IMPACT SEVEN INC.

Industrial Rd.
Turtle Lake, WI 54889
715/986-4171

Year Founded: 1970
Type: Community Development Corp.
Total Paid-In Capital: $4,000,000

1983 Investment History:

Stage	Dollars Invested	No. of Deals
Seed/Startup	N.A.	N.A.
Later Stage	N.A.	N.A.
Follow-On	N.A.	N.A.
Buyouts	N.A.	N.A.
Total Investments	$225,000	2
Average Investment	$112,500	

Project Preferences
Geographical: WI
Industries: Diversified
Stages: Any

Principals: William Bay, Pres.; Dileep Rao
Contact: Either

Wyoming

WYOMING INDUSTRIAL DEVELOPMENT CORP.

P.O. Box 612
145 S. Durbin, Suite 201
Casper, WY 82602
307/234-5351

Year Founded: 1967
Type: Private V.C. Firm
Total Paid-In Capital: $7,200,000

1983 Investment History:

Stage	Dollars Invested	No. of Deals
Seed/Startup	$ 125,000	1
Later Stage	$ 550,000	1
Follow-On	$ 20,000	1
Buyouts	$ 958,350	4
Total Investments	$1,653,350	7
Average Investment	$ 236,193	

Project Preferences
Geographical: WY
Industries: Diversified
Stages: Startup

Principals: Larry McDonald, Pres.; Robert Kemper, Exec. V.P.; Luella Brown, Asst. V.P.
Contact: Any of Above

VENTURE FIRMS UNDER $10 MIL

DOMESTIC LISTINGS

SMALL BUSINESS INVESTMENT COMPANIES: $3 MILLION AND UP

Alabama

FIRST SMALL BUSINESS INVESTMENT CO. OF ALABAMA

16 Midtown Park E.
Mobile, AL 36606
205/476-0700

Affiliation: First Alabama Capital Corp.
Year Founded: 1977
Total Private Funds: $3,000,000
Total SBA Leverage: $6,000,000

1983 Investment History:
Total Investments: $1,300,000
Deals: 24
Average Investment: $54,167

Project Preferences
Geographical: Mobile, Baldwin County
Industries: Diversified
Stages: Any

Principals: David C. Delaney, Pres.
Contact: David C. Delaney

Arkansas

SMALL BUSINESS INVESTMENT CAPITAL INC.

12103 Interstate 30
Little Rock, AR 72203
501/455-2234

Year Founded: 1976
Total Private Funds: $1,100,000
Total SBA Leverage: $3,300,000

1983 Investment History:
Total Investments: $1,000,000
Deals: 15
Average Investment: $66,667

Project Preferences
Geographical: AR, Northern LA
Industries: Food Distribution, Supermarkets
Stages: Seed, Startup, First, Second, Later

Principals: Hubert Fugett, Controller
Contact: Hubert Fugett

California

BANKAMERICA VENTURES INC.

555 California St., 42nd Floor
San Francisco, CA 94104
415/622-2230

Affiliation: Bank of America
Year Founded: 1959
Total Private Funds: $12,500,000
Total SBA Leverage: 0

1983 Investment History:
Total Investments: $1,400,000
Deals: 2
Average Investment: $700,000

Project Preferences
Geographical: Anywhere in U.S., West Coast
Industries: Diversified
Stages: Second, Later

Principals: Robert W. Gibson, Pres.; Philip J. Gioia, V.P.; Patrick J. Topolski, V.P.; Roger C. Drufva Jr., V.P.; Tina Moretti, Assoc. V.P.
Contact: Any of Above

BAY VENTURE GROUP

1 Embarcadero Ctr., Suite 3303
San Francisco, CA 94111
415/989-7680

Year Founded: 1981
Total Private Funds: $1,500,000
Total SBA Leverage: $2,500,000

1983 Investment History:
Total Investments: $500,000
Deals: 3
Average Investment: $166,667

Project Preferences
Geographical: San Francisco Bay Area
Industries: High Technology
Stages: Seed, Startup

Principals: William R. Chandler, Gen. Part.; Charles Slutzkin, Gen. Part.
Contact: William R. Chandler

BRENTWOOD CAPITAL CORP.

11661 San Vicente Blvd., Suite 707
Los Angeles, CA 90049
213/826-6581

Affiliation: Brentwood Associates II
Year Founded: 1972
Total Private Funds: $6,000,000
Total SBA Leverage: $11,500,000

1983 Investment History:
Total Investments: $2,900,000
Deals: 121
Average Investment: $138,095

Project Preferences
Geographical: Anywhere in U.S., West Coast
Industries: High Technology
Stages: Seed, Startup, First

Principals: George M. Crandell, Gen. Part.; B. Kipling Hagopian, Gen. Part.; Timothy M. Pennington, Gen. Part.; Frederick J. Warren, Gen. Part.; Roger C. Davisson, Gen. Part.; Michael J. Fourticq, Gen. Part.
Contact: G. Bradford Jones; Brian P. McDermott

CALIFORNIA CAPITAL INVESTORS

11812 San Vicente Blvd.
Los Angeles, CA 90049
213/820-7222

Year Founded: 1980
Total Private Funds: $1,200,000
Total SBA Leverage: $2,500,000

1983 Investment History:
Total Investments: $1,800,000
Deals: 15
Average Investment: $120,000

Project Preferences
Geographical: West Coast, Southwest
Industries: Diversified
Stages: Second

Principals: Arthur H. Bernstein, Gen. Part.; Harold A. Haytin, Gen. Part.
Contact: Either

FIRST INTERSTATE CAPITAL CORP.

515 S. Figueroa St.
Los Angeles, CA 90071
213/622-1922

Affiliation: First Interstate Bank Corp.
Year Founded: 1978
Total Private Funds: $9,000,000
Total SBA Leverage: $4,800,000

1983 Investment History:
Total Investments: $13,900,000
Deals: 25
Average Investment: $534,615

Project Preferences
Geographical: West Coast
Industries: High Technology, Semiconductors, Electronics,
    Software, Medical
Stages: Seed, Startup, First, Second

Principals: David B. Jones, Pres.; John Funk, V.P.; Kenneth M.
    Deemer, V.P.
Contact: Any of Above

Branch: 1300 SW Fifth St., Portland, OR 97201, 503/223-4334.
    Contact: Wayne Kingsley, Exec. V.P.

FIRST SBIC OF CALIFORNIA

4000 MacArthur Blvd., Suite 950
Newport Beach, CA 92660
714/754-4780

Affiliation: Security Pacific National Bank
Year Founded: 1960
Total Private Funds: $25,000,000
Total SBA Leverage: 0

1983 Investment History:
Total Investments: $13,000,000
Deals: 11
Average Investment: $1,181,818

Project Preferences
Geographical: Anywhere in U.S.
Industries: Diversified, Manufacturing, Chain Retailing,
    Communications, Healthcare Management
Stages: Any

Principals: Timothy Hay, Pres.; John Geer, Man. Part.; Brian Jones,
    Man. Part.; James B. McElwee, Man. Part.; Gregory Forrest, Exec.
    V.P.; Alvin Brizzard, V.P.; Everett Cox, Investment Off.; James
    McGoodwin, Investment Off.; Dimitri Bosky, Investment Off.
Contact: Brian Jones, James B. McElwee, John Geer

Branches: 333 S. Hope St., Los Angeles, CA 90071, 213/613-5215.
    Contact: John Padgett, Man. Part.; Tony Stevens, Man. Part.
50 Milk St., 15th Floor, Boston, MA 02109, 617/542-7601. *Contact:*
    Michael Cronin, Man. Part.
P.O. Box 512, Washington, PA 15301, 412/223-0707. *Contact:*
    Daniel Dye, Man. Part.

MARWIT CAPITAL CORP.

180 Newport Ctr. Dr.
Newport Beach, CA 92660
714/640-6234

Year Founded: 1962
Total Private Funds: $1,200,000
Total SBA Leverage: $1,500,000

1983 Investment History:
Total Investments: $1,000,000
Deals: 8
Average Investment: $125,000

Project Preferences
Geographical: CA
Industries: Diversified
Stages: Second, Later, Buyouts

Principals: Martin W. Witte, Pres.
Contact: Martin W. Witte

MERRILL, PICKARD, ANDERSON & EYRE

2 Palo Alto Square, Suite 425
Palo Alto, CA 94306
415/856-8880

Year Founded: 1980
Total Private Funds: $38,000,000
Total SBA Leverage: 0

1983 Investment History:
Total Investments: $8,000,000
Deals: 12
Average Investment: $666,667

Project Preferences
Geographical: Anywhere in U.S.
Industries: High Technology, Computers, Computer Peripherals,
    Telecommunications
Stages: Seed, Startup, First, Second

Principals: Steven L. Merrill, Man. Part.; James C. Anderson, Gen.
    Part.; Chris A. Eyre, Gen. Part.; W. Jeff Pickard, Gen. Part.;
    Stephen E. Coit, Gen. Part.
Contact: W. Jeff Pickard

NEW WEST VENTURES

4350 Executive Dr., Suite 206
San Diego, CA 92121
619/457-0722

Year Founded: 1981
Total Private Funds: $2,000,000
Total SBA Leverage: $3,000,000

1983 Investment History:
Total Investments: $1,400,000
Deals: 10
Average Investment: $140,000

Project Preferences
Geographical: West Coast
Industries: Diversified
Stages: Second, Later, Buyouts

Principals: Timothy P. Haidinger, Pres.
Contact: Timothy P. Haidinger

SBICs
$3 MIL AND UP

129

PCF VENTURE CAPITAL CORP.

Alpha Pacific Bldg.
3420 E. Third Ave., Suite 200
Foster City, CA 94404
415/571-5411

Affiliation: Pacific Capital Fund Inc.
Year Founded: 1983
Total Private Funds: $4,500,000
Total SBA Leverage: $4,500,000

1983 Investment History:
Total Investments: $1,500,000
Deals: 5
Average Investment: $300,000

Project Preferences
Geographical: West Coast
Industries: Diversified, Telecommunications, Financial Services, Software
Stages: Seed, Startup, First, Second

Principals: Benedicto V. Yujuico, Chair.; Jose Luis Cervero, Pres.
Contact: Either

SAN JOAQUIN CAPITAL CORP.

P.O. Box 2538
Bakersfield, CA 93303
805/323-7581

Year Founded: 1962
Total Private Funds: $837,330
Total SBA Leverage: $2,500,000

1983 Investment History:
Total Investments: $541,000
Deals: 8
Average Investment: $67,625

Project Preferences
Geographical: CA
Industries: Diversified
Stages: Second, Later

Principals: Jimmie Icardo, Chair.; Chester W. Troudy, Pres.
Contact: Chester W. Troudy

SAN JOSE SBIC INC.

100 Park Center Plaza, Suite 427
San Jose, CA 95113
408/293-7708

Affiliation: San Jose Capital Partners
Year Founded: 1977
Total Private Funds: $1,400,000
Total SBA Leverage: $1,800,000

1983 Investment History:
Total Investments: $1,300,000
Deals: 9
Average Investment: $144,444

Project Preferences
Geographical: West Coast
Industries: High Technology, Computers, Telecommunications, Electronics, Medical
Stages: Seed, Startup, First

Principals: Robert T. Murphy, Pres.; Daniel Hochman, Dir.
Contact: Either

SEAPORT VENTURES INC.

770 B St., Suite 420
San Diego, CA 92101
619/232-4069

Year Founded: 1982
Total Private Funds: $1,400,000
Total SBA Leverage: 0

1983 Investment History:
Total Investments: $1,000,000
Deals: 9
Average Investment: $111,111

Project Preferences
Geographical: Anywhere in U.S.
Industries: Diversified
Stages: Second

Principals: Michael Stolper, Pres.; Carole Rhoades, V.P.
Contact: Either

UNION VENTURE CORP.

445 S. Figueroa St.
Los Angeles, CA 90071
213/236-6287

Year Founded: 1967
Total Private Funds: $6,500,000
Total SBA Leverage: 0

1983 Investment History:
Total Investments: $4,500,000
Deals: 15
Average Investment: $300,000

Project Preferences
Geographical: Anywhere in U.S.
Industries: Diversified, Information Technologies, Medical, Communications, Specialty Materials, Electronics, Semiconductors
Stages: Any

Principals: Brent T. Rider, Pres.; Lee McCracken, Investment Off.; Jeffrey A. Watts, Sr. Investment Off.; John W. Ulrich, V.P.; Chris L. Rafferty, V.P.
Contact: Any of Above

WALDEN CAPITAL CORP.

303 Sacramento St.
San Francisco, CA 94111
415/391-7225

Affiliation: Walden Venture Capital Corp.
Year Founded: 1974
Total Private Funds: Not Provided
Total SBA Leverage: $2,500,000

1983 Investment History:
Total Investments: $1,000,000

Project Preferences
Geographical: West Coast
Industries: High Technology
Stages: Seed, Startup, First

Principals: Arthur S. Berliner, Gen. Part.; George S. Sarlo, Gen. Part.; Lip-Bu Tan, Gen. Part.
Contact: Any of Above

Branch: 1001 Logan Bldg., Seattle, WA 98101, 206/623-6550.
Contact: Ted Wight, Gen. Part.

SBICs $3 MIL AND UP

WELLS FARGO EQUITY CORP.

1 Embarcadero Ctr.
San Francisco, CA 94111
415/396-3291

Affiliation: Wells Fargo Bank
Year Founded: 1982
Total Private Funds: $5,000,000
Total SBA Leverage: 0

1983 Investment History:
Total Investments: Not Provided
Deals: Not Provided
Average Investment: $1,000,000

Project Preferences
Geographical: Anywhere in U.S.
Industries: Diversified
Stages: Later, Buyouts

Principals: Michael Park, Sr. V.P.
Contact: Michael Park

Connecticut

ASSET CAPITAL & MANAGEMENT CORP.

608 Ferry Blvd.
Stratford, CT 06497
203/375-0299

Affiliation: Asset Capital and Management Co.
Year Founded: 1960
Total Private Funds: $1,000,000
Total SBA Leverage: $13,000,000

1983 Investment History:
Total Investments: $650,000
Deals: 7
Average Investment: $92,857

Project Preferences
Geographical: Anywhere in U.S., Northeast
Industries: Manufacturing
Stages: Second, Later

Principals: Ralph Smith, Pres.; Edward L. Marcus, Sec.
Contact: Ralph Smith

CAPITAL IMPACT

234 Church St., Suite 804
New Haven, CT 06510
203/384-5670

Affiliation: CityTrust Bank Corp.
Year Founded: 1984
Total Private Funds: $3,000,000
Total SBA Leverage: 0

1983 Investment History: New Fund

Project Preferences
Geographical: Northeast
Industries: Diversified Non-High Technology
Stages: Second, Later

Principals: Kevin S. Tierney, Pres.; John Cuticelli, V.P.; Leonard Vignola, Consultant
Contact: Any of Above

CAPITAL RESOURCE CO. OF CONNECTICUT

699 Bloomfield Ave.
Bloomfield, CT 06002
203/243-1114

Year Founded: 1977
Total Private Funds: $934,365
Total SBA Leverage: $2,700,000

1983 Investment History:
Total Investments: $2,600,000
Deals: 33
Average Investment: $78,788

Project Preferences
Geographical: Northeast
Industries: High Technology, Taxicabs
Stages: Second, Later

Principals: I. Martin Fierberg, Gen. Part.; Janice M. Romanowski, Gen. Part.
Contact: Either

THE FIRST CONNECTICUT SMALL BUSINESS INVESTMENT CO.

177 State St.
Bridgeport, CT 06604
203/366-4726

Affiliation: The First Connecticut Capital Corp.
Year Founded: 1960
Total Private Funds: $9,300,000
Total SBA Leverage: $21,900,000

1983 Investment History:
Total Investments: $13,000,000
Deals: 102
Average Investment: $127,451

Project Preferences
Geographical: Northeast, NJ, FL
Industries: Diversified
Stages: Second

Principals: James Breiner, Chair.; David Engelson, Pres.; Lawrence Yurdin, V.P.; Stephen Breiner, V.P.
Contact: Any of Above

Branch: 680 Fifth Ave., New York, NY 10019. 212/541-6222. *Contact:* Sidney Kessler

REGIONAL FINANCIAL ENTERPRISES

51 Pine St.
New Canaan, CT 06840
203/966-2800

Affiliation: Regional Financial Enterprises Inc.
Year Founded: 1979
Total Private Funds: Not Provided
Total SBA Leverage: Not Provided

1983 Investment History:
Total Investments: $4,500,000
Deals: 11
Average Investment: $409,091

Project Preferences
Geographical: Anywhere in U.S.
Industries: High Technology, Computers, Healthcare, Communications
Stages: Any

Principals: Robert M. Williams, Part.; George E. Thomassy III, Part.; Howard C. Landis, Part.; Robert Sparacino, Part.; John V. Titsworth, Part.
Contact: Any of Above

District of Columbia

ALLIED INVESTMENT CORP.

1625 I Street, NW, Suite 603
Washington, DC 20006
202/331-1112

Affiliation: Allied Capital Corp.
Year Founded: 1959
Total Private Funds: $4,300,000
Total SBA Leverage: $8,200,000

1983 Investment History:
Total Investments: $3,200,000
Deals: 25
Average Investment: $128,000

Project Preferences
Geographical: Anywhere in U.S.
Industries: Diversified
Stages: Second, Later, Buyouts

Principals: David J. Gladstone, Pres.; George C. Williams, Chair.; Brooks Brown, Sr. V.P.; Joan Barra, Asst. V.P.
Contact: Joan Barra

Branch: 1 Financial Plaza, Suite 1614, Ft. Lauderdale, FL 33394, 305/763-8484.

COLUMBIA VENTURES INC.

1818 L St., NW
Washington, DC 20036
202/659-0033

Year Founded: 1971
Total Private Funds: $6,000,000
Total SBA Leverage: $3,000,000

1983 Investment History: Not Provided

Project Preferences
Geographical: East Coast
Industries: Diversified
Stages: Later, Buyouts

Principals: Richard Whitney, Pres.
Contact: Richard Whitney

Branch: 809 State St., Jackson, MS 39201, 601/354-1453. *Contact:* Maurice Reed, Chair.

Florida

FIRST AMERICAN INVESTMENT CORP.

2701 S. Bayshore Dr., Suite 402
Coconut Grove, FL 33133
305/854-6840

Affiliation: HMG Property Investors Inc.
Year Founded: 1961
Total Private Funds: $4,000,000
Total SBA Leverage: $4,100,000

1983 Investment History:
Total Investments: $1,300,000
Deals: 3
Average Investment: $433,333

Project Preferences
Geographical: Southeast
Industries: Real Estate, High Technology
Stages: Startup, Second

Principals: Maurice Wiener, Chair.; Joseph N. Hardin Jr., Pres.
Contact: Joseph N. Hardin Jr.

GOLD COAST CAPITAL CORP.

3550 Biscayne Blvd., Suite 601
Miami, FL 33137
305/576-2012

Year Founded: 1959
Total Private Funds: $860,000
Total SBA Leverage: $2,600,000

1983 Investment History: Not Provided

Project Preferences
Geographical: FL
Industries: Diversified, Electrical Engineering
Stages: Startup, First, Second, Later

Principals: William I. Gold, Pres.
Contact: William I. Gold

SMALL BUSINESS ASSISTANCE CORP. OF PANAMA CITY

2612 W. 15th St.
Panama City, FL 32401
904/785-9577

Year Founded: 1963
Total Private Funds: $3,600,000
Total SBA Leverage: $12,000,000

1983 Investment History:
Total Investments: $1,000,000
Deals: 5
Average Investment: $200,000

Project Preferences
Geographical: FL
Industries: Diversified, Hotels
Stages: Seed, Startup, First, Later

Principals: Charles S. Smith, Pres.; H.N. Tillman, Corp. Sec.
Contact: Either

SOUTHEAST VENTURE CAPITAL INC.

1 Southeast Financial Ctr.
Miami, FL 33131
305/375-6470

Affiliation: Southeast Banking Corp.
Year Founded: 1968
Total Private Funds: $3,000,000
Total SBA Leverage: $4,000,000

1983 Investment History:
Total Investments: $3,600,000
Deals: 14
Average Investment: $257,143

Project Preferences
Geographical: Anywhere in U.S., Southeast
Industries: Diversified
Stages: Seed, Startup, First

Principals: C.L. Hofmann, Pres.; John H. Lamothe, V.P.; James R. Fitzsimons Jr., V.P.; Anne Cario, Treas.
Contact: C.L. Hofmann

WESTERN FINANCIAL CAPITAL CORP.

1380 Miami Gardens Dr., NE
N. Miami Beach, FL 33179
305/949-5900

Affiliation: Pro-Med Capital
Year Founded: 1979
Total Private Funds: $2,600,000
Total SBA Leverage: $4,200,000

1983 Investment History:
Total Investments: $3,000,000
Deals: 62
Average Investment: $48,387

Project Preferences
Geographical: Anywhere in U.S.
Industries: Healthcare
Stages: Second, Later

Principals: Frederic Rosemore, Pres.; Lance Rosemore, V.P.
Contact: Either

Illinois

CONTINENTAL ILLINOIS VENTURE CORP.

231 S. LaSalle St.
Chicago, IL 60697
312/828-8021

Affiliation: Continental Illinois Corp.
Year Founded: 1970
Total Private Funds: Not Provided
Total SBA Leverage: 0

1983 Investment History:
Total Investments: $13,800,000
Deals: 23
Average Investment: $600,000

Project Preferences
Geographical: Anywhere in U.S.
Industries: Diversified
Stages: Seed, Startup, First, Second, Later

Principals: John L. Hines, Pres.; William Putze, Sr. V.P.; Scott E. Smith, 2nd V.P.; Samuel L. Freitag, 2nd V.P.; Seth L. Pierrepont, V.P.; Judith Bultman Meyer, V.P.
Contact: Seth L. Pierrepont, Scott E. Smith

FIRST CHICAGO VENTURE CAPITAL GROUP

1 First National Plaza
Chicago, IL 60670
312/732-5400

Affiliation: First Chicago Corp.
Year Founded: 1961
Total Private Funds: $23,500,000
Total SBA Leverage: $3,600,000

1983 Investment History:
Total Investments: $32,000,000
Deals: 33
Average Investment: $969,697

Project Preferences
Geographical: Anywhere in U.S.
Industries: High Technology, Communications, Healthcare, Computer Software
Stages: Any

Principals: John A. Canning Jr., Pres.; Kent P. Dauten, V.P.; Paul R. Wood, V.P.
Contact: Any of Above

Branch: 133 Federal St., Boston, MA 02110, 617/542-9185. *Contact:* Kevin McCafferty, V.P.

FRONTENAC CAPITAL CORP.

208 S. LaSalle St., Suite 1900
Chicago, IL 60604
312/368-0044

Affiliation: Frontenac Venture Co.
Year Founded: 1976
Total Private Funds: $6,400,000
Total SBA Leverage: $25,600,000

1983 Investment History: Not Provided

Project Preferences
Geographical: Midwest, Southwest
Industries: Medical Products & Services, Computer Products & Services
Stages: Buyouts

Principals: Martin J. Koldyke, Gen. Part.; David A.R. Dullum, Gen. Part.; Rodney L. Goldstein, Gen. Part.
Contact: Any of Above

MESIROW CAPITAL CORP.

135 S. LaSalle St.
Chicago, IL 60603
312/443-5757

Year Founded: 1982
Total Private Funds: Not Provided
Total SBA Leverage: Not Provided

1983 Investment History:
Total Investments: $2,300,000
Deals: 9
Average Investment: $255,556

Project Preferences
Geographical: Anywhere in U.S.
Industries: Diversified
Stages: Seed, Startup, First, Second, Later

Principals: James Tyree, Exec. V.P.
Contact: James Tyree

Indiana

HERITAGE VENTURE GROUP INC.

1 Indiana Square, Suite 2400
Indianapolis, IN 46204
317/635-5696

Year Founded: 1981
Total Private Funds: $3,000,000
Total SBA Leverage: 0

1983 Investment History:
Total Investments: $2,000,000
Deals: 7
Average Investment: $281,429

Project Preferences
Geographical: Midwest
Industries: Communications, Broadcasting, Light Manufacturing
Stages: Any

Principals: Arthur A. Angotti, Pres. & Dir.; Stephen M. Robbins, V.P. & Asst. Sec. & Treas.; Julia M. Rogers, Corp. Sec.
Contact: Arthur A. Angotti

Iowa

MORAMERICA CAPITAL CORP.

300 American Bldg.
Cedar Rapids, IA 52401
391/363-8249

Affiliation: MorAmerica Financial Corp.
Year Founded: 1959
Total Private Funds: $5,000,000
Total SBA Leverage: $12,000,000

1983 Investment History:
Total Investments: $3,200,000
Deals: 10
Average Investment: $320,000

Project Preferences
Geographical: Midwest
Industries: Diversified
Stages: Seed, Startup, First, Second, Buyouts

Principals: Jerry M. Burrows, Pres.; Donald E. Flynn, V.P.; David Schroder, V.P.; Phillip Suess, Investment Analyst
Contact: Jerry M. Burrows

Branches: 911 Main St., Kansas City, MO 64105, 816/842-0114. *Contact:* Kevin Mullane, V.P.
600 E. Mason St., Milwaukee, WI 53202, 414/276-3839. *Contact:* Steven Massey, Investment Off.

Kentucky

FINANCIAL OPPORTUNITIES INC.

981 S. Third St.
Louisville, KY 40203
502/584-1281

Affiliation: Conna Corp.
Year Founded: 1974
Total Private Funds: $900,000
Total SBA Leverage: $2,900,000

1983 Investment History:
Total Investments: $500,000
Deals: 15
Average Investment: $33,333

Project Preferences
Geographical: IN, NC, SC, TN, KY
Industries: Diversified, Retail
Stages: Second, Buyouts

Principals: Gary F. Duerr, Gen. Mgr.
Contact: Gary F. Duerr

Louisiana

COMMERCIAL CAPITAL INC.

P.O. Box 1776
Covington, LA 70434
504/893-5402

Affiliation: Diversified Commercial Investment Corp.
Year Founded: 1969
Total Private Funds: $860,000
Total SBA Leverage: $2,200,000

1983 Investment History:
Total Investments: $329,000
Deals: 10
Average Investment: $32,900

Project Preferences
Geographical: LA
Industries: Diversified
Stages: Any

Principals: Milton Coxe, Pres.; Michael Whitney, Treas.; Lou Braddock, Sec.
Contact: Michael Whitney, Lou Braddock

FIRST SOUTHERN CAPITAL CORP.

P.O. Box 14205
6161 Perkins Rd.
Baton Rouge, LA 70898
504/769-3004

Year Founded: 1961
Total Private Funds: $1,500,000
Total SBA Leverage: $2,500,000

1983 Investment History:
Total Investments: $789,000
Deals: 4
Average Investment: $197,250

Project Preferences
Geographical: South, Southwest
Industries: Diversified
Stages: Startup, First, Second, Later

Principals: John H. Crabtree, Pres.; Carol Perrin, Treas.
Contact: Either

LOUISIANA EQUITY CAPITAL

P.O. Box 1511
Baton Rouge, LA 70821
504/389-4421

Affiliation: Louisiana National Bank
Year Founded: 1974
Total Private Funds: $6,500,000
Total SBA Leverage: $1,000,000

1983 Investment History:
Total Investments: $675,000
Deals: 5
Average Investment: $135,000

Project Preferences
Geographical: Southeast, LA
Industries: Diversified
Stages: Seed, Startup, First, Second, Later

Principals: Charles W. McCoy, Chair.; G. Lee Griffin, V. Chair.; Melvin L. Rambin, Pres.
Contact: Melvin L. Rambin

WALNUT STREET CAPITAL CO.

231 Carondelet
New Orleans, LA 70130
504/525-2112

Affiliation: Delta Capital Corp.; Southgate Venture Partners II
Year Founded: 1962
Total Private Funds: $5,000,000
Total SBA Leverage: $1,500,000

1983 Investment History:
Total Investments: $1,200,000
Deals: 4
Average Investment: $300,000

Project Preferences
Geographical: Anywhere in U.S.
Industries: Diversified
Stages: Any

Principals: William D. Humphries, Man. Gen. Part.
Contact: William D. Humphries

Maryland

GREATER WASHINGTON INVESTORS INC.

5454 Wisconsin Ave.
Chevy Chase, MD 20815
301/656-0626

Year Founded: 1959
Total Private Funds: $25,000,000
Total SBA Leverage: $3,000,000

1983 Investment History:
Total Investments: $3,800,000
Deals: 16
Average Investment: $237,500

Project Preferences
Geographical: East Coast
Industries: High Technology
Stages: Seed, Startup, First

Principals: Don A. Christiansen, Pres.; Martin S. Pinson, Sr. V.P.; Cyril W. Draffin Jr., V.P.
Contact: Cyril W. Draffin

SUBURBAN CAPITAL CORP.

6610 Rockledge Dr.
Bethesda, MD 20817
301/493-7025

Affiliation: Suburban Bank
Year Founded: 1983
Total Private Funds: $5,000,000
Total SBA Leverage: 0

1983 Investment History:
Total Investments: $2,000,000
Deals: 5
Average Investment: $400,000

Project Preferences
Geographical: East Coast
Industries: Diversified
Stages: Any

Principals: Pete Linsert, Pres.; Steve Dubin, V.P.
Contact: Either

Massachusetts

BANCBOSTON VENTURES INC.

100 Federal St.
Boston, MA 02110
617/434-2442

Affiliation: Bank of Boston Corp.
Year Founded: 1959
Total Private Funds: $15,800,000
Total SBA Leverage: $7,500,000

1983 Investment History:
Total Investments: $12,500,000
Deals: 32
Average Investment: $390,625

Project Preferences
Geographical: Anywhere in U.S.
Industries: High Technology, Healthcare
Stages: Seed, Startup, First, Second, Later

Principals: Paul F. Hogan, Pres.; Jeffrey W. Wilson, V.P. & Treas.; Diana H. Frazier, V.P.; Edwin M. Kania, Investment Off.
Contact: Any of Above

BOSTON HAMBRO CORP.

1 Boston Pl., Suite 923
Boston, MA 02108
617/722-7055

Affiliation: Hambros Bank; The Boston Company
Year Founded: 1979
Total Private Funds: $5,400,000
Total SBA Leverage: $2,000,000

1983 Investment History:
Total Investments: $918,000
Deals: 13
Average Investment: $70,000

Project Preferences
Geographical: Anywhere in U.S.
Industries: Diversified
Stages: Seed, Startup, First

Principals: Robert S. Sherman, V.P.; Richard A. D'Amore, V.P.
Contact: Either

Branch: 17 E. 71st St., New York, N.Y. 10021, 212/288-7778.
    Contacts: Edwin A. Goodman, Pres.; Anders K. Brag, V.P.; Arthur C. Spinner, V.P.

MASSACHUSETTS CAPITAL CORP.

400 Washington St., Suite 200
Braintree, MA 02184
617/843-2927

Year Founded: 1960
Total Private Funds: $1,700,000
Total SBA Leverage: $3,300,000

1983 Investment History: Not Provided

Project Preferences
Geographical: Anywhere in U.S.
Industries: High Technology
Stages: Seed, Startup, First, Second

Principals: James W. Lavin, V.P.; Lee Gray, V.P.
Contact: James W. Lavin

Branch: 2701 S. Bayshore Dr., Suite 402, Coconut Grove, FL 33133, 305/854-6851. *Contact:* Warren Miller, V.P.

NEW ENGLAND CAPITAL CORP.

1 Washington Mall
Boston, MA 02108
617/722-6400

Affiliation: Bank of New England
Year Founded: 1961
Total Private Funds: $2,500,000
Total SBA Leverage: $875,000

1983 Investment History:
Total Investments: $2,500,000
Deals: 10
Average Investment: $250,000

Project Preferences
Geographical: Anywhere in U.S.
Industries: Diversified High Technology
Industries: Any

Principals: Z. David Patterson, Exec. V.P.: Melvin W. Ellis, V.P.;
    Thomas C. Tremblay, V.P.; Thomas A. Ballantyne, Asst.
    Investment Off.
Contact: Any of Above

TRANSATLANTIC CAPITAL CORP.

24 Federal St.
Boston, MA 02110
617/482-0015

Year Founded: 1979
Total Private Funds: $3,000,000
Total SBA Leverage: 0

1983 Investment History:
Total Investments: $1,400,000
Deals: 9
Average Investment: $155,556

Project Preferences
Geographical: New England, Boston
Industries: Diversified
Stages: Startup, First

Principals: Bayard Henry, Pres.; John O. Flender, V.P.
Contact: Either

UST CAPITAL CORP.

30 Court St.
Boston, MA 02108
617/726-7260

Affiliation: United States Trust Co.
Year Founded: 1961
Total Private Funds: $1,300,000
Total SBA Leverage: $1,300,000

1983 Investment History:
Total Investments: $1,400,000
Deals: 8
Average Investment: $175,000

Project Preferences
Geographical: Northeast
Industries: Diversified
Stages: Startup, First

Principals: Richard Koren, V.P.; Arthur Snyder, Dir.
Contact: Either

Michigan

DETROIT METROPOLITAN SBIC

150 Michigan Ave.
Detroit, MI 48226
313/963-8190

Year Founded: 1982
Total Private Funds: $500,000
Total SBA Leverage: $2,500,000

1983 Investment History:
Total Investments: $60,000
Deals: 2
Average Investment: $30,000

Project Preferences
Geographical: MI
Industries: Diversified
Stages: Seed, Startup, First, Second

Principals: Ruby Jones, Gen. Mgr.
Contact: Ruby Jones

DOAN RESOURCES CORP.

P.O. Box 1431
Midland, MI 48640
517/631-2471

Affiliation: Doan Associates; VCM II Services Co.
Year Founded: 1972
Total Private Funds: $3,800,000
Total SBA Leverage: $9,600,000

1983 Investment History: *

Project Preferences
Geographical: Anywhere in U.S.
Industries: Life Sciences, Computers & Peripherals, Software,
    Semiconductors, Communications & Information Systems,
    Industrial Automation
Stages: Seed, Startup, First

Principals: Ian R.N. Bund, Man. Gen. Part.
Contact: Ian R.N. Bund

*For investment history, see Doan Associates, page 62.

MICHIGAN CAPITAL & SERVICE INC.

500 First National Bldg.
201 S. Main
Ann Arbor, MI 48104
313/663-0702

Affiliation: NBD Bancorp Inc.
Year Founded: 1966
Total Private Funds: $4,200,000
Total SBA Leverage: $4,000,000

1983 Investment History:
Total Investments: $5,400,000
Deals: 23
Average Investment: $234,783

Project Preferences
Geographical: Anywhere in U.S.
Industries: High Technology, Communications
Stages: Any

Principals: Joseph F. Conway, Pres.; Gerard L. Buhrman Jr., V.P.;
    James A. Parsons, V.P.; Anthony F. Buffa, V.P.; Christopher
    Hampson, Investment Off.; Mary L. Campbell, Investment Analyst
Contact: Any of Above

Minnesota

CONTROL DATA CAPITAL CORP.

3601 W. 77th St.
Minneapolis, MN 55435
612/921-4118; 612/921-4391

Affiliation: Control Data Corp.
Year Founded: 1977
Total Private Funds: $4,500,000
Total SBA Leverage: $8,000,000

1983 Investment History: Not Provided

Project Preferences
Geographical: Anywhere in U.S., Midwest
Industries: Diversified, Computer Technology, Manufacturing, Medical, Telecommunications
Stages: Startup, First, Second

Principals: D.C. Curtis Jr., Pres.; W.D. Anderson, V.P.
Contact: Either

FBS SBIC

7515 Wayzata Blvd.
Minneapolis, MN 55426
612/544-2754

Affiliation: FBS Venture Capital Corp.; Community Investment Enterprises Inc.
Year Founded: 1984
Total Private Funds: $3,000,000
Total SBA Leverage: 0

1983 Investment History: New Fund

Project Preferences
Geographical: AZ, CO, MN
Industries: Diversified, Medical, Electronics, Computers
Stages: Startup, First, Second

Principals: W. Ray Allen, Exec. V.P.; John Howell Bullion
Contact: Either

Branches: 6900 E. Camelback Rd., Scottsdale, AZ 85251, 602/941-2160. *Principals:* William B. McKee, Pres.; R. Randy Stolworthy, V.P. *Contact:* Stephen Buchanan
3000 Pearl St., Suite 206, Boulder, CO 80301. *Contact:* Brian Johnson, V.P.

FIRST MIDWEST CAPITAL CORP.

1010 Plymouth Bldg.
12 S. Sixth St.
Minneapolis, MN 55402
612/339-9391

Affiliation: First Midwest Corp.
Year Founded: 1959
Total Private Funds: $1,600,000
Total SBA Leverage: $3,200,000

1983 Investment History:
Total Investments: $315,000
Deals: 5
Average Investment: $63,000

Project Preferences
Geographical: Anywhere in U.S., Midwest
Industries: Diversified, Computer-Related
Stages: Any

Principals: Alan K. Ruvelson, Chair; Dr. William R. Franta, Pres.; Walter L. Tiffin, V.P. & Treas.; Patricia A. Montgomery, Sec.
Contact: Dr. William R. Franta

NORTH STAR VENTURES INC.

1501 First Bank Pl. W.
Minneapolis, MN 55402
612/333-1133

Year Founded: 1974
Total Private Funds: $5,000,000
Total SBA Leverage: $17,800,000

1983 Investment History:
Total Investments: $9,300,000
Deals: 39
Average Investment: $238,462

Project Preferences
Geographical: Anywhere in U.S.
Industries: Diversified
Stages: Any

Principals: Terrence W. Glarner, Pres.; David W. Stassen, V.P.; Keith Eastman, V.P.
Contact: Terrence W. Glarner

Mississippi

INVESAT CAPITAL CORP.

162 E. Amite, Suite 204
Jackson, MS 39201
601/969-3242

Year Founded: 1974
Total Private Funds: $3,500,000
Total SBA Leverage: $4,100,000

1983 Investment History:
Total Investments: $1,600,000
Deals: 5
Average Investment: $320,000

Project Preferences
Geographical: Southeast, Southwest
Industries: Manufacturing, Healthcare, Broadcasting
Stages: Seed, Startup, First, Second, Later

Principals: J. Thomas Noojin, Chair. & Pres.; John R. Bise, V.P.
Contact: Either

Missouri

CAPITAL FOR BUSINESS INC.

911 Main St., Suite 2300
Kansas City, MO 64105
816/234-2472

Affiliation: Commerce Bancshares Inc.
Year Founded: 1959
Total Private Funds: $2,600,000
Total SBA Leverage: 0

1983 Investment History:
Total Investments: $2,000,000
Deals: 5
Average Investment: $400,000

Project Preferences
Geographical: Midwest
Industries: Manufacturing
Stages: Seed, Startup, First, Second, Later

Principals: James B. Hebenstreit, Pres.; Bart S. Bergman, V.P.; William O. Cannon, Investment Off.
Contact: Any of Above

Branch: County Tower Bldg., 11 S. Meramec, St. Louis, MO 63105, 314/854-7427.

SBICs $3 MIL AND UP

137

New Jersey

MONMOUTH CAPITAL CORP.

P.O. Box 335
125 Wycoff Rd.
Eatontown, NJ 07724
201/542-4927

Year Founded: 1961
Total Private Funds: $2,500,000
Total SBA Leverage: $6,300,000

1983 Investment History:
Total Investments: $1,000,000
Deals: 6
Average Investment: $166,667

Project Preferences
Geographical: Northeast
Industries: Diversified Non-High Technology
Stages: Second, Later

Principals: Eugene W. Landy, Pres.; Ralph B. Patterson, Exec. V.P.; Ernest V. Bencivenga, Sec. & Treas.
Contact: Ralph B. Patterson

RAYBAR SMALL BUSINESS INVESTMENT CORP.

255 W. Spring Valley Ave.
Maywood, NJ 07607
201/368-2280

Affiliation: H.K. Metalcraft Manufacturing Corp.
Year Founded: 1981
Total Private Funds: $510,000
Total SBA Leverage: $1,500,000

1983 Investment History:
Total Investments: $1,300,000
Deals: 26
Average Investment: $50,000

Project Preferences
Geographical: New York City
Industries: Diversified
Stages: Any

Principals: Patrick F. McCort, V.P. & Gen. Mgr.
Contact: Patrick F. McCort

UNICORN VENTURES/UNICORN VENTURES II LP

14 Commerce Dr.
Cranford, NJ 07016
201/276-7880

Year Founded: 1981
Total Private Funds: $6,100,000
Total SBA Leverage: $3,000,000

1983 Investment History:
Total Investments: $1,600,000
Deals: 8
Average Investment: $200,000

Project Preferences
Geographical: Anywhere in U.S.
Industries: Diversified
Stages: Any

Principals: Frank P. Diassi, Gen. Part.; Arthur B. Baer, Gen. Part.
Contact: Either

New Mexico

FLUID CAPITAL CORP.

8421-B Montgomery, NE
Albuquerque, NM 87111
505/292-4747

Affiliation: Fluid Corp.
Year Founded: 1979
Total Private Funds: $1,600,000
Total SBA Leverage: $3,900,000

1983 Investment History: Not Provided

Project Preferences
Geographical: Anywhere in U.S.
Industries: Diversified
Stages: Later

Principals: George T. Slaughter, Pres.
Contact: George T. Slaughter

NEW MEXICO CAPITAL CORP.

2900 Louisiana Blvd., NE, Suite 201
Albuquerque, NM 87110
505/884-3600

Year Founded: 1963
Total Private Funds: $3,000,000
Total SBA Leverage: $12,000,000

1983 Investment History: Not Provided

Project Preferences
Geographical: Southwest
Industries: Diversified
Stages: Seed, Startup, First

Principals: Phillip G. Larson, Pres. & Chair.; John C. Evans, V.P.
Contact: John C. Evans

SOUTHWEST CAPITAL INVESTMENTS INC.

3500 E. Comanche Rd., NE
Albuquerque, NM 87107
505/884-7161

Affiliation: Southwest Capital Corp.
Year Founded: 1976
Total Private Funds: $1,000,000
Total SBA Leverage: $2,500,000

1983 Investment History: Not Provided

Project Preferences
Geographical: Western
Industries: Diversified
Stages: Later

Principals: Martin J. Roe, Pres. & Treas.; Valerie Wetherill, V.P. & Sec.
Contact: Either

SBICs
$3 MIL AND UP

New York

AMERICAN COMMERCIAL CAPITAL CORP.

310 Madison Ave., Suite 1304
New York, NY 10017
212/986-3305

Year Founded: 1982
Total Private Funds: $1,000,000
Total SBA Leverage: $1,000,000

1983 Investment History:
Total Investments: $1,400,000
Deals: 12
Average Investment: $116,667

Project Preferences
Geographical: Northeast
Industries: Manufacturing
Stages: Later

Principals: Gerald J. Grossman, Pres.; Barbara Grossman, Sec.
Contact: Either

AMEV CAPITAL CORP.

1 World Trade Center, 50th Floor
New York, NY 10048
212/775-9100

Affiliation: AMEV Holdings Inc.
Year Founded: 1979
Total Private Funds: $4,500,000
Total SBA Leverage: $7,500,000

1983 Investment History:
Total Investments: $3,400,000
Deals: 9
Average Investment: $377,778

Project Preferences
Geographical: Anywhere in U.S.
Industries: Diversified, Healthcare, Communications, High Technology, Real Estate
Stages: Second

Principals: Martin S. Orland, Pres.; Joseph A. Lopez, V.P. & Man. Dir.; Robert S. Whyte, V.P.
Contact: Any of Above

BT CAPITAL CORP.

280 Park Ave., 10th Floor W.
New York, NY 10017
212/850-1916

Affiliation: Bankers Trust N.Y. Corp.
Year Founded: 1974
Total Private Funds: $22,600,000
Total SBA Leverage: $11,300,000

1983 Investment History:
Total Investments: $29,800,000
Deals: 13
Average Investment: $2,292,308

Project Preferences
Geographical: Anywhere in U.S.
Industries: Communications, Basic Industries, Diversified Non-High Technology
Stages: Later, Buyouts

Principals: James G. Hellmuth, Chair.; Noel D. Urben, Pres.; Keith R. Fox, V.P.; B. Martha Cassidy, Asst. Treas.
Contact: Any of Above

CITICORP VENTURE CAPITAL LTD.

153 E. 53rd St., 28th Floor
New York, NY 10043
212/559-1127

Affiliation: Citicorp
Year Founded: 1968
Total Private Funds: $37,500,000
Total SBA Leverage: $10,000,000

1983 Investment History:
Total Investments: $64,000,000
Deals: 56
Average Investment: $1,142,857

Project Preferences
Geographical: Anywhere in U.S.
Industries: Diversified, Healthcare, Information Processing, Energy, Transportation, Communications, Manufacturing
Stages: Any

Principals: James W. Stevens, Chair.; Peter G. Gerry, Pres.; George M. Middlemas, V.P.; Guy de Chazal, V.P.: Stanley Nitzburg, V.P.
Contact: Stanley Nitzburg

Branches: 1 Sansome St., Suite 2410, San Francisco, CA 94104, 415/627-6472. *Contact:* J. Matthew Mackowski, V.P.
220 Geng Rd., Suite 203, Palo Alto CA 94303, 415/424-8000. *Contact:* David A. Wegmann, V.P.; Allan Rosenberg, V.P.; Larry J. Wells, V.P.
Diamond Shamrock Tower, 717 Harwood St., Suite 2920-LB87, Dallas, TX 75221, 214/880-9670. *Contact:* Thomas F. McWilliams, V.P.; Newell Starks, V.P.

CLINTON CAPITAL CORP.

419 Park Ave. S.
New York, NY 10016
212/696-4334

Year Founded: 1980
Total Private Funds: $4,000,000
Total SBA Leverage: $9,000,000

1983 Investment History:
Total Investments: $6,000,000
Deals: 35
Average Investment: $171,429

Project Preferences
Geographical: East Coast
Industries: Diversified
Stages: Second, Later

Principals: Mark Scharfman, Pres.; Alan Leavitt, V.P.
Contact: Either

CMNY CAPITAL CO. INC.

77 Water St.
New York, NY 10005
212/437-7079

Affiliation: Carl Marks & Co.
Year Founded: 1962
Total Private Funds: $1,800,000
Total SBA Leverage: $5,900,000

1983 Investment History:
Total Investments: $4,900,000
Deals: 68
Average Investment: $72,059

Project Preferences
Geographical: Anywhere in U.S.
Industries: Diversified
Stages: Seed, Startup, First, Second, Later

Principals: Robert Boas, Pres.; Edwin Marks, V.P.; Robert Davidoff, V.P.
Contact: Any of Above

CORNELL CAPITAL CORP.

230 Park Ave., Suite 3440
New York, NY 10169
212/490-9198

Year Founded: 1979
Total Private Funds: $558,000
Total SBA Leverage: $1,100,000

1983 Investment History:
Total Investments: $1,200,000
Deals: 13
Average Investment: $92,308

Project Preferences
Geographical: Anywhere in U.S.
Industries: Retail & Fast-Food Franchises
Stages: Any

Principals: Barry M. Bloom, Pres.
Contact: Barry M. Bloom

Branch: 2049 Century Park E., 12th Floor, Century City, CA 90067, 213/277-7993. *Contact:* Alan B. Newman, Sec. & V.P.

CVC CAPITAL CORP.

666 Fifth Ave.
New York, NY 10019
212/319-7210

Year Founded: 1977
Total Private Funds: $3,000,000
Total SBA Leverage: $6,000,000

1983 Investment History:
Total Investments: $2,600,000
Deals: 5
Average Investment: $520,000

Project Preferences
Geographical: Anywhere in U.S.
Industries: Communications, Broadcasting
Stages: Startups

Principals: Joerg G. Klebe, Pres.
Contact: Joerg G. Klebe

EAB VENTURE CORP.

90 Park Ave.
New York, NY 10016
212/437-4182

Affiliation: European American Bank
Year Founded: 1980
Total Private Funds: $5,000,000
Total SBA Leverage: $9,000,000

1983 Investment History:
Total Investments: $3,400,000
Deals: 18
Average Investment: $188,889

Project Preferences
Geographical: Anywhere in U.S.
Industries: Diversified
Stages: Seed, Startup, First, Second

Principals: Richard C. Burcaw; Mark R. Littell, V.P.
Contact: Either

EDWARDS CAPITAL CORP.

215 Lexington Ave.
New York, NY 10016
212/686-2568

Year Founded: 1979
Total Private Funds: $3,200,000
Total SBA Leverage: $8,900,000

1983 Investment History:
Total Investments: $8,000,000
Deals: 200
Average Investment: $40,000

Project Preferences
Geographical: New York City
Industries: Taxicabs
Stages: Startup, Refinancing

Principals: Edward H. Teitelbaum, Pres.
Contact: Edward H. Teitelbaum

FAIRFIELD EQUITY CORP.

200 E. 42nd St., Suite 2300
New York, NY 10017
212/867-0150

Year Founded: 1958
Total Private Funds: $1,000,000
Total SBA Leverage: $3,000,000

1983 Investment History:
Total Investments: $825,000
Deals: 6
Average Investment: $137,500

Project Preferences
Geographical: East Coast
Industries: Publishing, Retailing, Light Manufacturing
Stages: Second, Later

Principals: Matthew A. Berdon, Pres.; S.L. Highleyman, V.P.; Joel Handel, Sec.
Contact: Matthew A. Berdon

FERRANTI HIGH TECHNOLOGY

515 Madison Ave.
New York, NY 10022
212/688-9691

Affiliation: American Corporate Services
Year Founded: 1982
Total Private Funds: $3,000,000
Total SBA Leverage: 0

1983 Investment History:
Total Investments: $1,400,000
Deals: 4
Average Investment: $350,000

Project Preferences
Geographical: Anywhere in U.S.
Industries: High Technology, Telecommunications, Semiconductors, Computer Hardware
Stages: Second

Principals: Sanford R. Simon, Pres.; Michael R. Simon, V.P.
Contact: Either

Branch: Ferranti Pl., Millbank Tower, Millbank, London, SW1 4QS, England, 44/1-834-6611.

FIFTY-THIRD STREET VENTURES LP

420 Madison Ave.
New York, NY 10017
212/752-8010

Affiliation: Tessler & Cloherty Inc.
Year Founded: 1976
Total Private Funds: $2,600,000
Total SBA Leverage: $5,500,000

1983 Investment History:
Total Investments: $2,500,000
Deals: 11
Average Investment: $227,273

Project Preferences
Geographical: Anywhere in U.S.
Industries: Diversified, Information Processing, Electronics
Stages: Any

Principals: Daniel Tessler, Chair.; Patricia Cloherty, Pres.
Contact: Either

JH FOSTER & CO. LP

437 Madison Ave.
New York, NY 10022
212/753-4810

Affiliation: Foster Management Co.
Year Founded: 1973
Total Private Funds: $2,100,000
Total SBA Leverage: $3,000,000

1983 Investment History: Not Provided

Project Preferences
Geographical: Anywhere in U.S.
Industries: Diversified, Broadcasting, Healthcare, Transportation, Energy, Home Furniture
Stages: Any

Principals: John H. Foster, Michael J. Connelly, Timothy E. Foster
Contact: Any of Above

THE FRANKLIN CORP.

1185 Ave. of the Americas
New York, NY 10036
212/719-4844

Year Founded: 1960
Total Private Funds: $20,000,000
Total SBA Leverage: $9,000,000

1983 Investment History:
Total Investments: $6,000,000
Deals: 20
Average Investment: $300,000

Project Preferences
Geographical: Anywhere in U.S.
Industries: Diversified, Automotive Products, Electronics, Computers
Stages: Any

Principals: Herman E. Goodman, Pres.; Alan A. Farkas, Exec. V.P.; James S. Eisberg, Gen. Counsel; Elliott Gorman, Controller.
Contact: Any of Above

IRVING CAPITAL CORP.

1290 Ave. of the Americas
New York, NY 10104
212/408-4800

Affiliation: Irving Trust Co.
Year Founded: 1976
Total Private Funds: $6,900,000
Total SBA Leverage: 0

1983 Investment History: Not Provided

Project Preferences
Geographical: Anywhere in U.S.
Industries: Diversified
Stages: Second, Later, Buyouts

Principals: J. Andrew McWethy, Exec. V.P. & Gen. Mgr.; Barry A. Solomon, V.P.; Kathleen M. Snyder, Asst. Sec.
Contact: Kathleen M. Snyder

KEY VENTURE CAPITAL CORP.

60 State St.
Albany, NY 12207
518/447-3227

Affiliation: Key Bank Inc.
Year Founded: 1983
Total Private Funds: $3,000,000
Total SBA Leverage: 0

1983 Investment History: New Fund

Project Preferences
Geographical: Anywhere in U.S.
Industries: High Technology
Stages: Seed, Startup, First

Principals: Mark R. Hursty, Exec. V.P.; James P. Galvin, Asst. V.P.; Richard C. VanAuken, Asst. V.P.
Contact: Mark R. Hursty

M&T CAPITAL CORP.

1 M&T Plaza
Buffalo, NY 14240
716/842-5881

Affiliation: Manufacturers & Traders Trust Co.
Year Founded: 1967
Total Private Funds: $5,000,000
Total SBA Leverage: $2,500,000

1983 Investment History:
Total Investments: $1,500,000
Deals: 4
Average Investment: $375,000

Project Preferences
Geographical: Anywhere in U.S.
Industries: Diversified
Stages: Any

Principals: Joseph V. Parlator, Pres.; Norma E. Gracia, Treas.
Contact: Either

SBIC
$3 M

MIDLAND VENTURE CAPITAL LTD.

950 Third Ave.
New York, NY 10022
212/753-7790

Affiliation: Midland Capital Corp.
Year Founded: 1981
Total Private Funds: $10,000,000
Total SBA Leverage: $10,700,000

1983 Investment History:
Total Investments: $2,000,000
Deals: 1

Project Preferences
Geographical: Anywhere in U.S.
Industries: Precision Manufacturing (Aerospace & Defense),
    Precious Metals, Energy
Stages: Second, Later, Buyouts

Principals: Robert. B. Machinist, Man. Dir.; Michael R. Stanfield, Man.
    Dir.; Edwin B. Hathaway, Asst. V.P.
Contact: Any of Above

PIERRE FUNDING CORP.

270 Madison Ave., Suite 1608
New York, NY 10016
212/689-9361

Year Founded: 1981
Total Private Funds: $1,400,000
Total SBA Leverage: $1,400,000

1983 Investment History:
Total Investments: $3,500,000
Deals: 55
Average Investment: $63,636

Project Preferences
Geographical: New York City
Industries: Transportation
Stages: Seed, Startup, First

Principals: Elias Debbas, Pres.
Contact: Elias Debbas

PIONEER INVESTORS CORP.

113 E. 55th St.
New York, NY 10022
212/980-9090

Affiliation: Pioneer Venture Co.
Year Founded: 1977
Total Private Funds: $2,500,000
Total SBA Leverage: $6,500,000

1983 Investment History:
Total Investments: $620,675
Deals: 5
Average Investment: $124,135

Project Preferences
Geographical: Anywhere in U.S.
Industries: Diversified, Healthcare, Agriculture, Oil & Gas, Food
Stages: Second, Later

Principals: Neil A. McConnell, Chair.; James G. Niven, Pres.; R. Scott
    Asen, V.P.
Contact: R. Scott Asen, James G. Niven

QUESTECH CAPITAL CORP.

600 Madison Ave., 21st Floor
New York, NY 10022
212/758-8522

Affiliation: Biotech Capital Corp.
Year Founded: 1981
Total Private Funds: $5,000,000
Total SBA Leverage: $5,000,000

1983 Investment History:
Total Investments: $2,700,000
Deals: 9
Average Investment: $300,000

Project Preferences
Geographical: Anywhere in U.S.
Industries: Telecommunications, Information Processing,
    Biotechnology
Stages: Seed, Startup, First

Principals: Dr. Earl W. Brian, Pres.
Contacts: Dr. Earl W. Brian

ROUNDHILL CAPITAL CORP.

44 Wall St.
New York, NY 10005
212/747-0144

Year Founded: 1981
Total Private Funds: $3,000,000
Total SBA Leverage: 0

1983 Investment History:
Total Investments: $2,000,000
Deals: 5
Average Investment: $400,000

Project Preferences
Geographical: Anywhere in U.S.
Industries: Diversified
Stages: Any

Principals: J. Morton Davis, Pres.
Contact: J. Morton Davis

S&S VENTURE ASSOCIATES LTD.

370 Seventh Ave.
New York, NY 10001
212/736-4530

Year Founded: 1979
Total Private Funds: $510,000
Total SBA Leverage: $1,500,000

1983 Investment History:
Total Investments: $1,000,000
Deals: 10
Average Investment: $100,000

Project Preferences
Geographical: New York City
Industries: Diversified, Service Industries
Stages: Seed, Startup, First

Principals: Donald Smith, Pres.; Mark Smith, V.P. & Treas.; Bernard J.
    Sandler, V.P. & Sec.
Contact: Bernard J. Sandler

TLC FUNDING CORP.

141 S. Central Ave.
Hartsdale, NY 10530
914/683-1144

Year Founded: 1979
Total Private Funds: $1,000,000
Total SBA Leverage: $2,200,000

1983 Investment History:
Total Investments: $1,300,000
Deals: 22
Average Investment: $59,091

Project Preferences
Geographical: Anywhere in U.S.
Industries: Dry Cleaners & Laundries, Restaurants, Taxicabs, Construction
Stages: Startup, First

Principals: Philip G. Kass, Pres.
Contact: Philip G. Kass

VEGA CAPITAL CORP.

720 White Plains Rd.
Scarsdale, NY 10583
914/472-8550

Year Founded: 1968
Total Private Funds: $2,400,000
Total SBA Leverage: $7,000,000

1983 Investment History:
Total Investments: $1,900,000
Deals: 8
Average Investment: $237,500

Project Preferences
Geographical: Anywhere in U.S., Northeast
Industries: Basic Manufacturing
Stages: Second, Later, Buyouts

Principals: Victor Harz, Chair. & Pres.; Ronald A. Linden, Exec. V.P.
Contact: Either

WINFIELD CAPITAL CORP.

237 Mamaroneck Ave.
White Plains, NY 10605
914/949-2600

Year Founded: 1972
Total Private Funds: $1,000,000
Total SBA Leverage: $2,000,000

1983 Investment History:
Total Investments: $2,000,000
Deals: 8
Average Investment: $250,000

Project Preferences
Geographical: East Coast
Industries: Manufacturing, Distribution
Stages: Second, Later

Principals: Stanley Pechman, Pres.
Contact: Stanley Pechman

Branch: 2670 W. Fairbank Ave., Winter Park, FL 32789, 305/629-0038. *Contact:* Sanford B. Sheber, Representative

WOOD RIVER CAPITAL CORP.

645 Madison Ave.
New York, NY 10022
212/750-9420

Affiliation: Sierra Ventures
Year Founded: 1979
Total Private Funds: $6,500,000
Total SBA Leverage: $18,000,000

1983 Investment History:
Total Investments: $2,500,000
Deals: 11
Average Investment: $227, 273

Project Preferences
Geographical: Anywhere in U.S.
Industries: Diversified
Stages: Seed, Startup, First

Principals: Elizabeth W. Smith, Pres.
Contact: Elizabeth W. Smith

Branch: 3000 Sand Hill Rd., Menlo Park, CA 94025, 415/854-7145. *Contact:* Peter C. Wendell, V.P.

North Carolina

DELTA CAPITAL INC.

227 N. Tryon St., Suite 201
Charlotte, NC 28202
704/372-1410

Affiliation: Southgate Venture Partners
Year Founded: 1971
Total Private Funds: $2,000,000
Total SBA Leverage: $4,500,000

1983 Investment History:
Total Investments: $2,000,000
Deals: 6
Average Investment: $333,333

Project Preferences
Geographical: Anywhere in U.S.
Industries: Diversified
Stages: Any

Principals: William F. Lane, Martha C. Riker, Alexander B. Wilkins Jr.
Contact: Any of Above

HERITAGE CAPITAL CORP.

2290 First Union Plaza
Charlotte, NC 28282
704/334-2867

Affiliation: Ruddick Corp.
Year Founded: 1962
Total Private Funds: $2,400,000
Total SBA Leverage: $2,400,000

1983 Investment History:
Total Investments: $750,000
Deals: 4
Average Investment: $187,500

Project Preferences
Geographical: Southeast
Industries: Diversified
Stages: Second

Principals: Herman B. McManaway, Pres.; William R. Starnes, V.P.
Contact: Either

KITTY HAWK CAPITAL INC.

20301 Tryon Ctr.
Charlotte, NC 28284
704/333-3777

Year Founded: 1980
Total Private Funds: $2,000,000
Total SBA Leverage: $1,500,000

1983 Investment History:
Total Investments: $1,800,000
Deals: 8
Average Investment: $225,000

Project Preferences
Geographical: Southeast
Industries: Diversified
Stages: Any

Principals: Walter H. Wilkinson Jr., Pres.; W. Chris Hegele, V.P.
Contact: Either

Ohio

CLARION CAPITAL CORP.

1801 E. 12th St., Suite 201
Cleveland, OH 44114
216/687-1096

Affiliation: First City Financial Corp. Ltd.
Year Founded: 1968
Total Private Funds: $11,000,000
Total SBA Leverage: $9,500,000

1983 Investment History: No Investments Made in 1983

Project Preferences
Geographical: East Coast, West Coast
Industries: Communications, Life Sciences, Specialty Chemicals
Stages: Seed, Startup, First

Principals: Morton A. Cohen, Chair. & CEO; Michael L. Boeckman, V.P. & CFO; Roger Eaglen, V.P.
Contact: Morton A. Cohen, Roger Eaglen

NATIONAL CITY CAPITAL CORP.

P.O. Box 5756
Cleveland, OH 44101
216/575-2491

Affiliation: National City Corp.
Year Founded: 1979
Total Private Funds: $2,500,000
Total SBA Leverage: $4,000,000

1983 Investment History:
Total Investments: $1,100,000
Deals: 7
Average Investment: $157,143

Project Preferences
Geographical: Anywhere in U.S.
Industries: Diversified
Stages: Second, Later

Principals: Michael Sherwin, Pres.; Martha A. Barry, V.P.; John B. Naylor, V.P.
Contact: Martha A. Barry

Oklahoma

ALLIANCE BUSINESS INVESTMENT CO.

1 Williams Ctr., Suite 2000
Tulsa, OK 74172
918/584-3581

Year Founded: 1959
Total Private Funds: $3,100,000
Total SBA Leverage: $2,800,000

1983 Investment History: Not Provided

Project Preferences
Geographical: Southwest
Industries: Natural Resources, Energy, Manufacturing, Healthcare, Robotics, Broadcasting, Specialty Chemicals
Stages: Second, Third, Later

Principals: Barry M. Davis, Pres.; John M. Holliman III, V.P.
Contact: Either

FIRST VENTURE CORP.

Venture Bldg., The Quarters
Bartlesville, OK 74006
918/333-8820

Affiliation: First Bancshares Inc.
Year Founded: 1973
Total Private Funds: $1,500,000
Total SBA Leverage: $6,000,000

1983 Investment History: Not Provided

Project Preferences
Geographical: Anywhere in U.S.
Industries: Diversified, High Technology, Energy, Medical, Airlines
Stages: Second

Principals: John R.K. Tinkle, Pres.; James G. Thompson, Sr. V.P.; Ralph B. Finkle Jr., V.P.
Contact: Any of Above

INVESTMENT CAPITAL INC.

P.O. Box 1071
300 N. Harrison
Cushing, OK 74023
918/225-5850

Affiliation: First National Bank and Trust Co.
Year Founded: 1978
Total Private Funds: $1,000,000
Total SBA Leverage: $2,800,000

1983 Investment History:
Total Investments: $400,000
Deals: 4
Average Investment: $100,000

Project Preferences
Geographical: OK
Industries: Manufacturing, Retail
Stages: Seed, Startup, First

Principals: James J. Wasson, Pres.; Edward J. Puckett, V.P.; Donna L. Bogle, Sec.
Contact: Donna L. Bogle

SBICs
$3 MIL AND UP

WESTERN VENTURE CAPITAL CORP.

4880 S. Lewis
Tulsa, OK 74170
918/749-7981

Affiliation: Western National Bank
Year Founded: 1980
Total Private Funds: $2,000,000
Total SBA Leverage: $2,000,000

1983 Investment History:
Total Investments: $2,000,000
Deals: 5
Average Investment: $400,000

Project Preferences
Geographical: OK, TX, KS, LA, CO
Industries: Diversified, Oil & Gas, Computers
Stages: Second, Later

Principals: Joe D. Tippens, V.P.
Contact: Joe D. Tippens

Puerto Rico

VENTURE CAPITAL PR INC.

Hideca Bldg., Second Floor
58 Caribe St.
Condado, PR 00907
809/721-3550

Year Founded: 1981
Total Private Funds: $1,200,000
Total SBA Leverage: $2,600,000

1983 Investment History:
Total Investments: $2,500,000
Deals: 50
Average Investment: $50,000

Project Preferences
Geographical: PR
Industries: Manufacturing, Real Estate
Stages: Startup

Principals: Frank Marino Hernandez, Chair,; Manuel L. Prats, Pres.
Contact: Either

Rhode Island

FLEET VENTURE RESOURCES INC.

111 Westminster St.
Providence, RI 02903
401/278-5597

Affiliation: Fleet Financial Group
Year Founded: 1969
Total Private Funds: $4,000,000
Total SBA Leverage: $1,500,000

1983 Investment History:
Total Investments: $2,400,000
Deals: 10
Average Investment: $240,000

Project Preferences
Geographical: Northeast, Middle Atlantic, Midwest, South, Southeast, Southwest
Industries: High Technology, Communications, Healthcare
Stages: Startup, First Second, Later, Buyouts

Principals: Robert M. Van Degna, Pres.
Contact: Robert M. Van Degna

Branch: 60 State St., Boston, MA 02109, 617/367-6700. *Contact:* Carlton B. Klein, V.P.

NARRAGANSETT CAPITAL CORP.

40 Westminster St.
Providence, RI 02903
401/751-1000

Affiliation: Narragansett Capital
Year Founded: 1959
Total Private Funds: $16,400,000
Total SBA Leverage: $32,000,000

1983 Investment History:
Total Investments: $6,500,000
Deals: 8
Average Investment: $812,500

Project Preferences
Geographical: Anywhere in U.S.
Industries: Diversified
Stages: Seed, Startup, First

Principals: Arthur D. Little, Chair.; Robert D. Manchester, Pres.; William P. Lane, V.P. & Treas.; Roger A. Vandenberg, V.P.; Gregory P. Barber, V.P.; Paul A. Giusti, V.P.
Contact: Any of Above

RIHT CAPITAL CORP.

1 Hospital Trust Plaza
Providence, RI 02903
401/278-8819

Affiliation: Rhode Island Hospital Trust National Bank
Year Founded: 1982
Total Private Funds: $85,400,000
Total SBA Leverage: $4,000,000

1983 Investment History:
Total Investments: $8,500,000
Deals: 19
Average Investment: $447,368

Project Preferences
Geographical: Anywhere in U.S., Midwest, Northeast
Industries: Diversified
Stages: First, Second, Later

Principals: Peter D. Van Oosterhout, Pres. & CEO; Robert A. Comey, V.P.
Contact: Either

Branch: 796 Huntington Bldg., Cleveland, OH 44115, 216/781-3655.

South Carolina

LOW COUNTRY INVESTMENT CORP.

P.O. Box 10447
Charleston, SC 29411
803/554-9886

Affiliation: Greenbax Enterprises Inc.
Year Founded: 1960
Total Private Funds: $1,900,000
Total SBA Leverage: $4,000,000

1983 Investment History:
Total Investments: $954,000
Deals: 6
Average Investment: $159,000

Project Preferences
Geographical: Southeast
Industries: Grocery Stores
Stages: Any

Principals: J.T. Newton Jr., Pres.; Harold F. Mahoney, V.P.; Joseph T. Newton III, V.P.; Burton R. Schools, Sec. & Treas.
Contact: Harold F. Mahoney

SBICs
$3 MIL AND UP

145

Tennessee

SUWANNEE CAPITAL CORP.

3030 Poplar Ave.
Memphis, TN 38111
901/325-4315

Affiliation: M&H Financial Corp.
Year Founded: 1978
Total Private Funds: $2,000,000
Total SBA Leverage: $1,500,000

1983 Investment History:
Total Investments: $1,500,000
Deals: 8
Average Investment: $187,500

Project Preferences
Geographical: Southeast
Industries: Food Retailers, Grocery Stores
Stages: Startups

Principals: Joseph R. Hyde III, Chair.; Peter R. Pettit, Pres.
Contact: Peter R. Pettit

Texas

ALLIED BANCSHARES CAPITAL CORP.

1000 Louisiana
Houston, TX 77002
713/226-1625

Affiliation: Allied Bancshares Inc.
Year Founded: 1979
Total Private Funds: $13,000,000
Total SBA Leverage: 0

1983 Investment History:
Total Investments: $2,400,000
Deals: 6
Average Investment: $400,000

Project Preferences
Geographical: Southwest
Industries: Diversified, Computer Software, Medical & Health, Robotics
Stages: Later

Principals: Phillip A. Tuttle, Pres.; Hollis L. Walters, V.P & Sec.; D. Kent Anderson
Contact: Phillip A. Tuttle

AMERICAN ENERGY INVESTMENT CORP.

1010 Lamar St., Suite 1680
Houston, TX 77002
713/651-0220; 212/752-1291

Year Founded: 1981
Total Private Funds: $2,500,000
Total SBA Leverage: $2,500,000

1983 Investment History:
Total Investments: $3,100,000
Deals: 7
Average Investment: $442,857

Project Preferences
Geographical: Anywhere in U.S., Mountain States, TX
Industries: Oil & Gas
Stages: Second, Later

Principals: John J. Hoey, Chair.; James Rhenos, Sec. & Treas.
Contact: John J. Hoey

AMERICAP CORP.

6363 Woodway, Suite 200
Houston, TX 77057
713/780-8084

Year Founded: 1983
Total Private Funds: $1,100,000
Total SBA Leverage: $1,000,000

1983 Investment History:
Total Investments: $1,100,000
Deals: 7
Average Investment: $157,143

Project Preferences
Geographical: Southwest
Industries: Diversified
Stages: Any

Principals: Joe E. Russo, Chair.; James L. Hurn, Pres.
Contact: James L. Hurn

BOW LANE CAPITAL CORP.

2401 Fountain View, Suite 950
Houston, TX 77057
713/977-7421

Year Founded: 1983
Total Private Funds: $2,500,000
Total SBA Leverage: $8,500,000

1983 Investment History:
Total Investments: $2,010,000
Deals: 7
Average Investment: $285,714

Project Preferences
Geographical: Anywhere in U.S.
Industries: High Technology
Stages: Second, Later

Principals: Stuart Schube, Pres.
Contact: Stuart Schube

Branch: 3305 Graybuck Rd., Austin, TX 78748, 512/282-9330.
    Contact: Hugh Batey

BRITTANY CAPITAL CORP.

2424 LTV Tower
Dallas, TX 75201
214/742-5810

Year Founded: 1968
Total Private Funds: $500,000
Total SBA Leverage: $1,400,000

1983 Investment History:
Total Investments: $1,500,000
Deals: 10
Average Investment: $150,000

Project Preferences
Geographical: Anywhere in U.S.
Industries: Diversified
Stages: Startup, First,Second

Principals: Robert E. Clements, Pres.
Contact: Robert E. Clements

CAPITAL MARKETING CORP.

P.O. Box 1000
Keller, TX 76248
817/656-7380

Year Founded: 1968
Total Private Funds: $8,900,000
Total SBA Leverage: $26,000,000

1983 Investment History:
Total Investments: $7,700,000
Deals: 34
Average Investment: $226,471

Project Preferences
Geographical: TX
Industries: Retail Grocery
Stages*: Seed, Startup, First

Principals: John King Myrick, Pres.; Roger P. Fryar, V.P.; Morris
 Whetstone, Gen. Mgr.
Contact: Morris Whetstone

*Loans only.

CAPITAL SOUTHWEST VENTURE CORP.

12900 Preston Rd., Suite 700
Dallas, TX 75230
214/233-8242

Affiliation: Capital Southwest Corp.
Year Founded: 1961
Total Private Funds: $6,500,000
Total SBA Leverage: $6,000,000

1983 Investment History:
Total Investments: $3,500,000
Deals: 8
Average Investment: $438,250

Project Preferences
Geographical: Anywhere in U.S.
Industries: High Technology, Energy
Stages: Later

Principals: William R. Thomas, Chair. & Pres.; J. Bruce Duty, V.P.,
 Sec. & Treas., Pat Hamner, Investment Assoc.
Contact: Any of Above

ENERGY CAPITAL CORP.

953 Esperson Bldg.
Houston, TX 77002
713/236-0006

Affiliation: Energy Capital
Year Founded: 1980
Total Private Funds: $11,500,000
Total SBA Leverage: $1,500,000

1983 Investment History:
Total Investments: $4,100,000
Deals: 8
Average Investment: $512,500

Project Preferences
Geographical: TX, LA, KS
Industries: Energy-Related, Oil & Gas
Stages: Seed, Startup, First

Principals: Herbert F. Poyner Jr., Pres.; Donald R. Henderson, V.P.;
 George Allman, Sec.
Contact: Any of Above

INTERCAPCO INC.

750 N. St. Paul, Suite 500
Dallas, TX 75201
214/969-0250

Year Founded: 1976
Total Private Funds: $5,000,000
Total SBA Leverage: $10,000,000

1983 Investment History:
Total Investments: $4,100,000
Deals: 13
Average Investment: $315,385

Project Preferences
Geographical: Anywhere in U.S.
Industries: High Technology, Telecommunications
Stages: Any

Principals: Thomas O. Hicks, Man. Dir.
Contact: Thomas O. Hicks

INTERFIRST VENTURE CORP.

P.O. Box 83644
Dallas, TX 75283
214/744-8050

Affiliation: InterFirst Corp.
Year Founded: 1961
Total Private Funds: $12,500,000
Total SBA Leverage: $10,000,000

1983 Investment History:
Total Investments: $12,000,000
Deals: 14
Average Investment: $857,143

Project Preferences
Geographical: Southwest, Southeast
Industries: High Technology, Healthcare
Stages: Any

Principals: James O'Donnell, Pres.; Mark Masur, V.P.; Frank Young,
 Asst. V.P.; Michael Novelli, Investment Off.
Contact: Any of Above

MAPLELEAF CAPITAL CORP.

1 W. Loop S., Suite 603
Houston, TX 77027
713/627-0752

Year Founded: 1980
Total Private Funds: $3,500,000
Total SBA Leverage: $2,000,000

1983 Investment History:
Total Investments: $1,700,000
Deals: 4
Average Investment: $425,000

Project Preferences
Geographical: Southwest, TX
Industries: Diversified
Stages: Later

Principals: Edward M. Fink, Pres.; Bernadette Obermeier, Treas.
Contact: Either

MVENTURE CORP.

P.O. Box 662090
1704 Main St.
Dallas, TX 75266-2090
214/741-1469

Affiliation: MBank of Dallas
Year Founded: 1976
Total Private Funds: $15,000,000
Total SBA Leverage: $30,000,000

1983 Investment History:
Total Investments: $28,400,000
Deals: 65
Average Investment: $436,923

Project Preferences
Geographical: Southwest
Industries: Healthcare, Communications, Basic Industries
Stages: Later

Principals: James B. Gardner, Chair. & Dir.; John G. Farmer, Pres. & Dir.; J. Wayne Gaylord, Exec. V.P., Sec., Asst. Treas. & Dir.; Thomas K. Mitchell, Investment Off. & Asst. Sec.; Edwin A. Walker, Investment Off.
Contact: J. Wayne Gaylord, Thomas K. Mitchell, Edwin A. Walker

REPUBLIC VENTURE GROUP INC.

P.O. Box 225961
Dallas, TX 75265
214/653-5078

Affiliation: Republic Bank of Dallas
Year Founded: 1961
Total Private Funds: $12,000,000
Total SBA Leverage: 0

1983 Investment History:
Total Investments: $4,000,000
Deals: 11
Average Investment: $363,636

Project Preferences
Geographical: Anywhere in U.S., Southwest
Industries: Diversified
Stages: Seed, Startup, First, Second

Principals: Robert H. Wellborn, Pres.; Christian A. Melhado, Investment Off.; Wayne C. Willcox, Investment Off.; Bart A. McLean, Investment Off.; William W. Richey, Investment Off.
Contact: Any of Above

RICE INVESTMENT CO.

3350 Rodgerdale
Houston, TX 77042
713/797-1990

Year Founded: 1961
Total Private Funds: $1,800,000
Total SBA Leverage: $3,700,000

1983 Investment History: Not Provided

Project Preferences
Geographical: TX, Southeast
Industries: Grocery Stores
Stages: Startup

Principals: Alvin Diamond, Sec.
Contact: Alvin Diamond

RUST CAPITAL LTD.

114 W. Seventh St., Suite 1300
Austin, TX 78701
512/479-0055

Year Founded: 1979
Total Private Funds: $7,000,000
Total SBA Leverage: $7,500,000

1983 Investment History:
Total Investments: $2,800,000
Deals: 5
Average Investment: $560,000

Project Preferences
Geographical: Anywhere in U.S.
Industries: High Technology, Healthcare, Medical Technology, Communications, Telecommunications
Stages: Seed, Startup, First

Principals: Jeffrey C. Garvey, Pres.; Kenneth P. DeAngelis, Man. Dir.; Joseph C. Aragona, V.P.; John J. Locy, V.P.; William P. Wood, V.P
Contact: Any of Above

SBI CAPITAL CORP.

P.O. Box 771668
Houston, TX 77215
713/975-1188

Year Founded: 1980
Total Private Funds: $1,800,000
Total SBA Leverage: $1,000,000

1983 Investment History:
Total Investments: $1,100,000
Deals: 8
Average Investment: $137,500

Project Preferences
Geographical: TX
Industries: Diversified, Computer-Related, Oil & Gas
Stages: Any

Principals: William E. Wright, Pres.; W. M. Wright, Sec., Treas. & V.P.; Paul W. Wright, V.P.
Contact: William E. Wright

TEXAS CAPITAL CORP.

333 Clay St., Suite 2100
Houston, TX 77002
713/658-9961

Affiliation: Telecom Corp.
Year Founded: 1959
Total Private Funds: $3,100,000
Total SBA Leverage: $7,700,000

1983 Investment History:
Total Investments: $3,000,000
Deals: 14
Average Investment: $214,286

Project Preferences
Geographical: Southwest
Industries: Diversified
Stages: Second, Later, Buyouts

Principals: W. Grogan Lord, Pres.; Larry W. Schumann, Exec. V.P.; David G. Franklin, V.P.; Tom Beecroft, Investment Mgr.
Contact: Larry W. Schumann, David G. Franklin, Tom Beecroft

SBICs $3 MIL AND UP

TEXAS COMMERCE INVESTMENT CO.

P.O. Box 2558
Houston, TX 77252
713/236-5332

Affiliation: Texas Commerce Bancshares
Year Founded: 1982
Total Private Funds: $7,500,000
Total SBA Leverage: 0

1983 Investment History:
Total Investments: $5,500,000
Deals: 8
Average Investment: $687,500

Project Preferences
Geographical: Anywhere in U.S., Southwest
Industries: Diversified, Natural Resources, Healthcare
Stages: Any

Principals: Fred R. Lummis, V.P.; Fred C. Hamilton, Investment Off.
Contact: Either

TSM CORP.

444 Executive Ctr. Blvd., Suite 237
El Paso, TX 79902
915/533-6375

Year Founded: 1976
Total Private Funds: $6,000,000
Total SBA Leverage: $1,200,000

1983 Investment History:
Total Investments: $300,000
Deals: 5
Average Investment: $60,000

Project Preferences
Geographical: Western TX, NM
Industries: Manufacturing
Stages: Any

Principals: Joe Justice, Gen. Mgr.
Contact: Joe Justice

Virginia

JAMES RIVER CAPITAL ASSOCIATES

9 S. 12th St.
Richmond, VA 23219
804/643-7358

Affiliation: Hillcrest Group
Year Founded: 1981
Total Private Funds: $1,200,000
Total SBA Leverage: $1,300,000

1983 Investment History:
Total Investments: $1,600,000
Deals: 10
Average Investment: $160,000

Project Preferences
Geographical: Middle Atlantic, Southeast
Industries: Diversified
Stages: Second, Later, Buyouts

Principals: A. Hugh Ewing III, Gen. Part.; James B. Farinholt Jr., Gen. Part.
Contact: Either

Branch: 1666 K. St., NW, Washington, D.C. 20006, 202/872-6054.
    Contact: J. Roderick Heller III, Gen Part.

UV CAPITAL

9 S. 12th St.
Richmond, VA 23219
804/643-7358

Affiliation: United Virginia Bankshares Inc.
Year Founded: 1984
Total Private Funds: $5,000,000
Total SBA Leverage: 0

1983 Investment History: New Fund

Project Preferences
Geographical: Middle Atlantic, Southeast
Industries: Diversified
Stages: Second, Later, Buyouts

Principals: A. Hugh Ewing III, Gen. Part.; James B. Farinholt Jr., Gen. Part.; John B. Funkhouser, Gen. Part.
    Contact: Any of Above

Branch: 1666 K. St., NW, Washington, DC 20006, 202/872-6054.
    Contact: J. Roderick Heller III, Gen. Part.

Washington

OLDSTONE CAPITAL CORP.

1417 Fourth Ave.
Seattle, WA 98101
206/682-5400

Affiliation: Oldstone Bank
Year Founded: 1961
Total Private Funds: $6,000,000
Total SBA Leverage: $16,000,000

1983 Investment History:
Total Investments: $830,000
Deals: 3
Average Investment: $276,667

Project Preferences
Geographical: Anywhere in U.S.
Industries: Consumer-Goods Manufacturing
Stages: Later

Principals: Arthur C. Barton, Exec. V.P.; Nikki Vaudette, Operations Mgr.
Contact: Arthur C. Barton

Branch: 150 S. Main St., Providence, RI 02903, 401/278-2859.
    Contact: Arthur C. Barton

SEAFIRST CAPITAL CORP.

Fourth & Blanchard Bldg.
Seattle, WA 98121
206/583-3278

Affiliation: Seafirst National Bank
Year Founded: 1980
Total Private Funds: $2,500,000
Total SBA Leverage: $3,000,000

1983 Investment History:
Total Investments: $3,700,000
Deals: 9
Average Investment: $411,111

Project Preferences
Geographical: Northwest
Industries: Real Estate
Stages: Any

Principals: Donald F. Rapp, V.P.
Contact: Donald F. Rapp

SBICs
$3 MIL AND UP

SEATTLE TRUST CAPITAL CORP.

804 Second Ave
Seattle, WA 98104
206/223-2237

Affiliation: Seattle Trust & Savings Bank
Year Founded: 1981
Total Private Funds: $1,000,000
Total SBA Leverage: 0

1983 Investment History:
Total Investments: $1,000,000
Deals: 5
Average Investment: $200,000

Project Preferences
Geographical: Northwest
Industries: Diversified
Stages: Startup, First, Second, Later

Principals: Donald M. McPhee, V.P.
Contact: Donald M. McPhee

Wisconsin

BANDO-McGLOCKLIN INVESTMENT CO. INC.

13555 Bishops Court, Suite 205
Brookfield, WI 53005
414/784-9010

Year Founded: 1980
Total Private Funds: $3,000,000
Total SBA Leverage: $12,400,000

1983 Investment History:
Total Investments: $5,000,000
Deals: 13
Average Investment: $384,615

Project Preferences
Geographical: Anywhere in U.S., WI
Industries: Manufacturing, Service, Wholesalers
Stages: Later

Principals: George Schonath, CEO; Sal L. Bando, Pres.; Jon McGlocklin, Exec. V.P.
Contact: Sal L. Bando

CAPITAL INVESTMENTS INC.

744 N. Fourth St., Suite 400
Milwaukee, WI 53203
414/273-6560

Year Founded: 1959
Total Private Funds: $2,500,000
Total SBA Leverage: $7,500,000

1983 Investment History:
Total Investments: $1,300,000
Deals: 3
Average Investment: $433,333

Project Preferences
Geographical: Anywhere in U.S.
Industries: Diversified
Stages: Later, Buyouts

Principals: Frank W. Norris, Pres.; Robert L. Banner, V.P.; Steven C. Rippl, Sec. & Treas.
Contact: Any of Above

SMALL BUSINESS INVESTMENT COMPANIES: UNDER $3 MILLION

Alabama

BENSON INVESTMENT CO.

504 S. Commerce St.
Geneva, AL 36340
205/684-2824

Year Founded: 1978
Total Private Funds: $1,000,000
Total SBA Leverage: $1,000,000

1983 Investment History:
Total Investments: $200,000
Deals: 3
Average Investment: $66,667

Project Preferences
Geographical: Southeast AL, GA, FL
Industries: Grocery-Store Franchises
Stages: Startup, First

Principals: Joe Dan Benson, Pres.; George Ward, V.P. & Sec.
Contact: Either

Arizona

FIRST SOUTHWEST SMALL BUSINESS INVESTMENT CO.

4350 E. Camelback, Suite 120-B
Phoenix, AZ 85018
602/840-6072

Year Founded: 1962
Total Private Funds: $540,000
Total SBA Leverage: 0

Investment History:
Total Investments: No Investments Made in 1983

Project Preferences
Geographical: Southwest, AZ
Industries: Diversified
Stages: Seed, Startup, First, Second, Later

Principals: William Howard O'Brien, Pres.
Contact: William Howard O'Brien

ROCKY MOUNTAIN EQUITY CORP.

4530 N. Central Ave.
Phoenix, AZ 85012
602/274-7534

Year Founded: 1981
Total Private Funds: $550,000
Total SBA Leverage: $500,000

1983 Investment History:
Total Investments: $200,000
Deals: 2
Average Investment: $100,000

Project Preferences
Geographical: AZ
Industries: Diversified
Stages: Later

Principals: Anthony J. Nicoli, Pres.
Contact: Anthony J. Nicoli

Arkansas

FIRST SBIC OF ARKANSAS INC.

1400 Worthen Bank Bldg.
Little Rock, AR 72201
501/378-1876

Affiliation: Worthen Banking Corp.
Year Founded: 1976
Total Private Funds: $600,000
Total SBA Leverage: 0

1983 Investment History: Not Provided

Project Preferences
Geographical: AR
Industries: Manufacturing
Stages: Second, Later

Principals: Fred C. Burns, Pres. & Gen. Mgr.; Michael F. Cissel, V.P.
Contact: Either

INDEPENDENCE FINANCIAL SERVICES INC.

12th & Main St.
Batesville, AR 72501
501/793-4533

Affiliation: Independence Federal Bank
Year Founded: 1982
Total Private Funds: $500,000
Total SBA Leverage: 0

1983 Investment History:
Total Investments: $325,000
Deals: 4
Average Investment: $81,250

Project Preferences
Geographical: Southeast, AR
Industries: Diversified
Stages: Any

Principals: Jeffrey Hance, Sec.
Contact: Jeffrey Hance

California

ALLIED BUSINESS INVESTORS INC.

482 S. Atlantic Blvd., Suite 201
Monterey Park, CA 91754
818/289-0186

Year Founded: 1982
Total Private Funds: $600,000
Total SBA Leverage: 0

1983 Investment History:
Total Investments: $580,000
Deals: 5
Average Investment: $116,000

Project Preferences
Geographical: Anywhere in U.S.
Industries: Diversified
Stages: Later

Principals: Jack Hong, Pres.
Contact: Jack Hong

SBICs UNDER $3 MIL

AMF FINANCIAL INC.

9910-D Mira Mesa Blvd.
San Diego, CA 92126
619/695-0233

Affiliation: American Mortgage Fund
Year Founded: 1982
Total Private Funds: $500,000
Total SBA Leverage: 0

1983 Investment History: Not Provided

Project Preferences
Geographical: Southern CA
Industries: Diversified
Stages: Later

Principals: Steven R. Jones, CEO; William Temple, Pres.
Contact: William Temple

BANCORP VENTURE CAPITAL INC.

2633 Cherry Ave.
Signal Hill, CA 90806
213/595-1177

Year Founded: 1984
Total Private Funds: $2,300,000
Total SBA Leverage: 0

1983 Investment History: New Fund

Project Preferences
Geographical: West Coast, CA
Industries: Diversified
Stages: Later, Buyouts

Principals: Paul Blair, Pres.
Contact: Paul Blair

BENOX INC.

17295 E. Railroad St.
City of Industry, CA 91749
818/965-1541

Affiliation: Utility Trailer Manufacturing Co.
Year Founded: 1980
Total Private Funds: $500,000
Total SBA Leverage: 0

1983 Investment History:
Total Investments: $100,000
Deals: 1

Project Preferences
Geographical: Anywhere in U.S.
Industries: Truck/Trailer Retail, Specialized Transport
Stages: Any

Principals: John C. Bennett, Chair.; Neil G. Smith, Pres.; Al J. Frazer, Sec.; M.J. Blum, CFO.
Contact: John C. Bennett; Neil G. Smith

CALIFORNIA FIRST BANK VENTURE CAPITAL CORP.

530 B St.
San Diego, CA 92112
619/230-4567

Affiliation: Bank of Tokyo*
Year Founded: 1983
Total Private Funds: $1,000,000
Total SBA Leverage: 0

1983 Investment History: New Fund

Project Preferences
Geographical: CA
Industries: High Technology
Stages: Startup, Later, Buyouts

Principals: Y. Shibusawa, Pres.; Yoji Anzai, V.P.
Contact: Either

*Syndicate with 20% of investors from Japan.

CFB VENTURE CAPITAL CORP.

530 B St.
San Diego, CA 92101
619/230-3304

Affiliation: California First Bank
Year Founded: 1983
Total Private Funds: $1,000,000
Total SBA Leverage: 0

1983 Investment History: New Fund

Project Preferences
Geographical: CA
Industries: High Technology
Stages: Later

Principals: Piet Westerbeck III, CFO; Richard J. Roncagliar, V.P.
Contact: Either

Branches: 616 W. Sixth St., Los Angeles, CA 90017, 213/972-5260.
350 California St., San Francisco, CA 94104, 415/445-0200.

CITY VENTURES INC.

404 N. Roxbury Dr., Suite 800
Beverly Hills, CA 90210
213/550-0416

Affiliation: City National Bank
Year Founded: 1982
Total Private Funds: $2,000,000
Total SBA Leverage: 0

1983 Investment History:
Total Investments: $500,000
Deals: 2
Average Investment: $250,000

Project Preferences
Geographical: Anywhere in U.S.
Industries: Diversified, Consumer, Manufacturing, High Technology
Stages: Later

Principals: Neill B. Lawton, Pres.
Contact: Neill B. Lawton

CROCKER CAPITAL CORP.

111 Sutter St., Suite 600
San Francisco, CA 94104
415/399-7889

Year Founded: 1970
Total Private Funds: $1,000,000
Total SBA Leverage: 0

1983 Investment History:
Total Investments: $1,000,000
Deals: 4
Average Investment: $250,000

Project Preferences
Geographical: West Coast, San Francisco Bay Area
Industries: Diversified, High Technology, Electronics, Biological Research
Stages: Any

Principals: Charles Crocker, Pres., William R. Dawson, V.P.
Contact: Either

DEVELOPERS EQUITY CAPITAL CORP.

9201 Wilshire Blvd., Suite 204
Beverly Hills, CA 90210
213/278-3611

Year Founded: 1964
Total Private Funds: $583,000
Total SBA Leverage: $550,000

1983 Investment History:
Total Investments: $850,000
Deals: 9
Average Investment: $94,444

Project Preferences
Geographical: Southern CA
Industries: Real Estate
Stages: Second

Principals: Larry Sade, Pres.
Contact: Larry Sade

ENTERPRISE VENTURE CAPITAL CORP.

1922 The Alameda, Suite 306
San Jose, CA 95126
408/246-7502

Year Founded: 1983
Total Private Funds: $750,000
Total SBA Leverage: $750,000

1983 Investment History:
Total Investments: $145,000
Deals: 3
Average Investment: $48,333

Project Preferences
Geographical: Anywhere in U.S., CA
Industries: Diversified, High Technology
Stages: Seed, Startup, First

Principals: Ernest de la Ossa, Pres.
Contact: Ernest de la Ossa

HAMCO CAPITAL CORP.

235 Montgomery St., Suite 530
San Francisco, CA 94104
415/576-3300

Affiliation: Hambrecht & Quist
Year Founded: 1982
Total Private Funds: $1,200,000
Total SBA Leverage: $1,000,000

1983 Investment History: Not Provided

Project Preferences
Geographical: Anywhere in U.S.
Industries: Diversified
Stages: Seed, Startup, First, Second

Principals: William R. Hambrecht, Pres.
Contact: William R. Hambrecht

IK CAPITAL LOANS

8601 Wilshire Blvd., Suite 600
Beverly Hills, CA 90211
213/657-0178

Year Founded: 1982
Total Private Funds: $1,000,000
Total SBA Leverage: 0

1983 Investment History: Not Provided

Project Preferences
Geographical: Anywhere in U.S., Southern CA
Industries: Diversified
Stages: Any

Principals: Iraj Kermanshahchi, Pres.; Joseph Forgatch, V.P.
Contact: Either

IVANHOE VENTURE CAPITAL LTD.

737 Pearl St., Suite 201
La Jolla, CA 92037
619/454-8882

Year Founded: 1983
Total Private Funds: $700,000
Total SBA Leverage: $500,000

1983 Investment History:
Total Investments: $1,100,000
Deals: 1

Project Preferences
Geographical: Southern CA
Industries: High Technology, Medical
Stages: Seed, Startup, First, Second, Later

Principals: Alan Toffler, Man. Gen. Part.
Contact: Alan Toffler

LATIGO CAPITAL PARTNERS

23410 Civic Center Way, Suite E-2
Malibu, CA 90265
213/456-5539

Affiliation: Latigo Ventures
Year Founded: 1982
Total Private Funds: $1,000,000
Total SBA Leverage: $1,000,000

1983 Investment History:
Total Investments: $700,000
Deals: 4
Average Investment: $175,000

Project Preferences
Geographical: Anywhere in U.S.
Industries: High Technology, Medical Technology,
    Restaurants
Stages: Seed, Startup, First, Second, Later

Principals: Robert Peterson, Gen. Part.; Donald Peterson, Gen. Part.
Contact: Robert Peterson

METROPOLITAN VENTURE CO. INC.

5757 Wilshire Blvd., Suite 670
Los Angeles, CA 90036-3636
213/938-3488

Year Founded: 1981
Total Private Funds: $1,000,000
Total SBA Leverage: 0

1983 Investment History:
Total Investments: $375,000
Deals: 4
Average Investment: $93,750

Project Preferences
Geographical: CA
Industries: Diversified, Real Estate, Financial Services
Stages: Buyouts

Principals: Esther Lowy, Pres.
Contact: Esther Lowy

MONTGOMERY VENTURES*

606 Wilshire Blvd., Suite 602
Santa Monica, CA 90401
213/458-1441

*See Peregrine Associates, page 39.

NSS INVESTMENT INC.

897 MacArthur Blvd., Suite 103
San Leandro, CA 94577
415/632-5833

Year Founded: 1980
Total Private Funds: $500,000
Total SBA Leverage: $1,200,000

1983 Investment History:
Total Investments: $422,000
Deals: 3
Average Investment: $140,667

Project Preferences
Geographical: Northern CA, NV
Industries: Diversified
Stages: Any

Principals: Bernie N. Nemerov, Pres; Beryl Stolper, Sec. & Treas.
Contact: Either

ROUND TABLE CAPITAL CORP.

601 Montgomery St.
San Francisco, CA 94111
415/392-7500

Affiliation: Round Table Pizza Inc.
Year Founded: 1959
Total Private Funds: $700,000
Total SBA Leverage: $1,500,000

1983 Investment History: Not Provided

Project Preferences
Geographical: West Coast, Midwest
Industries: Restaurants
Stages: Seed, Startup, First

Principals: Richard A. Dumke, Chair.; Scott Bergrem, Pres.;
    Micheline Chau, Exec. V.P.
Contact: Any of Above

WESCO CAPITAL LTD.

3471 Via Lido, Suite 204
Newport Beach, CA 92663
714/673-4733

Year Founded: 1983
Total Private Funds: $1,000,000
Total SBA Leverage: 0

1983 Investment History:
Total Investments: $200,000
Deals: 6
Average Investment: $33,333

Project Preferences
Geographical: Anywhere in U.S., CA
Industries: Diversified, Manufacturing
Stages: First, Second, Later, Buyouts

Principals: Peter J. Madigan, Gen. Part.
Contact: Peter J. Madigan

WESTAMCO INVESTMENT CO.

8929 Wilshire Blvd.
Beverly Hills, CA 90211
213/652-8288

Year Founded: 1961
Total Private Funds: $800,000
Total SBA Leverage: $275,000

1983 Investment History:
Total Investments: $800,000
Deals: 5
Average Investment: $160,000

Project Preferences
Geographical: Southern CA
Industries: Diversified
Stages: Second, Later

Principals: Leonard G. Muskin, Pres.
Contact: Leonard G. Muskin

Colorado

COLORADO GROWTH CAPITAL INC.

1600 Broadway, Suite 2125
Denver, CO 80202
303/629-0205

Year Founded: 1974
Total Private Funds: $1,100,000
Total SBA Leverage: 0

1983 Investment History: Not Provided

Project Preferences
Geographical: Mountain States
Industries: Oil Processing, Manufacturing
Stages: Second, Later

Principals: Debra Chavez, Financial Analyst
Contact: Debra Chavez

ENTERPRISE FINANCE CAPITAL DEVELOPMENT CORP.

P.O. Box 5840
Snowmass Village, CO 81615
303/923-4144

Affiliation: Enterprise Finance Co.
Year Founded: 1983
Total Private Funds: $1,000,000
Total SBA Leverage: 0

1983 Investment History:
Total Investments: $580,000
Deals: 3
Average Investment: $193,333

Project Preferences
Geographical: Anywhere in U.S.
Industries: Diversified
Stages: Later

Principals: Robert N. Hampton, Pres.
Contact: Robert N. Hampton

Connecticut

NORTHEASTERN CAPITAL CORP.

61 High St.
East Haven, CT 06512
203/469-7901

Year Founded: 1961
Total Private Funds: $500,000
Total SBA Leverage: $1,100,000

1983 Investment History:
Total Investments: $200,000
Deals: 12
Average Investment: $16,667

Project Preferences
Geographical: CT
Industries: Diversified
Stages: Any

Principals: Louis W. Mingione, Exec. Dir.
Contact: Louis W. Mingione

Florida

CARIBANK CAPITAL CORP.

255 E. Dania Beach Blvd.
Dania, FL 33004
305/925-2880

Affiliation: Caribank
Year Founded: 1982
Total Private Funds: $1,000,000
Total SBA Leverage: $500,000

1983 Investment History:
Total Investments: $750,000
Deals: 5
Average Investment: $150,000

Project Preferences
Geographical: Southeast
Industries: High Technology, Healthcare
Stages: Second, Later

Principals: Michael E. Chaney, Pres.; Harold F. Mezner, V.P.
Contact: Either

FIRST MIAMI SMALL BUSINESS INVESTMENT CO.

250 S. Ocean Blvd., Suite 18D
Boca Raton, FL 33432
305/392-4424

Year Founded: 1959
Total Private Funds: $830,500
Total SBA Leverage: $136,000

1983 Investment History: Not Provided

Project Preferences
Geographical: Southeast, Northeast
Industries: Entertainment, Real Estate
Stages: Later

Principals: Irve L. Libby, Pres.; Jay Linn, Sec.
Contact: Either

Branch: 1195 NE 125 St., North Miami, FL 305/891-2534.
   Contact: Irve L. Libby; Jay Linn

MARKET CAPITAL CORP.

P.O. Box 22667
Tampa, FL 33630
813/247-1357

Year Founded: 1964
Total Private Funds: $700,000
Total SBA Leverage: $1,000,000

1983 Investment History:
Total Investments: $800,000
Deals: 10
Average Investment: $80,000

Project Preferences
Geographical: FL
Industries: Grocery Stores
Stages: Any

Principals: Robert Taylor, Investment Mgr.
Contact: Robert Taylor

Georgia

INVESTOR'S EQUITY INC.

2629 First Atlanta Tower
Atlanta, GA 30383
404/523-3999

Year Founded: 1960
Total Private Funds: $2,200,000
Total SBA Leverage: 0

1983 Investment History: Not Provided

Project Preferences
Geographical: Southeast
Industries: Light Manufacturing, High Technology
Stages: Second

Principals: I. Walter Fisher, Pres.; Richard W. Bell, V.P.
Contact: Richard W. Bell

MIGHTY CAPITAL CORP.

50 Technology Park
Norcross, GA 30092
404/448-2232

Affiliation: Mighty Distributing System of America Inc.
Year Founded: 1983
Total Private Funds: $505,000
Total SBA Leverage: 0

1983 Investment History: New Fund

Project Preferences
Geographical: Anywhere in U.S.
Industries: Automotive
Stages: First, Second

Principals: Gary Korynoski, V.P. & Gen. Mgr.
Contact: Gary Korynoski

Illinois

ALPHA CAPITAL VENTURE PARTNERS

3 First National Plaza, Suite 1400
Chicago, IL 60602
312/372-1556

Year Founded: 1983
Total Private Funds: $1,300,000
Total SBA Leverage: 0

1983 Investment History:
Total Investments: $250,000
Deals: 1

Project Preferences
Geographical: Midwest
Industries: Diversified
Stages: Any

Principals: Andrew H. Kalnow, Man. Part.; Daniel W. O'Connell, Man. Part.
Contact: Either

Indiana

CIRCLE VENTURES INC.

20 N. Meridian St.
Indianapolis, IN 46204
317/636-7242

Affiliation: Raffensperger Hughes & Co. Inc.
Year Founded: 1983
Total Private Funds: $1,000,000
Total SBA Leverage: 0

1983 Investment History: New Fund

Project Preferences
Geographical: Central IN
Industries: Diversified
Stages: Any

Principals: Russell Breeden III, V.P.; Sam B. Sutphin II, Investment Off.
Contact: Russell Breeden III

EQUITY RESOURCE CO.

1 Plaza Pl.
202 S. Michigan St.
South Bend, IN 46601
219/237-5255

Year Founded: 1983
Total Private Funds: $2,000,000
Total SBA Leverage: 0

1983 Investment History: New Fund

Project Preferences
Geographical: Northern IN, Southern MI
Industries: Diversified Non-High Technology
Stages: Second, Later, Buyouts

Principals: Richard T. Doermer, Chair.; Richard A. Rosenthal, Pres.; Michael J. Hammes, V.P. & Sec.
Contact: Michael J. Hammes

FIRST SOURCE CAPITAL CORP.

100 N. Michigan St.
South Bend, IN 46601
219/236-2180

Affiliation: First Source Bank
Year Founded: 1983
Total Private Funds: $1,800,000
Total SBA Leverage: 0

1983 Investment History: New Fund

Project Preferences
Geographical: Midwest
Industries: Diversified
Stages: Later

Principals: Christopher J. Murphy III, Pres.; Eugene L. Cavanaugh Jr., V.P.
Contact: Eugene L. Cavanaugh Jr.

SBICs UNDER $3 MIL

WHITE RIVER CAPITAL CORP.

P.O. Box 929
500 Washington St.
Columbus, IN 47201
812/376-1759

Affiliation: Irwin Union Corp.; Corporation for Innovation
    Development
Year Founded: 1982
Total Private Funds: $1,100,000
Total SBA Leverage: 0

1983 Investment History:
Total Investments: $526,000
Deals: 5
Average Investment: $105,200

Project Preferences
Geographical: Midwest
Industries: Broadcasting, Communications, Software, Electronics
Stages: Second, Later, Buyouts

Principals: John H. Cragoes, Pres.; Thomas D. Washburn, V.P. &
    Treas.; David J. Blair, V.P. Investment
Contact: David J. Blair

Kentucky

BLACKBURN-SANFORD VENTURE CAPITAL CORP.

3120 First National Tower
Louisville, KY 40202
502/585-9612

Year Founded: 1983
Total Private Funds: $1,400,000
Total SBA Leverage: 0

1983 Investment History: Not Provided

Project Preferences
Geographical: South, Middle Atlantic, Midwest
Industries: Diversified, Service
Stages: Seed, Startup, First, Second

Principals: Charles S. Arensberg, Exec. V.P. & Gen. Mgr.
Contact: Charles S. Arenberg

MOUNTAIN VENTURES INC.

911 N. Main St.
London, KY 40741
606/878-6635

Affiliation: Kentucky Highlands Investment Co.
Year Founded: 1978
Total Private Funds: $1,600,000
Total SBA Leverage: $170,000

1983 Investment History:
Total Investments: $170,000
Deals: 2
Average Investment: $85,000

Project Preferences
Geographical: KY
Industries: Diversified
Stages: Seed, Startup, First

Principals: Ray Moncrief, Pres.
Contact: Ray Moncrief

Louisiana

CADDO CAPITAL CORP.

3010 Knight, Suite 240
Shreveport, LA 71105
318/869-1689

Year Founded: 1979
Total Private Funds: $530,000
Total SBA Leverage: $1,000,000

1983 Investment History:
Total Investments: $250,000
Deals: 6
Average Investment: $41,667

Project Preferences
Geographical: Anywhere in U.S., Southwest
Industries: Diversified, Medical, Computers
Stages: Second

Principals: Thomas L. Young Jr., Pres.; Debby S. Wauson, V.P.
Contact: Debby S. Wauson

CAPITAL EQUITY CORP.

1885 Wooddale Blvd.
Baton Rouge, LA 70806
504/924-9205

Affiliation: Capital Bank & Trust Co.
Year Founded: 1983
Total Private Funds: $1,100,000
Total SBA Leverage: 0

1983 Investment History:
Total Investments: $400,000
Deals: 3
Average Investment: $133,333

Project Preferences
Geographical: LA
Industries: Diversified
Stages: Startup, First, Second, Later

Principals: Arthur J. Mitchell, Gen. Mgr.
Contact: Arthur J. Mitchell

DIXIE BUSINESS INVESTMENT CO.

P.O. Box 588
Lake Providence, LA 71254
318/559-1558

Affiliation: Bank of Dixie
Year Founded: 1974
Total SBA Leverage: $1,200,000

1983 Investment History:
Total Investment: $500,000
Deals: 7
Average Investment: $71,429

Project Preferences
Geographical: South
Industries: Real Estate, Construction
Stages: Second

Principals: Wayne Baker, Pres.; George S. Linsing, Mgr.; Jamie
    Scott, Asst. Mgr.
Contact: Jamie Scott

Maine

MAINE CAPITAL CORP.

70 Center St.
Portland, ME 04101
207/772-1001

Year Founded: 1980
Total Private Funds: $1,000,000
Total SBA Leverage: 0

1983 Investment History:
Total Investments: $200,000
Deals: 3
Average Investment: $66,667

Project Preferences
Geographical: ME
Industries: Diversified
Stages: Any

Principals: David Coit, Pres.
Contact: David Coit

Massachusetts

NORTHEAST SBIC CORP.

16 Cumberland St.
Boston, MA 02115
617/267-3983

Year Founded: 1974
Total Private Funds: $387,000
Total SBA Leverage: $1,100,000

Investment History:
Total Investments: $900,000
Deals: 8
Average Investment: $112,500

Project Preferences
Geographical: Northeast
Industries: High Technology
Stages: Second

Principals: Morris Isseroff, Treas.
Contact: Morris Isserott

WORCESTER CAPITAL CORP.

446 Main St.
Worcester, MA 01608
617/793-4508

Affiliation: Shawmut Worcester County Bank
Year Founded: 1967
Total Private Funds: $1,000,000
Total SBA Leverage: $200,000

1983 Investment History:
Total Investments: $200,000
Deals: 2
Average Investment: $100,000

Project Preferences
Geographical: New England
Industries: Diversified
Stages: Second, Later

Principals: W. Kenneth Kidd, V.P. & Gen. Mgr.
Contact: W. Kenneth Kidd

Michigan

MICHIGAN TECH CAPITAL CORP.

1414 College Ave.
Houghton, MI 49931
906/487-2643

Year Founded: 1982
Total Private Funds: $600,000
Total SBA Leverage: 0

1983 Investment History:
Total Investments: $150,000
Deals: 2
Average Investment: $75,000

Project Preferences
Geographical: Anywhere in U.S., MI
Industries: High Technology, Electronics,
   Metallurgy, Chemicals, Software
Stages: Seed, Startup, First

Principals: Edward J. Koepel, Pres,; Clark L. Pellegrini, Treas.;
   Richard E. Tieder, Sec.
Contact: Richard E. Tieder

Minnesota

CONSUMER GROWTH CAPITAL INC.

8200 Humboldt Ave. S.
Bloomington, MN 55431
612/888-9561

Year Founded: 1977
Total Private Funds: $1,500,000
Total SBA Leverage: $1,000,000

1983 Investment History:
Total Investments: $100,000
Deals: 1

Project Preferences
Geographical: Midwest
Industries: Consumer Goods
Stages: Seed, Startup, First, Second

Principals: Bruce A. Thomson, Pres.; David S. Sommers, Asst. Sec.
Contact: David S. Sommers

NORTHLAND CAPITAL CORP.

613 Missabe Bldg.
227 W. First St.
Duluth, MN 55802
218/772-0545

Year Founded: 1967
Total Private Funds: $800,000
Total SBA Leverage: $400,000

1983 Investment History:
Total Investments: $300,000
Deals: 10
Average Investment: $30,000

Project Preferences
Geographical: Northern MN, Upper MI, Northern WI
Industries: Diversified
Stages: Seed, Startup, First, Second, Later

Principals: George G. Barnum Jr., Pres.
Contract: George G. Barnum

RETAILERS GROWTH FUND INC.

2318 Park Ave. S.
Minneapolis, MN 55404
612/872-4929

Affiliation: Lease Moore Equipment Inc.
Year Founded: 1962
Total Private Funds: $700,000
Total SBA Leverage: $1,900,000

1983 Investment History:
Total Investments: $600,000
Deals: 5
Average Investment: $120,000

Project Preferences
Geographical: Anywhere in U.S.
Industries: Retail, Transportation
Stages: Second, Buyouts

Principals: Cornell L. Moore, Pres.; Rick Olson, Controller
& Treas.
Contact: Either

SHARED VENTURES INC.

6550 York Ave. S.
Minneapolis, MN 55435
612/925-3411

Year Founded: 1981
Total Private Funds: $750,000
Total SBA Leverage: $500,000

1983 Investment History: Not Provided

Project Preferences
Geographical: Anywhere in U.S., Upper Midwest
Industries: Diversified
Stages: Any

Principals: Howard Weiner, Pres.; Frederick Weiner, V.P.
Contact: Either

Mississippi

DELTA SBIC CAPITAL CORP.

P.O. Box 588
Greenville, MS 38701
601/335-5291

Affiliation: Delta Foundation
Year Founded: 1972
Total Private Funds: $2,000,000
Total SBA Leverage: 0

1983 Investment History:
Total Investments: Not Provided
Deals: Not Provided
Average Investment: $100,000

Project Preferences
Geographical: Anywhere in U.S.
Industries: Communications
Stages: Any

Principals: Charles Bannerman, Pres.; Howard Bouttee, V.P. & Gen.
Mgr.
Contact: Howard Bouttee

VICKSBURG SBIC

Box 852
Vicksburg, MS 39180
601/636-4762

Year Founded: 1960
Total Private Funds: $700,000
Total SBA Leverage: $500,000

1983 Investment History:
Total Investments: $600,000
Deals: 6
Average Investment: $100,000

Project Preferences
Geographical: MS
Industries: Diversified Non-High Technology
Stages: Startup

Principals: David L. May, Pres.
Contact: David L. May

Missouri

BANKERS CAPITAL CORP.

4049 Pennsylvania St.
Kansas City, MO 64111
816/531-1600

Year Founded: 1976
Total Private Funds: $302,000
Total SBA Leverage: $900,000

1983 Investment History:
Total Investments: $400,000
Deals: 5
Average Investment: $80,000

Project Preferences
Geographical: Anywhere in U.S., Midwest
Industries: Diversified
Stages: Second, Later

Principals: Raymond R. Glasnapp, Pres.; Lee Glasnapp, V.P.
Contact: Either

INTERCAPCO WEST INC.

7800 Bonhomme
St. Louis, MO 63105
314/863-0600

Year Founded: 1976
Total Private Funds: $525,000
Total SBA Leverage: $2,000,000

1983 Investment History:
Total Investments: $500,000
Deals: 9
Average Investment: $55,556

Project Preferences
Geographical: Midwest
Industries: Diversified
Stages: Second, Later, Buyouts

Principals: Thomas E. Phelps, Chair., Mark Lincoln, Pres.
Contact: Either

New Hampshire

GRANITE STATE CAPITAL INC.

10 Fort Eddy Rd.
Concord, NH 03301
603/228-9090

Affiliation: New Hampshire Business Development Corp.
Year Founded: 1983
Total Private Funds: $1,000,000
Total SBA Leverage: $350,000

1983 Investment History: New Fund

Project Preferences
Geographical: NH
Industries: Diversified
Stages: Seed, Startup, First

Principals: Stuart D. Pompian, Man. Dir.
Contact: Stuart D. Pompian

HAMPSHIRE CAPITAL CORP.

P.O. Box 468
500 Spalding Tpke.
Portsmouth, NH 03801
603/431-7755

Affiliation: Business Investment Advisory
Year Founded: 1979
Total Private Funds: $525,000
Total SBA Leverage: 0

1983 Investment History:
Total Investments: $120,000
Deals: 2
Average Investment: $60,000

Project Preferences
Geographical: Anywhere in U.S.
Industries: Diversified
Stages: Seed, Startup, First, Second, Later

Principals: Philip G. Baker, Pres.; Lauren E. Wright, V.P.
Contact: Either

New Jersey

CAPITAL SBIC INC.

691 State Highway 33
Trenton, NJ 08619
609/394-5221

Year Founded: 1963
Total Private Funds: $1,000,000
Total SBA Leverage: 0

1983 Investment History: Not Provided

Project Preferences
Geographical: Anywhere in U.S.
Industries: Real Estate
Stages: Later

Principals: Isadore Cohen, Pres.; Esther Cohen, Sec.
Contact: Either

ESLO CAPITAL CORP.

2401 Morris Ave., Suite 220
Union, NJ 07083
201/467-2545

Year Founded: 1979
Total Private Funds: $639,323
Total SBA Leverage: $1,000,000

1983 Investment History:
Total Investments: $600,000
Deals: 9
Average Investment: $66,667

Project Preferences
Geographical: NY, NJ, MA
Industries: Diversified
Stages: Seed, Startup, First, Second, Later

Principals: Leo Katz, Pres. & Treas.; Estelle Katz, V.P. & Sec.;
Rachelle Katz, V.P.
Contact: Any of Above

FIRST PRINCETON CAPITAL CORP.

227 Hamburg Tpke.
Pompton Lakes, NJ 07442
201/831-0330

Year Founded: 1983
Total Private Funds: $1,300,000
Total SBA Leverage: 0

1983 Investment History:
Total Investments: Not Provided
Deals: Not Provided
Average Investment: $200,000

Project Preferences
Geographical: Anywhere in U.S., NY, CT, NJ
Industries: Diversified
Stages: Later

Principals: S. Lawrence Goldstein, Pres.
Contact: S. Lawrence Goldstein

New Mexico

ALBUQUERQUE SMALL BUSINESS INVESTMENTS CO.

P.O. Box 487
501 Tijeras Ave., NW
Albuquerque, NM 87103
505/247-0145

Year Founded: 1977
Total Private Funds: $502,000
Total SBA Leverage: 0

1983 Investment History:
Total Investments: $200,000
Deals: 2
Average Investment: $100,000

Project Preferences
Geographical: NM
Industries: Diversified
Stages: Second

Principals: Albert T. Ussery, Pres.
Contact: Albert T. Ussery

SBICs UNDER $3 MIL

161

New York

BENEFICIAL CAPITAL CORP.

880 Third Ave.
New York, NY 10022
212/752-1291

Year Founded: 1961
Total Private Funds: $575,000
Total SBA Leverage: $1,500,000

1983 Investment History:
Total Investments: $883,761
Deals: 5
Average Investment: $176,752

Project Preferences
Geographical: Anywhere in U.S.
Industries: Diversified, Real Estate
Stages: Buyouts

Principals: John Hoey, Pres.; James Rhinos, V.P.
Contact: Either

CENTRAL NY SBIC INC.

351 S. Warren St.
Syracuse, NY 13202
315/478-5026

Year Founded: 1961
Total Private Funds: $150,000
Total SBA Leverage: $180,000

1983 Investment History: Not Provided

Project Preferences
Geographical: Upstate NY
Industries: Vending Machines, Services
Stages: Later

Principals: Albert Wertheimer, Pres.; Angelo Rinaldi, Treas.
Contact: Either

CROYDEN CAPITAL CORP.

45 Rockefeller Plaza, Suite 2165
New York, NY 10111
212/974-0184

Year Founded: 1984
Total Private Funds: $1,500,000
Total SBA Leverage: 0

1983 Investment History: New Fund

Project Preferences
Geographical: Anywhere in U.S., Northeast
Industries: Diversified Non-High Technology, Manufacturing,
   Healthcare, Communications, Sophisticated Services, Distribution
Stages: First, Second, Later, Buyouts

Principals: Harry Freund, Chair.; Jay Goldsmith, Co-Chair.; Victor
   Hecht, Pres.; Donald Cecil, Dir.
Contact: Victor Hecht

HANOVER CAPITAL CORP.

150 E. 58th St., Suite 2710
New York, NY 10155
212/980-9670

Year Founded: 1964
Total Private Funds: $850,000
Total SBA Leverage: $1,500,000

1983 Investment History:
Total Investments: Not Provided
Deals: 4

Project Preferences
Geographical: Anywhere in U.S., Northeast
Industries: Diversified, Manufacturing
Stages: Any

Principals: Benson A. Selzer, Chair.; John A. Selzer, Pres.; Alan I.
   Tencer, V.P.; Stephen E. Levenson, V.P.
Contact: Stephen E. Levenson

KWIAT CAPITAL CORP.

576 Fifth Ave.
New York, NY 10036
212/391-2461

Affiliation: Kwiat Management Associates
Year Founded: 1981
Total Private Funds: $500,000
Total SBA Leverage: $1,000,000

1983 Investment History: Not Provided

Project Preferences
Geographical: Anywhere in U.S.
Industries: High Technology
Stages: Seed, Startup, First, Second

Principals: Jeffrey M. Greene, Pres.
Contact: Jeffrey M. Greene

MULTI-PURPOSE CAPITAL CORP.

31 S. Broadway
Yonkers, NY 10701
914/963-2733

Year Founded: 1969
Total Private Funds: $225,000
Total SBA Leverage: $244,000

1983 Investment History: Not Provided

Project Preferences
Geographical: New York City
Industries: Diversified, Construction, Real Estate
Stages: Any

Principals: Eli B. Fine, Pres.
Contact: Eli B. Fine

NELSON CAPITAL CORP.

591 Stewart Ave.
Garden City, NY 11530
516/222-2555

Affiliation: Reprise Capital Corp.
Year Founded: 1972
Total Private Funds: $665,000
Total SBA Leverage: $1,500,000

1983 Investment History:
Total Investments: $900,000
Deals: 9
Average Investment: $100,000

Project Preferences
Geographical: Anywhere in U.S.
Industries: Diversified Non-High Technology, Manufacturing,
    Construction, Land Development
Stages: Second, Buyouts

Principals: Irwin B. Nelson, Pres.
Contact: Irwin B. Nelson

Branches: 8550 Bryn Mawr Ave., Suite 515, Chicago, IL 60631,
    312/693-5990.
10000 Santa Monica Blvd., Suite 300, Los Angeles, CA 90067,
    213/556-1944. *Contact:* Norman Tulchin, Chair.

NPD CAPITAL INC.

375 Park Ave.
New York, NY 10152
212/826-8500

Year Founded: 1983
Total Private Funds: $1,000,000
Total SBA Leverage: 0

1983 Investment History:
Total Investments: $50,000
Deals: 1

Project Preferences
Geographical: East Coast
Industries: Medical, Healthcare
Stages: Any

Principals: Jerome I. Feldman, Chair.
Contact: Jerome I. Feldman

NYBDC CAPITAL CORP.

41 State St.
Albany, NY 12207
518/463-2268

Affiliation: New York Business Development Corp.
Year Founded: 1973
Total Private Funds: $500,000
Total SBA Leverage: $270,000

1983 Investment History: Not Provided

Project Preferences
Geographical: NY
Industries: Manufacturing
Stages: Second

Principals: Marshall R. Lustig, Pres.; Robert W. Lazar, Sr. V.P.; John
    D. Wasson, V.P. & Asst. Sec.
Contact: Marshall R. Lustig

PREFERENTIAL CAPITAL CORP.

16 Court St.
Brooklyn, NY 11241
718/855-2728

Year Founded: 1979
Total Private Funds: $500,000
Total SBA Leverage: $1,000,000

1983 Investment History:
Total Investments: $250,000
Deals: 3
Average Investment: $83,333

Project Preferences
Geographical: New York City
Industries: Diversified
Stages: Any

Principals: Bruce Bayroff, Sec. & Treas.
Contact: Bruce Bayroff

R&R FINANCIAL CORP.

1451 Broadway
New York, NY 10036
212/790-1400

Affiliation: Rosenthal & Rosenthal Inc.
Year Founded: 1962
Total Private Funds: $525,000
Total SBA Leverage: $300,000

1983 Investment History:
Total Investments: $500,000
Deals: 6
Average Investment: $83,333

Project Preferences
Geographical: Middle Atlantic
Industries: Diversified
Stages: Second

Principals: Imre J. Rosenthal, Chair.; Martin Eisenstadt, V.P.
Contact: Martin Eisenstadt

RAND SBIC INC.

1300 Rand Bldg.
Buffalo, NY 14203
716/853-0802

Affiliation: Rand Capital Corp.
Year Founded: 1969
Total Private Funds: $1,600,000
Total SBA Leverage: $600,000

1983 Investment History: No Investments Made in 1983

Project Preferences
Geographical: Northeast
Industries: Diversified, Communications, Cable Applications
Stages: Any

Principals: George F. Rand III, Chair.; Donald A. Ross, Pres., CEO
    & Treas.; Keith B. Wiley, V.P. & Sec.
Contact: Any of Above

SBICs UNDER $3 MIL

REALTY GROWTH CAPITAL CORP.

575 Lexington Ave.
New York, NY 10022
212/755-9044

Year Founded: 1963
Total Private Funds: $500,000
Total SBA Leverage: $1,500,000

1983 Investment History:
Total Investments: Not Provided
Deals: 15
Average Investment: $70,000

Project Preferences
Geographical: Anywhere in U.S., New York City
Industries: Taxicabs, Real Estate
Stages: *

Principals: Lawrence A. Benenson, Pres.
Contact: Lawrence A. Benenson

*Will consider highly collateralized loans only.

TAPPAN ZEE CAPITAL CORP.

120 N. Main St.
New City, NY 10956
914/634-8822

Year Founded: 1963
Total Private Funds: $800,000
Total SBA Leverage: $1,300,000

1983 Investment History: Not Provided

Project Preferences
Geographical: Northeast
Industries: Diversified, Real Estate
Stages: Second

Principals: Jack Birnberg, V.P.
Contact: Jack Birnberg

TRANSGULF CAPITAL CORP.

80 Broad St., 29th Floor
New York, NY 10004
212/785-8370

Year Founded: 1981
Total Private Funds: Not Provided
Total SBA Leverage: Not Provided

1983 Investment History:
Total Investments: Not Provided
Deals: 2

Project Preferences
Geographical: Anywhere in U.S.
Industries: Manufacturing, Distribution, Consumer Products, Industrial Products & Equipment
Stages: Buyouts

Principals: James V. Hoey, Pres.; Douglas H. Bagin, Exec. V.P.; George D. Armiger, Exec V.P.
Contact: Any of Above

TRANSWORLD VENTURES LTD.

331 West End Ave.
New York, NY 10023
212/496-1010

Year Founded: 1982
Total Private Funds: $517,000
Total SBA Leverage: 0

1983 Investment History:
Total Investments: Not Provided
Deals: 3
Average Investment: $100,000

Project Preferences
Geographical: NY, CT, NJ
Industries: Diversified, Service Industries
Stages: First, Second

Principals: Jack H. Berger, Pres.
Contact: Jack H. Berger

North Carolina

FALCON CAPITAL CORP.

311 Evans St.
Greenville, NC 27834
919/752-5918

Year Founded: 1964
Total Private Funds: $58,000
Total SBA Leverage: $75,000

1983 Investment History: Not Provided

Project Preferences
Geographical: Anywhere in U.S., Midwest, East Coast
Industries: Diversified
Stages: Seed, Startup, First, Second, Later

Principals: P.S. Prasad, Pres.
Contact: P.S. Prasad

North Dakota

DAKOTA FIRST CAPITAL CORP.

51 Broadway, Suite 601
Fargo, ND 58102
701/237-0450

Affiliation: Dakota Bankshares Inc.
Year Founded: 1973
Total Private Funds: $1,000,000
Total SBA Leverage: $1,000,000

1983 Investment History:
Total Investments: $300,000
Deals: 3
Average Investment: $100,000

Project Preferences
Geographical: Upper Midwest
Industries: Diversified
Stages: Seed, Startup, First, Second

Principals: David Johnson, Chair.; Donald Scott, V.P.
Contact: Donald Scott

Ohio

BANC ONE CAPITAL CORP.

100 E. Broad St.
Columbus, OH 43215
614/463-5832

Affiliation: Banc One Corp.
Year Founded: 1959
Total Private Funds: $400,000
Total SBA Leverage: 0

1983 Investment History:
Total Investments: $200,000
Deals: 1

Project Preferences
Geographical: OH, CA
Industries: Diversified, Medical, Electronics
Stages: Startup

Principals: John G. McCoy, Pres.; James E. Kolls, V.P.
Contact: James E. Kolls

FIRST OHIO CAPITAL CORP.

606 Madison Ave.
Toledo, OH 43604
419/259-7146

Affiliation: First National Bank of Toledo
Year Founded: 1982
Total Private Funds: $2,000,000
Total SBA Leverage: $300,000

1983 Investment History:
Total Investments: $710,000
Deals: 6
Average Investment: $118,333

Project Preferences
Geographical: IN, KY, PA, WV, OH
Industries: Diversified
Stages: Later

Principals: John T. Rogers, Pres.; Michael Aust, V.P.
Contact: Michael Aust

GRIES INVESTMENT CO.

720 Statler Office Tower
Cleveland, OH 44115
216/861-1146

Year Founded: 1964
Total Private Funds: $1,000,000
Total SBA Leverage: $1,500,000

1983 Investment History: Not Provided

Project Preferences
Geographical: Anywhere in U.S.
Industries: Diversified
Stages: Seed, Startup, First, Second

Principals: Robert D. Gries, Pres.; Richard F. Brezick, V.P.
Contact: Either

MIAMI VALLEY CAPITAL INC.

131 N. Ludlow St., Suite 315
Dayton, OH 45402
513/222-7222

Year Founded: 1980
Total Private Funds: $1,500,000
Total SBA Leverage: $1,300,000

1983 Investment History:
Total Investments: $635,000
Deals: 6
Average Investment: $105,833

Project Preferences
Geographical: Southwestern OH
Industries: Manufacturing
Stages: Seed, Startup, First, Second, Buyouts

Principals: Walker Lewis, Chair.; Everett Telljohann, Pres.
Contact: Either

TAMCO INVESTORS SBIC INC.

P.O. Box 1588
375 Victoria Rd.
Youngstown, OH 44501
216/792-3811

Affiliation: Giant Eagle Inc.
Year Founded: 1977
Total Private Funds: $300,000
Total SBA Leverage: $950,000

1983 Investment History:
Total Investments: $500,000
Deals: 8
Average Investment: $62,500

Project Preferences
Geographical: OH, Western PA
Industries: Grocery Stores
Stages: Startup

Principals: Nathan H. Monus, Pres.
Contact: Nathan H. Monus

TOMLINSON CAPITAL CORP.

3055 E. 63rd St.
Cleveland, OH 44127
216/271-2103

Affiliation: Meyer Co.
Year Founded: 1974
Total Private Funds: $550,000
Total SBA Leverage: $1,400,000

1983 Investment History:
Total Investments: $750,000
Deals: 20
Average Investment: $37,500

Project Preferences
Geographical: Anywhere in U.S.
Industries: Diversified
Stages: Startup, First

Principals: H.F. Meyer, Pres.; John A. Chernak, V.P.; Donald R. Calkins, V.P.; John M. Matras, Sec. & Treas.
Contact: Donald R. Calkins

Oregon

NORTHERN PACIFIC CAPITAL CORP.

Century Tower
1201 SW 12th Ave., Suite 608
Portland, OR 97205
503/241-1255

Year Founded: 1961
Total Private Funds: $750,000
Total SBA Leverage: $1,200,000

1983 Investment History:
Total Investments: $350,000
Deals: 3
Average Investment: $116,667

Project Preferences
Geographical: Northwest
Industries: Manufacturing, Distribution, Real Estate
Stages: Second

Principals: Joseph P. Tennant, Pres.; John J. Tennant Jr., V.P.
Contact: Either

Pennsylvania

FIRST VALLEY CAPITAL CORP.

Hamilton Financial Ctr.
1 Center Sq., Suite 201
Allentown, PA 18101
215/776-6760

Affiliation: First Valley Bank
Year Founded: 1983
Total Private Funds: $510,000
Total SBA Leverage: 0

1983 Investment History: New Fund

Project Preferences
Geographical: Eastern PA
Industries: Diversified
Stages: Seed, First

Principals: Matthew W. Thomas, President
Contact: Matthew W. Thomas

MERIDIAN CAPITAL CORP.

Bluebell W., Suite 122
Bluebell, PA 19422
215/278-8900

Affiliation: Meridian Bancorp Inc.
Year Founded: 1977
Total Private Funds: $1,500,000
Total SBA Leverage: 0

1983 Investment History:
Total Investments: $500,000
Deals: 4
Average Investment: $125,000

Project Preferences
Geographical: Middle Atlantic
Industries: Manufacturing, Distribution
Stages: Second, Buyouts

Principals: Knute C. Albrecht, Pres.; Jay M. Ackerman, Asst. V.P.
Contact: Either

PNC CAPITAL CORP.

Fifth Ave. & Wood St., 19th Floor
Pittsburgh, PA 15222
412/355-2245

Affiliation: Pittsburgh National Bank
Year Founded: 1982
Total Private Funds: $2,500,000
Total SBA Leverage: 0

1983 Investment History:
Total Investments: $450,000
Deals: 3
Average Investment: $150,000

Project Preferences
Geographical: PA, Middle Atlantic
Industries: Diversified
Stages: Second, Later, Buyouts

Principals: David M. McL. Hillmann, Exec. V.P.; Jeffrey H. Schutz, V.P.
Contact: Either

Rhode Island

MONETA CAPITAL CORP.

Governor Financial Ctr.
285 Governor St.
Providence, RI 02906
401/861-4600

Year Founded: 1984
Total Private Funds: $505,000
Total SBA Leverage: 0

1983 Investment History: New Fund

Project Preferences
Geographical: East Coast
Industries: Diversified
Stages: Later, Buyouts

Principals: Arnold Kilberg, Pres.; Dominic Voragine, V.P.
Contact: Arnold Kilberg

South Carolina

CAROLINA VENTURE CAPITAL CORP.

14 Archer Rd.
Hilton Head Island, SC 29928
803/842-3101

Year Founded: 1980
Total Private Funds: $800,000
Total SBA Leverage: $500,000

1983 Investment History:
Total Investments: $600,000
Deals: 7
Average Investment: $85,714

Project Preferences
Geographical: Southeast
Industries: Diversified
Stages: Seed, Startup, First, Second, Later

Principals: Thomas H. Harvey III, Pres.
Contact: Thomas H. Harvey III

CHARLESTON CAPITAL CORP.

111 Church St.
Charleston, SC 29401
803/723-6464

Year Founded: 1958
Total Private Funds: $1,000,000
Total SBA Leverage: $1,800,000

1983 Investment History:
Total Investments: $920,000
Deals: 7
Average Investment: $131,429

Project Preferences
Geographical: Southeast
Industries: Diversified Retail, Real Estate, Manufacturing
Stages: Any

Principals: Henry Yaschik, Pres.; Thomas M. Ervin, Pres.
Contact: Either

REEDY RIVER VENTURES

P.O. Box 17526
400 Haywood Rd.
Greenville, SC 29606
803/297-9198

Year Founded: 1981
Total Private Funds: $1,200,000
Total SBA Leverage: $1,700,000

1983 Investment History:
Total Investments: $700,000
Deals: 4
Average Investment: $175,000

Project Preferences
Geographical: Southeast
Industries: Diversified
Stages: Buyouts

Principals: Tecumseh Hooper, Gen. Part.; John M. Sterling, Gen. Part.
Contact: Either

Tennessee

DESOTO CAPITAL CORP.

60 N. Third St.
Memphis, TN 38103
901/523-6894

Year Founded: 1977
Total Private Funds: $500,000
Total SBA Leverage: $500,000

1983 Investment History:
Total Investments: Not Provided
Deals: Not Provided
Average Investment: $100,000

Project Preferences
Geographical: Anywhere in U.S.
Industries: Diversified
Stages: Any

Principals: Damon S. Arney, Pres.
Contact: Damon S. Arney

FINANCIAL RESOURCES INC.

2800 Sterick Bldg.
Memphis, TN 38103
901/527-9411

Year Founded: 1961
Total Private Funds: $751,000
Total SBA Leverage: 0

1983 Investment History: Not Provided

Project Preferences
Geographical: Anywhere in U.S.
Industries: Manufacturing
Stages: Any

Principals: Milton C. Picard, Chair. & Treas.
Contact: Milton C. Picard

TENNESSEE VENTURE CAPITAL CORP.

P.O. Box 2657
162 Fourth Ave. N., Suite 125
Nashville, TN 37219
615/244-6935

Year Founded: 1979
Total Private Funds: $1,000,000
Total SBA Leverage: $500,000

1983 Investment History:
Total Investments: $115,000
Deals: 2
Average Investment: $57,500

Project Preferences
Geographical: TN
Industries: Diversified
Stages: Startup, First, Second, Later

Principals: Wendell P. Knox, Pres.
Contact: Wendell P. Knox

Texas

BANCTEXAS CAPITAL INC.

1601 Elm St., Suite 200
Dallas, TX 75201
214/969-6421

Affiliation: Banctexas Group Inc.
Year Founded: 1981
Total Private Funds: $1,000,000
Total SBA Leverage: 0

1983 Investment History: Not Provided

Project Preferences
Geographical: Southwest, TX
Industries: Diversified
Stages: Any

Principals: Byron G. Berger, Exec. V.P.
Contact: Byron G. Berger

BUSINESS CAPITAL CORP. OF ARLINGTON

1112 Copeland Rd., Suite 420
Arlington, TX 76011
817/261-4936

Year Founded: 1982
Total Private Funds: $510,000
Total SBA Leverage: $500,000

1983 Investment History:
Total Investments: $400,000
Deals: 4
Average Investment: $100,000

Project Preferences
Geographical: Southwest
Industries: Diversified
Stages: Seed, Startup, First, Second, Later

Principals: Keith Martin, Pres.
Contact: Keith Martin

CENTRAL TEXAS SBIC CORP.

P.O. Box 829
Waco, TX 76703
817/753-6461

Affiliation: Republic Bank Corp. of Waco
Year Founded: 1962
Total Private Funds: $300,000
Total SBA Leverage: $100,000

1983 Investment History:
Total Investments: $300,000
Deals: 3
Average Investment: $100,000

Project Preferences
Geographical: TX
Industries: Diversified
Stages: Second

Principals: David G. Horner, Pres.; David Senior, Sec.
Contact: Either

FSA CAPITAL LTD.

301 W. Sixth St.
Austin, TX 78701
512/472-7171

Affiliation: Financial Services of Austin Inc.
Year Founded: 1982
Total Private Funds: $1,950,000
Total SBA Leverage: 0

1983 Investment History: Not Provided

Project Preferences
Geographical: TX
Industries: Diversified
Stages: Seed, Startup, First, Second

Principals: G. Felder Thornhill, Pres.; William Ward Greenwood, Sec.
Contact: Either

OMEGA CAPITAL CORP.

755 S. 11th St.
Beaumont, TX 77701
409/832-0221

Year Founded: 1982
Total Private Funds: $500,000
Total SBA Leverage: 0

1983 Investment History:
Total Investments: $400,000
Deals: 4
Average Investment: $100,000

Project Preferences
Geographical: Anywhere in U.S., TX
Industries: Diversified
Stages: Seed, Startup, First

Principals: Theodrick E. Moore Jr., Pres.; Frank Ryan, Gen. Mgr.
Contact: Frank Ryan

RETZLOFF CAPITAL CORP.

15000 NW Freeway, Suite 310A
Houston, TX 77040
713/466-4690

Affiliation: Retzloff Industries
Year Founded: 1983
Total Private Funds: $2,500,000
Total SBA Leverage: 0

1983 Investment History: New Fund

Project Preferences
Geographical: Anywhere in U.S.
Industries: Diversified, Manufacturing, Medical
Stages: Seed, Startup, First

Principals: A.F. Retzloff, Chair.; James K. Hines, Pres. & CEO; George Martinez, V.P. & Treas.
Contact: James K. Hines

RICHARDSON CAPITAL CORP.

P.O. Box 8
12700 Park Central Dr., Suite 1500
Dallas, TX 75251
214/980-2441

Affiliation: Richardson Savings & Loan Association
Year Founded: 1982
Total Private Funds: $2,000,000
Total SBA Leverage: 0

1983 Investment History: Not Provided

Project Preferences
Geographical: Southwest
Industries: Diversified
Stages: Seed, Startup, First, Later

Principals: Robert Young, V.P.
Contact: Robert Young

SAN ANTONIO VENTURE GROUP INC.

2300 W. Commerce St.
San Antonio, TX 78207
512/223-3633

Year Founded: 1978
Total Private Funds: $1,100,000
Total SBA Leverage: 0

1983 Investment History:
Total Investments: $360,000
Deals: 3
Average Investment: $120,000

Project Preferences
Geographical: San Antonio
Industries: Diversified
Stages: Seed, Startup, First, Second, Later

Principals: Ruben M. Saenz, V.P.
Contact: Ruben M. Saenz

SOUTH TEXAS SBIC

P.O. Box 1698
120 S. Main St.
Victoria, TX 77902
512/573-5151

Affiliation: Victoria Bank & Trust Co.
Year Founded: 1961
Total Private Funds: $1,000,000
Total SBA Leverage: $1,000,000

1983 Investment History:
Total Investments: $826,552
Deals: 11
Average Investment: $75,141

Project Preferences
Geographical: Southern TX
Industries: Diversified
Stages: Second, Later

Principals: D.F. Peyton Jr., Pres.; Robert Coffey, Treas.
Contact: Either

SOUTHWESTERN VENTURE CAPITAL OF TEXAS INC.

1336 E. Court St., Second Floor
Seguin, TX 78155
512/379-0380

Year Founded: 1981
Total Private Funds: $1,100,000
Total SBA Leverage: $500,000

1983 Investment History:
Total Investments: $650,000
Deals: 7
Average Investment: $92,857

Project Preferences
Geographical: Anywhere in U.S.
Industries: Diversified
Stages: Startup, First, Second

Principals: James A. Bettersworth, Pres.; Joe A. Mueller, V.P.
Contact: Either

Branch: 1250 NE Loop 410, Suite 700, San Antonio, TX 78209, 512/822-9949. *Contact:* Kurt Nestman, V.P.

Vermont

VERMONT INVESTMENT CAPITAL INC.

P.O. Box 590
S. Windsor St.
South Royalton, VT 05068
801/763-7716

Year Founded: 1971
Total Private Funds: $228,344
Total SBA Leverage: $675,000

1983 Investment History:
Total Investments: $400,000
Deals: 9
Average Investment: $44,444

Project Preferences
Geographical: NY, VT, NH
Industries: Diversified
Stages: Any

Principals: Harold Jacobs, Pres.
Contact: Harold Jacobs

Virginia

TIDEWATER SMALL BUSINESS INVESTMENT CORP.

1300 First Virginia Bank Tower
Norfolk, VA 23510
804/627-2315

Year Founded: 1965
Total Private Funds: $1,000,000
Total SBA Leverage: $675,000

1983 Investment History: No Investments Made in 1983

Project Preferences
Geographical: VA
Industries: Diversified, Manufacturing
Stages: Any

Principals: Robert H. Schmidt, Pres.
Contact: Robert H. Schmidt

Washington

CAPITAL RESOURCE CORP.

1001 Logan Bldg.
Seattle, WA 98101
206/623-6550

Year Founded: 1980
Total Private Funds: $1,100,000
Total SBA Leverage: $1,100,000

1983 Investment History:
Total Investments: $700,000
Deals: 7
Average Investment: $100,000

Project Preferences
Geographical: Anywhere in U.S.
Industries: High Technology, Electronics, Medical
Stages: Any

Principals: Theodore M. Wight, Pres.
Contact: Theodore M. Wight

CLIFTON CAPITAL CORP.

1408 Washington Bldg.
Tacoma, WA 98402
206/272-1875

Year Founded: 1982
Total Private Funds: $650,000
Total SBA Leverage: 0

1983 Investment History:
Total Investments: $325,000
Deals: 4
Average Investment: $81,250

Project Preferences
Geographical: West Coast
Industries: Manufacturing, Distribution, Telecommunications
Stages: Second, Later

Principals: James H. Wiborg, Pres.; John S. Wiborg, V.P.; James H. Morton, Sec. & Treas.
Contact: John S. Wiborg

NORTHWEST BUSINESS INVESTMENT CORP.

W. 929 Sprague Ave.
Spokane, WA 99204
509/838-3111

Affiliation: Metropolitan Mortgage & Securities Co. Inc.
Year Founded: 1961
Total Private Funds: $250,000
Total SBA Leverage: $550,000

1983 Investment History: Not Provided

Project Preferences
Geographical: WA
Industries: Real Estate
Stages: Any

Principals: E. Paul Sandifur Sr., Chair.; Irv Marcus, V.P.
Contact: Either

AMERICAN CAPITAL INC.

300 N. Kanawha St.
Beckley, WV 25801
304/255-1494

Affiliation: Associated Cemetary Estates Inc.
Year Founded: 1984
Total Private Funds: $750,000
Total SBA Leverage: 0

1983 Investment History: New Fund

Project Preferences
Geographical: WV, VA, PA, MD, OH, KY
Industries: Diversified
Stages: Any

Principals: Darryl J. Roberts, Pres.; Thomas B. Briers, V.P.; Gary A. Peck, Gen. Mgr. & Investment Advisor
Contacts: Any of Above

BANKIT FINANCIAL CORP.

111 E. Wisconsin Ave., Suite 1900
Milwaukee, WI 53202
414/271-5050

Affiliation: Farm House Foods Corp.
Year Founded: 1972
Total Private Funds: $150,000
Total SBA Leverage: $350,000

1983 Investment History:
Total Investments: $140,000
Deals: 2
Average Investment: $70,000

Project Preferences
Geographical: Anywhere in U.S.
Industries: Retail Food
Stages: Second

Principals: Donald E. Runge, Pres.
Contact: Donald Runge

MADISON CAPITAL CORP.

102 State St.
Madison, WI 53703
608/256-8185

Year Founded: 1983
Total Private Funds: $1,300,000
Total SBA Leverage: 0

1983 Investment History: New Fund

Project Preferences
Geographical: WI
Industries: Diversified
Stages: Any

Principals: Roger H. Ganser, Exec. V.P.
Contact: Roger H. Ganser

CAPITAL CORPORATION OF WYOMING INC.

P.O. Box 612
145 S. Durbin, Suite 201
Casper, WY 82602
307/234-5438

Affiliation: Wyoming Industrial Development Corp.
Year Founded: 1979
Total Private Funds: $1,000,000
Total SBA Leverage: $700,000

1983 Investment History:
Total Investments: $100,000
Deals: 1

Project Preferences
Geographical: WY
Industries: Diversified, Light Manufacturing
Stages: Seed, Startup

Principals: Larry J. McDonald, Pres.; Robert Kemper, Exec. V.P.; Luella Brown, Asst. V.P.
Contact: Any of Above

MINORITY ENTERPRISE SMALL BUSINESS INVESTMENT COMPANIES: $1.5 MILLION AND UP

Alabama

FIRST ALABAMA CAPITAL CORP.

16 Midtown Park E.
Mobile, AL 36606
205/476-0700

Affiliation: First SBIC of Alabama
Year Founded: 1981
Total Private Funds: $764,000
Total SBA Leverage: $1,500,000

1983 Investment History:
Total Investments: $1,400,000
Deals: 37
Average Investment: $37,838

Project Preferences
Geographical: AL
Industries: Diversified
Stages: Any

Principals: David C. Delaney, Pres.
Contact: David C. Delaney

Alaska

CALISTA BUSINESS INVESTMENT CORP.

16 Denali St.
Anchorage, AK 99501
907/277-0425

Affiliation: Calista Corp.
Year Founded: 1983
Total Private Funds: $750,000
Total SBA Leverage: $750,000

1983 Investment History:
Total Investments: $900,000
Deals: 14
Average Investment: $64,286

Project Preferences
Geographical: AK (Continental)
Industries: Diversified Non-High Technology, General
   Merchandising
Stages: Any

Principals: Nelson Angapak, Pres.; Matthew Nicolai, V.P.; Sue
   Gamache, Dir. of Public Relations
Contact: Any of Above

Arkansas

KARMAL VENTURE CAPITAL

610 Plaza W. Bldg.
Little Rock, AR 72205
501/661-0010

Year Founded: 1978
Total Private Funds: $500,000
Total SBA Leverage: $1,000,000

1983 Investment History:
Total Investments: $550,000
Deals: 5
Average Investment: $110,000

Project Preferences
Geographical: Anywhere in U.S.
Industries: Diversified, Retailing
Stages: Any

Principals: Thomas A. Karam, Pres.
Contact: Thomas A. Karam

WORTHEN FINANCE & INVESTMENT INC.

Worthen Bank Bldg.
200 E. Capital
Little Rock, AR 72201
501/378-1000

Affiliation: Worthen Banking Corp.
Year Founded: 1983
Total Private Funds: $3,000,000
Total SBA Leverage: 0

1983 Investment History: New Fund

Geographical: AR, New York City, Los Angeles
Industries: Diversified
Stages: Second

Principals: James P. Jett, Pres.; Mickey Freeman, V.P. & Gen. Mgr.
Contact: Mickey Freeman

Branches: 2121 K. St., NW, Suite 830, Washington, DC 20037, 202/
   659-9427. *Contact:* A. Vernon Weaver, V. Chair.
535 Madison Ave., New York, NY 10022, 212/750-9100. *Contact:*
   Guy Meeker
3660 Wilshire Blvd., Third Floor, Los Angeles, CA 90010,
   213/480-1111. *Contact:* Ellis Chane

California

ALLY FINANCE CORP.

9100 Wilshire Blvd., Suite 408
Beverly Hills, CA 90212
213/550-8100

Year Founded: 1982
Total Private Funds: $600,000
Total SBA Leverage: $950,000

1983 Investment History:
Total Investments: $300,000
Deals: 3
Average Investment: $100,000

Geographical: Anywhere in U.S.
Industries: Diversified
Stages: Startup

Principals: Percy P. Lin, Pres.
Contact: Percy P. Lin

ASSOCIATES VENTURE CAPITAL CORP.

425 California St.
San Francisco, CA 94104
415/956-1444

Year Founded: 1978
Total Private Funds: $600,000
Total SBA Leverage: $1,200,000

1983 Investment History:
Total Investments: $1,400,000
Deals: 3
Average Investment: $466,667

Project Preferences
Geographical: Anywhere in U.S.
Industries: High Technology, Energy Development, Medical
   Technology
Stages: Seed, Startup, First, Second

Principals: Walter P. Strycker, Pres.
Contact: Walter P. Strycker

BUSINESS EQUITY & DEVELOPMENT CORP.

1411 W. Olympic Blvd.
Los Angeles, CA 90015
213/385-0351

Affiliation: Los Angeles Economic Development Corp.
Year Founded: 1970
Total Private Funds: $1,800,000
Total SBA Leverage: $1,000,000

1983 Investment History: No Investments Made in 1983

Project Preferences
Geographical: Los Angeles
Industries: Diversified, Telecommunications
Stages: Second, Later

Principals: Ricardo J. Olivarez, Pres.; Art Garcia, Chair.; Victor Madrid, Treas.
Contact: Ricardo J. Olivarez

CHARTERWAY INVESTMENT CORP.

222 S. Hill St., Suite 800
Los Angeles, CA 90012
213/687-8534

Year Founded: 1984
Total Private Funds: $2,000,000
Total SBA Leverage: $1,000,000

1983 Investment History: New Fund

Project Preferences
Geographical: Southern CA
Industries: High Technology
Stages: Second, Later, Buyouts

Principals: Harold Chuang, Pres.
Contact: Harold Chuang

LASUNG INVESTMENT & FINANCE CO.

3600 Wilshire Blvd., Suite 1410
Los Angeles, CA 90010
213/384-7548

Year Founded: 1979
Total Private Funds: $1,300,000
Total SBA Leverage: $2,600,000

1983 Investment History:
Total Investments: $1,900,000
Deals: 42
Average Investment: $45,238

Project Preferences
Geographical: Southern CA
Industries: Diversified, Restaurants, Gas Stations
Stages: Any

Principals: Jung S. Lee, Pres.
Contact: Jung S. Lee

MCA NEW VENTURES INC.

100 Universal City Plaza
Universal City, CA 91608
818/508-2933

Affiliation: MCA Inc.
Year Founded: 1976
Total Private Funds: $3,100,000
Total SBA Leverage: $3,000,000

1983 Investment History:
Total Investments: $750,000
Deals: 4
Average Investment: $187,500

Project Preferences
Geographical: Anywhere in U.S., CA
Industries: Diversified, Broadcasting, Food Franchising, Manufacturing
Stages: Second

Principals: W. Roderick Hamilton, Pres.
Contact: W. Roderick Hamilton

MYRIAD CAPITAL INC.

8820 Sepulveda Blvd., Suite 204
Los Angeles, CA 90045
213/641-7936

Year Founded: 1979
Total Private Funds: $1,300,000
Total SBA Leverage: $2,700,000

1983 Investment History:
Total Investments: $3,000,000
Deals: 16
Average Investment: $187,500

Project Preferences
Geographical: West Coast, Southeast
Industries: Diversified
Stages: Second, Later

Principals: Chung-I Lin, Pres,; Betty C. Lin, CFO.; Kuo-Hung Chen, Sec.
Contact: Kuo-Hung Chen

OPPORTUNITY CAPITAL CORP.

50 California St., Suite 2505
San Francisco, CA 94111
415/421-5935

Year Founded: 1970
Total Private Funds: $2,900,000
Total SBA Leverage: $3,300,000

1983 Investment History: Not Provided

Project Preferences
Geographical: West Coast
Industries: Diversified
Stages: Any

Principals: J. Peter Thompson, Pres.
Contact: J. Peter Thompson

MESBICs
$1.5 MIL AND UP

PACIFIC CAPITAL FUND INC.

Alpha Pacific Bldg.
3420 E. Third Ave.
Foster City, CA 94404
415/571-5411

Affiliation: P.C.F. Venture Capital Corp.
Year Founded: 1981
Total Private Funds: $1,000,000
Total SBA Leverage: $2,000,000

1983 Investment History:
Total Investments: $800,000
Deals: 2
Average Investment: $400,000

Project Preferences
Geographical: West Coast
Industries: High Technology, Telecommunications, Software,
   Financial Services
Stages: First

Principals: Benedicto V. Yujuico, Chair.; Jose Luis Cervero, Pres.
Contact: Jose Luis Cervero

SPACE VENTURES INC.

3931 MacArthur Blvd., Suite 212
Newport Beach, CA 92660
714/851-0855

Affiliation: First California Business Development Corp.
Year Founded: 1974
Total Private Funds: $1,100,000
Total SBA Leverage: $1,000,000

1983 Investment History:
Total Investments: $600,000
Deals: 4
Average Investment: $150,000

Project Preferences
Geographical: CA
Industries: Diversified, Manufacturing, Real Estate Development
Stages: Startup, Second

Principals: Leslie R. Brewer, Pres.
Contact: Leslie R. Brewer

Branch: 130 Montgomery St., Sixth Floor, San Francisco, CA 94104,
   415/392-5410.

District of Columbia

BROADCAST CAPITAL INC.

1711 N St., NW, Suite 404
Washington, DC 20036
202/293-3575

Affiliation: Broadcast Capital Fund Inc.
Year Founded: 1980
Total Private Funds: $2,000,000
Total SBA Leverage: $2,000,000

1983 Investment History:
Total Investments: $1,700,000
Deals: 7
Average Investment: $242,857

Project Preferences
Geographical: Anywhere in U.S.
Industries: Diversified, Communications, Radio & Television
   Station Ownership
Stages: Any

Principals: John E. Oxendine, Pres.
Contact: John E. Oxendine

FULCRUM VENTURE CAPITAL CORP.

2021 K St., NW, Suite 301
Washington, DC 20006-1085
202/833-9590

Year Founded: 1978
Total Private Funds: $5,000,000
Total SBA Leverage: $2,000,000

1983 Investment History: Not Provided

Project Preferences
Geographical: Anywhere in U.S.
Industries: High Technology, Manufacturing
Stages: Second

Principals: Divakar R. Kamath, Pres.; Renate K. Todd, Portfolio Mgr.
Contact: Either

MINORITY BROADCAST & INVESTMENT CORP.

1220 19th St., NW, Suite 501
Washington, DC 20036
202/293-1166

Affiliation: Storer Communications Inc.
Year Founded: 1979
Total Private Funds: $3,000,000
Total SBA Leverage: $2,000,000

1983 Investment History:
Total Investments: $100,000
Deals: 1

Project Preferences
Geographical: Anywhere in U.S.
Industries: Broadcasting
Stages: Startup

Principals: Walter L. Threadgill, Chair.; Larry Edler, Pres.; Peter
   Storer, Dir.; Kenneth Mosher, Dir.; Stuart Law, Dir. & Sec.; Warren
   Zwicke, V.P.; Minta Branham, Asst. V.P.
Contact: Larry Edler, Minta Branham

SYNCOM CAPITAL CORP.

1625 I St., NW, Suite 412
Washington, DC 20006
202/293-9428

Affiliation: Syndicated Communications Inc.
Year Founded: 1978
Total Private Funds: $2,300,000
Total SBA Leverage: $7,100,000

1983 Investment History:
Total Investments: $1,700,000
Deals: 5
Average Investment: $340,000

Project Preferences
Geographical: Anywhere in U.S.
Industries: Telecommunications
Stages: Startup

Principals: Herbert P. Wilkins, Pres.; Terry L. Jones, V.P.
Contact: Either

WASHINGTON FINANCE & INVESTMENT CORP.

2600 Virginia Ave., NW
Washington, DC 20037
202/338-2900

Year Founded: 1982
Total Private Funds: $500,000
Total SBA Leverage: $1,000,000

1983 Investment History:
Total Investments: $900,000
Deals: 12
Average Investment: $75,000

Project Preferences
Geographical: DC, MD, VA
Industries: Diversified
Stages: Startup, First, Second, Later

Principals: Nicolas M. Salgo, Chair.; Chang Ho Lie, Pres.
Contact: Chang Ho Lie

Florida

JETS VENTURE CAPITAL CORP.

615 Park St.
Jacksonville, FL 32204
904/356-2032

Affiliation: Allied Management Corp.
Year Founded: 1978
Total Private Funds: $1,000,000
Total SBA Leverage: $520,000

1983 Investment History:
Total Investments: $600,000
Deals: 4
Average Investment: $150,000

Project Preferences
Geographical: Southeast
Industries: Diversified, Service
Stages: Startup

Principals: James L. Morrell, Pres.
Contact: James L. Morrell

SAFECO CAPITAL INC.

835 SW 37th Ave.
Miami, FL 33135
305/443-7953

Year Founded: 1978
Total Private Funds: $500,000
Total SBA Leverage: $1,000,000

1983 Investment History:
Total Investments: $750,000
Deals: 15
Average Investment: $50,000

Project Preferences
Geographical: Southern FL
Industries: Diversified
Stages: Any

Principals: Rene J. Leonard, Pres.
Contact: Rene J. Leonard

UNIVERSAL FINANCIAL SERVICES INC.

2301 Collins Ave., Mezzanine 109
Miami Beach, FL 33139
305/538-5464

Year Founded: 1978
Total Private Funds: $505,000
Total SBA Leverage: $502,000

1983 Investment History:
Total Investments: $1,500,000
Deals: 12
Average Investment: $125,000

Project Preferences
Geographical: Anywhere in U.S.
Industries: Transportation, Real Estate Rehabilitation
Stages: Startup, First, Second, Later

Principals: Norman Zipkin, Pres.
Contact: Norman Zipkin

VENTURE OPPORTUNITIES CORP.

444 Brickell Ave., Suite 650
Miami, FL 33131
305/358-0359

Year Founded: 1978
Total Private Funds: $575,000
Total SBA Leverage: $1,700,000

1983 Investment History:
Total Investments: $500,000
Deals: 4
Average Investment: $125,000

Project Preferences
Geographical: East, Southeast
Industries: High Technology
Stages: Second

Principals: A. Fred March, Pres.
Contact: A. Fred March

VERDE CAPITAL CORP.

6701 Sunset Dr.
Miami, FL 33143
305/666-8789

Year Founded: 1978
Total Private Funds: $1,400,000
Total SBA Leverage: $4,000,000

1983 Investment History:*
Total Investments: $600,000
Deals: 4
Average Investment: $150,000

Project Preferences
Geographical: Southeast
Industries: Diversified
Stages: First

Principals: Jose Dearing, Pres. & Chair.; Maxwell Homberger, Sec. & Dir.
Contact: Jose Dearing

*Figures represent fiscal year ending May 31, 1984.

MESBICs
$1.5 MIL AND UP

Illinois

AMOCO VENTURE CAPITAL CO.

200 E. Randolph Dr., Mail Code 2908
Chicago, IL 60601
312/856-6523

Affiliation: Amoco Technology Co. (subsidiary of Standard Oil Co. of
    Indiana)
Year Founded: 1970
Total Private Funds: $1,400,000
Total SBA Leverage: $3,600,000

1983 Investment History:
Total Investments: $1,100,000
Deals: 11
Average Investment: $100,000

Project Preferences
Geographical: Anywhere in U.S.
Industries: High Technology*
Stages: Startup, First, Second

Principals: Gordon E. Stone, Gen. Mgr.
Contact: Gordon E. Stone

*Goods or services that Standard Oil can purchase.

CHICAGO COMMUNITY VENTURES INC.

108 N. State St., Suite 902
Chicago, IL 60602
312/726-6084

Year Founded: 1971
Total Private Funds: $1,500,000
Total SBA Leverage: $2,000,000

1983 Investment History: Not Provided

Project Preferences
Geographical: Chicago
Industries: Diversified
Stages: Second

Principals: Phyllis E. George, Pres.
Contact: Phyllis E. George

URBAN FUND OF ILLINOIS

1525 E. 53rd St.
Chicago, IL 60615
312/753-9620

Year Founded: 1970
Total Private Funds: $650,000
Total SBA Leverage: $1,300,000

1983 Investment History: Not Provided

Geographical: Midwest
Industries: Diversified
Stages: First, Second

Principals: E. Patric Jones, Gen. Mgr.
Contact: E. Patric Jones

Kentucky

EQUAL OPPORTUNITY FINANCE

420 Hurstborne Lane
Louisville, KY 40222
502/423-1943

Affiliation: Ashland Oil; *The Courier-Journal Times*
Year Founded: 1971
Total Private Funds: $1,100,000
Total SBA Leverage: $1,700,000

1983 Investment History:
Total Investments: $417,000
Deals: 14
Average Investment: $29,786

Project Preferences
Geographical: KY, OH, IN, WV
Industries: Diversified
Stages: Startup, First, Second, Later

Principals: Frank P. Justice Jr., Pres.; Gary B. Dodd, Exec. V.P.;
    David A. Sattich, V.P. & Investment Mgr.; Donald L. Davis, Asst.
    Treas. & Sec.
Contact: David A. Sattich, Donald L. Davis

Louisiana

SCDF INVESTMENT CORP.

1006 Surrey St.
Lafayette, LA 70502
318/232-3769

Affiliation: Southern Cooperative Development Fund
Year Founded: 1973
Total Private Funds: $2,000,000
Total SBA Leverage: $2,400,000

1983 Investment History:
Total Investments: $1,500,000
Deals: 11
Average Investment: $135,364

Project Preferences
Geographical: Southeast
Industries: Diversified
Stages: Startup, Second

Principals: Rev. Albert J. McKnight, Pres.; Martial Mirabeau, Sr. V.P.;
    Martin Beaulieu, Exec. V.P.
Contact: Any of Above

Massachusetts

MASSACHUSETTS VENTURE CAPITAL CORP.

59 Temple Pl.
Boston, MA 02111
617/426-0208

Year Founded: 1973
Total Private Funds: $710,000
Total SBA Leverage: $1,000,000

1983 Investment History: No Investments Made in 1983

Project Preferences
Geographical: Northeast
Industries: Diversified
Stages: Any

Principals: Thomas J. Brown, Chair.; Irene E. Sax, V.P.; Herbert L.
    Lyken, Treas.
Contact: Irene E. Sax

NEW ENGLAND MESBIC INC.

50 Kearney Rd., Suite 3
Needham, MA 02194
617/449-2066

Year Founded: 1982
Total Private Funds: $500,000
Total SBA Leverage: $500,000

1983 Investment History:
Total Investments: $1,000,000
Deals: 9
Average Investment: $111,111

Project Preferences
Geographical: Anywhere in U.S.
Industries: High Technology
Stages: Startup

Principals: Etang Chen, Pres.
Contact: Etang Chen

Michigan

DEARBORN CAPITAL CORP.

P.O. Box 1729
Dearborn, MI 48121
313/337-8577

Affiliation: Ford Motor Co.
Year Founded: 1978
Total Private Funds: $1,700,000
Total SBA Leverage: $1,000,000

1983 Investment History: Not Provided

Project Preferences
Geographical: Anywhere in U.S., Midwest
Industries: Diversified Non-High Technology, Manufacturing &
  Services, Automobile-Related Industries
Stages: First, Second

Principals: Stephen M. Aronson, Pres.; Michael L. LaManes, V.P. &
  Sec.
Contact: Stephen M. Aronson

INNERCITY CAPITAL ACCESS CO.

1505 Woodward Ave., Suite 700
Detroit, MI 48226
313/961-2470

Affiliation: Innercity Business Improvement Forum
Year Founded: 1973
Total Private Funds: $2,300,000
Total SBA Leverage: $4,000,000

1983 Investment History:
Total Investments: $600,000
Deals: 3
Average Investment: $200,000

Project Preferences
Geographical: MI
Industries: Diversified
Stages: Any

Principals: Walter M. McMurtry, Pres.
Contact: Walter M. McMurtry

MOTOR ENTERPRISES

3044 W. Grand Blvd., #13-152 GM Bldg.
Detroit, MI 48202
313/556-4273

Affiliation: General Motors Corp.
Year Founded: 1970
Total Private Funds: $2,000,000
Total SBA Leverage: $2,000,000

1983 Investment History:
Total Investments: $1,200,000
Deals: 19
Average Investment: $63,158

Project Preferences
Geographical: Anywhere in U.S.*
Industries: Diversified, Manufacturing
Stages: Second, Later

Principals: James Kobus, Mgr.
Contact: James Kobus

*Within 50 miles of a General Motors plant.

Minnesota

CONTROL DATA COMMUNITY VENTURES FUND INC.

3601 W. 77th St.
Minneapolis, MN 55435
612/921-4352; 612/921-4391

Affiliation: Control Data Corp.
Year Founded: 1979
Total Private Funds: $2,000,000
Total SBA Leverage: $4,000,000

1983 Investment History: Not Provided

Project Preferences
Geographical: Anywhere in U.S., Midwest
Industries: Diversified, Computer-Related, Manufacturing,
  Telecommunications
Stages: Startup, First, Second

Principals: T. F. Hunt Jr., Pres.; W.D. Anderson, V.P.
Contact: Either

Nebraska

COMMUNITY EQUITY CORP. OF NEBRASKA

6421 Ames Ave.
Omaha, NE 68104
402/455-7722

Year Founded: 1977
Total Private Funds: $775,000
Total SBA Leverage: $1,400,000

1983 Investment History:
Total Investments: $1,000,000
Deals: 13
Average Investment: $76,923

Project Preferences
Geographical: Omaha
Industries: Diversified
Stages: Second

Principals: William C. Moore, Pres.; Alvin M. Goodwin, Treas.;
   Herbert M. Patten, Mgr.
Contact: Herbert M. Patten

New Jersey

RUTGERS MINORITY INVESTMENT CO.

92 New St.
Newark, NJ 07102
201/648-5627

Affiliation: Rutgers University Graduate School of Management
Year Founded: 1970
Total Private Funds: $1,000,000
Total SBA Leverage: $1,000,000

1983 Investment History:
Total Investments: $100,000
Deals: 3
Average Investment: $33,333

Project Preferences
Geographical: Northeast
Industries: Diversified
Stages: First

Principals: Oscar Figueroa, Pres.
Contact: Oscar Figueroa

New Mexico

ASSOCIATED SOUTHWEST INVESTORS INC.

124 10th St., NW
Albuquerque, NM 87102
505/842-5955

Year Founded: 1971
Total Private Funds: $750,000
Total SBA Leverage: $2,000,000

1983 Investment History:
Total Investments: $600,000
Deals: 4
Average Investment: $150,000

Project Preferences
Geographical: Anywhere in U.S., Southwest
Industries: Diversified
Stages: Any

Principals: John R. Rice, Pres.
Contact: John R. Rice

New York

AVDON CAPITAL CORP.

576 Fifth Ave., Suite 305
New York, NY 10036
212/391-1119

Year Founded: 1983
Total Private Funds: $500,000
Total SBA Leverage: $1,000,000

1983 Investment History:
Total Investments: $1,200,000
Deals: 12
Average Investment: $100,000

Project Preferences
Geographical: Anywhere in U.S.
Industries: Diversified
Stages: Seed, Startup, First, Second, Later

Principals: A.M. Donner, Pres.
Contact: A.M. Donner

BANCAP CORP.

155 E. 42nd St.
New York, NY 10017
212/687-6470

Year Founded: 1971
Total Private Funds: $1,000,000
Total SBA Leverage: $1,000,000

1983 Investment History:
Total Investments: $500,000
Deals: 3
Average Investment: $166,667

Project Preferences
Geographical: Anywhere in U.S.
Industries: Diversified
Stages: Second

Principals: William L. Whitely, Pres.
Contact: William L. Whitely

COLUMBIA CAPITAL CORP.

419 Park Ave. S.
New York, NY 10016
212/696-4334

Year Founded: 1983
Total Private Funds: $530,000
Total SBA Leverage: $1,000,000

1983 Investment History:
Total Investments: $1,100,000
Deals: 10
Average Investment: $110,000

Project Preferences
Geographical: East Coast
Industries: Diversified
Stages: Any

Principals: Mark Scharfman, Pres.; Alan Leavitt, V.P.
Contact: Either

ELK ASSOCIATES FUNDING CORP.

277 Park Ave., Suite 4300
New York, NY 10172
212/888-7574

Year Founded: 1979
Total Private Funds: $1,900,000
Total SBA Leverage: $4,200,000

1983 Investment History:
Total Investments: $4,000,000
Deals: 75
Average Investment: $53,333

Project Preferences
Geographical: NY, NJ, CT, PA
Industries: Diversified, Transportation, Taxicabs
Stages: Seed*, Second

Principals: Gary C. Granoff, Pres.; Ellen M. Walker, V.P. & Gen.
   Counsel; N. Henry Granoff, V.P.
Contact: Gary C. Granoff

*Seed for taxicabs only.

EQUICO CAPITAL CORP.

1290 Ave. of the Americas, Suite 3400
New York, NY 10019
212/554-8413

Affiliation: The Equitable Life Assurance Society of the U.S.
Year Founded: 1971
Total Private Funds: $10,000,000
Total SBA Leverage: $10,000,000

1983 Investment History:
Total Investments: $1,500,000
Deals: 8
Average Investment: $187,500

Project Preferences
Geographical: Anywhere in U.S.
Industries: Diversified
Stages: Second, Later

Principals: Duane E. Hill, Pres. & CEO
Contact: Duane E. Hill

IBERO-AMERICAN INVESTORS CORP.

Chamber of Commerce Bldg.
Rochester, NY 14604
716/262-3440

Year Founded: 1979
Total Private Funds: $1,900,000
Total SBA Leverage: $2,100,000

1983 Investment History:
Total Investments: $2,000,000
Deals: 20
Average Investment: $100,000

Project Preferences
Geographical: Anywhere in U.S., NY
Industries: Diversified, Franchising, Electronics
Stages: Second

Principals: Emilio L. Serrano, Pres.
Contact: Emilio L. Serrano

JAPANESE AMERICAN CAPITAL CORP.

19 Rector St.
New York, NY 10006
212/344-4588

Year Founded: 1979
Total Private Funds: $500,000
Total SBA Leverage: $1,500,000

1983 Investment History:
Total Investments: $500,000
Deals: 8
Average Investment: $62,500

Project Preferences
Geographical: Anywhere in U.S.
Industries: Diversified
Stages: Second

Principals: Benjamin Lin, Pres.
Contact: Benjamin Lin

MINORITY EQUITY CAPITAL CO. INC.

275 Madison Ave.
New York, NY 10016
212/686-9710

Year Founded: 1971
Total Private Funds: $2,600,000
Total SBA Leverage: $2,600,000

1983 Investment History:
Total Investments: $750,000
Deals: 3
Average Investment: $250,000

Project Preferences
Geographical: Anywhere in U.S.
Industries: Diversified
Stages: Any

Principals: Patrick Owen Burns, Pres.; Donald F. Greene Sr.,
   Investment Off.
Contact: Donald F. Greene Sr.

NORTH STREET CAPITAL CORP.

250 North St.
White Plains, NY 10625
914/335-7901

Affiliation: General Foods
Year Founded: 1970
Total Private Funds: $1,200,000
Total SBA Leverage: $1,700,000

1983 Investment History:
Total Investments: $300,000
Deals: 3
Average Investment: $100,000

Project Preferences
Geographical: Anywhere in U.S.
Industries: Diversified
Stages: Any

Principals: Ralph L. McNeal Sr., Pres.
Contact: Ralph L. McNeal Sr.

MESBICs
$1.5 MIL AND UP

ODA CAPITAL CORP.

82 Lee Ave.
Brooklyn, NY 11211
212/963-9270

Year Founded: 1975
Total Private Funds: $401,000
Total SBA Leverage: $1,200,000

1983 Investment History:
Total Investments: $650,000
Deals: 26
Average Investment: $25,000

Project Preferences
Geographical: Brooklyn
Industries: Diversified
Stages: Startup, First, Second

Principals: Philip Klein, Exec. Dir.
Contact: Philip Klein

SITUATION VENTURES CORP.

502 Flushing Ave.
Brooklyn, NY 11205
718/855-1835

Year Founded: 1975
Total Private Funds: $1,000,000
Total SBA Leverage: $2,500,000

1983 Investment History:
Total Investments: $1,000,000
Deals: 15
Average Investment: $66,667

Project Preferences
Geographical: NY, NJ, CT
Industries: Manufacturing Services
Stages: Startup, Second

Principals: Sam Hollander, Pres.
Contact: Sam Hollander

SQUARE DEAL VENTURE CAPITAL

Village of New Square and Jefferson Ave.
New Square, NY 10977
914/354-7774

Year Founded: 1979
Total Private Funds: $500,000
Total SBA Leverage: $1,200,000

1983 Investment History:
Total Investments: $500,000
Deals: 4
Average Investment: $125,000

Project Preferences
Geographical: Northeast
Industries: Diversified
Stages: Second

Principals: Mordechai Z. Feldman, Pres.; Meyer Steier, Mgr.
Contact: Either

TAROCO CAPITAL CORP.

19 Rector St.
New York, NY 10006
212/344-6690

Year Founded: 1976
Total Private Funds: $505,000
Total SBA Leverage: $2,000,000

1983 Investment History:
Total Investments: $450,000
Deals: 10
Average Investment: $45,000

Project Preferences
Geographical: New York City
Industries: Diversified
Stages: Second

Principals: David Chang, Pres.; Tom Lee, Treas.
Contact: Tom Lee

TRANSPORTATION SBIC INC.

60 E. 42nd St., Suite 3126
New York, NY 10165
212/697-4885

Year Founded: 1979
Total Private Funds: $2,500,000
Total SBA Leverage: $7,500,000

1983 Investment History:
Total Investments: $4,000,000
Deals: 40
Average Investment: $100,000

Geographical: NY, PA, MA
Industries: Diversified, Transportation
Stages: Any

Principals: Melvin L. Hirsch, Pres.; Susan R. Hirsch, V.P.; Paul M. Thorna, V.P.; Dorothy T. Hirsch, Treas.
Contact: Any of Above

YANG CAPITAL CORP.

41-40 Kissena Blvd.
Flushing, NY 11355
718/445-4585

Year Founded: 1983
Total Private Funds: $500,000
Total SBA Leverage: $1,000,000

1983 Investment History:
Total Investments: $800,000
Deals: 12
Average Investment: $66,667

Project Preferences
Geographical: Queens
Industries: Diversified
Stages: Startup, First

Principals: Maysing Yang, Pres.
Contact: Maysing Yang

MESBICs
$1.5 MIL AND UP

Ohio

GLENCO ENTERPRISES

1464 E. 105th St., Suite 101
Cleveland, OH 44106
216/721-1200

Year Founded: 1973
Total Private Funds: $500,000
Total SBA Leverage: $1,500,000

1983 Investment History:
Total Investments: $150,000
Deals: 3
Average Investment: $50,000

Project Preferences
Geographical: OH, Western PA
Industries: Diversified, Manufacturing
Stages: Startup, Second

Principals: Lewis F. Wright, V.P.
Contact: Lewis F. Wright

Pennsylvania

ALLIANCE ENTERPRISE CORP.

1801 Market St., Third Floor
Philadelphia, PA 19103
215/972-4230

Affiliation: Sun Company Inc.
Year Founded: 1971
Total Private Funds: $3,000,000
Total SBA Leverage: $2,700,000

1983 Investment History: Not Provided

Project Preferences
Geographical: Southeast, Southwest
Industries: Diversified Non-High Technology
Stages: Any

Principals: Duane C. McNight, V.P.
Contact: Duane C. McNight

GREATER PHILADELPHIA VENTURE CAPITAL

225 S. 15th St., Suite 920
Philadelphia, PA 19102
215/732-3415; 215/732-1666

Affiliation: Capital Corp. of America
Year Founded: 1972
Total Private Funds: $800,000
Total SBA Leverage: $1,500,000

1983 Investment History:
Total Investments: $100,000
Deals: 2
Average Investment: $50,000

Project Preferences
Geographical: Middle Atlantic
Industries: Diversified
Stages: Second

Principals: Martin M. Newman, Gen. Mgr.
Contact: Martin M. Newman

Puerto Rico

FIRST PUERTO RICO CAPITAL INC.

P.O. Box 816
52 McKinley St.
Mayaguez, PR 00709
809/832-9171

Affiliation: Banco de Ahorro FSB
Year Founded: 1981
Total Private Funds: $500,000
Total SBA Leverage: $1,000,000

1983 Investment History:
Total Investments: $600,000
Deals: 10
Average Investment: $60,000

Project Preferences
Geographical: PR
Industries: Diversified
Stages: Startup, First

Principals: Eliseo E. Font, Pres.; Jaime Montilla, Gen. Mgr.
Contact: Either

Texas

MESBIC FINANCIAL CORP. OF DALLAS

7701 N. Stemmons Freeway, Suite 836
Dallas, TX 75247
214/637-0445

Year Founded: 1970
Total Private Funds: $2,500,000
Total SBA Leverage: $2,100,000

1983 Investment History:
Total Investments: $700,000
Deals: 16
Average Investment: $43,750

Project Preferences
Geographical: TX, OK, LA, NM
Industries: Diversified
Stages: Second

Principals: Walter W. Durham, Chair.; Norman D. Campbell, V.P.; Thomas G. Gerron, V.P. & Controller
Contact: Thomas G. Gerron, Norman D. Campbell

MESBICs
$1.5 MIL AND UP

MESBIC FINANCIAL CORP. OF HOUSTON

1801 Main St., Suite 320
Houston, TX 77002
713/228-8321

Year Founded: 1976
Total Private Funds: $854,900
Total SBA Leverage: $854,900

1983 Investment History: Not Provided

Project Preferences
Geographical: Houston
Industries: Diversified
Stages: Second, Later

Principals: Richard Rothfeld, Pres.
Contact: Richard Rothfeld

MESBIC OF SAN ANTONIO INC.

2300 Commerce St.
San Antonio, TX 78207
512/223-3633

Affiliation: San Antonio Venture Group Inc.
Year Founded: 1979
Total Private Funds: $750,000
Total SBA Leverage: $350,000

1983 Investment History:
Total Investments: $1,000,000
Deals: 6
Average Investment: $166,667

Project Preferences
Geographical: San Antonio
Industries: Diversified
Stages: Startup, First, Second, Later

Principals: Ruben M. Saenz, V.P.
Contact: Ruben M. Saenz

Virginia

NORFOLK INVESTMENT CO.

100 W. Plume St., Suite 208
Norfolk, VA 23510
804/623-1042

Year Founded: 1974
Total Private Funds: $700,000
Total SBA Leverage: $1,400,000

1983 Investment History:
Total Investments: $475,000
Deals: 5
Average Investment: $95,000

Project Preferences
Geographical: VA
Industries: High Technology
Stages: Startup, First, Buyouts

Principals: Kirk W. Saunders, Pres.
Contact: Kirk W. Saunders

MINORITY ENTERPRISE SMALL BUSINESS INVESTMENT COMPANIES: UNDER $1.5 MILLION

Alabama

TUSKEGEE CAPITAL CORP.

P.O. Drawer GG
Tuskegee Institute, AL 36088
205/727-2850

Year Founded: 1983
Total Private Funds: $500,000
Total SBA Leverage: 0

1983 Investment History: New Fund*

Geographical: AL
Industries: Diversified, Small Rural Businesses
Stages: Any

Principals: E. Taylor Harmon, Pres.
Contact: E. Taylor Harmon

*Investments limited to $137,500.

California

ASIAN AMERICAN CAPITAL

1251 W. Tennyson Rd., Suite 4
Hayward, CA 94544
415/887-6888

Year Founded: 1981
Total Private Funds: $510,000
Total SBA Leverage: $500,000

1983 Investment History:
Total Investments: $450,000
Deals: 10
Average Investment: $45,000

Project Preferences
Geographical: Anywhere in U.S., CA
Industries: Diversified
Stages: Startup, First

Principals: David Der, Pres.; Gennie Chen, Mgr.
Contact: Gennie Chen

FIRST AMERICAN CAPITAL FUNDING INC.

18662 MacArthur Blvd., Suite 400
Irvine, CA 92715
714/833-8100

Year Founded: 1984
Total Private Funds: $734,000
Total SBA Leverage: $734,000

1983 Investment History: New Fund

Project Preferences
Geographical: Southern CA
Industries: High Technology
Stages: Second, Later

Principals: Luu Trankiem, Pres.
Contact: Luu Trankiem

Colorado

MILE HI SBIC

1355 S. Colorado Blvd., Suite 400
Denver, CO 80222
303/830-0087

Year Founded: 1984
Total Private Funds: $560,000
Total SBA Leverage: 0

1983 Investment History: New Fund

Project Preferences
Geographical: CO
Industries: Diversified Communications
Stages: Second, Later

Principals: Preston Summer, V.P. & Investment Adviser
Contact: Preston Summer

District of Columbia

ALLIED FINANCIAL CORP.

1625 I St., NW, Suite 603
Washington, DC 20006
202/331-1112

Affiliation: Allied Capital Corp.
Year Founded: 1983
Total Private Funds: $500,000
Total SBA Leverage: $500,000

1983 Investment History:
Total Investments: $429,000
Deals: 5
Average Investment: $85,800

Project Preferences
Geographical: Anywhere in U.S.
Industries: Diversified
Stages: Second, Later, Buyouts

Principals: George Cabell Williams II, Chair.; David J. Gladstone, Pres.; Brooks Brown, Sr. V.P.; Joan Barra, Asst. V.P.
Contact: Joan Barra

Branch: 1 Financial Plaza, Suite 1614, Ft. Lauderdale, FL 33394, 305/763-8484.

NBL CAPITAL CORP.

4324 Georgia Ave., NW
Washington, DC 20011
202/829-1154

Year Founded: 1981
Total Private Funds: $250,000
Total SBA Leverage: 0

1983 Investment History:
Total Investments: $175,000
Deals: 4
Average Investment: $43,750

Project Preferences
Geographical: Anywhere in U.S.
Industries: Franchises
Stages: Later

Principals: Arthur E. Teele, Pres.
Contact: Arthur E. Teele

Florida

FIRST AMERICAN LENDING CORP.

401 N. Lakes Blvd.
N. Palm Beach, FL 33408
305/863-9826

Affiliation: First American Bank & Trust
Year Founded: 1979
Total Private Funds: $500,000
Total SBA Leverage: $500,000

1983 Investment History:
Total Investments: $650,000
Deals: 7
Average Investment: $92,857

Project Preferences
Geographical: South FL
Industries: Diversified
Stages: Second

Principals: Sidney H. Kooperl, Pres,; G. Michael Caughlin, Dir.
Contact: Either

VENTURE GROUP INC.

5433 Buffalo Ave.
Jacksonville, FL 32208
904/353-7313

Year Founded: 1983
Total Private Funds: $500,000
Total SBA Leverage: $500,000

1983 Investment History:
Total Investments: $500,000
Deals: 12
Average Investment: $41,667

Geographical: Southeast FL, GA
Industries: Automotive
Stages: Any

Principals: Ellis W. Hitzing, Pres.
Contact: Ellis W. Hitzing

Hawaii

PACIFIC VENTURE CAPITAL LTD.

1405 N. King St., Suite 302
Honolulu, HI 96817
808/847-6502

Affiliation: Hawaii Economic Development Corp.
Year Founded: 1975
Total Private Funds: $721,000
Total SBA Leverage: $700,000

1983 Investment History:
Total Investments: $150,000
Deals: 3
Average Investment: $50,000

Project Preferences
Geographical: HI
Industries: Diversified
Stages: Later

Principals: Dexter J. Taniguchi, Pres.
Contact: Dexter J. Taniguchi

Illinois

CEDCO CAPITAL CORP.

180 N. Michigan Ave.*
Chicago, IL 60601
312/984-5971

Year Founded: 1972
Total Private Funds: $750,000
Total SBA Leverage: $500,000

1983 Investment History:
Total Investments: $400,000
Deals: 3
Average Investment: $133,333

Project Preferences
Geographical: Chicago
Industries: Diversified, Manufacturing, Retail
Stages: First

Principals: Frank B. Brooks, Pres.
Contact: Frank B. Brooks

*The Contractor's Division is located at 1339 S. Michigan, Chicago, IL 60605, 312/341-1380.

COMBINED OPPORTUNITIES

1525 E. 53rd St.
Chicago, IL 60615
312/753-9650

Affiliation: Combined Insurance Co. of America
Year Founded: 1971
Total Private Funds: $500,000
Total SBA Leverage: $500,000

1983 Investment History:
Total Investments: $500,000
Deals: 3
Average Investment: $166,667

Project Preferences
Geographical: Midwest
Industries: Diversified
Stages: First

Principals: E. Patric Jones, Asst. V.P.
Contact: E. Patric Jones

THE NEIGHBORHOOD FUND INC.

1950 E. 71st St.
Chicago, IL 60649
312/684-8074

Affiliation: South Shore Bank of Chicago
Year Founded: 1978
Total Private Funds: $500,000
Total SBA Leverage: $500,000

1983 Investment History:
Total Investments: $350,000
Deals: 5
Average Investment: $70,000

Project Preferences
Geographical: Chicago
Industries: Diversified
Stages: Second

Principals: James Fletcher, Pres.
Contact: James Fletcher

PETERSON FINANCE & INVESTMENT CO.

3300 Peterson Ave., Suite A
Chicago, IL 60659
312/539-0502

Year Founded: 1984
Total Private Funds: $501,000
Total SBA Leverage: 0

1983 Investment History: New Fund

Project Preferences
Geographical: IL
Industries: Diversified
Stages: Startup, Second

Principals: Thomas Lhee, Pres.
Contact: Thomas Lhee

Maryland

SECURITY FINANCIAL & INVESTMENT CORP.

7720 Wisconsin Ave., Suite 207
Bethesda, MD 20814
301/951-4288

Year Founded: 1984
Total Private Funds: $535,000
Total SBA Leverage: $500,000

1983 Investment History: New Fund

Project Preferences
Geographical: DC, MD, VA
Industries: Small Retail Stores
Stages: Any

Principals: Gus Lebathes, Exec. V.P.; James Kae, Acct.
Contact: Either

Mississippi

SUN DELTA CAPITAL ACCESS CENTER

819 Main St.
Greenville, MS 38701
601/335-5291

Year Founded: 1979
Total Private Funds: $1,200,000
Total SBA Leverage: 0

1983 Investment History: Not Provided

Average Investment: $75,000

Project Preferences
Geographical: Anywhere in U.S.
Industries: Communications
Stages: Any

Principals: Howard Boutte, Gen. Mgr.
Contact: Howard Boutte

New York

FAIR CAPITAL CORP.

175 Fifth Ave., Suite 3019
New York, NY 10010
212/696-4410

Year Founded: 1982
Total Private Funds: $500,000
Total SBA Leverage: $500,000

1983 Investment History:
Total Investments: $300,000
Deals: 4
Average Investment: $75,000

Project Preferences
Geographical: Anywhere in U.S.
Industries: Diversified
Stages: Later

Principals: James Chen, Asst. Mgr.
Contact: James Chen

FRESHSTART VENTURE CAPITAL CORP.

250 W. 57th St., Suite 612
New York, NY 10107
212/265-2249

Year Founded: 1982
Total Private Funds: $500,000
Total SBA Leverage: 0

1983 Investment History:
Total Investments: $500,000
Deals: 26
Average Investment: $19,231

Project Preferences
Geographical: New York City
Industries: Diversified, Taxicabs
Stages: Second

Principals: Zindel Zelmanovich, Pres.
Contact: Zindel Zelmanovich

PIONEER CAPITAL CORP.

113 E. 55th St.
New York, NY 10022
212/980-9090

Affiliation: Pioneer Ventures Co.
Year Founded: 1969

1983 Investment History:
Total Investments: $670,175
Deals: 12
Average Investment: $55,848

Project Preferences
Geographical: Anywhere in U.S.
Industries: Diversified, Healthcare & Services, Oil & Gas, Food
Stages: Second, Later

Principals: James G. Niven, Pres.; R. Scott Asen, V.P.
Contact: Either

TRIAD CAPITAL CORP.

7 Hugh Grant Circle
Bronx, NY 10462
212/597-4387

Year Founded: 1983
Total Private Funds: $500,000
Total SBA Leverage: 0

1983 Investment History:
Total Investments: $225,000
Deals: 2
Average Investment: $112,510

Project Preferences
Geographical: NY
Industries: Manufacturing, Franchising, Distributorships
Stages: Any

Principals: James Barrera, Pres.
Contact: James Barrera

Ohio

CENTER CITY MESBIC

762 Centre City Office Bldg.
Dayton, OH 45402
513/461-6164

Year Founded: 1981
Total Private Funds: $500,000
Total SBA Leverage: $500,000

1983 Investment History:
Total Investments: $350,000
Deals: 4
Average Investment: $87,500

Project Preferences
Geographical: Southwestern OH
Industries: Diversified
Stages: Later

Principals: Michael A. Robinson, Pres.
Contact: Michael A. Robinson

Tennessee

CHICKASAW CAPITAL CORP.

60 N. Third St.
Memphis, TN 38103
901/523-6404

Affiliation: Union Planters Corp.
Year Founded: 1977
Total Private Funds: $424,861
Total SBA Leverage: $500,000

1983 Investment History:
Total Investments: $110,000
Deals: 2
Average Investment: $55,000

Project Preferences
Geographical: Southeast
Industries: Diversified Non-High Technology, Basic Manufacturing
Stages: Second, Later

Principals: H. Morgan Brookfield III, Mgr.
Contact: H. Morgan Brookfield III

TENNESSEE EQUITY CAPITAL CORP.

1102 Stonewall Jackson
Nashville, TN 37220
615/373-4502

Affiliation: Tennessee Equity Capital Fund
Year Founded: 1978
Total Private Funds: $502,000
Total SBA Leverage: $750,000

1983 Investment History: Not Provided

Project Preferences
Geographical: Anywhere in U.S.
Industries: Diversified
Stages: Startup, First, Second, Later, Buyouts

Principals: Walter S. Cohen, Pres. & CEO
Contact: Walter S. Cohen

VALLEY CAPITAL CORP.

Krystal Blvd., Suite 806
Chattanooga, TN 37402
612/265-1557

Year Founded: 1982
Total Private Funds: $1,200,000
Total SBA Leverage: 0

1983 Investment History:
Total Investments: $250,000
Deals: 3
Average Investment: $83,333

Geographical: Tennessee Valley
Industries: Diversified
Stages: Startup, First

Principals: Lamont J. Partridge, Pres.
Contact: Lamont J. Partridge

WEST TENNESSEE VENTURE CAPITAL CORP.

P.O. Box 300
152 Beale St.
Memphis, TN 38101
901/527-6091

Year Founded: 1982
Total Private Funds: $1,300,000
Total SBA Leverage: 0

1983 Investment History:
Total Investments: $500,000
Deals: 5
Average Investment: $100,000

Geographical: Southeast, TN
Industries: Diversified, Communications, Manufacturing
Stages: Second

Principals: Bennie L. Marshall, Mgr.; Osbie L. Howard, Pres.
Contact: Bennie L. Marshall

Texas

SOUTHERN ORIENT CAPITAL CORP.

2419 Fannin St., Suite 200
Houston, TX 77002
713/225-3369

Year Founded: 1980
Total Private Funds: $550,000
Total SBA Leverage: $550,000

1983 Investment History:
Total Investments: $500,000
Deals: 15
Average Investment: $33,333

Project Preferences
Geographical: TX
Industries: Retail
Stages: Any

Principals: Min-Hsiung Liang, Pres.; Cheng Ming Lee, Dir.
Contact: Either

Virginia

BASIC INVESTMENT CORP.

6723 Whittier Ave., Suite 201
McLean, VA 22102
703/356-4300

Year Founded: 1983
Total Private Funds: $505,000
Total SBA Leverage: 0

1983 Investment History: New Fund

Project Preferences
Geographical: MD, VA, DC
Industries: Diversified, Motels
Stages: Any

Principals: Frank Luwis, Pres.; Ed Sandler, Dir.
Contact: Either

EAST WEST UNITED INVESTMENT CO.

6723 Whittier Ave.
McLean, VA 22101
703/821-6616

Year Founded: 1976
Total Private Funds: $500,000
Total SBA Leverage: $500,000

1983 Investment History:
Total Investments: $128,500
Deals: 5
Average Investment: $25,700

Project Preferences
Geographical: DC, VA, MD
Industries: Diversified, Restaurants, Retail, Grocery, Services
Stages: Startup, First, Second

Principals: Doug Bui, Pres.
Contact: Doug Bui

Wisconsin

SC OPPORTUNITIES INC.

1112 Seventh Ave.
Monroe, WI 53566
608/328-8400

Affiliation: The Swiss Colony Inc.
Year Founded: 1976
Total Private Funds: $300,000
Total SBA Leverage: $600,000

1983 Investment History:
Total Investments: $100,000
Deals: 2
Average Investment: $50,000

Project Preferences
Geographical: Anywhere in U.S.
Industries: Swiss Colony Franchises
Stages: Startup

Principals: Raymond R. Rubly, Pres. & Treas.; Robert L. Ablema, Sec.; Michael C. Rubly, V.P.; Richard E. Becker, Asst. Sec. & Treas.
Contact: Richard E. Becker

MESBICs UNDER $1.5 MIL

CANADA

Alberta

AEONIAN CAPITAL CORP.

602 12th Ave., SW, Suite 400
Calgary T2R 1J3
Alberta
403/264-4394

Year Founded: 1982
Type: Private V.C. Firm
Total Paid-In Capital: 7,000,000 CAN ($5,300,000)

1983 Investment History:
Total Investments: 300,000 CAN ($227,273)
Deals: 1

Project Preferences
Geographical:
Domestic: Anywhere in Canada
Industries: Resource & Resource-Related, Oil & Gas,
    Petrochemicals, Forestry, Manufacturing, Energy-Related
Stages: Startup, Later, Buyouts

Principals: C. Alan Smith, Pres.; Drew S. Burgess, V.P.

ALTA-CAN TELECOM INC.

411 First St., SE
71 26-H
Calgary T2G 4Y5
Alberta
403/231-8535

Year Founded: 1983
Type: Corp. V.C. Subsidiary
Total Paid-In Capital: 10,000,000 CAN ($7,580,000)

1983 Investment History:
Total Investments: 550,000 CAN ($416,667)
Deals: 1

Project Preferences
Geographical:
Domestic: Anywhere in Canada, Alberta
Foreign: U.S.
Industries: Electronics, Manufacturing & Distribution,
    Telecommunications, Software
Stages: Startup, Buyouts

Principals: Archie A. MacKinnon, Pres.

ALTAVENTURES CORP.

9411 20th Ave.
Research Centre One
Edmonton TGN 1E5
Alberta
403/450-2468

Affiliation: Alberta Small Business Equity Corp.
Year Founded: 1984
Type: Government Economic Development Agency
Total Paid-In Capital: 1,000,000 CAN ($760,000)

1983 Investment History:
Total Investments: Not Provided
Deals: Not Provided
Average Investment: 250,000 CAN ($189,394)

Project Preferences
Geographical:
Domestic: Alberta
Industries: Diversified, High Technology
Stages: Seed, Startup

Principals: E.A. Clarke, Pres.

AVF INVESTMENTS LTD.

300 Mount Royal Village
1550 Eighth St., SW
Calgary TZR 1K1
Alberta
403/228-9152

Year Founded: 1980
Type: Private V.C. Firm
Total Paid-In Capital: 13,250,000 CAN ($10,000,000)

1983 Investment History:
Total Investments: 3,500,000 CAN ($2,650,000)
Deals: 3
Average Investment: 1,116,667 CAN ($883,839)

Project Preferences
Geographical:
Domestic: Anywhere in Canada, Alberta, Western Canada
Foreign: U.S.
Industries: Resources & Energy, High Technology
Stages: Startup, Later

Principals: Clifford M. James, Pres.; Robert W. Ruff, V.P. Finance &
    Administration

CAPITAL MARKETS WEST LTD.

P.O. Box 1213
Ponoka TOC 2H0
Alberta
403/783-3453

Year Founded: 1980
Type: Investment Banking Firm
Total Paid-In Capital: Not Provided

1983 Investment History:
Total Investments: 500,000 CAN ($378,888)
Deals: 2
Average Investment: 250,000 CAN ($189,394)

Project Preferences
Geographical:
Domestic: Alberta
Industries: Diversified, High Technology, Transportation, Publishing
Stages: Startup

CAPWEST CAPITAL SERVICES LTD.

1102 Empire Bldg.
10080 Jasper Ave.
Edmonton T5J 1V9
Alberta
403/426-7117

Year Founded: 1973
Type: Private V.C. Firm
Total Paid-In Capital: Not Provided

1983 Investment History:
Total Investments: Not Provided
Deals: 3
Average Investment: Not Provided

Project Preferences
Geographical:
Domestic: Anywhere in Canada
Foreign: U.S.
Industries: Diversified, Manufacturing
Stages: Startup, Later, Buyouts

Principals: M. Adam Miles, Pres.; Richard E. Shuhany, V.P.; Pamela
    S. Miles, V.P.

CONGRESS RESOURCES LTD.

999 Eighth St., SW, Suite 600
Calgary T2R 1J5
Alberta

Year Founded: 1975
Type: Private V.C. Firm
Total Paid-In Capital: Not Provided

1983 Investment History:
Total Investments: 2,500,000 CAN ($400,000)
Deals: 3
Average Investment: 166,667 CAN ($126,263)

Project Preferences
Geographical:
Domestic: Western Canada, Alberta
Foreign: U.S.
Industries: Diversified, Oil-Related, Manufacturing
Stages: Startup, Later, Buyouts

Principals: Roger S. Hegan, Gen. Mgr.

GT MANAGEMENT

510 Fifth St., SW, Suite 1430
Calgary T2P 2S2
Alberta
403/262-8185

Year Founded: 1982
Type: Financial Consultants
Total Paid-In Capital: Not Provided

1983 Investment History:
Total Investments: 30,000,000 CAN ($22,700,000)
Deals: 8
Average Investment: 3,750,000 CAN ($2,840,909)

Project Preferences
Geographical:
Domestic: Anywhere in Canada
Foreign: U.S.
Industries: Oil & Gas Consulting
Stages: Later, Buyouts

Principals: Gar Beacom, Part.; Terry Gibson, Part.

VENCAP EQUITIES ALBERTA LTD.

10025 Jasper Ave., Suite 816
Edmonton T5J 1S6
Alberta
403/420-1171

Year Founded: 1983
Type: Public V.C. Firm
Total Paid-In Capital: 240,000,000 CAN ($182,000,000)

1983 Investment History:
Total Investments: New Fund

Project Preferences
Geographical:
Domestic: Alberta
Industries: Diversified
Stages: Any

Principals: Derek H. Mather, Pres.

Branch: 2410 Pallister Square, 125 Ninth Ave., SE, Calgary T2G 0P6, Alberta, 403/237-8101. *Contact:* Ted Mills, Investment Off.

BAWLF MANAGEMENT & ASSOCIATES

550 Burrard St., Suite 410
Vancouver V6C 2S6
British Columbia
604/682-6336

Year Founded: 1983
Type: Private V.C. Firm
Total Paid-In Capital: 250,000 CAN ($190,000)

1983 Investment History:
Total Investments: Not Provided

Project Preferences
Geographical:
Domestic: Western Canada
Foreign: Northwestern U.S.
Industries: Diversified, Resources, Manufacturing, Real Estate
Stages: Startup, Later

Principals: Charles Bawlf, Part.; Frank Heaps, Part.; Howard Jones, Assoc.

DORCHESTER CAPITAL CORP.

1066 W. Hastings St., Suite 1710
Vancouver V6E 3X2
British Columbia
604/683-0345

Year Founded: 1983
Type: Private V.C. Firm
Total Paid-In Capital: 10,000,000 CAN ($7,580,000)

1983 Investment History:
Total Investments: Not Provided
Deals: Not Provided
Average Investment: 500,000 CAN ($3,800,000)

Project Preferences
Geographical:
Domestic: Western Canada
Foreign: U.S.
Industries: Diversified, High Technology
Stages: First

Principals: Joseph Micallef, Pres.; Vince Micallef, V.P.

PRIMROSE TECHNOLOGY CORP.

1750-609 Granville St.
Vancouver V7Y 1G5
British Columbia
604/682-2296

Year Founded: 1982
Type: Public V.C. Firm
Total Paid-In Capital: 5,000,000 CAN ($3,800,000)

1983 Investment History:
Total Investments: 1,500,000 CAN ($1,100,000)
Deals: 1

Project Preferences
Geographical:
Domestic: Anywhere in Canada
Foreign: North America
Industries: Diversified, Computer-Related, Infrared Products
Stages: Seed, Startup

Principals: Alistair MacLennan, Pres.; David Patterson, Sec. & Dir.; Jerry Bradley, V.P.

VENTURES WEST CAPITAL LTD.

321 Water St., Suite 400
Vancouver V6B 1B8
British Columbia
604/688-9495

Year Founded: 1973
Type: Private V.C. Firm
Total Paid-In Capital: 26,000,000 CAN ($19,700,000)

1983 Investment History:
Total Investments: 10,000,000 CAN ($7,600,000)
Deals: 10
Average Investment: 1,000,000 CAN ($760,000)

Project Preferences
Geographical:
Domestic: Anywhere in Canada
Foreign: U.S.
Industries: High Technology, Technology-Related
Stages: Startup, Second

Principals: Michael J. Brown, Pres.; J. Haig Farris, V.P.; Sam Znaimer, Analyst

Manitoba

CANERTECH INC.

1003-213 Notre Dame Ave.
Winnipeg R3B 1N3
Manitoba
204/949-1160

Affiliation: Petro Canada
Year Founded: 1980
Type: V.C. Subsidiary of Government-Held Corp.
Total Paid-In Capital: 30,000,000 CAN ($22,700,000)

1983 Investment History:
Total Investments: 3,300,000 CAN ($2,500,000)
Deals: 4
Average Investment: 825,000 CAN ($625,000)

Project Preferences
Geographical:
Domestic: Anywhere in Canada
Industries: Diversified, Conservation, Alternative & Renewable Energy Technology
Stages: Any

Principals: Lorne Dyke, Pres., & CEO; Kim Aagaard, V.P. & CFO

CANWEST CAPITAL CORP.

1900-155 Carlton St.
Winnipeg R3C 3H8
Manitoba
204/956-2025

Year Founded: 1977
Type: Merchant Banking Firm
Total Paid-In Capital: 50,000,000 CAN ($37,900,000)

1983 Investment History:
Total Investments: 50,000,000 CAN ($37,900,000)
Deals: 16
Average Investment: 3,125,000 CAN ($2,367,424)

Project Preferences
Geographical:
Domestic: Anywhere in Canada
Foreign: U.S.
Industries: Communications, Financial Services
Stages: Buyouts

Principals: Israel Asper, Chair.; Stephen Gross, V.P.

Nova Scotia

SMALL BUSINESS EQUITY LTD.

P.O. Box 3638
Halifax B3J 3K6
Nova Scotia
902/422-9260

Year Founded: 1982
Type: Private V.C. Firm
Total Paid-In Capital: 500,000 CAN ($380,000)

1983 Investment History:
Total Investments: 750,000 CAN ($568,000)
Deals: 6
Average Investment: 125,000 CAN ($94,697)

Project Preferences
Geographical:
Domestic: Anywhere in Nova Scotia
Industries: Manufacturing, Tourism, Mineral Resources
Stages: Startup, Later

Principals: E.W. Twohig, Pres.; E.R. Bustin, Sec.-Treas.

Ontario

ANDROCAN INC.

50 Bartor Rd.
Weston M9M 2G5
Ontario
416/745-3333

Year Founded: 1970
Type: Private V.C. Firm
Total Paid-In Capital: Not Provided

1983 Investment History:
Total Investments: 4,000,000 CAN ($3,000,000)
Deals: 4
Average Investment: 1,000,000 CAN ($800,000)

Project Preferences
Geographical:
Domestic: Anywhere in Canada
Foreign: North America
Industries: Diversified Non-High Technology
Stages: Startup, Later

Principals: Barry D. Rose, Chair. & CEO; F.E. Ross, Pres.; B.S. McCubbin, Exec. V.P.

BG ACORN CAPITAL FUND

2300 Young St., Suite 1201
Toronto M4P 1E4
Ontario
406/485-1010

Year Founded: 1984
Type: Private V.C. Firm
Total Paid-In Capital: 18,000,000 CAN ($13,700,000)

1983 Investment History:
Total Investments: New Fund

Project Preferences
Geographical:
Domestic: Anywhere in Canada
Foreign: U.S.
Industries: Diversified
Stages: Startup, Later, Buyouts

Principals: Michael M. Boyd, Pres.; Ted Higgins, V.P.

BUSINESS VENTURE CO. INC.

22 St. Clair Ave. E., Suite 1703
Toronto M4T 2S4
Ontario
416/961-1888

Year Founded: 1980
Type: Small Business Development Corp.
Total Paid-In Capital: Not Provided

1983 Investment History:
Total Investments: 700,000 CAN ($530,303)
Deals: 1

Project Preferences
Geographical:
Domestic: Ontario
Industries: Manufacturing & Processing
Stages: Later

Principals: Millard S. Roth, Pres.; Marvin Mandell, V.P.

CANADA OVERSEAS INVESTMENTS LTD.

P.O. Box 62
S. Tower, Suite 2301
Royal Bank Plaza
Toronto M5J 2J2
Ontario
416/865-0266

Year Founded: 1959
Type: Private V.C. Firm
Total Paid-In Capital: Not Provided

1983 Investment History: Not Provided

Project Preferences
Geographical:
Domestic: Anywhere in Canada
Foreign: North America
Industries: Manufacturing & Processing, Communications
Stages: Startup, Later

Principals: Michael M. Koerher, Pres.

CANADIAN CORPORATE FUNDING LTD.

330 Bay St., Suite 717
Toronto M5H 2S8
Ontario
416/363-3717

Year Founded: 1979
Type: Private V.C. Firm, Pension Fund Management Vehicle
Total Paid-In Capital: 20,000,000 CAN ($15,200,000)

1983 Investment History:
Total Investments: 6,500,000 CAN ($4,900,000)
Deals: 3
Average Investment: 2,166,677 CAN ($1,641,414)

Project Preferences
Geographical:
Domestic: Anywhere in Canada
Industries: Diversified Non-High Technology
Stages: Later, Buyouts

Principals: Paul Lowenstein, Chair.; Robert Ogilvie, Pres.; Peter Snucins, V.P.; Lorna Ford, V.P. Admin.

Branch: 1010 Sherbrooke St. W., Suite 2210, Montreal H3A 2R7, Quebec, 514/287-9884.

CANADIAN VENTURE CAPITAL CORP. LTD.

120 Adelaide St. W., 11th Floor
Toronto M5H 1V1
Ontario
416/364-2271

Affiliation: Triarch Corp. Ltd.
Year Founded: 1974
Type: Private V.C. Firm
Total Paid-In Capital: 5,000,000 CAN ($3,800,000)

1983 Investment History:
Total Investments: 300,000 CAN ($227,272)
Deals: Not Provided

Project Preferences
Geographical:
Domestic: Anywhere in Canada
Foreign: North America
Industries: Diversified
Stages: Later, Buyouts

Principals: James F.C. Stewart

CARRIAGE SMALL BUSINESS VENTURES INC.

270 Bridge St.
Fergus N1M 1T6
Ontario
519/843-2811

Affiliation: Fergus Venture Capital Corp.; Lewis Venture Capital Corp.
Year Founded: 1983
Type: Public Small Business Development Corp.
Total Paid-In Capital: 500,000 CAN ($378,788)

1983 Investment History: New Fund

Project Preferences
Geographical:
Domestic: Ontario
Industries: High Technology, Hotels, Tourism, Defense, Processing, Medical & Pharmaceutical
Stages: Later

Principals: George K. Lewis, Pres.

CAVENDISH INVESTING LTD.

130 Adelaide St. W.
Toronto M5H 3P5
Ontario
416/367-9285

Year Founded: 1978
Type: Private V.C. Firm
Total Paid-In Capital: 126,000,000 CAN ($95,500,000)

1983 Investment History:
Total Investments: Not Provided
Deals: Not Provided
Average Investment: 5,000,000 CAN ($3,800,000)

Project Preferences
Geographical:
Domestic: Anywhere in Canada
Foreign: U.S.
Industries: Real Estate, Technology-Related
Stages: Later, Buyouts

Principals: M.A. Lloyd, Mgr.; G. Wotchorn, Pres.

CHARTERHOUSE CANADA LTD.

150 York St., Suite 800
Toronto M5H 3S5
Ontario
416/362-7791

Year Founded: 1952
Type: Private V.C. Firm
Total Paid-In Capital: Not Provided

1983 Investment History:
Total Investments: 4,500,000 CAN ($3,409,091)
Deals: 5
Average Investment: 900,000 CAN ($681,818)

Project Preferences
Geographical:
Domestic: Anywhere in Canada
Foreign: U.S.
Industries: Diversified, High Technology
Stages: Later, Buyouts

Principals: J.C. Hardy, Pres.

CITIBANK CANADA CAPITAL MARKETS GROUP

123 Front St. W., Suite 1900
Toronto M5J 2M3
Ontario
416/947-5500

Affiliation: Citibank Canada
Year Founded: 1980
Type: Corporate V.C. Subsidiary
Total Paid-In Capital: Not Provided

1983 Investment History:
Total Investments: Not Provided
Deals: Not Provided
Average Investment: 800,000 CAN ($606,061)

Project Preferences
Geographical:
Domestic: Anywhere in Canada
Industries: Diversified, High Technology, Manufacturing, Services
Stages: Startup, Later, Buyouts

Principals: Paul Donaldson, V.P.; John Puddington, V.P.; Robert Gilson, Asst. V.P.; Jim Woodes, Asst. V.P.

FERGUS VENTURE CAPITAL CORP.

270 Bridge St.
Fergus N1M 1T6
Ontario
519/843-2811

Affiliation: Carriage Small Business Ventures Inc.; Lewis Venture Capital Corp.
Year Founded: 1983
Type: Private Small Business Development Corp.
Total Paid-In Capital: 2,800,000 CAN ($2,120,000)

1983 Investment History:
Total Investments: 2,000,000 CAN ($1,500,000)
Deals: 12
Average Investment: 166,667 CAN ($126,263)

Project Preferences
Geographical:
Domestic: Ontario
Industries: Hotel, Tourism, Defense, Medical & Pharmaceutical, Manufacturing
Stages: Later

Principals: George K. Lewis, Pres.

GORDON CAPITAL CORP.

Toronto Dominion Centre, Suite 5500
P.O. Box 67
Toronto M5K 1E7
Ontario
416/364-9393

Year Founded: 1968
Type: Investment Banking Firm
Total Paid-In Capital: Not Provided

1983 Investment History:
Total Investments: 1,800,000 CAN ($1,363,636)
Deals: 4
Average Investment: 450,000 CAN ($340,909)

Project Preferences
Geographical:
Foreign: U.S.—Northwest, South, Southwest
Industries: High Technology, Information Processing
Stages: First, Second, Later, Buyouts

Principals: Richard Reed, Mgr. Venture Investments
Contact: Richard Reed

GRIEVE HORNER & ASSOCIATES LTD.

20 Victoria St., Suite 405
Toronto M5C 2N8
Ontario
416/362-7668

Year Founded: 1976
Type: Private V.C. Firm
Total Paid-In Capital: Not Provided

1983 Investment History:
Total Investments: 700,000 CAN ($530,303)
Deals: 3
Average Investment: 233,333 CAN ($176,767)

Project Preferences
Geographical:
Domestic: Ontario
Foreign: Northeastern U.S.
Industries: Diversified, High Technology, Media, Entertainment
Stages: Startup, Later

Principals: Alan Grieve, Part.; Ralph Horner, Part.; Anthony Brown, Part.

HELIX INVESTMENTS LTD.

401 Bay St., Suite 2400
Toronto M5H 2Y4
Ontario
416/367-1290

Year Founded: 1969
Type: Private V.C. Firm
Total Paid-In Capital: Not Provided

1983 Investment History:
Total Investments: 13,000,000 CAN ($9,850,000)*
Deals: 17
Average Investment: 765,000 CAN ($579,000)

Project Preferences
Geographical:
Domestic: Anywhere in Canada
Foreign: Anywhere
Industries: High Technology
Stages: Startup, First, Later, Buyouts

Principals: Donald C. Webster, Pres.; Michael Needman, Sr. V.P. & Sec.; Peter Tolrai, V.P.; Kenneth W. Soehna, Treas.

*Figure represents 18-month period in 1983–1984.

IDEA CORP. □

33 Yonge St., Suite 800
Toronto M5E 1V3
Ontario
416/362-4400

Affiliation: Canadian Ministry of Industry and Trade
Year Founded: 1982
Type: Government Economic Development Agency
Total Paid-In Capital: 107,000,000 CAN ($81,100,000)*

1983 Investment History:
Total Investments: 4,100,000 CAN ($3,100,000)
Deals: 18
Average Investment: 227,778 CAN ($172,559)

Project Preferences
Geographical:
Domestic: Ontario
Industries: High Technology
Stages: Seed, Startup, First, Second, Later

Principals: Loren Chudy, V.P. Corporate Affairs; Barry Schachter, V.P. Marketing; George Lyn, V.P. Finance; Dr. Ignace Krizancic, V.P. Technology; Larry Robinson, V.P. Technology Transfer & Licensing.
Contact: Any of Above

*Investment period limited to five years.

IPS INDUSTRIAL PROMOTION SERVICES LTD.

65 Queen St. W., Suite 1402
Toronto M5H 2M5
Ontario
416/364-6478

Affiliation: IPS (Switzerland)
Year Founded: 1979
Type: Corp. V.C. Subsidiary
Total Paid-In Capital: Call-In Fund

1983 Investment History: Not Provided

Project Preferences
Geographical:
Domestic: Anywhere in Canada
Industries: Manufacturing, Controlled Farming, Services
Stages: Startup, Later, Buyouts

Principals: N. Sultan, Sec.

LEWIS VENTURE CAPITAL CORP.

270 Bridge St.
Fergus N1M 1T6
Ontario
519/843-2811

Affiliation: Carriage Small Business Ventures Inc.; Fergus Venture Capital Corp.
Year Founded: 1980
Type: Private Small Business Development Corp.
Total Paid-In Capital: 4,000,000 CAN ($3,030,000)

1983 Investment History:
Total Investments: 600,000 CAN ($454,545)
Deals: 3
Average Investment: 200,000 CAN ($151,515)

Project Preferences
Geographical:
Domestic: Ontario
Industries: High Technology, Hotels, Tourism, Medical & Pharmaceutical, Manufacturing, Defense
Stages: Later

Principals: George K. Lewis, Pres.

MAPLEBROOK INVESTMENTS LTD.

P.O. Box 199
2 First Canadian Pl.
Toronto M5X 1A6
Ontario
416/869-3945

Year Founded: 1974
Type: Private V.C. Firm
Total Paid-In Capital: Not Provided

1983 Investment History:
Total Investments: Not Provided
Deals: 3
Average Investment: Not Provided

Project Preferences
Geographical:
Domestic: Anywhere in Canada
Foreign: North America
Industries: Diversified Non-High Technology
Stages: Later, Buyouts

Principals: P.J.M. Bloemen, Pres.; J.E. Sands, V.P.

McCONNELL & CO. LTD.

8 King St. E.
Toronto M5C 1B5
Ontario
416/364-4461

Year Founded: 1983
Type: Brokerage House Specializing in Venture Capital
Total Paid-In Capital: Not Provided

1983 Investment History:
Total Investments: 6,000,000 CAN ($4,500,000)
Deals: 4
Average: 1,500,000 CAN ($1,100,000)

Project Preferences
Geographical:
Domestic: Anywhere in Canada
Foreign: North America
Industries: Diversified
Stages: Startup, Buyouts

Principals: Frank E. McConnell, Pres.; Mark H. von Roeder, V.P.; John Glover, V.P.

MINISTRY OF REVENUE: ONTARIO SMALL BUSINESS DEVELOPMENT CORPS. PROGRAM

P.O. Box 625
33 King St. W.
Oshawa L1H 8H9
Ontario
416/433-6469

Year Founded: 1974
Type: Government Economic Development Agency
Total Paid-In Capital: Not Provided

1983 Investment History: Not Provided

Project Preferences
Geographical:
Domestic: Ontario
Industries: Creation of Small-Business Development Companies in Ontario.*

*Investors receive a one-third nontaxed incentive grant, which is equivalent to SBA leverage.

□ Member of the European Venture Capital Association.

NORANDA ENTERPRISE LTD.

90 Sparks St., Suite 1128
Ottawa K1P 5T8
Ontario
613/230-6205

Affiliation: Noranda Inc.
Year Founded: 1983
Type: Corp. V.C. Subsidiary
Total Paid-In Capital: Call-In Fund

1983 Investment History:
Total Investments: Not Provided
Deals: Not Provided
Average Investment: 2,500,000 CAN ($1,900,000)

Project Preferences
Geographical:
Domestic: Anywhere in Canada
Foreign: North America
Industries: High Technology
Stages: Second, Later

Principals: Douglas C. Cameron, Pres.

NORTH AMERICAN VENTURES FUND I & II

85 Bloor St. E.
Toronto M4W 1A9
Ontario
416/967-5774

Affiliation: Inco Ltd.; SB Capital Corp.
Year Founded: 1981
Type: Private V.C. Firm
Total Paid-In Capital: 58,000,000 CAN ($43,900,000)

1983 Investment History:
Total Investments: 9,000,000 CAN ($6,800,000)
Deals: 20
Average Investment: 450,000 CAN ($340,909)

Project Preferences
Geographical:
Domestic: Anywhere in Canada
Foreign: North America, Taiwan
Industries: Diversified, High Technology
Stages: Startup, Later, Buyouts

Principals: George Fells, Pres.; Mitchell Kostuch, V.P.

NORTHERN TELECOM VENTURE CAPITAL DIVISION

33 City Centre Dr.
Mississanga L5B 3A2
Ontario
416/275-0960

Affiliation: Northern Telecom Ltd.
Year Founded: 1981
Type: Corp. V.C. Subsidiary
Total Paid-In Capital: Not Provided

1983 Investment History:
Total Investments: 3,000,000 CAN ($2,300,000)
Deals: 7
Average Investment: 428,571 CAN ($324,675)

Project Preferences
Geographical:
Domestic: Anywhere in Canada
Foreign: North America
Industries: Telecommunications, Electronics, Office Systems
Stages: Startup, Later

Principals: Raymond J. Herpers
Contact: Raymond J. Herpers

ONTARIO CENTRE FOR RESOURCE MACHINERY TECHNOLOGY

127 Cedar St.
Sudbury P3E 1B1
Ontario
705/673-6606

Affiliation: Canadian Ministry of Industry and Trade
Year Founded: 1982
Type: Government Economic Development Agency
Total Paid-In Capital: 16,400,000 CAN ($12,400,000)*

1983 Investment History:
Total Investments: 2,100,000 CAN ($1,590,000)
Deals: 7
Average Investment: 300,000 CAN ($227,273)

Project Preferences
Geographical:
Domestic: Ontario
Industries: Mining & Forestry, Manufacturing
Stages: Any

Principals: John L. Dodge, Pres.
Contact: John L. Dodge

*Investment period limited to five years.

ONTARIO DEVELOPMENT CORP.

56 Wellesley St. W., Fifth Floor
Toronto M5S 1C3
Ontario
416/965-4622

Year Founded: 1966
Type: Government Economic Development Agency
Total Paid-In Capital: Call-In Fund

1983 Investment History:*
Total Investments: 95,000,000 CAN ($72,000,000)
Deals: 561
Average Investment: 169,340 CAN ($123,288)

Project Preferences
Geographical:
Domestic: Ontario
Industries: Secondary Manufacturing Industries, Tourism
Stages: Any

Principals: David Goodyear, Information Off.
Contact: David Goodyear

Branches: U.S.—Atlanta, Boston, Chicago, Dallas, Los Angeles, New York, Philadelphia, San Francisco; Foreign—Brussels, Frankfurt, Hong Kong, London, Paris, Tokyo.

*Figures represent fiscal year April 1983–April 1984.

ONTARIO ENERGY VENTURES LTD.

101 Bloor St. W., Fifth Floor
Toronto M5S 1P7
Ontario
416/926-4200

Year Founded: 1983
Type: Government Economic Development Agency
Total Paid-In Capital: Not Provided

1983 Investment History:
Total Investments: Not Provided
Deals: Not Provided
Average Investment: 500,000 CAN ($378,788)

Project Preferences
Geographical:
Domestic: Anywhere in Canada
Industries: Energy-Related Industries
Stages: First, Second, Later

Principals: Peter Szego, V.P

SB CAPITAL CORP. LTD.

85 Bloor St. E., Suite 506
Toronto M4W 1A9
Ontario
416/967-5439

Affiliation: Inco Ltd.; North American Ventures Fund I & II
Year Founded: 1973
Type: Private V.C. Firm
Total Paid-In Capital: 2,000,000 CAN ($1,560,000)

1983 Investment History: No Investments Made in 1983

Project Preferences
Geographical:
Domestic: Anywhere in Canada
Foreign: North America
Industries: Diversified, High Technology
Stages: Startup, First, Second, Later

Principals: George Fells, Pres.; Mitchell Kostuch, V.P.

SHARWOOD & CO. LTD.

20 Victoria St., Suite 405
Toronto M5C 2N8
Ontario
416/869-1598

Year Founded: 1976
Type: Merchant Banking Firm
Total Paid-In Capital: Not Provided

1983 Investment History:
Total Investments: 107,000,000 CAN ($81,100,000)
Deals: 13
Average Investment: 8,230,769 CAN ($6,235,431)

Project Preferences
Geographical:
Domestic: Anywhere in Canada
Foreign: Anywhere
Industries: Diversified, High Technology, Real Estate, Chemicals, Abrasives
Stages: Buyouts

Principals: Gordon R. Sharwood, Pres.; Kenneth L. Cutts, Exec. V.P.

TRIARCH CORP. LTD.

120 Adelaide St. W., 11th Floor
Toronto M5H 1V1
Ontario
416/364-2271

Affiliation: Canadian Venture Capital Corp.
Year Founded: 1962
Type: Private V.C. Firm
Total Paid-In Capital: 10,000,000 CAN ($7,600,000)

1983 Investment History:
Total Investments: 15,000,000 CAN ($11,400,000)
Deals: 5
Average Investment: 3,000,000 CAN ($2,300,000)

Project Preferences
Geographical:
Domestic: Anywhere in Canada
Foreign: North America
Industries: Diversified Non-High Technology
Stages: Buyouts*

Principals: James F.C. Stewart, Pres. & CEO; Peter E. Rood, V.P.

*Company must have sales greater than 5,000,000 CAN.

TRUCENA INVESTMENTS LTD.

Exchange Tower, Suite 1020
P.O. Box 199
2 First Canadian Pl.
Toronto M5X 1A6
Ontario
416/869-3945

Year Founded: 1969
Type: Private V.C. Firm
Total Paid-In Capital: Not Provided

1983 Investment History: Not Provided

Project Preferences
Geographical:
Domestic: Anywhere in Canada
Foreign: North America
Industries: Diversified
Stages: Later, Buyouts

Principals: J.F. Sands, V.P.; P.J.M. Bloeman, Pres.

VENGROWTH CAPITAL FUNDS

111 Richmond St. W., Suite 805
Toronto M5H 2G4
Ontario
416/947-9123

Year Founded: 1982
Type: Private V.C. Firm
Total Paid-In Capital: 34,000,000 CAN ($25,800,000)

1983 Investment History:
Total Investments: 9,600,000 CAN ($7,300,000)
Deals: 12
Average Investment: 800,000 CAN ($606,061)

Project Preferences
Geographical:
Domestic: Anywhere in Canada
Foreign: North America, Northeast U.S.
Industries: General Manufacturing, High Technology
Stages: Startup, Second

Principals: Harry Mortimer, Gen. Part.; R. Earl Storie, Gen. Part.; Andrew Gutman, Assoc.

Quebec

ALEXIS NITTON CORP.

6380 Cote de Liesse
Montreal H4T 1E3
Quebec
514/731-3344

Year Founded: 1946
Type: Private V.C. Firm
Total Paid-In Capital: Not Provided

1983 Investment History: Not Provided

Project Preferences
Geographical:
Domestic: Anywhere in Canada
Foreign: Anywhere
Industries: Diversified, High Technology
Stages: Any

Principals: Jean Rastoul, V.P. Corporate Finance
Contact: Jean Rastoul

ALTAMIRA CAPITAL CORP.

475 Michel Jasmin
Dorval H9P 1C2
Quebec
514/631-2682

Year Founded: 1984
Type: Private V.C. Firm
Total Paid-In Capital: 30,000,000 CAN ($22,700,000)

1983 Investment History: New Fund

Project Preferences
Geographical:
Domestic: Anywhere in Canada
Foreign: North America
Industries: High Technology
Stages: Any

Principals: Eric E. Baker, Pres.; Christopher J. Winn, Exec. V.P;
    Robert Mee, V.P.

CONSORTIUM INVESTMENT CORP.

6600 Cote des Neiges
Montreal H3S 2A9
Quebec
514/341-5511

Year Founded: 1967
Type: Private V.C. Firm
Total Paid-In Capital: 12,000,000 CAN ($9,100,000)

1983 Investment History:
Total Investments: Not Provided
Deals: Not Provided
Average Investment: 200,000 CAN ($151,515)

Project Preferences
Geographical:
Domestic: Ontario & Quebec
Foreign: Anywhere*
Industries: Food, Manufacturing
Stages: First, Second, Later

Principals: Murray Lippman, Pres.

*Co-investment only.

FEDERAL BUSINESS DEVELOPMENT BANK

P.O. Box 47
800 Victoria Sq./Sixth Floor
Montreal H4Z 1A8
Quebec
514/283-5904

Affiliation: Canadian Government
Year Founded: 1975
Type: Investment Banking Firm
Total Paid-In Capital: 35,600,000 CAN ($27,000,000)

1983 Investment History:
Total Investments: 28,000,000 CAN ($21,200,000)
Deals: 60
Average Investment: 466,667 CAN ($353,536)

Project Preferences
Geographical:
Domestic: Anywhere in Canada
Industries: Diversified, High Technology
Stages: Any

Principals: R.J.G. LaFond, Asst. V.P. Investment Banking

INNOCAN INVESTMENTS LTD.

7707 Sherbrook St. W.
Montreal H3A 1G1
Quebec
514/281-1944

Year Founded: 1973
Type: Private V.C. Firm
Total Paid-In Capital: 70,000,000 CAN ($53,000,000)

1983 Investment History:
Total Investments: Not Provided
Deals: 6
Average Investment: 5,000,000 CAN ($3,800,000)

Project Preferences
Geographical:
Domestic: Anywhere in Canada
Industries: Transportation Management, Information Systems,
    Chemicals
Stages: Startup, Later, Buyouts

Principals: Stephen Kauser, Pres.; Jonathan Hurstfield-Meyer, V.P.;
    John Hobbs, V.P.; Bernard Matte, V.P.

INVESTISSEMENTS NOVACAP INC.

1981 McGill College, Suite 465
Montreal H3A 2W9
Quebec
514/282-1383

Year Founded: 1981
Type: Private V.C. Firm
Total Paid-In Capital: 20,000,000 CAN ($15,200,000)

1983 Investment History:
Total Investments: 1,800,000 CAN ($1,400,000)
Deals: 3
Average Investment: 600,000 CAN ($454,545)

Project Preferences
Geographical:
Domestic: Anywhere in Canada
Foreign: North America
Industries: Diversified, High Technology
Stages: Any

Principals: Marc Beauchamp, Pres.; Jacques Tousignant, V.P.; Abe Rolnick, V.P.

Branch: 199 Bay St., Suite 1100, Toronto M5J 1L4, Ontario, 416/868-1458. *Contact:* Abe Rolnick, V.P.

SOCIÉTÉ D'INVESTISSEMENT DESJARDINS

Bureau 1222
1 Complexe Desjardins
760 Succurale Desjardins
Montreal H5B 1B8
Quebec
514/281-7676

Affiliation: Movement des Caisses Populaires Desjardins
Year Founded: 1976
Type: Investment Arm of Credit Union
Total Paid-In Capital: 60,000,000 CAN ($45,500,000)

1983 Investment History:
Total Investments: 12,000,000 CAN ($9,100,000)
Deals: 3
Average Investment: 4,000,000 CAN ($3,000,000)

Project Preferences
Geographical:
Domestic: Quebec
Industries: Diversified, High Technology
Stages: Later

Principal: Mr. Riopel

Saskatchewan

SASKATCHEWAN ECONOMIC DEVELOPMENT CORP.

P.O. Box 5024
1106 Winnepeg St.
Regina S4P 3M3
Saskatchewan
306/565-7200

Affiliation: Province of Saskatchewan
Year Founded: 1963
Type: Government Economic Development Agency
Total Paid-In Capital: 19,000,000 CAN ($14,400,000)

1983 Investment History:
Total Investments: 21,000,000 CAN ($15,900,000)
Deals: 26
Average Investment: 807,692 CAN ($611,888)

Project Preferences
Geographical:
Domestic: Saskatchewan
Industries: Real Estate Development
Stages: Startup, Later

Principals: Doug Preiss, Pres,; G. Wayne Thompson, V.P.
Contact: G. Wayne Thompson

UNITED KINGDOM

UNITED KINGDOM

England

ABINGWORTH PLC

26 St. James's St.
London SW1 A 1HA
44/1-839-6745

Year Founded: 1973
Type: Public V.C. Firm
Total Paid-In Capital: 65,000,000 ENG ($75,400,000)

1983 Investment History:
Total Investments: 15,000,000 ENG ($17,400,000)
Deals: 23
Average Investment: 652,174 ENG ($756,522)

Project Preferences
Geographical:
Domestic: Anywhere in U.K.
Foreign: U.S.
Industries: Diversified, Semiconductors, Telecommunications, Computers, Biotechnology, Software
Stages: Startup, Later, Buyouts

Principals: Anthony Montagn, Chair. CEO; Peter Dicks, Exec. Dir.; David Quysner, Exec. Dir.

ADVENT LTD.□

25 Buckingham Gate
London SW1 E 6LD
44/1-630-9811

Affiliation: TA Associates (U.S.)
Year Founded: 1981
Type: Private V.C. Firm
Total Paid-In Capital: 20,000,000 ENG ($23,200,000)

1983 Investment History:
Total Investments: 11,300,000 ENG ($13,100,000)
Deals: 31
Average Investment: 364,516 ENG ($422,839)

Project Preferences
Geographical:
Domestic: Anywhere in U.K.
Foreign: Europe, U.S.
Industries: High Technology
Stages: Startup, Later, Buyouts

Principals: David Cooksey, Man. Dir.

ALLIED IRISH INVESTMENT BANK LTD.□

Pinners Hall
8-9 Austin Friars
London EC2 N 2AE
44/1-920-9155

Affiliation: Allied Irish Investment Bank Ltd.
Year Founded: 1983
Type: Bank Subsidiary
Total Paid-In Capital: Call-In Fund

1983 Investment History:
Total Investments: Not Provided
Deals: 2
Average Investment: 200,000 ENG ($232,000)

Project Preferences
Geographical:
Domestic: Anywhere in U.K.
Foreign: U.S.
Industries: Diversified, High Technology
Stages: Startup, Later, Buyouts

Principals: Nicholas Condon, Asst. Dir.; Brian Stephens, Mgr.

ALTA BERKELEY ASSOCIATES□

25 Berkeley Sq.
London W1 X 5HB
44/1-629-1550

Year Founded: 1982
Type: Private V.C. Firm
Total Paid-In Capital: 34,500,000 ENG ($40,000,000)

1983 Investment History:
Total Investments: 7,800,000 ENG ($9,000,000)
Deals: 14
Average Investment: 554,187 ENG ($642,857)

Project Preferences
Geographical:
Domestic: Anywhere in U.K.
Foreign: Europe, U.S.
Industries: Diversified, Electronics, Healthcare
Stages: Startup, Later, Buyouts

Principals: Bryan Wood, Man. Dir.; Mark Diskin, Man. Dir.; Robert Drummond, Man. Dir.

BARCLAYS DEVELOPMENT CAPITAL LTD.□

Chatsworth House
66-70 St. Mary Ave.
London EC3 A 8BD
44/1-623-4321

Affiliation: Barclays Bank PLC
Year Founded: 1974
Type: Bank Subsidiary
Total Paid-In Capital: 15,000,000 ENG ($17,400,000)

1983 Investment History:
Total Investments: 7,100,000 ENG ($8,200,000)
Deals: 12
Average Investment: 591,667 ENG ($686,334)

Project Preferences
Geographical:
Domestic: Anywhere in U.K.
Foreign: France, U.S.
Industries: Diversified, High Technology
Stages: Later, Buyouts

Principals: Michael Cumming, Man. Dir.

BARING BROTHERS HAMBRECHT & QUIST LTD.□

8 Queen St.
London EC4 N 1SP
44/1-626-5133

Year Founded: 1984
Type: Private V.C. Firm
Total Paid-In Capital: 10,000,000 ENG ($11,600,000)

1983 Investment History: New Fund

Project Preferences
Geographical:
Domestic: Anywhere in U.K.
Foreign: Western Europe
Industries: Diversified, High Technology
Stages: Any

Principals: Richard A. Ontans, Exec.; Paul T. Bailey, Dir.

□ Member of the European Venture Capital Association.

BARONSMEAD ASSOCIATES LTD.

59 London Wall
London EC2 M 5TP
44/1-638-6826

Year Founded: 1982
Type: Private V.C. Firm
Total Paid-In Capital: 4,000,000 ENG ($4,600,000)

1983 Investment History:
Total Investments: 1,600,000 ENG ($1,900,000)
Deals: 9
Average Investment: 177,778 ENG ($206,222)

Project Preferences
Geographical:
Domestic: Anywhere in U.K.
Foreign: U.S.
Industries: High Technology, Robotics, Computers
Stages: Startup, Later, Buyouts

Principals: Dr. Richard Hargreaves, Man. Dir.

BRITISH RAILWAYS PENSION FUND

50 Liverpool St.
London EC2 P 2BQ
44/1-247-7600

Affiliation: British Railways
Year Founded: 1970
Type: Pension Fund
Total Paid-In Capital: 3,500,000 ENG ($4,100,000)

1983 Investment History:
Total Investments: 3,000,000 ENG ($3,500,000)
Deals: 5
Average Investment: 600,000 ENG ($696,000)

Project Preferences
Geographical:
Domestic: Anywhere in U.K.
Industries: Diversified, High Technology
Stages: Later, Buyouts

Principals: Peter Croft, Dir.; Nicholas Fitzpatrick,
   Investment Mgr.

BROWN, SHIPLEY & CO. LTD.

Founders Court
Lothbury, London EC2 R 7HE
44/1-606-9833

Year Founded: 1810
Type: Private V.C. Firm
Total Paid-In Capital: 40,000,000 ENG ($46,400,000)

1983 Investment History: Not Provided

Project Preferences
Geographical:
Domestic: Anywhere in U.K.
Foreign: U.S.
Industries: Diversified, High Technology
Stages: Later

Principals: P.J. Thurbin, Joint Man. Dir.; R.M. Mansell-Jones, Joint
   Man. Dir.

BUCKMASTER & MOORE

Stock Exchange
London EC2 P 2JT
44/1-588-2868

Year Founded: 1981
Type: Private V.C. Firm
Total Paid-In Capital: 1,800,000 ENG ($2,100,000)

1983 Investment History:
Total Investments: 1,000,000 ENG ($1,200,000)
Deals: 7
Average Investment: 142,857 ENG ($165,714)

Project Preferences
Geographical:
Domestic: Anywhere in U.K.
Industries: Diversified, Electronics, Hotels, Software
Stages: Startup, Later, Buyouts

Principals: J.E.A. Mocatta, Head of Corp. Finance

CANDOVER INVESTMENTS PLC

4-7 Red Lion Court
London EC4 A 3EB
44/1-583-5090

Affiliation: Chappell & Co.
Year Founded: 1980
Type: Public V.C. Firm
Total Paid-In Capital: 15,000,000 ENG ($17,400,000)

1983 Investment History:
Total Investments: 1,500,000 ENG ($1,700,000)
Deals: 15
Average Investment: 100,000 ENG ($116,000)

Project Preferences
Geographical:
Domestic: Anywhere in U.K.
Foreign: U.S.
Industries: Diversified, High Technology
Stages: Startup, Buyouts

Principals: Roger Brooke, CEO; Stephen Curran, Deputy CEO

CAPITAL FOR COMPANIES LTD.

Coverdale House
14 E. Parade
Leeds LS1 2BH
44/532-438043

Year Founded: 1983
Type: Private V.C. Firm
Total Paid-In Capital: 1,200,000 ENG ($1,400,000)

1983 Investment History:
Total Investments: 400,000 ENG ($464,000)
Deals: 5
Average Investment: 80,000 ENG ($92,800)

Project Preferences
Geographical:
Domestic: Yorkshire & N. Humberside, London & Lancashire
Industries: Diversified Non-High Technology
Stages: Startup, Later, Buyouts

Principals: Alan J. Hird, Chair.; Barry A. Anysz, CEO

CAPITAL VENTURES LTD.

The Priory
37 London Rd.
Cheltenham, Gloucestershire GL52 6HA
44/2/42-584380

Year Founded: 1981
Type: Private V.C. Firm
Total Paid-In Capital: Not Provided

1983 Investment History:
Total Investments: 6,000,000 ENG ($7,000,000)
Deals: 20
Average Investment: 300,000 ENG ($348,000)

Project Preferences
Geographical:
Domestic: Anywhere in England
Industries: Diversified, High Technology
Stages: Startup, Later, Buyouts

Principals: Dennis Frendjohn, Man. Dir.

CASTLE FINANCE LTD.

P.O. Box 52
Surrey St.
Norwich, Norfolk NR1 3TE
44/603-222000

Affiliation: Norwich Union Insurance Group
Year Founded: 1979
Type: Corp. V.C. Subsidiary
Total Paid-In Capital: Not Provided

1983 Investment History:
Total Investments: 3,600,000 ENG ($4,200,000)
Deals: 14
Average Investment: 257,143 ENG ($298,286)

Project Preferences
Geographical:
Domestic: Anywhere in U.K.
Industries: Diversified, High Technology, Manufacturing
Stages: Startup, Later

Principals: David Faulke, Mgr.

CHARTERHOUSE DEVELOPMENT LTD.□

65 Holborn Viaduct
London EC1 A 2DR
44/1-248-4000

Affiliation: Charterhouse G. Rothschild PLC
Year Founded: 1933
Type: Corp. V.C. Subsidiary
Total Paid-In Capital: Call-In Fund

1983 Investment History:
Total Investments: 4,000,000 ENG ($4,600,000)
Deals: 15
Average Investment: 500,000 ENG ($580,000)

Project Preferences
Geographical:
Domestic: Anywhere in U.K.
Foreign: France, U.S., Canada
Industries: Diversified, High Technology
Stages: Startup, Later, Buyouts

Principals: Paul Brooks, Mkt. Dir.

CHARTERHOUSE JAPHET VENTURE FUND MANAGEMENT LTD.□

10 Hortsord St.
London W1 Y 7DX
44/1-409-3232

Affiliation: Charterhouse G. Rothschild, PLC
Year Founded: 1984
Type: Corp. V.C. Subsidiary
Total Paid-In Capital: 17,500,000 ENG ($20,300,000)

1983 Investment History: New Fund

Project Preferences
Geographical:
Domestic: Anywhere in U.K.
Foreign: Orient, U.S., Europe
Industries: High Technology, Telecommunications, Semi-conductors, Computer-Related
Stages: Any

Principals: R. Sheldon, Dir.; Dr. G. Walker, Dir.

CITICORP VENTURE CAPITAL LTD.□

33 Melbourne Pl.
Aldwych
London WC2 B 4ND
44/1-438-1266

Year Founded: 1981
Type: Bank Subsidiary
Total Paid-In Capital: Call-In Fund

1983 Investment History:
Total Investments: 6,300,000 ENG ($7,300,000)
Deals: 10
Average Investment: 630,000 ENG ($730,000)

Project Preferences
Geographical:
Domestic: Anywhere in U.K.
Foreign: Ireland
Industries: Diversified, High Technology
Stages: Startup, Later, Buyouts

Principals: Jon Moutlon, Gen. Mgr.; Eric Cater, Sec. & Sr. Investment Mgr.

CLOSE BROTHERS GROUP PLC

36 Great St. Helens
London EC3
44/1-283-2241

Year Founded: 1953
Type: Merchant Banking Firm
Total Paid-In Capital: Not Provided

1983 Investment History:
Total Investments: 1,500,000 ENG ($1,700,000)
Deals: 6
Average Investment: 250,000 ENG ($290,000)

Project Preferences
Geographical:
Domestic: Anywhere in U.K.
Foreign: North America
Industries: Diversified, High Technology
Stages: Startup, Later, Buyouts

Principals: R.D. Kent, Exec. Dir.; P.L. Winkworth, Exec. Dir.

□ Member of the European Venture Capital Association.

UNITED KINGDOM

COMMONWEALTH DEVELOPMENT FINANCE LTD.

Colechurch House
1 London Bridge Walk
London SE1 2SS
44/1-407-9711

Year Founded: 1954
Type: Private V.C. Firm
Total Paid-In Capital: 7,300,000 ENG ($8,500,000)

1983 Investment History:
Total Investments: 3,000,000 ENG ($3,500,000)
Deals: 6
Average Investment: 500,000 ENG ($580,000)

Project Preferences
Geographical:
Domestic: Anywhere in U.K.
Foreign: Canada, Australia, Hong Kong, Singapore, U.S.
Industries: Diversified, High Technology
Stages: Later, Buyouts

Principals: C.N.G. Hobbs, Investment Mgr.; P.J. Dale, Head of Investments

COUNTY BANK DEVELOPMENT CAPITAL LTD.□

11 Old Broad St.
London EC2 N 1BB
44/1-638-6000

Year Founded: 1969
Type: Bank Subsidiary
Total Paid-In Capital: Not Provided

1983 Investment History:
Total Investments: 7,000,000 ENG ($8,100,000)
Deals: 20
Average Investment: 350,000 ENG ($406,000)

Project Preferences
Geographical:
Domestic: Anywhere in U.K.
Foreign: North America, Europe
Industries: Diversified, High Technology
Stages: Startup, Later, Buyouts

Principals: Andrew J. Davidson, Man. Dir.

DEVELOPMENT CAPITAL GROUP LTD.

88 Baker St.
London W1M 1DL
44/1-468-5021

Affiliation: Lazard Brothers & Co.
Total Paid-In Capital: Not Provided

1983 Investment History: Not Provided

Project Preferences
Geographical:
Domestic: Anywhere in U.K.
Industries: Diversified
Stages: Any

Principals: N. Falkner, Man. Dir.
Contact: N. Falkner

EAST ANGLIAN SECURITIES TRUST LTD.

3 Colegate
Norwich, Norfolk WR3 1BN
44/603-660931

Year Founded: 1972
Type: Merchant Banking Firm
Total Paid-In Capital: Not Provided

1983 Investment History:
Total Investments: 160,000 ENG ($185,600)
Deals: 8
Average Investment: 20,000 ENG ($23,200)

Project Preferences
Geographical:
Domestic: East Anglia
Industries: Diversified, High Technology
Stages: Startup, Later, Buyouts

Principals: Francis Madden, Deputy Man. Dir.; Stephen Allen, Corp. Financial Mgr.

ELECTRA RISK CAPITAL PLC□

Electra House
Temple Pl.
Victoria Embankment
London WC2 3HP
44/1-836-7766

Affiliation: Electra Investment Trust
Year Founded: 1981
Type: Corp. V.C. Subsidiary
Total Paid-In Capital: Not Provided

1983 Investment History:
Total Investments: 20,000,000 ENG ($23,200,000)
Deals: 45
Average Investment: 444,444 ENG ($515,555)

Project Preferences
Geographical:
Domestic: Anywhere in U.K.
Foreign: U.S.
Industries: Diversified, High Technology
Stages: Startup, Later, Buyouts

Principals: Michael Walton, Man. Dir.

ENGLISH & CALEDONIAN INVESTMENT PLC

Cayzer House
2-4 St. Mary Axe
London EC3 A 8BP
44/1-283-4343

Year Founded: 1981
Type: Private V.C. Firm
Total Paid-In Capital: 5,000,000 ENG ($5,800,000)

1983 Investment History:
Total Investments: 2,000,000 ENG ($2,300,000)
Deals: 3
Average Investment: 666,667 ENG ($773,333)

Project Preferences
Geographical:
Domestic: Anywhere in U.K.
Industries: Diversified, High Technology
Stages: Startup, Later, Buyouts

Principals: Anne Higgins, Exec. Dir.

□ Member of the European Venture Capital Association.

EQUITY CAPITAL FOR INDUSTRY LTD.▫

Leith House
47-57 Gresham St.
London EC2
44/1-606-1000

Affiliation: Paragon Partners
Year Founded: 1976
Type: Private V.C. Firm
Total Paid-In Capital: 47,000,000 ENG ($54,500,000)

1983 Investment History:
Total Investments: 39,000,000 ENG ($45,200,000)
Deals: 54
Average Investment: 722,222 ENG ($837,778)

Project Preferences
Geographical:
Domestic: Anywhere in U.K.
Foreign: Europe, U.S.
Industries: Diversified, High Technology
Stages: Startup, Later, Buyouts

Principals: Tony Lorenz, Man. Dir.; David Wansbrough, Investment
  Dir.; Jonathan Baker, Investment Dir.

FOREIGN & COLONIAL MANAGEMENT LTD.

1 Laurence Pountney Hill
London EC4 R 0BA
44/1-623-4680

Year Founded: 1868
Type: Investment Banking Firm
Total Paid-In Capital: 30,000,000 ENG ($34,800,000)

1983 Investment History:
Total Investments: 8,000,000 ENG ($9,300,000)
Deals: 33
Average Investment: 242,424 ENG ($281,222)

Project Preferences
Geographical:
Domestic: Anywhere in U.K.
Foreign: U.S., Europe, Far East
Industries: Diversified
Stages: Second, Later, Buyouts

Principals: James Nelson, Dir. of Venture Capital Activities

FOUNTAIN DEVELOPMENT CAPITAL LTD.

100 Wood St.
London EC2 P 2AJ
44/1-628-8011

Affiliation: Hill Samuel Merchant Bank
Year Founded: 1982
Type: Bank Subsidiary
Total Paid-In Capital: 7,000,000 ENG ($8,100,000)

1983 Investment History:
Total Investments: 1,900,000 ENG ($2,200,000)
Deals: 6
Average Investment: 316,667 ENG ($367,334)

Project Preferences
Geographical:
Domestic: Anywhere in U.K.
Industries: Diversified, High Technology
Stages: Startup, Later, Buyouts

Principals: David Osborne, Mgr.; Anthony Wheaton, Mgr.

GRANVILLE VENTURE CAPITAL LTD.▫

27-28 Lovat Lane
London EC3 R 8EB
44/1-621-1212

Year Founded: 1983
Type: Private V.C. Firm
Total Paid-In Capital: 10,000,000 ENG ($11,600,000)

1983 Investment History:
Total Investments: 3,800,000 ENG ($4,400,000)
Deals: 8
Average Investment: 468,750 ENG ($543,750)

Project Preferences
Geographical:
Domestic: Anywhere in U.K.
Foreign: France, Germany, The Netherlands
Industries: Diversified, Advanced Manufacturing
Stages: Startup, Later, Buyouts

Principals: David Steeds, CEO; Ernest Bachrach, Dir.

GREATER LONDON ENTERPRISE BOARD

63-67 Newington Causeway
London SE1 6BD
44/1-403-0300

Year Founded: 1982
Type: Government Economic Development Agency
Total Paid-In Capital: 30,000,000 ENG ($34,800,000)

1983 Investment History:
Total Investments: 30,000,000 ENG ($34,800,000)
Deals: 120
Average Investment: 250,000 ENG ($290,000)

Project Preferences
Geographical:
Domestic: Greater London
Industries: Diversified
Stages: Startup, Later, Buyouts

Principals: Alan McGarvey, CEO

GRESHAM TRUST PLC

Barrington House
Gresham St.
London EC2 V 7HE
44/1-606-6474

Year Founded: 1958
Type: Merchant Banking Firm
Total Paid-In-Capital: 10,000,000 ENG ($11,600,000)

1983 Investment History: Not Provided

Project Preferences
Geographical:
Domestic: Anywhere in U.K.
Industries: Diversified, High Technology
Stages: Any

Principals: Trevor Jones, Dir.

▫ Member of the European Venture Capital Association.

GROSVENOR DEVELOPMENT CAPITAL LTD.

Commerce House
2-6 Bath Rd.
Slough, Berkshire SL1 3R2
44/7-53-32623

Year Founded: 1981
Type: Private V.C. Firm
Total Paid-In Capital: 10,000,000 ENG ($11,600,000)

1983 Investment History:
Total Investments: 6,800,000 ENG ($7,900,000)
Deals: 8
Average Investment: 843,750 ENG ($978,750)

Project Preferences
Geographical:
Domestic: Anywhere in U.K.
Industries: High Technology
Stages: Later, Buyouts

Principals: David Beattie, Man. Dir.; Tony Crook, Assoc. Dir.

GUINNESS MAHON INC.

32 St. Mary at Hill
London EC3 P 3AJ
44/1-623-9333

Year Founded: 1825
Type: Investment Banking Firm
Total Paid-In Capital: 10,000,000 ENG ($11,600,000)

1983 Investment History:
Total Investments: 2,400,000 ENG ($2,800,000)
Deals: 8
Average Investment: 300,000 ENG ($348,000)

Project Preferences
Geographical:
Domestic: Anywhere in U.K.
Industries: Diversified
Stages: Later, Buyouts

Principals: Bruce A. Ursell, Dir.

HAMBROS ADVANCED TECHNOLOGY TRUST

41 Bishopsgate
London EC2 P 2AA
44/1-588-2851

Affiliation: Hambros Bank
Year Founded: 1982
Type: Bank Subsidiary
Total Paid-In Capital: 3,500,000 ENG ($4,100,000)

1983 Investment History:
Total Investments: 1,000,000 ENG ($1,160,000)
Deals: 15
Average Investment: 66,667 ENG ($77,334)

Project Preferences
Geographical:
Domestic: Anywhere in U.K.
Industries: Advanced Technology
Stages: Startup, Second, Later

Principals: Alan Rydem, Investment Mgr.

INNOTECH LTD.

28 Buckingham Gate
London SW1 E 6LD
44/1-834-2492

Year Founded: 1981
Type: Private V.C. Firm
Total Paid-In Capital: 1,000,000 ENG ($1,160,000)

1983 Investment History:
Total Investments: 7,000,000 ENG ($8,100,000)
Deals: 10
Average Investment: 700,000 ENG ($812,000)

Project Preferences
Geographical:
Domestic: Southern U.K.
Foreign: France, U.S.
Industries: Computer Peripherals Systems & Software, Electronic Testing Equipment, Biotechnology
Stages: Startup, Later, Buyouts

Principals: Frank Phaxton, Man. Dir.

INTEX EXECUTIVES (UK) LTD.

Chancery House
53-64 Chancery Lane
London WC2 A 1QU
44/1-831-6925

Year Founded: 1973
Type: Private V.C. Firm
Total Paid-In Capital: Not Provided

1983 Investment History: Not Provided

Project Preferences
Geographical:
Domestic: Anywhere in U.K.
Industries: Diversified, High Technology
Stages: Any

Principals: D.C. Lueck, Man. Dir.; Mark Swan, Assoc. Exec.

LEOPOLD JOSEPH & SONS LTD.

31-45 Gresham St.
London EC2 V 7EA
44/1-588-2323

Affiliation: Leopold Joseph Holdings PLC
Year Founded: 1919
Type: Merchant Banking Firm
Total Paid-In Capital: Call-In Fund

1983 Investment History:
Total Investments: 13,500,000 ENG ($15,700,000)
Deals: 4
Average Investment: 3,375,000 ENG ($3,900,000)

Project Preferences
Geographical:
Domestic: Anywhere in U.K.
Foreign: Europe
Industries: Diversified, High Technology
Stages: Any

Principals: Bernard Heymann, Consultant for Corporate Finance

KLEINWORT BENSON DEVELOPMENT CAPITAL LTD.

20 Fenchurch St.
London EC3 P 3DB
44/1-623-8000

Affiliation: Kleinwort Benson Ltd.
Year Founded: 1981
Type: Bank Subsidiary
Total Paid-In Capital: Call-In Fund

1983 Investment History:
Total Investments: 4,000,000 ENG ($4,600,000)
Deals: 10
Average Investment: 400,000 ENG ($460,000)

Project Preferences
Geographical:
Domestic: Anywhere in U.K.
Foreign: U.S., East Coast, West Coast
Industries: Diversified, High Technology
Stages: Any

Principals: A.J. Sumner, Man. Dir.; B.M. Dean, Mgr.

MATHERCOURT SECURITIES LTD.

1 Lincoln's Inn Fields
London WC2 A 3AA
44/1-831-9001

Year Founded: 1980
Type: Investment Consultants
Total Paid-In Capital: Not Provided

1983 Investment History:
Total Investments: Not Provided
Deals: 10

Project Preferences
Geographical:
Domestic: Anywhere in U.K.
Foreign: Luxembourg, U.S.
Industries: Diversified, High Technology, Healthcare Services, Light Industry, Oil
Stages: Any

Principals: Ian Taylor, Dir.

MERCIA VENTURE CAPITAL LTD.

126 Colmore Row
Birmingham B33AP
West Midlands
44/21-233-3404

Year Founded: 1982
Type: Private V.C. Firm
Total Paid-In Capital: 1,500,000 ENG ($1,700,000)

1983 Investment History:
Total Investments: 1,300,000 ENG ($1,500,000)
Deals: 19
Average Investment: 68,421 ENG ($79,368)

Project Preferences
Geographical:
Domestic: Anywhere in U.K.*, Midlands
Industries: Diversified, High Technology
Stages: Any

Principals: R.P. Barnsley, Man. Dir.

*Excludes London.

MIDLAND & NORTHERN LTD.

1 Waterloo St.
Birmingham B25PG
44/21-643-3941

Affiliation: Centreway Trust PLC
Year Founded: 1958
Type: Corp. V.C. Subsidiary
Total Paid-In Capital: 50,000 ENG ($58,000)

1983 Investment History:
Total Investments: 1,100,000 ENG ($1,300,000)
Deals: 8
Average Investment: 137,500 ENG ($159,500)

Project Preferences
Geographical:
Domestic: Anywhere in U.K.
Industries: Diversified, High Technology
Stages: Any

Principals: Roger Storey, Man. Dir.; John Naylor, Investment Exec.; Paul Whelan, Investment Exec.; Kevin Caley, Investment Exec.

MIDLAND BANK EQUITY GROUP□

47 Cannon St.
London EC4 M 5SQ
44/1-638-8861

Affiliation: Midland Bank PLC
Year Founded: 1968
Type: Bank Subsidiary
Total Paid-In Capital: Call-In Fund

1983 Investment History:
Total Investments: 9,000,000 ENG ($10,400,000)
Deals: 40
Average Investment: 225,000 ENG ($261,000)

Project Preferences
Geographical:
Domestic: Anywhere in U.K.
Industries: Diversified, High Technology
Stages: Any

Principals: Brian Warnes, Man. Dir.

MINSTER TRUST LTD.

Minster House
Arthur St.
London EC4 R 9BH
44/1-623-1050

Year Founded: 1928
Type: Private V.C. Firm
Total Paid-In Capital: 800,000 ENG ($928,000)

1983 Investment History:
Total Investments: 1,200,000 ENG ($1,400,000)
Deals: 6
Average Investment: 200,000 ENG ($232,000)

Project Preferences
Geographical:
Domestic: Anywhere in U.K.
Industries: Diversified, High Technology
Stages: Any

Principals: H.J.H. Hildreth, Dir.

□ Member of the European Venture Capital Association.

MTI MANAGERS LTD.

70 St. Albans Rd.
Watford WD1 1RP
44/9-235-0244

Year Founded: 1983
Type: Private V.C. Firm
Total Paid-In Capital: 9,100,000 ENG ($10,600,000)

1983 Investment History:
Total Investments: 700,000 ENG ($812,000)
Deals: 2
Average Investment: 350,000 ENG ($406,000)

Project Preferences
Geographical:
Domestic: Anywhere in U.K.
Industries: High Technology
Stages: Any

Principals: Dr. Paul Castle, CEO

PA DEVELOPMENTS

Hyde Park House
60A Knightsbridge
London SW1 X 7LE
44/1-235-6060; 44/1-584-2863

Year Founded: 1977
Type: Private V.C. Firm
Total Paid-In Capital: Call-In Fund

1983 Investment History:
Total Investments: 2,500,000 ENG ($2,900,000)
Deals: 5
Average Investment: 500,000 ENG ($580,000)

Project Preferences
Geographical:
Domestic: Anywhere in U.K.
Industries: Diversified, High Technology
Stages: Any

Principals: Peter Grundy, Dir.; David Hemming, Associate

ALAN PATRICOF ASSOCIATES LTD.□

24 Upper Brook St.
London W1 Y 1PD
44/1-493-3633

Affiliation: Alan Patricof Associates Inc. (U.S.)
Year Founded: 1981
Type: Private V.C. Firm
Total Paid-In Capital: 40,000,000 ENG ($46,400,000)

1983 Investment History:
Total Investments: 3,000,000 ENG ($3,500,000)
Deals: 300
Average Investment: 10,000 ENG ($11,600)

Project Preferences
Geographical:
Domestic: Anywhere in U.K.
Foreign: U.S.
Industries: Diversified, High Technology
Stages: Startup, Later, Buyouts

Principals: Ronald Cohen, Exec. Chair.; Rhys Williams, Man. Dir.;
  Adrian Beecroft, Dir.; Peter Englander, Dir.

PRETEC LTD.

17 Buckingham Gate
London SW1 E 6LN
44/1-828-2082

Affiliation: Prudential Assurance Co.
Year Founded: 1980
Type: Corp. V.C. Subsidiary
Total Paid-In Capital: 15,000,000 ENG ($17,400,000)

1983 Investment History:
Total Investments: 7,000,000 ENG ($8,100,000)
Deals: 8
Average Investment: 875,000 ENG ($1,000,000)

Project Preferences
Geographical:
Domestic: Anywhere in U.K.
Foreign: U.S., FL, MA; The Netherlands
Industries: High Technology
Stages: Seed, Startup

Principals: Dr. Derrick Allam, CEO

PRUVENTURE□

142 Holborn Bars
London EC1 N 2NH
44/1-405-9222

Affiliation: Prudential Portfolio Managers Ltd.
Year Founded: 1981
Type: Corp. V.C. Subsidiary
Total Paid-In Capital: 15,000,000 ENG ($17,400,000)

1983 Investment History:
Total Investments: 12,000,000 ENG ($13,900,000)
Deals: 24
Average Investment: 500,000 ENG ($580,000)

Project Preferences
Geographical:
Domestic: Anywhere in U.K.
Industries: Diversified, High Technology
Stages: Startup, First, Second, Later

Principals: Ian R. Hawkins, Exec. Dir.; Richard Gawthorne, Gen. Mgr.

RAINFORD VENTURE CAPITAL LTD.

Rainford House
Crank Rd.
Crank
St. Helens, Merseyside WA1 1 7RP
44/7-443-7227

Year Founded: 1981
Type: Private V.C. Firm
Total Paid-In Capital: 2,500,000 ENG ($2,900,000)

1983 Investment History:
Total Investments: 350,000 ENG ($406,000)
Deals: 7
Average Investment: 50,000 ENG ($58,000)

Project Preferences
Geographical:
Domestic: Northwest England
Industries: High Technology
Stages: Any

Principals: J.P. Shepardson, Advertising Dir.; D.B.M. Johnston, Dir.

□ Member of the European Venture Capital Association.

UNITED KINGDOM

SABRELANCE LTD.

20-21 Princess St.
Hanover Square
London W1 R 8PX
44/1-493-3599

Year Founded: 1983
Type: Investment Advisor
Total Paid-In Capital: 250,000 ENG ($290,000)

1983 Investment History:
Total Investments: 1,500,000 ENG ($1,700,000)
Deals: 5
Average Investment: 300,000 ENG ($348,000)

Project Preferences
Geographical:
Domestic: Anywhere in U.K.
Foreign: U.S.
Industries: Diversified, High Technology
Stages: Any

Principals: David Shaw, Man. Dir.

THE ST. JAMES'S VENTURE CAPITAL FUND LTD.

66 St. James's St.
London SW1 A 1NE
44/1-493-8111

Affiliation: Charterhouse G. Rothschild PLC
Year Founded: 1984
Type: Corp. V.C. Subsidiary
Total Paid-In Capital: Call-In Fund

1983 Investment History: New Fund

Project Preferences
Geographical:
Domestic: Anywhere in U.K.
Foreign: U.S.
Industries: High Technology
Stages: Startup, Later

Principals: Dr. S. Hochhauser, Man. Dir.

SAPLING (NORTHWEST) LTD.

East Cliff County Offices
East Cliff, Preston
Lancashire PR1 3EX
44/77-226-4382

Year Founded: 1982
Type: Private V.C. Firm
Total Paid-In Capital: 5,000,000 ENG ($5,800,000)

1983 Investment History:
Total Investments: Not Provided
Deals: Not Provided
Average Investment: 80,000 ENG ($92,800)

Project Preferences
Geographical:
Domestic: Lancashire, Merseyside
Industries: Diversified, High Technology
Stages: Startup, Later

Principals: Alan Payne, Man. Dir.

SINGER & FRIEDLANDER LTD.

21 New St.
Bishopsgate
London EC2 M 4HR
44/1-623-3000

Affiliation: Brittannia Arrow
Year Founded: 1908
Type: Bank Subsidiary
Total Paid-In Capital: Call-In Fund

1983 Investment History:
Total Investments: 6,000,000 ENG ($7,000,000)
Deals: 28
Average Investment: 214,286 ENG ($248,572)

Project Preferences
Geographical:
Domestic: Anywhere in U.K.
Industries: Diversified, High Technology
Stages: Later

Principals: Panton Corbett, Man. Dir.; Sir Timothy Harford, Man. Dir.

SMITHDOWN INVESTMENT LTD.

15 S. Molton St.
London W1 Y 1DE
44/1-278-5199

Year Founded: 1977
Type: Private V.C. Firm
Total Paid-In Capital: Not Provided

1983 Investment History:
Total Investments: 500,000 ENG ($580,000)
Deals: 9
Average Investment: 55,556 ENG ($64,445)

Project Preferences
Geographical:
Domestic: England
Industries: Diversified
Stages: Startup, First, Second, Buyouts

Principals: G.L. Taylor, Man. Dir.

SUMIT LTD.

Edmund House
12 Newhall St.
Birmingham B33ER
44/21-236-5801

Year Founded: 1980
Type: Private V.C. Firm
Total Paid-In Capital: 8,500,000 ENG ($9,900,000)

1983 Investment History:
Total Investments: 2,000,000 ENG ($2,300,000)
Deals: 4
Average Investment: 500,000 ENG ($580,000)

Project Preferences
Geographical:
Domestic: Anywhere in U.K.
Foreign: Anywhere
Industries: Diversified, High Technology, Forestry, Technical Education, Engine Parts
Stages: Any

Principals: S.D. Sharp, Chair.; Meinert Hages, Dir.; Nick Talbot Rice, Dir.

THOMPSON CLIVE & PARTNERS LTD.

24 Old Bond St.
London W1
44/1-491-4809

Year Founded: 1980
Type: Private V.C. Firm
Total Paid-In Capital: 20,000,000 ENG ($23,200,000)

1983 Investment History:
Total Investments: 3,000,000 ENG ($3,480,000)
Deals: 10
Average Investment: 300,000 ENG ($348,000)

Project Preferences
Geographical:
Domestic: Anywhere in U.K.
Foreign: U.S., West Coast
Industries: High Technology, Medical
Stages: Second, Buyouts

Principals: Charles Fitzherbert, Dir.

TRUST OF PROPERTY SHARES PLC

6 Welbeck St.
London W1 N 8BS
44/1-486-4684

Year Founded: 1978
Type: Public V.C. Firm
Total Paid-In Capital: 500,000 ENG ($580,000)

1983 Investment History:
Total Investments: 1,200,000 ENG ($1,400,000)
Deals: 30
Average Investment: 40,000 ENG ($46,400)

Project Preferences
Geographical:
Domestic: Anywhere in U.K.
Industries: Retail Shops, Real Estate
Stages: Startup, Second, Later

Principals: E.N. Goodman, Dir.; S. Kon, Dir.

VENTURE FOUNDERS LTD.

39 The Green
South Bar
Banbury, Oxfordshire OX16 9AE
44/295-65881

Year Founded: 1979
Type: Private V.C. Firm
Total Paid-In Capital: 12,000,000 ENG ($13,900,000)

1983 Investment History:
Total Investments: Not Provided
Deals: Not Provided
Average Investment: 250,000 ENG ($290,000)

Project Preferences
Geographical:
Domestic: Anywhere in U.K.
Industries: High Technology
Stages: Startup, Later

Principals: Charles Cox, Man. Dir.

SG WARBURG & CO. LTD.

33 King William St.
London EC4
44/1-280-2800

Year Founded: 1982
Type: Merchant Banking Firm
Total Paid-In Capital: Call-In Fund

1983 Investment History:
Total Investments: 7,000,000 ENG ($8,100,000)
Deals: 15
Average Investment: 466,667 ENG ($541,334)

Project Preferences
Geographical:
Domestic: Anywhere in U.K.
Foreign: U.S., Canada, Denmark, Hong Kong
Industries: Diversified
Stages: Any

Principals: R.M. Palmer, Dir.; S.C. O'Neil, Dir.

WEST MIDLANDS ENTERPRISE BOARD

Lloyds Bank Chambers
75 Edmund St.
Birmingham B33 HD
44/21-236-8855

Year Founded: 1982
Type: Government Economic Development Agency
Total Paid-In Capital: 7,000,000 ENG ($8,100,000)

1983 Investment History:
Total Investments: 5,600,000 ENG ($6,500,000)
Deals: 18
Average Investment: 311,111 ENG ($360,889)

Project Preferences
Geographical:
Domestic: W. Midlands
Industries: Manufacturing
Stages: Second, Later

Principals: Norman Holmes, CEO

Scotland

CLYDESDALE BANK EQUITY LTD.

30 St. Vincent Pl.
Glasgow Gl 2HL
44/41-248-7070

Year Founded: 1981
Type: Bank Subsidiary
Total Paid-In-Capital: 5,000,000 ENG ($5,800,000)

1983 Investment History:
Total Investments: 1,000,000 ENG ($1,160,000)
Deals: 3
Average Investment: 333,333 ENG ($386,666)

Project Preferences
Geographical:
Domestic: Scotland
Industries: Diversified, High Technology
Stages: Later, Buyouts

Principals: D.L. Walker, Mgr.; S.B. Keir, Financial Exec.

JAMES FINLAY CORP. LTD.

Finlay House
10-14 W. Nile St.
Glasgow GI 2PP
44/41/204-1321

Year Founded: 1975
Type: Private V.C. Firm
Total Paid-In-Capital: 6,000,000 ENG ($7,000,000)

1983 Investment History:
Total Investments: 1,000,000 ENG ($1,160,000)
Deals: 6
Average Investment: 66,667 ENG ($193,333)

Project Preferences
Geographical:
Domestic: Anywhere in U.K.
Foreign: U.S., CT, CA
Industries: Manufacturing, Oil & Coal
Stages: Later, Buyouts

Principals: R.G. Capper, Man. Dir.

HIGHLANDS & ISLANDS DEVELOPMENT BOARD

Bridge House
27 Bank St.
Inverness IV1 1QR
44/46-323-4171

Year Founded: 1965
Type: Government Economic Development Agency
Total Paid-In Capital: 7,000,000 ENG ($8,100,000)

1983 Investment History:
Total Investments: 22,900,000 ENG ($26,600,000)
Deals: 132
Average Investment: 17,192 ENG ($19,943)

Project Preferences
Geographical:
Domestic: Highlands & Islands of Scotland
Industries: Diversified, High Technology
Stages: Startup, Later

Principals: Ian MacAskill, Sec.

HODGSON MARTIN VENTURES LTD.

4A St. Andrew Sq.
Edinburgh EH2 2BD
44/31-557-3560

Affiliation: Hodgson Martin Ltd.
Year Founded: 1982
Type: Investment Management Co.
Total Paid-In Capital: Call-In Fund

1983 Investment History:
Total Investments: 1,300,000 ENG ($1,500,000)
Deals: 17
Average Investment: 76,471 ENG ($88,706)

Project Preferences
Geographical:
Domestic: Northern England, Scotland
Industries: Diversified, High Technology
Stages: Any

Principals: Allan Hodgson, Man. Dir.; Richard Martin, Dir.

MELVILLE STREET INVESTMENTS (EDINBURGH) LTD.

4 Melville St.
Edinburgh EH3 7NZ
44/31-226-4071

Year Founded: 1976
Type: Private V.C. Firm
Total Paid-In Capital: 17,000,000 ENG ($19,700,000)

1983 Investment History:
Total Investments: 3,000,000 ENG ($3,500,000)
Deals: 14
Average Investment: 214,286 ENG ($248,542)

Project Preferences
Geographical:
Domestic: Anywhere in U.K.
Industries: Diversified, High Technology
Stages: Any

Principals: J.D. Anderson, Dir.

MURRAY JOHNSTONE LTD.

163 Hope St.
Glasgow G2 2UH
44/41-221-5521

Year Founded: 1907
Type: Private V.C. Firm
Total Paid-In Capital: Not Provided

1983 Investment History:
Total Investments: 20,000,000 ENG ($23,200,000)
Deals: 40
Average Investment: 500,000 ENG ($580,000)

Project Preferences
Geographical:
Domestic: Anywhere in U.K.
Foreign: U.S.
Industries: Diversified, High Technology
Stages: Any

Principals: Ross Peters; Ken Pelton

NOBLE GROSSART INVESTMENTS LTD.

48 Queen St.
Edinburgh EH2 3WR
44/31-226-7011

Affiliation: Noble Grossart Ltd.
Year Founded: 1969
Type: Private V.C. Firm
Total Paid-In Capital: 5,000,000 ENG ($5,800,000)

1983 Investment History:
Total Investments: 2,000,000 ENG ($2,300,000)
Deals: 6
Average Investment: 333,333 ENG ($386,666)

Project Preferences
Geographical:
Domestic: Anywhere in U.K.
Industries: Diversified
Stages: Any

Principals: Peter Stevenson, Dir.; Angus Grossart, Dir.

QUAYLE MUNRO LTD.

42 Charlotte Sq.
Edinburgh EH2 4HQ
44/31-226-4421

Year Founded: 1983
Type: Merchant Banking Firm
Total Paid-In Capital: 25,000,000 ENG ($29,000,000)

1983 Investment History:
Total Investments: 2,000,000 ENG ($2,300,000)
Deals: 10
Average Investment: 200,000 ENG ($230,000)

Project Preferences
Geographical:
Domestic: Anywhere in U.K.
Industries: Diversified, Oil
Stages: Later, Buyouts

Principals: J.C. Elliot, Mgr.

SCOTTISH DEVELOPMENT AGENCY □

120 Bothwell St.
Glasgow G2 7JP
44/41-248-2700

Year Founded: 1975
Type: Government Economic Development Agency
Total Paid-In Capital: Call-In Fund

1983 Investment History:
Total Investments: 14,000,000 ENG ($16,200,000)
Deals: 314
Average Investment: 44,586 ENG ($51,720)

Project Preferences
Geographical:
Domestic: Scotland
Industries: Diversified
Stages: Any

Principals: Donald Patience, Dir.

STEWART FUND MANAGERS

45 Charlotte Sq.
Edinburgh EH2 4HW
44/31-226-3271

Year Founded: 1970
Type: Private V.C. Firm
Total Paid-In Capital: 30,000,000 ENG ($34,800,000)

1983 Investment History:
Total Investments: 5,000,000 ENG ($5,800,000)
Deals: 18
Average Investment: 277,778 ENG ($322,222)

Project Preferences
Geographical:
Domestic: Anywhere in U.K.
Foreign: U.S.
Industries: Diversified, High Technology
Stages: Seed, Startup, First, Second, Later

Principals: John H. Murray, Dir.

Wales

HAFRON INVESTMENT FINANCE LTD.

Pearl House
Greyfriars Rd.
Cardiff CF1 3XX
South Glamorgan
44/2-223-2955

Year Founded: 1982
Type: Government Economic Development Agency
Total Paid-In Capital: 2,000,000 ENG ($2,300,000)

1983 Investment History:
Total Investments: 669,000 ENG ($776,040)
Deals: 14
Average Investment: 47,786 ENG ($55,432)

Project Preferences
Geographical:
Domestic: Wales
Industries: Diversified, High Technology
Stages: Startup, Later

Principals: Stephen Haigh, Sr. Investment Analyst

Bermuda

NEWMARKET COMPANY LTD.

30 Cedar Ave.
Hamilton 5
809/295-7169

Affiliation: Venrock Associates
Year Founded: 1972
Type: Public V.C. Firm
Total Paid-In Capital: 1,600,000 ENG ($1,800,000)

1983 Investment History:
Total Investments: 88,800,000 ENG ($103,000,000)
Deals: 79
Average Investment: 1,123,963 ENG ($1,300,000)

Project Preferences
Geographical:
Domestic: Anywhere in U.K.
Foreign: Canada, Europe, U.S., Australia
Industries: Medical, Technology
Stages: Startup, Later

Principals: John Nettleton, Mgr.

UNITED KINGDOM

□ Member of the European Venture Capital Association.

EUROPE

Belgium

ADVENT MANAGEMENT NV□

Industriepark Keiberg
Excelsiorlaan 7, bus 4
Zaventem B 1930
32/2-720-70-07

Year Founded: 1982
Type: Private V.C. Firm
Total Paid-In Capital: 632,000,000 BFR ($10,000,000)

1983 Investment History:
Total Investments: 189,600,000 BFR ($3,000,000)
Deals: 9
Average Investment: 21,066,645 BFR ($333,333)

Project Preferences
Geographical:
Domestic: Anywhere in Belgium
Foreign: U.S.
Industries: High Technology
Stages: Any

Principals: Paul de Vrée, Man. Dir.

GEWESTELIJKE INVESTERINGSMAATSCHAPPIJ VOOR VLAANDEREN□

Anneessensstraat 1-3
Antwerp B 2018
32/31-233-83-83

Year Founded: 1980
Type: Private V.C. Firm
Total Paid-In Capital: 1,896,000,000 BFR ($30,000,000)

1983 Investment History:
Total Investments: 948,000,000 BFR ($15,000,000)
Deals: 10
Average Investment: 94,800,000 BFR ($1,500,000)

Project Preferences
Geographical:
Domestic: Flanders
Foreign: U.S.—Palo Alto, Pittsburgh, Denver
Industries: Technology-Related
Stages: Startup, Later, Buyóuts

Principals: R. Van Outryve d'Vdewalle, Man. Dir.

INVESTCO NV□

Regentlaan 54, bus 2
Brussels B 1000
32/2-513-45-20

Year Founded: 1943
Type: Investment Banking Firm
Total Paid-In Capital: 189,600,000 BFR ($3,000,000)

1983 Investment History:
Total Investments: 158,000,000 BFR ($2,500,000)
Deals: 10
Average Investment: 15,800,000 BFR ($250,000)

Project Preferences
Geographical:
Domestic: Anywhere in Belgium
Foreign: U.S.—East Coast, West Coast; The Netherlands
Industries: Diversified, High Technology, Low Technology, Consumer Goods
Stages: Any

Principals: G. Declercq, Pres.

SA PROMINVEST NV□

Marnixlaan 24
Brussels B 1050
32/2-517-21-11

Year Founded: 1973
Type: Private V.C. Firm
Total Paid-In Capital: 630,000,000 BFR ($10,000,000)

1983 Investment History:
Total Investments: 364,000,000 BFR ($5,800,000)
Deals: 24
Average Investment: 15,200,000 BFR ($200,000)

Project Preferences
Geographical:
Domestic: Anywhere in Belgium
Industries: Diversified, High Technology
Stages: Startup, Later

Principals: Marc Van der Stichele, Pres.

VLAAMSE INVESTERINGSVENNOOTSCHAP NV□

Kouter 8
Ghent B 9000
32/91-24-08-94

Year Founded: 1981
Type: Private V.C. Firm
Total Paid-In Capital: 500,000,000 BFR ($7,900,000)

1983 Investment History:
Total Investments: 189,600,000 BFR ($3,000,000)
Deals: 18
Average Investment: 10,500,000 BFR ($166,667)

Project Preferences
Geographical:
Domestic: Anywhere in Belgium, Flanders
Foreign: Countries Where Belgian Companies Have Affiliates
Industries: High Technology, Food, Construction, Telecommunications
Stages: Startup, Later

Principals: Jozef Schoonjans, Man. Dir.

Denmark

DANVENTURE MANAGEMENT A/S□

Købmagergade 53
Copenhagen DK 1150
45/1-15-38-15

Year Founded: 1983
Type: Private V.C. Firm
Total Paid-In Capital: 7,500,000 DKR ($700,000)

1983 Investment History:
Total Investments: 600,000 DKR ($53,333)
Deals: 1

Project Preferences
Geographical:
Domestic: Anywhere in Denmark
Industries: High Technology
Stages: Startup, Later

Principals: Klaus Pildal, Exec. Dir.

□ Member of the European Venture Capital Association.

EUROPE

PRIVATBANKENS INITIATIVFOND□

Torvegade 2
Copenhagen DK 1400
45/1-11-11-11

Affiliation: Privatbankens
Year Founded: 1979
Type: Bank Subsidiary
Total Paid-In Capital: 50,000,000 DKR ($4,400,000)

1983 Investment History:
Total Investments: 15,000,000 DKR ($1,300,000)
Deals: 10
Average Investment: 1,500,000 DKR ($1,333,333)

Project Preferences
Geographical:
Domestic: Anywhere in Denmark
Industries: Diversified
Stages: Startup, First, Second

Principals: Bent Kiemer, Mgr.

France

AGRINOVA□

Tour Maine Montparnasse
33 avenue de Maine, 41ème étage
Paris F 75755, Cedex 15
33/1-323-28-22

Affiliation: Crediagricole Banc
Year Founded: 1982
Type: Bank Subsidiary
Total Paid-In Capital: 25,000,000 FFR ($2,600,000)

1983 Investment History:
Total Investments: 11,000,000 FFR ($1,100,000)
Deals: 20
Average Investment: 550,000 FFR ($57,113)

Project Preferences
Geographical:
Domestic: Anywhere in France
Foreign: Europe, U.S.
Industries: High Technology
Stages: Any

Principals: Bernard de Valroger, Dir.

ALPHA ASSOCIES SA

89 rue Taitbout
Paris 75009
33/1 526 7929

Year Founded: 1984
Type: Private V.C. Firm
Total Paid-In Capital: 200,000,000 FFR ($20,800,000)

1983 Investment History: New Fund

Project Preferences
Geographical:
Domestic: Anywhere in France
Industries: High Technology
Stages: Startup, First, Second, Later

Principals: Guy Eugene, Part.; Hervé Legoupil, Part.

FINOVELEC SA□

6 rue Ancelle
Neuilly F 92200
33/1-747-69-00

Year Founded: 1981
Type: Private V.C. Firm
Total Paid-In Capital: 30,000,000 FFR ($3,100,000)

1983 Investment History:
Total Investments: 10,000,000 FFR ($1,000,000)
Deals: 8
Average Investment: 1,250,000 FFR ($129,802)

Project Preferences
Geographical:
Domestic: Anywhere in France
Industries: Electrical Equipment
Stages: Startup, First, Second

Principals: Paul Caseou, Chair.

IDIANOVA SA□

35 avenue Franklin Roosevelt
Paris F 75008
33/1-359-91-41

Year Founded: 1981
Type: Merchant Banking Firm
Total Paid-In Capital: 50,000,000 FFR ($5,200,000)

1983 Investment History:
Total Investments: 7,000,000 FFR ($700,000)
Deals: 15
Average Investment: 466,667 FFR ($48,460)

Project Preferences
Geographical:
Domestic: Paris
Foreign: Anywhere
Industries: Food, Biotechnology
Stages: Startup, Later

INNOVEST SA□

Le Sébastopol
3 quai Kléber
Strasbourg F 67055
33/88-32-98-50

Affiliation: Société Financement Innovation
Year Founded: 1983
Type: Government Industrial Development Agency
Total Paid-In-Capital: 14,400,000 FFR ($1,500,000)

1983 Investment History:
Total Investments: 3,800,000 FFR ($400,000)
Deals: 6
Average Investment: 642,003 FFR ($66,667)

Project Preferences
Geographical:
Domestic: Eastern France
Foreign: Germany, Switzerland
Industries: High Technology, Biomedical,
  Micromechanics, Lasers, Data Processing
Stages: Startup, Later

Principals: Jean-Marc Nicolas, Man. Dir.

EUROPE

□ Member of the European Venture Capital Association.

INOVELF SA□

7 rue Nélaton
Paris F 75015
33/1-571-7273

Affiliation: ELF Technologies Inc.
Year Founded: 1979
Type: Corp. V.C. Subsidiary
Total Paid-In-Capital: 541,500,000 FFR ($56,200,000)

1983 Investment History: Not Provided

Project Preferences
Geographical:
Domestic: Anywhere in France
Foreign: Europe, U.S., Japan
Industries: Diversified, Energy, Biotechnology, General
   Pharmaceuticals, Specialty Chemicals, Agribusiness
Stages: Any

Principals: Michel Ronc, CEO; Christine Civiale, Asst. CEO
Contact: Either

IRDI DE MIDI-PYRENEES□

64 rue Raymond IV
Toulouse F 31000
33/61-63-99-95

Year Founded: 1982
Type: Private V.C. Firm
Total Paid-In Capital: 83,000,000 FFR ($8,600,000)

1983 Investment History:
Total Investments: 20,000,000 FFR ($2,100,000)
Deals: 20
Average Investment: 1,000,000 FFR ($103,842)

Project Preferences
Geographical:
Domestic: Southwestern France
Industries: High Technology
Stages: Startup, Later

Principals: Henri Perrier, Pres.

PARIBAS TECHNOLOGY—FRANCE□

3 rue d'Antin
75002 Paris
33/1-298-0560

Affiliation: Bank Paribas
Year Founded: 1872
Type: Private V.C. Firm
Total Paid-In-Capital: 385,200,000 FFR ($40,000,000)

1983 Investment History:
Total Investments: 9,600,000 FFR ($1,000,000)
Deals: 6
Average Investment: 1,605,003 FFR ($166,667)

Project Preferences
Geographical:
Domestic: Anywhere in France
Foreign: Western Europe
Industries: Luxury Goods, Telecommunications, Computers,
   Biotechnology, Healthcare
Stages: Any

Principals: Michel Jaugey, Prin.; Robert Lattes, Prin.
Contact: Either

ALAN PATRICOF ASSOCIES□

67 rue de Monceau
Paris F 75008
33/1-563-28-12

Affiliation: Alan Patricof Associates (U.S. & U.K.)
Year Founded: 1983
Type: Private V.C. Firm
Total Paid-In Capital: 100,000,000 FFR ($10,400,000)

1983 Investment History: New Fund

Project Preferences
Geographical:
Domestic: Anywhere
Foreign: U.K., U.S.
Industries: Diversified, Technology-Related
Stages: Any

Principals: Maurice Tchénio, Man. Dir.

SOFINETI□

12 avenue Georges V
Paris F 75008
33/1-720-65-88

Year Founded: 1983
Type: Private V.C. Firm
Total Paid-In Capital: 60,000,000 FFR ($6,200,000)

1983 Investment History:
Total Investments: Not Provided
Deals: Not Provided
Average Investment: 3,000,000 FFR ($300,000)

Project Preferences
Geographical:
Domestic: Anywhere in France
Foreign: Countries Where French Companies Have Subsidiaries
Industries: High Technology, Telecommunications
Stages: Startup, Second

Principals: Christian Cleiftie, Man. Dir.

SOFININDEX SA□

51 rue Saint Georges
Paris F 75009
33/1-280-68-70

Year Founded: 1983
Type: Private V.C. Firm
Total Paid-In Capital: 50,000,000 FFR ($5,200,000)

1983 Investment History:
Total Investments: 15,400,000 FFR ($1,600,000)
Deals: 16
Average Investment: 962,500 FFR ($99,948)

Project Preferences
Geographical:
Domestic: Anywhere in France
Foreign: U.S., Europe
Industries: Diversified, Mechanical, Electronics, Technology-
   Related, Electricity, Agribusiness
Stages: Any

Principals: Michel Fraiche, Chair.; Dominique Oger, Mgr.

□ Member of the European Venture Capital Association.

SOFINNOVA SA□

51 rue Saint Georges
Paris F 75009
33/1-280-68-70

Year Founded: 1972
Type: Private V.C. Firm
Total Paid-In Capital: 150,000,000 FFR ($15,600,000)

1983 Investment History:
Total Investments: 25,000,000 FFR ($2,600,000)
Deals: 15
Average Investment: 1,700,000 FFR ($173,070)

Project Preferences
Geographical:
Domestic: Anywhere in France
Foreign: U.S.
Industries: High Technology
Stages: Startup, Second, Later

Principals: Hervé Hamon, Man. Dir.

SOGINNOVE SA□

5 rue Boudreau
Paris F 75009
33/1-298-26-22

Year Founded: 1972
Type: Private V.C. Firm
Total Paid-In Capital: 100,000,000 FFR ($10,400,000)

1983 Investment History:
Total Investments: 18,000,000 FFR ($1,900,000)
Deals: 29
Average Investment: 620,690 FFR ($64,454)

Project Preferences
Geographical:
Domestic: Anywhere in France
Industries: Diversified, Biotechnology, Hardware, Software, Pharmaceuticals, Energy Alternatives
Stages: Any

Principals: Jacque Stouff, Man. Dir.

Germany, Federal Republic of

DEUTSCHE WAGNISFINANZIERUNGS-GESELLSCHAFT MBH□

Ulmenstrasse 37-39
D 6000 Frankfurt-am-Main 1
49/611-69-71-0040

Year Founded: 1975
Type: Private V.C. Firm
Total Paid-In Capital: 180,000,000 DMK ($57,100,000)

1983 Investment History:
Total Investments: 20,000,000 DMK ($6,400,000)
Deals: 14
Average Investment: 1,400,000 DMK ($400,000)

Project Preferences
Geographical:
Domestic: Anywhere in Germany
Foreign: U.S.
Industries: Diversified, High Technology
Stages: Startup, First, Second, Later

Principals: Karl-Heinz Fanselow, Pres.

TECHNO VENTURES MANAGEMENT□

Ismaninger Strasse 51
D 8000 Munich 80
49/89-41-80-1172

Affiliation: TA Associates (U.S.)
Year Founded: 1984
Type: Private V.C. Firm
Total Paid-In Capital: 166,000,000 DMK ($52,700,000)

1983 Investment History: New Fund

Project Preferences
Geographical:
Domestic: Anywhere
Foreign: U.S., U.K., Japan, Singapore, Austria
Industries: Diversified, High Technology
Stages: Any

Principals: Dr. Hellmut Kirchner, Man. Part.; Rolf Dienst, Man. Part.

Ireland

ALLIED COMBINED TRUST, LTD.□

Bankcentre
Ballsbridge
IRL Dublin 4
353/1-604-733

Affiliation: Allied Irish Investment Bank Ltd.
Year Founded: 1972
Type: Bank Subsidiary
Total Paid-In Capital: Call-In Fund

1983 Investment History:
Total Investments: 2,000,000 IRE ($2,000,000)
Deals: 6
Average Investment: 333,333 IRE ($333,333)

Project Preferences
Geographical:
Domestic: Anywhere in Ireland
Foreign: Europe, U.S.
Industries: Diversified, High Technology, Electronics, Chemicals, Pharmaceuticals
Stages: Startup, Later, Buyout

Principals: Niall Carroll, Dir.; Aidain Byrnes, Dir.

DEVELOPMENT CAPITAL CORP. LTD.□

DCC House
Stillorgan, Blackrock
IRL Co. Dublin
353/1-831-011

Year Founded: 1976
Type: Private V.C. Firm
Total Paid-In Capital: 17,000,000 IRE ($17,000,000)

1983 Investment History:
Total Investments: 2,000,000 IRE ($2,000,000)
Deals: 5
Average Investment: 400,000 IRE ($400,000)

Project Preferences
Geographical:
Domestic: Anywhere in Ireland
Foreign: U.K., Europe, U.S.
Industries: Diversified, High Technology
Stages: Startup, Later

Principals: James Flavin, CEO

EUROPE

□ Member of the European Venture Capital Association.

219

INDUSTRIAL CREDIT CO. LTD.□

31-34 Harcourt St.
IRL Dublin 2
353/1-720-055

Year Founded: 1933
Type: State-Owned Development Bank
Total Paid-In Capital: Not Provided

Project Preferences
Geographical:
Domestic: Anywhere in Ireland
Industries: Diversified, High Technology
Stages: Any

Principals: David Fassbender, Dir. Corp. Finance

Italy

SOCIETA FINANZIARIA DI PARTECIPAZIONE SPA□

Via Saverio Mercadente 9
Rome IT 00198
39/6-84-40-641

Year Founded: 1982
Type: Private V.C. Firm
Total Paid-In Capital: 25,129,000,000 LIT ($13,000,000)

1983 Investment History: Not Provided

Project Preferences
Geographical:
Domestic: Anywhere in Italy
Industries: Diversified, High Technology
Stages: Any

Principals: Giorgio Tellini, Man. Dir.

VENTURE CAPITAL SPA

Corso Moncalieri 77
Turin 10133
39/11-65-05-979

Affiliation: Italfinanziaria Internazionale SPA
Year Founded: 1984
Type: Private V.C. Firm
Total Paid-In Capital: 5,000,000,000 LIT ($2,600,000)

1983 Investment History: New Fund

Project Preferences
Geographical:
Domestic: Anywhere in Italy
Industries: Diversified, Agribusiness, Software, Electronics
Stages: Startup, Later

Principals: Jimmy Bonaveglio, Man. Dir.

Luxembourg

INTERNATIONAL VENTURE CAPITAL PARTNER (IVCP) SA HOLDING□

35 rue Glesener
Luxembourg L 1631
49/2234-590-76

Year Founded: 1983
Type: Private V.C. Firm
Total Paid-In Capital: 18,000,000 DMK ($5,700,000)

1983 Investment History: New Fund

Project Preferences
Geographical:
Foreign: Europe, U.S.
Industries: High Technology
Stages: Second, Later

Principals: Thomas Kühr, Man. Dir.

The Netherlands

GILDE VENTURE FUND BV□

Herculesplein 261A
Utrecht NL 3584 AA
31/30-51-05-34

Year Founded: 1983
Type: Private V.C. Firm
Total Paid-In Capital: 30,000,000 HFL ($8,400,000)

1983 Investment History:
Total Investments: 6,000,000 HFL ($1,700,000)
Deals: 6
Average Investment: 1,000,000 HFL ($300,000)

Project Preferences
Geographical:
Domestic: Anywhere in The Netherlands
Foreign: U.S.
Industries: Diversified, High Technology
Stages: Later, Buyouts

Principals: Lex A.J. Schellings, Dir.; Leendert J. Van Driel, Dir.

HOLLAND VENTURE BV□

Eekholt 54
Diemen 1112 XH
31/20-99-11-11

Year Founded: 1981
Type: Private V.C. Firm
Total Paid-In Capital: 12,000,000 HFL ($3,400,000)

1983 Investment History:
Total Investments: 6,500,000 HFL ($1,800,000)
Deals: 10
Average Investment: 650,000 HFL ($182,584)

Project Preferences
Geographical:
Domestic: Anywhere in The Netherlands
Industries: Diversified, High Technology
Stages: Any

Principals: E.R. Deves, Man. Dir.

□ Member of the European Venture Capital Association.

EUROPE

ONDERNEMEND VERMOGEN NEDERLAND CV□

Van Houten Industriepark 11
MZ Weesp NL 1381
31/2940-19-440

Year Founded: 1982
Type: Private V.C. Firm
Total Paid-In Capital: Call-In Fund

1983 Investment History:
Total Investments: 1,500,000 HFL ($400,000)
Deals: 3
Average Investment: 500,000 HFL ($140,449)

Project Preferences
Geographical:
Domestic: Anywhere in The Netherlands
Industries: Diversified, High Technology, Trade, Service
Stages: Any

Principals: J.C.M. van Heesbeen, Man. Dir.

ORANJE-NASSAU PARTICIPATIES BV□

Nassauplein 25
Postbus 85578
Den Haag NL 2508 CG
31/70-46-96-70

Year Founded: 1891
Type: Private V.C. Firm
Total Paid-In Capital: 35,600,000 HFL ($10,000,000)

1983 Investment History:
Total Investments: 7,100,000 HFL ($2,000,000)
Deals: 5
Average Investment: 1,400,000 HFL ($400,000)

Project Preferences
Geographical:
Domestic: Anywhere in The Netherlands
Foreign: Belgium, Germany, Luxembourg, U.K.
Industries: Automotive, Plastics, Microelectronics
Stages: Startup, Buyouts

Principals: René Smit, Pres.

OVERIJSSELSE ONTWIKKELINGS MAATSCHAPPIJ NV (OOM)□

Burg van Roijensingel 12
P.O. Box 561
AN Zwolle NL 8000
31/38-214-772

Year Founded: 1975
Type: Government Economic Development Agency
Total Paid-In Capital: 46,000,000 HFL ($12,900,000)

1983 Investment History:
Total Investments: 10,000,000 HFL ($2,800,000)
Deals: 15
Average Investment: 666,667 HFL ($187,266)

Project Preferences
Geographical:
Domestic: Overijsselse
Industries: Industrial Production & Services
Stages: Startup, Second, Later

Principals: F.J. Gastkemper, Man. Dir.; Jean Roell, Asst. Dir.

PARCOM BEHEER BV□

Carnegieplein 5
Den Haag NL 2517 KJ's
31/70-65-59-10

Year Founded: 1982
Type: Private V.C. Firm
Total Paid-In Capital: 50,000,000 HFL ($14,000,000)

1983 Investment History:
Total Investments: 11,000,000 HFL ($3,100,000)
Deals: 7
Average Investment: 1,571,429 HFL ($441,413)

Project Preferences
Geographical:
Domestic: Anywhere in The Netherlands
Foreign: Europe
Industries: High Technology, Services, Engineering, Software
Stages: Any

Principals: Aris Wateler, Man. Dir.

EUROPE

□ Member of the European Venture Capital Association.

FOREIGN LISTINGS

ISRAEL

Israel

DISCOUNT INVESTMENT CORP.

16-18 Beith Hashoeva Lane
Tel Aviv 61016
972/3-622-256

Year Founded: 1962
Type: Public V.C. Firm
Total Paid-In Capital: 7,600,000,000 ISR ($12,700,000)

1983 Investment History:
Total Investments: 3,302,200,000 ISR ($5,500,000)
Deals: 10
Average Investment: 330,220,000 ISR ($550,000)

Project Preferences
Geographical:
Domestic: Anywhere in Israel
Industries: Diversified, High Technology
Stages: Startup, Later

Principals: Raphael Recanati, Chair.; Gideon Tolkowsky, Man. Dir.

EITAM ISRAEL ADVANCED INDUSTRIES LTD.

Industry House, Suite 1120
29 Hamered St.
Tel Aviv 68125
972/3-657-515; 972/3-657-753

Year Founded: 1982
Type: Public V.C. Firm
Total Paid-In Capital: Not Provided

1983 Investment History: Not Provided

Project Preferences
Geographical:
Domestic: Anywhere in Israel
Industries: High Technology
Stages: Any

Principals: Eli Shilani, Man. Dir.
Contact: Eli Shilani

ELRON ELECTRONIC INDUSTRIES

P.O. Box 1573
Advanced Technology Center
Haifa 31015
972/4-5-29-925

Affiliation: Elron Technologies
Year Founded: 1962
Type: Industrial Holding Co.
Total Paid-In Capital: 12,008,000,000 ISR ($20,000,000)

1983 Investment History:
Total Investments: Not Provided
Deals: Not Provided
Average Investment: 900,600,000 ISR ($1,500,000)

Project Preferences
Geographical:
Domestic: Anywhere in Israel
Foreign: U.S.
Industries: High Technology
Stages: Startup

Principals: Carlos Zorea, Sr. V.P.; Gideon Tolkowsky, V.P.

MEDIVENT LTD.

9 Montifiori St.
Tel Aviv 65252
972/3-653-027

Affiliation: Leumi and Co. Investment Bankers Ltd.
Year Founded: 1984
Type: Private V.C. Firm
Total Paid-In Capital: 2,521,700,000 ISR ($4,200,000)

1983 Investment History: New Fund

Project Preferences
Geographical:
Domestic: Anywhere in Israel
Foreign: U.S.
Industries: Healthcare Products, Computerized Telecommunications
Stages: Any

Principals: E. Sharvit, Head; Amnon Portugaly, Gen. Mgr.

ISRAEL

FOREIGN LISTINGS

ASIA

Japan

BANK OF TOKYO LTD.

Financial Services Dept.
P.O. Box 8, Nihonbashi
Tokyo 103-91
81/3-245-1111, Ext. 4150

Year Founded: 1980
Type: Investment Advisor
Total Paid-In Capital: Not Provided

1983 Investment History: Not Provided

Project Preferences
Geographical:
Foreign: U.S.
Industries: High Technology
Stages: Any

Principals: Mutsuo Murai, Gen. Mgr. Financial Services Dept.;
Kuninari Kato, Asst. to Gen. Mgr.
Contact: Either

DIAMOND CAPITAL

3-6-3 Kanga
Kadicho Chuo-Ku
Chuo-Ku
Tokyo 103
8/3-252-4591

Affiliation: Mitsubishi Bank
Year Founded: 1974
Type: Bank Subsidiary
Total Paid-In Capital: 500,000,000 YEN ($2,000,000)

1983 Investment History: Not Provided

Project Preferences
Geographical:
Domestic: Anywhere in Japan
Industries: Diversified, High Technology
Stages: Startup, Later, Buyouts

Principals: Kapfushipo Yamada, Pres.

FUJI INVESTMENT CO.

Kaguruagashi
Shinujuku-Ku
Tokyo 162
81/3-235-0141

Affiliation: Fuji and Yasuda Banks
Year Founded: 1983
Type: Bank Subsidiary
Total Paid-In Capital: 450,000,000 YEN ($1,800,000)

1983 Investment History: Not Provided

Project Preferences
Geographical:
Domestic: Anywhere in Japan
Industries: Diversified, High Technology
Stages: Startup, Later, Buyouts

Principals: Mr. Seya, Pres.

NEW JAPAN FINANCE CO.

1-70-10 Nihonbashi
Shuo-Ku
Tokyo 103
81/3-273-2311

Year Founded: 1982
Type: Private V.C. Firm
Total Paid-In Capital: 3,000,000,000 YEN ($11,900,000)

1983 Investment History:
Total Investments: Not Provided
Deals: 53
Average Investment: 250,000,000 YEN ($1,000,000)

Project Preferences
Geographical:
Domestic: Anywhere in Japan
Foreign: Anywhere
Industries: High Technology
Stages: Any

Principals: A. Takahashi, Dir.

NIPPON ENTERPRISE DEVELOPMENT

107 Minatoku
3-11-3 Akasaka-KA
Tokyo 103
81/3-586-4451

Affiliation: Long-Term Credit Bank of Japan
Year Founded: 1972
Type: Bank Subsidiary
Total Paid-In Capital: 10,000,000,000 YEN ($39,800,000)

1983 Investment History:
Total Investments: 301,700,000 YEN ($1,200,000)
Deals: 6
Average Investment: 50,300,000 YEN ($200,000)

Project Preferences
Geographical:
Domestic: Tokyo
Foreign: U.S.
Industries: Computer Software & Hardware
Stages: Later

Principals: Mr. Hara, Pres.

OKASAN FINANCE

1-16-3 Nihonbashi
Thuo-Ku 20
Tokyo 103
81/3-272-2211

Affiliation: Nihonbashi Securities
Year Founded: 1983
Type: Corp. V.C. Subsidiary
Total Paid-In Capital: 100,000,000 YEN ($400,000)

1983 Investment History: New Fund

Project Preferences
Geographical:
Domestic: Anywhere in Japan
Industries: Electric Appliances, Service Industry, Machinery,
Chemicals
Stages: Any

Principals: T. Ogawa, Pres.

ASIA

ORIENT CAPITAL CO. LTD.

World Trade Center Bldg. 2-4-1, 37th Floor
Hamana Tsu-Cho
Mianto-Ku
Tokyo 105
81/3-435-4890

Year Founded: 1983
Type: Private V.C. Firm
Total Paid-In Capital: 300,000,000 YEN ($1,200,000)

1983 Investment History:
Total Investments: Not Provided
Deals: Not Provided
Average Investment: 50,000,000 YEN ($200,000)

Project Preferences
Geographical:
Domestic: Anywhere in Japan
Foreign: U.S.
Industries: High Technology
Stages: Startup, Later, Buyouts

Principals: Kimai Shimamoto, Pres.

PARIBAS TECHNOLOGY—JAPAN

CPO Box 20
Yurakucho Denki Bldg., 19th Floor
1-7-1 Yurakucho Chiyoda-Ku
Tokyo 100-91
81/3-214-5881

Affiliation: Bank Paribas (France)
Year Founded: 1983
Type: Private V.C. Firm
Total Paid-In Capital: 5,028,000,000 YEN ($20,000,000)

1983 Investment History:
Total Investments: 1,508,400,000 YEN ($6,000,000)
Deals: 33
Average Investment: 45,700,000 YEN ($181,818)

Project Preferences
Geographical:
Domestic: Anywhere in Japan
Industries: Mechatronics (Robotics & Manufacturing), Electronic Components, New Materials, Computer Software, Life Sciences
Stages: Startup, First

Principals: Tad Ota, Prin.; Jacques Mecheri, Prin.
Contact: Either

SANWA CAPITAL CO. LTD.

1-1
1-Chome
Otemachi
Chiyoda-Ku
Tokyo 100
81/3-216-3111

Affiliation: Sanwa Bank
Year Founded: 1983
Type: Bank Subsidiary
Total Paid-In Capital: 200,000,000 YEN ($800,000)

1983 Investment History:
Total Investments: Not Provided
Deals: Not Provided
Average Investment: 30,000,000 YEN ($100,000)

Project Preferences
Geographical:
Domestic: Anywhere in Japan
Foreign: Anywhere
Industries: Diversified, High Technology
Stages: Later, Buyouts

Principals: Jiro Isukahara, Pres.

SANYO FINANCE CO. LTD.

Landic
Nihonbashi Bldg. 13-16
Nihonbashi 2 Chome
Chuo-Ku
Tokyo 103
81/3-666-1233

Affiliation: Sanyo Securities
Year Founded: 1982
Type: Corp. V.C. Subsidiary
Total Paid-In Capital: 500,000,000 YEN ($2,000,000)

1983 Investment History:
Total Investments: 78,100,000 YEN ($310,660)
Deals: 8
Average Investment: 9,800,000 YEN ($38,982)

Project Preferences
Geographical:
Domestic: Anywhere in Japan
Industries: Electronics, Computers, Biotechnology
Stages: Any

Principals: Ryohei Iwase, Pres.

TOKYO VENTURE CAPITAL

2-4-1 Muromachi
Nihonbashi
Chuo-Ku
Tokyo 103
81/245-0375

Affiliation: Dai-Ichi Kangyo Bank
Year Founded: 1974
Type: Bank Subsidiary
Total Paid-In Capital: 60,000,000 YEN ($200,000)

1983 Investment History:
Total Investments: 2,000,000,000 YEN ($8,000,000)
Deals: 20
Average Investment: 100,000,000 YEN ($400,000)

Project Preferences
Geographical:
Domestic: Anywhere in Japan
Foreign: U.S.
Industries: High Technology
Stages: Startup, Later, Buyouts

Principals: Takuzo Hayashida, Pres.

WAKO FINANCE CO.

651 Koamicho
Nihonbashi
Chuo-Ku
Tokyo 103
81/3-667-8111

Year Founded: 1982
Type: Private V.C. Firm
Total Paid-In Capital: 300,000,000 YEN ($1,200,000)

1983 Investment History: Not Provided

Project Preferences
Geographical:
Domestic: Anywhere in Japan
Industries: High Technology
Stages: Any

Principals: H. Tamura, Dir.

ASIA

227

YAMAICHI UNIVEN CO. LTD.

5-1 Kabutocho, Nihonbashi
Chuo-Ku
Tokyo 103
81/3-660-5974

Affiliation: Yamaichi Securities
Year Founded: 1983
Type: Private V.C. Firm
Total Paid-In Capital: 9,300,000,000 YEN ($37,000,000)

1983 Investment History:
Total Investments: 3,400,000,000 YEN ($13,500,000)
Deals: 25
Average Investment: 136,000,000 YEN ($500,000)

Project Preferences
Geographical:
Domestic: Tokyo
Foreign: CA
Industries: High Technology, Semiconductors, Electrical
  Parts
Stages: Second, Later

Principals: Yukio Ibi, Assoc. Mgr.

Singapore

SOUTH EAST ASIA VENTURE INVESTMENT CO. NV

c/o Venture Services (SEA) Private Ltd. *
24-01 UIC Bldg.
5 Shenton Way
Singapore 0106
65/225-5855

Affiliation: South East Asia Venture Investment Program; Oranje-
  Nassau BV; TA Associates
Year Founded: 1983
Type: Private V.C. Firm
Total Paid-In Capital: 61,000,000 SIN ($28,000,000)

1983 Investment History:
Total Investments: Not Provided
Deals: Not Provided
Average Investment: 1,100,000 SIN ($500,000)

Project Preferences
Geographical:
Domestic: Anywhere in Singapore
Foreign: Southeast Asia—Malaysia, Philippines, Thailand, Brunei
Industries: Electronics, Agribusiness, Healthcare, Energy Products
  & Services
Stages: Startup, Later, Buyouts

Principals: Agustin V. Que, Man. Dir.

Other Address: c/o ABN Trust Co. (Curaçao) NV, P.O. Box 564,
  Pietermaai 15, Willemstad, Curaçao, The Netherlands Antilles.

VENTURE INVESTMENT (SINGAPORE) LTD.

24-01 UIC Bldg.
5 Shenton Way
Singapore 0106
65/225-5855

Affiliation: South East Asia Venture Investment Program; Oranje-
  Nassau BV; TA Associates; National Iron & Steel Mills Ltd.
  (Singapore); The Development Bank of Singapore Ltd.
Year Founded: 1983
Type: Private V.C. Firm
Total Paid-In Capital: 15,300,000 SIN ($7,000,000)

1983 Investment History:
Total Investments: Not Provided
Deals: Not Provided
Average Investment: 654,000 SIN ($300,000)

Project Preferences
Geographical:
Domestic: Anywhere in Singapore
Industries: High Technology, Biotechnology
Stages: Startup, Later, Buyouts

Principals: Agustin V. Que, Man. Dir.

Malaysia

MALAYSIAN VENTURES BERHAD

Ninth Floor
Bangunan Datod Zainal
Jalan Melaka
Kuala Lumpur
60/3-91-99-67

Affiliation: South East Asia Venture Investment Program; Oranje-
  Nassau BV; TA Associates; Arab-Malaysian Merchant Bank
  Berhad
Year Founded: 1984
Type: Private V.C. Firm
Total Paid-In Capital: 14,600,000 MAL ($6,000,000)

1983 Investment History:
Total Investments: New Fund

Project Preferences
Geographical:
Domestic: Anywhere in Malaysia
Industries: Agribusiness, Electronics, Energy Products & Services
Stages: Any

Principals: Agustin V. Que, Man. Dir.

ASIA

ASSOCIATIONS

AMERICAN ASSOCIATION OF MINORITY ENTERPRISE SMALL BUSINESS INVESTMENT COMPANIES (AAMESBIC)

915 15th St., NW, Suite 700
Washington, DC 20005
202/347-8600

Officers: JoAnn Price, Pres.; Diane Thomas, Dir. of Gov. Affairs
Members: 150
Year Founded: 1971

Represents minority investment-company industry in legislative, regulatory, and program development. Conducts seminars. Publishes a minority business journal, two monthly newsletters, and a membership directory, which is available for $3.

NATIONAL ASSOCIATION OF SMALL BUSINESS INVESTMENT COMPANIES (NASBIC)

1156 15th St., NW
Washington, DC 20005
202/833-8230

Members: 500
Year Founded: 1958

Lobbies for regulation. Runs educational programs for venture capitalists. Publishes annual directory containing all SBICs in U.S.; directory available for $1.

NATIONAL VENTURE CAPITAL ASSOCIATION (NVCA)

1655 N. Fort Myer Dr.
Arlington, VA 22209
703/528-4370

Officers: Dan Kingsley, Exec. Dir.; Daniel Gregory, Chair.; B. Kipling Hagopian, Pres.; Christopher Brody, Pres.-Elect; Burton McMurtry, V.P. & Sec.; Daniel Haggerty, Treas.
Members: 181
Year Founded: 1973

Aims to foster understanding of venture capital in U.S., to stimulate flow of capital, and to affect regulation of venture capital activity and public policy.

WESTERN ASSOCIATION OF VENTURE CAPITALISTS (WAVC)

3000 Sand Hill Rd., Bldg. Z, Suite 260
Menlo Park, CA 94025
415/854-1322

Officers: Fran Cannon, Sec.
Members: 118
Year Founded: 1968

Holds monthly meetings; offers lectures on energy, technology, and so forth. Publishes directory, which is available for $25, and membership roster, which is available at no cost.

Canada

ASSOCIATION OF CANADIAN VENTURE CAPITAL COMPANIES (ACVCC)

c/o VenGrowth Capital Funds
111 Richmond St. W., Suite 805
Toronto M5H 264
Ontario
416/947-9123

Officers: Earl Storie, Pres.; Peter Standeven, Sec.
Members: 50 Full; 40 Assoc. (includes investment banking firms and
   accounting firms)
Year Founded: 1972

Association for all active Canadian venture capital firms; aims to
foster venture capital activity. Holds annual conferences for
prospective entrepreneurs and investors, monitors activities within
the industry, and publishes statistics.

Europe

EUROPEAN VENTURE CAPITAL ASSOCIATION (EVCA)

Clos de Parnasse, 11F
B-1040 Brussels
Belgium
322/511-5251

Officers: Robert A. Ceurvorst, Sec. Gen.; M. Philippe Roelandt,
   Admin.
Members: 50 Full; 27 Assoc.
Year Founded: 1983

Collects and disseminates information on venture capital and the
organization's activities; promotes the profession to the outside
world; stimulates contacts within the profession; maintains contacts
with other organizations; operates seminars for both members and
nonmembers. Publishes quarterly newsletter in French, English, and
German; also publishes annual guide to venture capital services in
Europe.

Note: An open box (☐) next to a listing's title denotes membership
   in the European Venture Capital Association.

ASSOCIATIONS

FIRMS

INDEX

D

E

INDEX
FIRMS

N

O

P

INDEX FIRMS

241

DOMESTIC LOCATIONS

INDEX

INDEX
DOMESTIC
LOCATIONS

INDEX DOMESTIC LOCATIONS

INDEX
DOMESTIC
LOCATIONS

VERMONT

VIRGINIA

WASHINGTON

WEST VIRGINIA

WISCONSIN

WYOMING

PREFERENCE

INDEXES

INDUSTRY PREFERENCES

INDEX

COMPUTER HARDWARE

COMPUTER-RELATED TECHNOLOGY & SERVICES

COMPUTER SOFTWARE

INDEX
INDUSTRY
PREFERENCES

261

ELECTRICAL EQUIPMENT

ELECTRONICS/COMPONENTS & INSTRUMENTATION

ELECTRONICS/SEMICONDUCTORS

ENERGY

ENGINEERING

ENTERTAINMENT

INDEX
INDUSTRY
PREFERENCES

HOTELS/MOTELS

INDUSTRIAL AUTOMATION

INDUSTRIAL PRODUCTS & EQUIPMENT

INFORMATION TECHNOLOGIES

TELEPHONE-RELATED TECHNOLOGY

TOURISM

TRANSPORTATION

TRANSPORTATION/TAXICABS

WHOLESALING

INDEX
INDUSTRY
PREFERENCES

GEOGRAPHICAL PREFERENCES

INDEX

Regions

EAST

NORTHEAST

MIDDLE ATLANTIC

SOUTH

MIDWEST

MOUNTAIN STATES

SOUTHWEST

Cities

NEW YORK CITY

NEW YORK CITY—BROOKLYN

NEW YORK CITY—QUEENS

OMAHA

PALO ALTO

PHILADELPHIA

PITTSBURGH

SAN ANTONIO

SAN FRANCISCO

SUBSCRIPTION INFORMATION

If you would like to subscribe to VENTURE, The Magazine for Entrepreneurs, call VENTURE's toll-free number, 1-800-247-5470, or write, VENTURE, Subscription Department, 521 Fifth Avenue, 15th Floor, New York, N.Y. 10175.

A one-year subscription costs $18, which is a 50% savings over the $36 newsstand price for 12 issues; a two-year subscription is $27, or 63% off the $72 newsstand price for 24 issues; for even greater savings, a three-year subscription is only $36, a 67% discount on the $108 newsstand price for 36 issues. (In Canada, add $5 per subscription year; all other foreign, add $7 per subscription year.)

Your subscription is tax-deductible as a business expense, and comes with a money-back guarantee. Please allow four to six weeks for delivery.